RENEWALS 458-4574

DATE DUE

GAYLORD			PRINTED IN U.S.A.

Employment with a Human Face

EMPLOYMENT WITH A HUMAN FACE

Balancing Efficiency, Equity, and Voice

JOHN W. BUDD

ILR Press
an imprint of
Cornell University Press

ITHACA AND LONDON

First published 2004 by Cornell University Press
Printed in the United States of America

Library of Congress Cataloging-in-Publication Data
Budd, John W.
   Employment with a human face : balancing efficiency, equity, and voice / John W. Budd.
      p. cm.
Includes bibliographical references and index.
   ISBN 0-8014-4208-7 (cloth : alk. paper)
   1. Industrial relations.   I. Title.
   HD6971.B83 2004
   331—dc22   2003020154

Cornell University Press strives to use environmentally responsible suppliers and materials to the fullest extent possible in the publishing of its books. Such materials include vegetable-based, low-VOC inks and acid-free papers that are recycled, totally chlorine-free, or partly composed of nonwood fibers. For further information, visit our website at www.cornellpress.cornell.edu.

Cloth printing   10 9 8 7 6 5 4 3 2 1

*To all my parents and grandparents, who worked so hard
to make things better for their children,*

And to my wife and children, who make it worthwhile

Contents

Preface

THE GENESIS OF THIS BOOK is at odds with most modern academic scholarship. This book grew not out of an explicit research agenda but out of my efforts to create a richer, deeper, and more engaging class for labor relations and labor policy at the University of Minnesota. Labor relations instruction is often dominated by the detailed examination of existing processes, such as how collective bargaining works, and the resulting belief, as explicitly stated by one leading textbook, that labor relations is about work rules. But labor relations is not about work rules; work rules are simply a means of achieving more important ends. Industrial relations systems should not be created to promote work rules; they should be established to promote more important ends. But what are these ends? What behaviors and systems effectively promote these ends? Are the current behaviors and systems around the world succeeding? If not, why not? And what can be done to change this? These are the critical, engaging, and exciting topics for students to tackle.

Structuring a labor relations course around these topics, however, requires a major shift from the conventional process-based approach to a theme-based approach. This book, then, started as a project on a theme-based approach to teaching labor relations. But as I started writing, it quickly became apparent that these themes had tremendous relevance and ramifications far beyond a labor relations classroom. In my view, the academic field of industrial relations—my intellectual home—is in the doldrums largely because of this process-based focus. A theme-based approach has the potential to reinvigorate the field and to lay the groundwork for richer connections with other fields that share similar perspectives on these broad themes, but not on the narrow processes. More important, the themes address central issues about the nature of employment that should be of interest to anyone concerned with the employment relationship—even if my normative conclusions are not shared by all.

Examination of the employment relationship can be a fascinating adventure. Employment involves market forces, individuals' emotions, social dynamics, managerial and union strategies, forms of work organization, constitutional and legal issues, history, technology, questions of human rights, negotiation and conflict resolution strategies, debates over globalization, and ethical challenges. It has been influenced by everything from violent strikes to religious writings, from libertarians to Marxists, from radical union leaders to great industrialists. The differing perspectives on employment are ultimately a microcosm of broader debates in society over the nature of freedom and justice, and over the extent to which economic markets adequately serve everyone's needs. This book is therefore the product of my efforts to get at the heart of employment—the objectives of the employment relationship and the alternatives for their achievement—to not only stimulate a richer understanding of employment in the classroom but to stimulate interest in the employment relationship from a variety of perspectives, and to explore how the nature of employment relates to the nature of the society we live in.

Like so much else, this book has greatly benefited from the time and effort of others who had little to gain personally. In particular, my University of Minnesota colleagues Mike Bognanno and John Fossum read my entire first draft and provided numerous comments, suggestions, and questions that greatly enriched the final product. Roy Adams and Bruce Kaufman commented on an early draft of a paper on the field of human resources and industrial relations. Bruce later served as a reviewer for Cornell University Press and I am grateful for his constructive comments, his encouragement, and his continued scholarship on the intellectual history of industrial relations. A second reviewer's comments revealed several areas that needed clarification and emphasized the need to add corporate governance and the early AFL model of governance to the analyses. Thanks to Bruce, participants in the International Industrial Relations Association's January 2003 study group on industrial relations theory—including John Godard, John Kelly, Tony Giles, and Gregor Gall—also suggested stimulating issues for me to wrestle with as I made the final revisions to the manuscript.

The University of Minnesota has long been a stimulating place for studying all aspects of employment, and in working on this book I have had the pleasure of benefiting from the discussions, comments, support, and friendship of Steve Befort, Morrie Kleiner, Brian McCall, Andy Miner, Jim Scoville (who read substantial portions of the manuscript), and Connie Wanberg. I thank Norm Bowie for sharing his expertise with a beginner in ethics, and David Weissbrodt for sharing his expertise with a beginner in human rights. I am grateful to the Industrial Relations Center (IRC), the Carlson School of Management, and the University of Minnesota for intellectual and financial support, to the University of Minnesota Law School for providing quiet office space during a sabbatical, and to the IRC staff for their helpfulness and good humor. The staff of the IRC's Georgianna Herman Reference Room also deserve special thanks for their helpfulness in identifying references and sources.

Matt Slaughter continues to be an excellent coauthor on international labor market issues and I have benefited from our conversations on globalization. Though it took many steps to get here, the genesis of this project occurred when Daphne Taras asked me to write a symposium article on using technology to teach labor relations. My advisors at Princeton more than a decade ago, especially David Card and Tim Guinnane, laid the foundation by encouraging me to pursue my institutional interests even though they clashed with the norms of mainstream economics. Fran Benson at Cornell University Press helped guide my book through the editorial process and I am grateful for her patience, support, and encouragement as the project evolved into a book that bears little resemblance to my initial proposal. Last, but by no means least, I thank my family for their help, patience, encouragement, support, and sacrifice. I hope we can now find time to go sailing.

Abbreviations

AFL	American Federation of Labor
AFL-CIO	American Federation of Labor-Congress of Industrial Organizations
CGT	*Confédération générale du travail* (General Confederation of Labor)
ECA	Employment Contracts Act
ENA	Experimental Negotiating Agreement
EU	European Union
EWC	European Works Council
FDI	Foreign Direct Investment
FLSA	Fair Labor Standards Act
GATT	General Agreement on Tariffs and Trade
GDP	Gross Domestic Product
HRIR	Human Resources and Industrial Relations
HRM	Human Resource Management
HUCTW	Harvard Union of Clerical and Technical Workers
IATSE	International Alliance of Theatrical and Stage Employees
ICCPR	International Covenant on Civil and Political Rights
ICESR	International Covenant on Economic, Social and Cultural Rights
ICFTU	International Confederation of Free Trade Unions
ILO	International Labour Organization
IR	Industrial Relations
ITF	International Transport Workers Federation
NAALC	North American Agreement on Labor Cooperation
NAFTA	North American Free Trade Agreement
NAO	National Administrative Office
NLRA	National Labor Relations Act

NLRB	National Labor Relations Board
OECD	Organization for Economic Cooperation and Development
PATCO	Professional Air Traffic Controllers Association
SEIU	Service Employees International Union
UAW	United Automobile, Aerospace, and Agricultural Implement Workers of America (United Auto Workers)
UN	United Nations
UNITE	Union of Needletrades, Industrial, and Textile Employees
WTO	World Trade Organization

Employment with a Human Face

Introduction

EMPLOYMENT IS A CRITICAL feature of modern society. The nature of employment determines the quality of individuals' lives, the operation of the economy, the viability of democracy, and the degree of respect for human dignity. It is therefore essential that modern society establish societal goals for employment. Economic prosperity demands that employment be productive, but economic performance should not be the sole standard of the employment relationship. Work is not simply an economic transaction; respect for the importance of human life and dignity requires that the fair treatment of workers also be a fundamental standard of the employment relationship—as are the democratic ideals of freedom and equality. Furthermore, the importance of self-determination for both human dignity and democracy mandate employee input and participation in work-related decisions that affect workers' lives. In short, the objectives of the employment relationship are efficiency, equity, and voice. This book is about these objectives and the alternative ways in which they can be achieved.

In some situations, efficiency, equity, and voice are mutually reinforcing. A productive workforce provides the economic resources for equitable working conditions that include employee voice in decision making. And equitable treatment and employee participation can provide the avenues for reducing turnover, increasing employee commitment, and harnessing workers' ideas for improving productivity and quality. But the more important question is: What should happen when efficiency, equity, and voice conflict with each other? This is the critical question that makes the analysis of the employment relationship a dynamic topic with diverse perspectives. Should efficiency—and the closely related property rights of employers—automatically trump equity and voice concerns? Or should the reverse be true—should equity and voice have priority over efficiency needs? Neither of these extreme options is preferable;

rather, a democratic society should seek to *balance* efficiency, equity, and voice. The power of free economic markets to provide efficiency and economic prosperity is important and should be encouraged, but respect for human dignity and democratic ideals further requires that the power of economic markets be harnessed to serve the quality of human life and provide broadly shared prosperity. As such, the imperative for the drivers of employment—individuals, markets, institutions, organizational strategies, and public policies—is to provide employment with a human face, which I define as a productive and efficient employment relationship that also fulfills the standards of human rights. The International Labour Organization (1999) calls this simply "decent work."

This imperative is underscored by the turbulence of the employment relationship in the twenty-first century. Expectations of stable, lifetime employment have all but vanished, and information technologies empower employees to harness information in remote locations while subjecting them to increased monitoring and demands for around-the-clock responsiveness to coworkers and customers. Globalization continues to put downward pressure on employment standards as well as on the ability of corporations and nations to compete with others. More workplaces are abandoning traditional, hierarchical forms of work organization; compensation is becoming more contingent and at-risk; demographic changes continue to force organizations to confront diversity and issues involving the balance of work and life; and disparities in labor market outcomes are widening.[1] The trend worldwide is for flexible employment relationships—employment flexibility, pay flexibility, functional flexibility, and procedural flexibility (see chapter 8). As a result, the institutions that traditionally have provided checks and balances on economic markets in the employment relationship, such as government standards and labor unions, are under attack and in decline.[2]

But the principle of adding checks and balances to economic markets is not limited to the employment relationship and should not be an idea in decay.[3] The United Nations continues to call for the creation of markets with a human face. Its *Human Development Report 1999* has the subtitle "Globalization with a Human Face" and opens with the following: "The real wealth of a nation is its people. And the purpose of development is to create an enabling environment for people to enjoy long, healthy, and creative lives. This simple but powerful truth is too often forgotten in the pursuit of material and financial wealth" (United Nations Development Programme 1999, 1). Replace "development" with "employment" and add "productive" to "long, healthy, and creative lives" and the resulting statement perfectly describes the need for employment with a human face. The report continues:

> But today's globalization is being driven by market expansion—opening national borders to trade, capital, information—outpacing governance of these markets and their repercussions for people. More progress has been made in norms, standards, policies and institutions for open global markets than for people and their

rights. . . . Competitive markets may be the best guarantee of efficiency, but not necessarily of equity. . . . The challenge of globalization in the new century is not to stop the expansion of global markets. The challenge is to find the rules and institutions for stronger governance—local, national, regional and global—to preserve the advantages of global markets and competition, but also to provide enough space for human, community and environmental resources to ensure that globalization works for people—not just for profits. (2)

In other words, markets should be respected and largely allowed to function, but with protections and safeguards—a set of checks and balances—that will help respect and serve human life (Flexner 1989; Hartmann 2002; Korten 1995) and democracy (Frank 2000; Kelly 2001; Phillips 2002). In 1999, the United Nations initiated a Global Compact with business in which corporations would respect human, labor, and environmental concerns while the United Nations would promote open markets so that "business could then be left to do what it does best, create jobs and wealth while giving the global market more of a 'human face.'"[4]

Another mainstream institution, the Catholic Church, also advocates improving markets with checks and balances. In reaffirming Pope Leo XIII's famous encyclical *Rerum Novarum* ("On the Condition of Workers," 1891), Pope John Paul II's *Centesimus Annus* ("The Hundredth Year," 1991) declared that

> The State must contribute to the achievement of [dignity at work, a just and secure wage, and humane working conditions] both directly and indirectly. Indirectly and according to the principle of subsidiarity, by creating favorable conditions for the free exercise of economic activity, which will lead to abundant opportunities for employment and sources of wealth. Directly and according to the principle of solidarity, by defending the weakest, by placing certain limits on the autonomy of the parties who determine working conditions, and by ensuring in every case the necessary minimum support for the unemployed worker. (§15)[5]

The Catholic Church, which represents hundreds of millions of Catholics worldwide, roots this doctrine in the belief that labor markets fall short of the theoretical ideal of economics textbooks—that is, labor markets are imperfect. Consequently, employers and employees, capital and labor, are not equals, and unregulated market-based outcomes will favor employers at the expense of employees, with the potential for abuse. Checks and balances are needed to restore equality between labor and capital:

> The State, however, has the task of determining the juridical framework within which economic affairs are to be conducted, and thus of safeguarding the prerequisites of a free economy, which presumes a certain equality between the parties, such that one party would not be so powerful as practically to reduce the other to subservience. (*Centesimus Annus*, §15)

Pursuit of a balance between efficiency, equity, and voice in employment therefore raises fundamental questions about the nature of work, the operation of labor markets, conflict and power in the employment relationship, and the role of employment in a democratic, capitalist society. Differing views on these questions lead to contrasting visions of the employment relationship. Economic models of competitive markets emphasize laissez-faire employment policies free of regulatory and institutional interference. Critical theories based on the Marxist view of capitalist employment as a fundamentally unequal relationship, rooted in mutually reinforcing ideological and power differences, envision an employment relationship in which capitalism is challenged by worker control. Human resource management theories produce balanced employment outcomes by assuming that conflict between employers and employees can be resolved by effective corporate policies that will align the interests of corporations and workers. Mainstream U.S. industrial relations principles embrace the benefits of economic markets but also include a necessary role for nonmarket institutions—such as government regulations and labor unions—to balance unequal bargaining power between employers and employees and to therefore produce outcomes that create economic prosperity and respect for human life.

Explicit analyses of fundamental issues pertaining to the nature of work, the operation of labor markets, conflict and power in the employment relationship, and the nature of employment in capitalism, however, is not a hallmark of contemporary scholarship on employment, especially in the United States. In the golden age of U.S. industrial relations that followed World War II, for example, there was a widespread belief among industrial relations scholars that collective bargaining was "self-evidently good" (Reynolds 1988, 123). Today, the subject of labor relations is often presented to students of industrial relations—traditional students in a classroom, policymakers, and the general public—from this same self-evident perspective. The same is true for human resource management. This is perhaps most visibly illustrated by the numerous textbooks that focus uncritically on labor relations or human resource management *processes*.[6] This process-based focus is also reflected in policy debates over labor law reform in which lawmakers hear about the need to weaken wage and hours laws or ban strike replacements because *processes*—for compensating employees or bargaining contracts—are handicapped by them. Process-based treatments are typically closely related to an emphasis on work rules, as if they are ends in themselves.[7]

Furthermore, the rhetoric of competitive markets and efficiency dominates public discourse (Frank 2000; Phillips 2002; Yergin and Stanislaw 1998). Social welfare is conceived simply as "economic welfare" (Osterman et al. 2001) and justice as "marginal productivity justice"—that is, whatever worth is determined by the market must be fair (McClelland 1990).[8] Critics of labor unions generally paint a narrow picture of labor union monopolies as harmful to efficiency, competitiveness, and the smooth operation of free markets.[9] The concern with competitiveness and efficiency is so strong that the last major U.S. government commission on industrial relations under a Democratic president was charged with investigating how to improve efficiency, not justice.[10] And even while for the most part supportive of unionism, the large literature on the positive effects of union voice spawned by the seminal book *What Do Unions Do?* (Freeman and Medoff 1984) focuses on the economic effects of unions and reduces debates over unions to whether they enhance productivity. In fact, U.S. research on employment issues increasingly focuses on the narrow issues of competitiveness and quality (that is, efficiency) of work policies and practices.

Adding to the rhetorical power of efficiency is the close association of efficiency with property rights. Shareholders—the owners of corporate property—desire efficiency to maximize profits and therefore the returns on their investments. Standard economic theory emphasizes the importance of well-defined property rights for market-based economies to produce efficient outcomes. Government regulations and labor unions are seen as restrictions on property rights and efficiency to the extent that they constrain the freedom to allocate resources to their most economically productive use. But property rights are also considered a fundamental basis of liberty and, therefore, a basic human right. In contrast, equity and voice stem from concern about the treatment and rights of employees as human beings. Of particular interest is ensuring that markets, or corporations, do not produce outcomes that undermine the value of human life. As such, conflicts between efficiency, on the one hand, and equity and voice, on the other, can be considered conflicts between the conflicting human rights of property and labor—or, in popular discourse, freedom versus justice.

To balance these competing human rights, the employment relationship should, therefore, balance efficiency, equity, and voice. Can markets or corporations be relied on to balance these goals in the absence of unions, government regulation, or other institutions? Or is seeking a balance a futile exercise because of the fundamentally unequal employment relationship in a capitalist society? Is collective bargaining more effective at balancing efficiency, equity, and voice than other methods of governing the workplace? What forms of employee representation and statutory regulation are best suited for specific contexts? Do human resource management policies achieve efficiency with the help of, or at the expense of, equity and voice? These are the central questions of the employment relationship. Explicit examination of these questions is essential for the study of employment, but it also has broader importance because many of the contemporary social and political debates—whether over tax policy, welfare, globalization, or public education—are rooted in the same debates over visions of freedom and justice and over the extent to which free markets benefit everyone.

Robert Hoxie (1917, 3) asked why labor unions should be studied: "What is the vital problem which [trade unionism] presents to us as individuals and which we must strive to solve through its study? . . . What vital human and social interests does unionism touch and affect through its aims, principles, policies, demands, methods, and attitudes?" These same questions apply to the study of employment more generally. What "vital problem" does employment present to us that we "must strive to solve through its study?" The vital problem is not a narrow focus on work rules or how processes work, nor is it a limited focus on efficiency.[11] The vital problem is how to balance efficiency, equity, and voice in the face of the conflicting human rights of property and labor. The "vital human and social interests" is the fulfillment of employment with a human face.

Studying the World of Work

The employment relationship can be studied from various academic perspectives, but the academic field that defines itself as the study of the employment relationship is industrial relations. Its roots extend back into the 19th century and the rise of dissatisfaction with both the nature of wage labor and classical economic theory and the writings of Karl Marx, Richard Ely, Sidney and Beatrice Webb, and, most notably for U.S. industrial relations, John R. Commons in the first few decades of the twentieth century.[12] The field's development in the United States can best be understood in terms of the early twentieth-century "labor problem": undesirable outcomes that stemmed from an inequitable and contentious, or perhaps even oppressive and exploitative, employment relationship. Workers suffered through long hours at low wages in dangerous working conditions; employers faced problems of turnover and labor conflict; and society suffered from the resulting costs of unemployment, poverty, and social unrest.

Two major schools of thought on the labor problem emerged: an institutional school that saw the labor problem as rooted in imperfections in labor markets that caused an inequality in bargaining power between labor and management, and a personnel management school that believed that the labor problem stemmed from short-sighted management practices that ignored the human needs of workers. The personnel management school focused on improving management principles, while the institutional school focused on using institutions, especially labor unions and government regulation, to address the labor problem.

Modern industrial relations subscribes to the pluralist or institutional belief in an inherent conflict of interest in the employment relationship and, as a consequence, believes in a productive role of unions and government regulation. Modern human resource management follows the unitarist belief that effective management policies can align the interests of employees and employers and thereby remove conflicts of interest. From their point of view, unions and government regulations are either unnecessary or intrusive. A third alternative is the critical industrial relations school that views employment relationship conflict as class-based or social rather than limited to either a pluralist or unitarist view of conflict confined to the employment relationship.[13] In this book, I define "human resources and industrial relations" (HRIR) as the academic discipline that includes all three schools (see epilogue). It includes scholars from multiple disciplines, including economics, history, law, political science, psychology, and sociology. The normative perspective of this book generally reflects a modern restatement of the pluralist conception of industrial relations, but the three schools within HRIR—pluralist industrial relations, unitarist human resource management, and critical industrial relations—will be compared at important junctures (especially in chapter 5). Most significantly, the analyses of the efficiency, equity, and voice framework have great relevance for all three schools—and anyone interested in the employment relationship—and draw on diverse scholarship from the disciplines just mentioned as well as moral philosophy and theology.

The need to balance competing objectives has a distinguished intellectual history in industrial relations. In discussing consumption and production decisions, Webb and Webb (1897, 823) asserted that none of the "interminable series of decisions can be allowed to run counter to the consensus of expert opinion representing the consumers on the one hand, the producers on the other, and the nation that is paramount over both." As the Webbs explicitly highlighted the welfare of workers as being in the national interest, their statement implies the need for a balance. Commons (1919, 43) discussed the need for "the equilibrium of capital and labor" rather than the domination of one or the other. Kochan (1980, 21, emphasis in original) stresses that "industrial relations theories, research, and policy prescriptions must be conscious of the relationships among the goals of workers, employers, and the larger society and seek ways of achieving a workable and equitable *balance* among these interests." My analysis seeks to refocus attention on the basic goals of the employment relationship; to create the industrial relations trilogy of efficiency, equity, *and* voice; to strengthen the need for a balance by grounding it not only in the traditional view of an imbalance of power between employees and employers but also in contemporary thought on human rights, property rights, and ethics; and to consider alternative methods to achieve this balance.

Plan of the Book

Analysis of employment starts with the objectives of the employment relationship. Chapter 1 argues that the employment relationship objectives are efficiency, equity, and voice. Efficiency is the common economic standard of effective use of scarce resources, and a critical issue is the extent to which workplace efficiency can be achieved by relying on laissez-faire market policies. Equity in the employment relationship is a set of fair employment standards that respect human dignity, the sanctity of human life, and liberty and cover both material outcomes and personal treatment. Essential elements include fair outcomes pertaining to wages, hours, safety and health, child labor, retirement, health and disability insurance, and family leave as well as equal opportunity (nondiscrimination) and just cause dismissal policies. In other words, equity entails fairness in both the distribution of economic rewards (such as wages and benefits) and the administration of employment policies (such as nondiscriminatory hiring and firing). Voice is the ability to have meaningful employee input into decisions. This includes not only free speech, supported by protection against unfair dismissal and grievance procedures, but also direct and indirect participation in workplace decision making.

Although efficiency dominates popular discussions, efficiency and equity are traditionally considered the core industrial relations goals. Some might argue that voice is part of equity, but they should be treated separately. Efficiency and equity are instrumental standards in that they provide the means to greater ends (such as purchasing basic necessities), while voice is an intrinsic standard. Voice may increase efficiency and thus be instrumental, but irrespective of this participation is valued for its own sake in support of both democratic and human dignity ideals. When voice is included as part of equity, instrumental and intrinsic standards are being mixed. Equity pertains to distribution and administration, voice involves participation. Equity can be unilaterally provided, voice requires employee involvement. Thus, some methods of governing the workplace may more effectively deliver equity than voice, or vice versa. Some forms of unionism may also be better suited to providing voice than equity, or vice versa. Thus, for both theoretical and applied reasons, voice should be elevated to an equal and distinct standard alongside efficiency and equity. The objectives of the employment relationship are efficiency, equity, and *voice*.

The basic objectives of efficiency, equity, and voice can be complementary, but they often are in conflict. The drive for global competitiveness can negatively affect workers and communities through reduced employment opportunities, wage and benefit reductions, and plant closings. Employee voice can reduce efficiency by making managerial decision making more cumbersome. Equitable wage structures and seniority-based promotion and layoff policies can reduce managerial flexibility and efficiency. Chapter 2 argues that these clashes are fundamentally conflicts between competing human rights—property rights and labor rights. The theme of conflicting human rights is therefore an integral part of studying the employment relationship. The intellectual history of the nature of human rights, including both property rights and labor rights, supports the need to seek a balance between property rights and labor rights.

To analyze the determinants of efficiency, equity, and voice, a necessary foundation is the understanding of the factors that shape employment outcomes. Chapters 3 and 4 present a model in which employment outcomes are the product of interactions between employees and employers as influenced by both the work environment and the nature of human decision making, including ethics. In economics and industrial relations, the environment has long been recognized as a key determinant of employment outcomes. At the same time, research in psychology, sociology, and organizational behavior emphasizes the importance of the behavioral aspects of human decision making. Finally, as Kochan, Katz, and McKersie (1986) highlight, employer-employee and labor-management interactions can take place at several levels within an organization and society. Chapter 3 brings this scholarship together. The richer set of human needs and wants beyond income—biological, psychological, and social—that have been identified in the scholarship of individual decision making reinforces the need to conceptualize work as a fully human activity. And, thus, a fuller set of employment relationship objectives beyond efficiency is required. At the same time, the importance of the environment for employment outcomes implies that the controllable portions of the environment, such as the legal environment, should be structured to balance property rights and labor rights to promote a balance between efficiency, equity, and voice.

Inherent in this model of employment outcomes, and as emphasized by Kochan, Katz, and McKersie (1986), is that employees, managers, policy makers, and their organizations have choices. These choices are shaped by various factors, but a critical factor that is typically overlooked is ethics. Chapter 4 applies business ethics scholarship to the employment relationship. Given the close connection between the employment relationship and concerns for dignity, respect, justice, and fairness, a serious treatment of ethics in human resources and industrial relations is long overdue. Kantian moral philosophy, Rawlsian conceptions of justice, and Aristotelian virtue ethics provide compelling support for the central premise of balancing efficiency, equity, and voice. But ethics is more than a normative subject; explicit ethical theories can be used to better understand the choices that individuals make in the employment relationship.

This book therefore presents the study of employment—human resources and industrial relations—as the analysis of the contributions of individuals, markets, institutions, organizational strategies, and public policies toward the employment-relationship objectives of efficiency, equity, and voice in the workplace, as influenced by the environment and individual decision making, including ethics. This broad conception provides the basis for not only examining specific processes and practices but for addressing more fundamental questions regarding the potential need for reform of employment and labor law, management strategies, and union behavior. The trilogy of efficiency, equity, and voice builds on the important questions in human resources and industrial relations while providing a modern restatement of the field by explicitly including voice and by grounding these principles in the scholarship on human rights and ethics. Various institutions and employment-relationship patterns emphasize different combinations of efficiency, equity, and voice. With efficiency, equity, and voice as the three points of a triangle, the study of employment becomes the analysis of the geometry of the employment relationship.[14] The application of this conceptual framework from chapters 1–4 to important topics in human resources and industrial relations is the focus of chapters 5–9.

Chapter 5 addresses the question of how to broadly structure the employment relationship to achieve a balance between efficiency, equity, and voice.

Compensation and other terms and conditions of the employment relationship can be established by labor market forces, human resource management strategies, worker control, government regulation, or negotiations between employers and independent employee representatives (Weiler 1990). Each workplace governance mechanism has strengths and weaknesses, and explicit discussion of these issues reveals the importance of nonmarket institutions as a component of the employment relationship system for balancing efficiency, equity, and voice. Chapter 5 further distinguishes these alternative workplace governance mechanisms on the basis of differing beliefs concerning four fundamental assumptions about the nature of labor markets, work, conflict, and voice. The central beliefs of pluralist industrial relations yield a critical role for independent employee representation, as through labor unions, to provide equity and voice.

Chapter 6 analyzes the New Deal industrial relations system as favoring a certain system of workplace governance relying on particular mechanisms to achieve efficiency, equity, and voice. Seven decades of legal decisions and labor-management practices have tried to balance property and labor rights. Continuing debates, such as those over employee involvement, flexible work practices, or nonunion employee representation, reflect differing perspectives on how to balance these conflicting rights and achieve efficiency, equity, and voice in the geometry of the employment relationship.

Comparative research should be an important component of human resources and industrial relations. Chapter 7 applies the geometry of the employment relationship paradigm to the commonly discussed features of industrial relations systems in other industrialized market economies: social partnerships, sectoral bargaining, centralized awards, enterprise unionism, exclusive representation, codetermination, and voluntarism. The standards of efficiency, equity, and voice provide an important framework for analyzing these institutional arrangements and provide a common focus for comparative employment research. That the comparative framework of chapter 7 demonstrates the trade-offs between efficiency, equity, and voice inherent in different institutions further reinforces the value of the geometry of the employment relationship paradigm.

As with comparative institutional arrangements, alternative union strategies can be analyzed with the standards of efficiency, equity, and voice. Chapter 8 presents the principal U.S. postwar model of job control unionism and two broad alternatives. Within the constraints of the dominant scientific-management paradigm, job control unionism sought to balance efficiency, equity, and voice, but as management strategies move away from scientific management, the effectiveness of job control unionism is waning. Moreover, proponents of strong unions are critical of the narrow workplace focus of business unionism and the passive servicing model of representation embedded in job control unionism. Within business unionism's focus on the workplace, I outline a model of employee empowerment unionism in which workers are empowered to determine their own outcomes within a union-negotiated framework of procedures. Minimum standards and procedural safeguards are created through collective bargaining, while individual employees are empowered to make decisions, with the institutional support of union representation, as needed. Employee empowerment unionism is consistent with high-performance work systems, episodic employment patterns, desires to blend individual and collective representation, and an organizing model of representation—and can balance efficiency, equity, and voice. Social unionism alternatives to business unionism are also presented and analyzed in the context of the geometry of the employment relationship.

Globalization continues to pressure the employment relationship in very challenging ways, and chapter 9 examines efficiency, equity, and voice in the global economy. In particular, I focus on the question of who should govern the global workplace. The basic options for governing the workplace in the international arena are considered: free markets (free trade policies promulgated by the World Trade Organization), human resource management (corporate codes of conduct), government regulation (International Labour Organization or North American Free Trade Agreement side agreements), or independent employee representation (European Works Councils and transnational collective bargaining or labor solidarity). Each of these options represents different mechanisms for balancing efficiency, equity, and voice as well as property rights versus labor rights in the global economic system.

The concluding chapter revisits the problem of creating employment with a human face in light of the intellectual framework and analyses developed in the preceding chapters. It has long been recognized that there is no U.S. consensus on the nature of public policies pertaining to employment (Dunlop 1961; Brown and Myers 1962), and this continues to be true.[15] As a consequence, either policy changes do not occur or they occur as an overreaction to specific events and special-interest-group power. A necessary first step toward consensus is explicit recognition of the goals of the employment relationship. Constructing detailed reform proposals for creating employment with a human face in the complex world of the twenty-first century would require a second book; the goal here is to articulate the apparatus for considering such reforms by developing the intellectual framework for thinking about the objectives of the employment relationship and the alternatives for their achievement. Chapters 6–8 largely focus on the role of different types of unions and industrial relations systems in providing equity and voice because of their traditional importance in delivering these critical objectives of the employment relationship. But unions are not necessarily the only mechanism for serving these ends. The intent of this book is not to answer how equity and voice should be provided but to provide a solid intellectual justification for the importance of this question and a useful framework for analysis. The analysis of the geometry of the employment relationship implies that the U.S. employment system is not balancing efficiency, equity, and voice and points to new institutional arrangements, union strategies, and methods for governing the global workplace that would more effectively achieve this balance; but the options considered here are not intended to be exhaustive.

For readers specifically interested in the future of the academic field of industrial relations, a separate epilogue explores the implications of the efficiency, equity, and voice framework for the definition of an inclusive academic field of human resources and industrial relations. Contrary to deep-seated traditions, human resources and industrial relations does not need a single theory; it needs a common vision of the unique domain of the field. The major themes of efficiency, equity, and voice, combined with the alternatives for achieving these goals (ranging from competitive labor markets to government regulation, from human resource management to labor relations), encompass several key theories or paradigms, and one unifying vision of a renewed academic discipline. This framework also provides the basis for a shift in teaching from a process-based approach, which focuses on the operation of the current processes, to a theme-based approach in which the current processes, as well as alternatives, can be better understood and evaluated in the context of the goals of the employment relationship. An emphasis on employment with a human face, rather than specific processes, also provides the basis for stronger links with other disciplines.

Employment with a Human Face proceeds from the abstract to the concrete. Objectives of the employment relationship that move beyond efficiency and are rooted in human dignity involve philosophical questions about the nature of human life. A detailed examination of these philosophical questions is necessary to establish the case for equity and voice with intellectual rigor and thoroughness. The contemporary efficiency discourse is powerful; careful philosophical analysis is needed to counter this power. Moreover, my intent is to establish a broadly applicable characterization of the employment relationship goals—not objectives limited to a particular time and place—and this requires abstraction. For those who associate employment with processes, or industrial relations theory with John Dunlop's *Industrial Relations Systems* (1958), this book may seem to take a long time to get to specific processes and conventional thought. But my argument is that the examination of employment processes and conventional thought should start with first principles—the objectives of the employment relationship and their relative importance. Efficient work systems, equitable treatment of workers, and employee voice are critical human resources and industrial relations issues, and these are ultimately the subjects of the beginning chapters.

These issues are so critical, in fact, that they should lay the foundation for all other work. For this reason, they precede the later, more concrete chapters. Without an explicit statement of first principles, there is no basis for evaluating employment trends and practices. Is growing inequality a problem? Is the decline in union representation a cause for concern? Is the breakdown of the employment relationship's social contract troublesome? Is the lack of powerful employee voice in many employee participation programs worrisome? These questions can only be answered against standards for the objectives of the employment relationship. And only when such standards are in place can researchers, practitioners, and policy makers turn their attention to the design of institutions, policies, and practices that achieve the desired objectives.

1   *The Objectives of the*
Employment Relationship

THE STARTING POINT for analyses of the employment relationship should be the objectives of this relationship. Research in human resource management, industrial relations, and other disciplines as well as public debates should be grounded in the employment relationship objectives—the goals of employers, employees, and also of society. These objectives are efficiency, equity, and voice. Efficiency is the well-known standard of economic performance, equity encompasses fair employment standards in material outcomes and personal treatment, and voice is the ability to have meaningful input into decisions. Efficiency is an instrumental standard of economic performance—the effective use of scarce resources that provides the means for consumption and investment—and is the primary objective of employers. Equity and voice are the objectives of labor. Equity is an instrumental standard of treatment—a fair wage, basic social or private insurance coverage, vacation time, and nondiscriminatory treatment are instrumental in providing the means toward greater ends such as food, shelter, health care, and leisure. Voice is an *intrinsic* standard of participation—participation in decision making is an end in itself for rational human beings in a democratic society. Intrinsic voice is important whether or not it improves economic performance, and whether or not it alters the distribution of economic rewards.

Efficiency is paramount in mainstream economics, human resource management, and public debates. It is important to move beyond this narrow focus. Within industrial relations, efficiency and equity are often viewed as the classic standards as illustrated by Noah Meltz's 1989 title "Industrial Relations: Balancing Efficiency and Equity." Moreover, the industrial relations conception of equity sometimes includes voice. Barbash (1989, 116–17), for example, defines equity as "fairness, voice, security and work of consequence." It is also common to refer to both protection and participation

(Weiler 1990) or protection and democratic rights (Godard and Delaney 2000) as the key industrial relations principles. It is time to formalize these principles into distinct components of equity and voice, and to make them more than *industrial relations* principles.

There are several important reasons to explicitly distinguish between equity and voice as separate objectives of the employment relationship. First, equity is often used more narrowly in other disciplines.[1] Consequently, a revised industrial relations conception of equity that excludes voice is more consistent with popular usage. Second, even in industrial relations, equity sometimes excludes voice. Meltz's (1989, 110) definition of equity is "the fair treatment of human beings in a work place free from arbitrary decisions, discrimination, favoritism, and free from reliance only on the narrowest measures of short-run contributions to productivity." Similarly, Kaufman (1993, 13) states that the early industrial relations scholars sought "greater equity in the distribution of economic rewards, the utilization of labor, and the administration of employment policies in the workplace." Neither of these usages of equity include the principle of noneconomic voice. Third, equity is an instrumental standard of treatment whereas voice is an intrinsic standard of participation. This distinction has important implications for both the justification and the implementation of each standard. It bears emphasizing that equity is how employees are treated—paid a fair wage, provided safe working conditions, and dealt with in a nondiscriminatory fashion. In contrast, voice is not how one is treated—it is independent of distributional issues—but is rather an activity workers engage in (Klare 1985). Voice cannot be accomplished unilaterally—a specific participation vehicle is required.

An explicit distinction between the instrumental concept of equity and the intrinsic concept of voice is strengthened by similar distinctions in industrial and organizational psychology. First, there is a well-accepted distinction between extrinsic and intrinsic work motivation (Campbell and Pritchard 1976; Herzberg, Mausner, and Snyderman 1959; Kanfer 1992). Extrinsic factors include pay, working conditions, and job security. Intrinsic factors include stimulation or satisfaction from achievement, interest in a task, and self-determination or responsibility. This parallels the needed distinction between equity (which is instrumental) and voice (which is intrinsic). Second, there is also a well-established distinction between distributive justice and procedural justice (Cropanzano et al. 2001; Folger and Cropanzano 1998; Folger and Konovsky 1989; Greenberg 1987; Thibaut and Walker 1975). Distributive justice focuses on the fairness of outcomes whereas procedural justice focuses on the fairness of the process that determines outcomes. Although my definitions of equity and voice do not perfectly equate to distributive and procedural justice, respectively, the longstanding distinction between these two components of organizational justice reinforces the need to carefully distinguish between different standards, such as equity versus voice.[2] Thus, the popular emphasis on "efficiency" and the traditional industrial relations dyad of "efficiency and equity" should be replaced by the triad of "efficiency, equity, and voice" as the central employment relationship objectives.

The remainder of this chapter describes the dimensions and justifications for these three objectives. The three objectives are intentionally broad so that they can characterize the fundamental employment relationship goals for all democratic societies. The methods to achieve these objectives might vary with different cultures, technologies, and resource endowments, but the basic principles do not. As a consequence, the development of these basic principles in this chapter is abstract. Moreover, efficiency, equity, and voice are rooted in diverse thought in economics, law, political theory, moral philosophy, and theology so the discussion is necessarily theoretical and philosophical. As noted in the introduction, contemporary debates over employment are largely dominated by efficiency concerns. To advance a framework that moves beyond efficiency requires a careful examination of philosophical questions pertaining to basic elements of human dignity in order to rigorously and convincingly establish the case for equity and voice. Later chapters delve into concrete applications of the abstract framework established in the early chapters.

Efficiency

Efficiency is the effective use of scarce resources. The standard economic definition of efficiency is Pareto optimality: when no one can be made better off without making someone else worse off (Hausman and McPherson 1996).[3] Otherwise, if someone's welfare can be improved without harming someone else, the current situation is wasteful (inefficient) and scare resources are not being utilized as effectively as they could be.[4] In more familiar terms, efficiency is closely associated with the business objective of maximizing profits. With its emphasis on effective use of scarce resources and the resulting benefits of economic prosperity, efficiency is an important objective of the employment relationship. Individuals differ, however, on their beliefs of what an efficient employment relationship should look like and how to best achieve it. The powerful link between efficiency and free market competition is revealed by the first fundamental theorem of welfare economics: every (perfectly) competitive equilibrium is Pareto optimal. Consequently, mainstream economics (the familiar neoclassical economics paradigm) emphasizes the importance of competitive markets: under some assumptions (such as perfect information and no transaction costs), voluntary economic transactions between self-interested, rational, informed agents in competitive markets result in efficient, Pareto optimal outcomes. In other words, economic welfare is maximized by the invisible hand of economic activity in competitive markets. The common law elements of well-defined property rights, freedom to enter into economic relationships (liberty of "contract"), and the law of torts to protect property damage support free exchange and are assumed to promote efficiency because of the behavior of self-interested individuals and companies (Epstein 1984; Posner 1986; Schwab 1997). Moreover, with no transaction costs, the famous Coase Theorem demonstrates that optimal efficient outcomes will result from competition irrespective of the initial distribution of property rights (Coase 1960).

These economic and legal theories are mutually reinforcing. Consumers, workers, corporations, suppliers, investors, and other economic agents will maximize their individual welfare and profits. If they can interact as equals in competitive markets, pursuit of their self-interest yields socially optimal, efficient outcomes—outcomes that cannot be improved via government intervention or other means. Unless the textbook assumptions are violated, laissez-faire economic and legal policies allow freely adjusting prices for inputs and outputs to signal scarcity and relative worth and guide the participants to efficiency, profit maximization, and economic prosperity.

This laissez-faire approach is the baseline theoretical model for judging efficiency. However, even some laissez-faire proponents admit that the classical, textbook assumptions are suspect, especially in the employment relationship. Thus, market failures can interfere with efficiency. While bearing in mind that some argue that in many cases trying to correct a market failure can exacerbate rather than improve an inefficient outcome, there are three broad categories of market failures to consider.[5] One, even in competitive markets, there can be externalities—essentially, spillovers in which an individual's or an organization's behavior benefits or harms someone else—in which case individual self-interest will not necessarily produce socially desirable outcomes. Two, if labor markets are not perfectly competitive, unregulated economic activity does not necessarily produce efficient outcomes. Three, the mainstream, neoclassical economics calculus often downplays the human side of labor, and it may be possible to increase efficiency by incorporating psychological and social concerns. In sum, in all three of the categories, economic outcomes can be improved by supplementing the invisible hand of free markets, for example with a law, a union, or a human resource management policy. In other words, "often the invisible guiding hand of competition is all thumbs" (Mangum and Philips 1988, 4–5).

One example of an externality (a spillover) involves workplace public goods such as safety provisions, lighting and ventilation, just-cause discipline and discharge provisions, or grievance procedures. By definition, an individual benefits from a public good regardless of whether they have directly paid for it. Consider an employee who can choose a lower wage in return for additional workplace safety protections that are freely available to all employees. Pure self-interest creates a free rider problem: rather than pay for this public good, let the others pay for it while you enjoy the benefits, that is, you can get a "free ride." In the extreme, when everyone is a free rider, no public goods will be produced even if the aggregate benefits outweigh the aggregate costs. The problem is that self-interest ignores the spillover benefits to others. Thus, even in competitive markets, the free rider problem can cause lower than optimal or desired levels of workplace public goods to be produced or offered because individual employees do not account for the social benefits in their own decision making (Freeman and Medoff 1984; Kaufman and Levine 2000).

A host of other externality problems may arise if there are social costs to competitive outcomes, that is, if there is a negative spillover.[6] For example, suppose a competitive labor market yields low wages, dangerous working conditions, and lack of health insurance coverage for unskilled workers. This can impose negative externalities on the rest of the community because taxpayers foot the bill for welfare, subsidized food purchases, public housing, and pubic health clinics. Or approaching the problem from the opposite angle, provision of family and medical leave, for example, can have positive externalities if it results in a healthier, better-nurtured populace. Providing advance notification of layoffs generates positive externalities if this advance warning lessens social costs to the community.

Negative externalities are also implicit in the legislative justification for the Wagner Act, which was enacted during the Great Depression to encourage workers to unionize. The reasoning was that strikes and other industrial disputes weaken the economy while (destructively) competitive labor market outcomes with low wages depress aggregate purchasing power (Kaufman 1996). By stabilizing industrial relations conflict, and by increasing workers' bargaining power (and therefore compensation) through unionization, the Wagner Act would stimulate the economy, or so the New Deal thinking went.

Last, there can be externalities and problems stemming from coordination failures in trying to move from a mass manufacturing to a high-performance employment system (Levine 1995). Starting from a mass manufacturing equilibrium, consider what happens if one company tries to switch to a high-performance paradigm. If a high-performance workplace has narrower wage differentials than the competitive market (to foster group cohesiveness, for example), then high-performance workplaces will have difficulty attracting higher skilled employees who can earn a higher wage elsewhere (Levine 1995). As a second example, if a high-performance workplace offers a just cause dismissal policy while the rest of the market does not, this firm will suffer from adverse selection problems in which workers with the greatest need for just cause protections—perhaps because of absenteeism or other undesirable habits—will disproportionately join this firm (Addison and Hirsch 1997; Levine 1995; Schwab 1997).

Many of these externality arguments are closely related to the second market-failures category of arguments that undermine the achievement of efficiency solely through laissez-faire economic and legal policies: information asymmetries, mobility costs, liquidity constraints (imperfect capital markets for workers), and transactions costs can impede the operation of competitive labor markets.[7] Employees likely have incomplete information about dismissal policies, accident risks, or pensions and therefore do not behave optimally (Weiler 1990; Addison and Hirsch 1997). The old institutional labor economists emphasized that labor market imperfections gave employers superior bargaining power relative to individual employees, which caused workers to engage in excessive labor market competition (Kaufman 1997b). Recent increases in globalization, and the international mobility of capital, have increased employer bargaining power in some industries and occupations (Befort 2002). Modern internal labor markets, unvested pension benefits, and employer-specific health insurance plans can also increase a firm's leverage over workers by increasing workers' mobility costs and therefore making it more difficult for employees to find an equivalent job elsewhere (Buchmueller and Valletta 1996; Ghilarducci 1990; Weiler 1990). At its worst, superior employer bargaining power can result in low wages, long hours, dangerous conditions, and arbitrary or abusive supervisory practices.[8] In addition to the negative social costs mentioned above, these labor problems can be detrimental to efficiency by undermining trust, cooperation, and motivation.[9]

This foreshadows the third category of efficiency-enhancing arguments. Contemporary human resource management emphasizes fair treatment, or distributive and procedural justice, as an important mechanism for reducing turnover and improving employee loyalty, motivation, and performance (Folger and Cropanzano 1998; Hammer 2000). Moreover, some form of employee voice is an important part of many recent corporate efforts to improve competitiveness and quality via employee involvement programs and the creation of high-performance work systems.[10] Employee representation can potentially enhance efficiency by addressing problems stemming from asymmetric information (Freeman and Lazear 1995), transactions costs (Kaufman and Levine 2000), and lack of procedural justice (Hammer 2000). And the possibility that unions can increase productivity by providing worker voice was famously demonstrated by Freeman and Medoff (1984).

In sum, because of the importance of using scarce resources effectively and therefore creating economic prosperity, efficiency is a primary objective of the employment relationship—and in other spheres of economic activity. In an ideal, textbook world, perfect competition yields efficient outcomes. But in real world labor markets, there is less agreement about how to achieve efficiency. This section has suggested a number of possible efficiency enhancements to the employment relationship (see table 1.1). They are not all well-accepted—in fact, market proponents argue that these enhancements cause more harm than good—and they are not presented here as truths. Rather, wide-ranging possibilities are presented to enable us to think broadly about the possible elements of an efficient employment relationship.

Equity

Equity in the employment relationship is a set of fair employment standards covering both material outcomes and personal treatment that respect human dignity and liberty. In industrial relations, the emphasis on equity can be

Table 1.1 Dimensions of Efficiency, Equity, and Voice

Objective	Rationale
Efficiency	
Market-based transactions and contracts	Allocative efficiency
Minimum labor standards (wages, hours, safety, family leave, advance notice, child labor)	Externalities (social cost, purchasing power), asymmetric information
Income maintenance (unemployment insurance, workers' compensation, pension standards)	Asymmetric information, costly dispute resolution, liquidity constraints
Industrial peace	Externalities (social cost)
Increased labor bargaining power	Externalities (social cost, purchasing power), mobility costs
Workplace public goods	Externalities (free riders)
Equality of opportunity	Externalities (social cost)
Employee representation/participation	Coordination failure, asymmetric information
Just cause dismissal	Coordination failure, costly dispute resolution
Equity	
Minimum labor standards (wages, hours, safety, family leave, advance notice, child labor)	Human dignity (moral and religious)
Balanced distribution of income	Political equality/liberty
Equality of opportunity	Human dignity (moral and religious), political equality/liberty, due process rights
Just cause dismissal	Human dignity (moral and religious), political equality/liberty, due process rights
Voice	
Industrial democracy	Political equality/liberty/democracy
Employee decision making and autonomy	Human dignity (moral and religious), psychological/social needs, property rights (stakeholder theory)
Free speech	Liberty/human dignity (moral)
Political employee voice	Political equality/liberty

traced to the early twentieth-century concern with excessive labor market competition among employees leading to employment practices that were sometimes abusive and exploitive. This was labeled the "labor problem" and was characterized by long hours at low wages in dangerous working conditions (Kaufman 1993, 1997b). As such, the drive for equitable employment outcomes focused to a large degree on minimum standards—minimum wages, maximum hours, minimum safety standards, protections against arbitrary discharge and favoritism, and restrictions on child labor.

In human resource management, the emphasis on equity is focused less on minimum standards and more on general fairness. This is perhaps classically illustrated through the equity theory of Adams (1965) in which a person views the distribution of outcomes as fair if the ratio of the individual's outputs to inputs equals the analogous ratio for someone else. In other words, equity stems from perceived consistency between effort and reward. In the labor movement, this is associated with the famous slogan "a fair day's pay for a fair day's work." Contemporary theories of organizational justice also include procedural justice, which focuses on the fairness of procedures (Cropanzano et al. 2001; Folger and Cropanzano 1998; Folger and Konovsky 1989; Greenberg 1987; Thibaut and Walker 1975).[11]

Equity as a standard of the employment relationship contains all three of these concepts: a set of minimum standards, distributive justice, and procedural justice.[12] Equity is therefore fairness in the employment relationship such that employees receive the treatment they deserve including both minimum conditions worthy of any free human being and fair conditions based on objective standards of performance.[13] Equitable minimum standards include minimum wages, maximum hours, safety and health protections, child labor restrictions, family leave, and the provision of retirement, health, and disability insurance (see table 1.1). Equity also includes work rewards that are fair and a balanced distribution of income. Equity also requires nondiscrimination policies so that people have equal opportunities and also protections against unjust dismissal. The importance of these precepts are underscored by their wide-ranging justifications including moral views of human dignity, religious beliefs about the sanctity of human life, humanistic psychology theories of human nature, and political theories of liberty and democracy.[14]

The employment relationship objective of equity can be supported by various ethical theories.[15] In the philosophy of Immanuel Kant, our actions must "always treat humanity, whether in your own person or in the person of any other, never simply as a means, but always at the same time as an end" (Sullivan 1989, 148). This stems from the basic value of human life and yields equity as an important standard of the employment relationship—for example, paying unfair wages or managing people in a discriminatory fashion treats them as a means, not as an end (Bowie 1999). Unjust dismissal without due process similarly violates Kantian moral principles (Bowie 1999; Pincoffs 1977). In the Aristotelian moral tradition, Nussbaum (2000, 5) argues that human beings have a moral right to pursue basic human capabilities—"what people are actually able to do and to be." Of particular relevance for the workplace, the universal capabilities that everyone is entitled to include "being able to live to the end of a human life of normal length" (78), "being able to have good health, including . . . to be adequately nourished" (78), and "having the right to seek employment on an equal basis with others" (80). Although emphasizing capabilities instead of explicit outcomes, this is another moral argument for important dimensions of employment relationship equity such as a minimum and fair wage, safety standards, and nondiscriminatory treatment. This is again based on the basic value of human dignity. More broadly, Goodin

(1985) argues that standard moral theories imply, or are at least consistent with, a particular responsibility for protecting the vulnerable. This includes vulnerabilities stemming from the employment relationship and is therefore essentially a moral theory of workplace minimum standards and equity.

Religious views on the sanctity of human life and respect for human dignity often closely resemble secular ethical conceptions of human dignity. It is thus no surprise that the standard of equity in the employment relationship also derives from religious thought (Ryan 1912).[16] In the form of papal encyclicals, the Catholic Church has been the most explicit. In the first encyclical on social thought, *Rerum Novarum* ("On the Condition of Workers," 1891), Pope Leo XIII wrote "justice demands that the dignity of human personality be respected in [workers] . . . It is shameful and inhuman, however, to use men as things for gain and to put no more value on them that what they are worth in muscle and energy" (§31).[17] Why? Because "no one may with impunity outrage the dignity of man, which God Himself treats with great reverence, nor impede his course to that level of perfection which accords with eternal life in heaven" (§57). Consequently, *Rerum Novarum* advocates workplace equity: a living wage, a limit on working hours, health standards, and restrictions on child labor.

These principles are reaffirmed in Pope John Paul II's *Centesimus Annus* ("The Hundredth Year," 1991):

> God has imprinted his own image and likeness on man (cf. Gen. 1:26), conferring upon him an incomparable dignity, as [*Rerum Novarum*] frequently insists. In effect, beyond the rights which man acquires by his own work, there exist rights which do not correspond to any work he performs, but which flow from his essential dignity as a person. (§11)[18]

While also affirming the importance of private property, the efficiency of the "modern business economy," and the "legitimate role of profit," *Centesimus Annus* asserts that the market should be "appropriately controlled by the forces of society and by the State, so as to guarantee that the basic needs of the whole of society are satisfied" (§32 and 35). Thus, to fulfill moral and spiritual development in human beings created by God, a fair set of material standards and fair treatment are necessary in the employment relationship.

Although Catholic labor policy has been the most explicit, Protestant, Jewish, and Islamic traditions also champion the dignity of human life and therefore the need for workplace justice.[19] According to Perry (1993, 1), in Judaism, "a social justice imperative appears repeatedly in Talmudic decisions concerning worker rights." This yields important standards regarding the payment of wages, hours of work, and sick and disability pay (Weisfeld 1974; Perry 1993). In Islam, one hadith of the Holy Prophet can be interpreted as requiring a living wage for workers and many teachings emphasize justice and fairness. Equitable distribution of wealth and lack of discrimination or favoritism are also important (Khalil-ur-Rehman 1995).

In addition to secular and religious beliefs about human dignity, the equity standard can also be constructed from political theories of justice. One line of argument is that the goal of a political system should be to provide the basic standards needed for self-development and self-actualization (Hill 1997). Humanistic psychology maintains that self-actualization flows from a hierarchy of needs that includes physiological and security needs as the building blocks (Maslow 1968).[20] As such, the standards of workplace equity that provide for these basic needs—including a living wage, safe working conditions, job security, and health insurance—are necessary for self-development and self-actualization and should therefore be provided by the political system.[21] In other words, workplace equity should be an important societal goal.

Another political theory in support of workplace equity stems from John Rawls's landmark *A Theory of Justice* (1971). A centerpiece of this framework is that social and economic inequalities are acceptable only if opportunities are available to all and if the inequalities benefit the worst-off members of society. This conception of justice implies that everyone is entitled to a minimum of resources and to equal opportunities—in the workplace this amounts to minimum material standards and policies of fair, nondiscriminatory treatment.[22] This is a political theory because it can be justified on the basis of the requirements for free and equal citizens in a political democracy; that is, on the basis of political liberalism (Rawls 1993, 2001). In other words, the lack of equity—discriminatory treatment and a lack of minimum standards—is counter to the basic ideals of political democracy. This assertion has two strains (West 2001). First, citizens are not able to function as political equals when they lack a basic level of material well-being (Cohen and Rogers 1983; Sandel 1996). Second, irrespective of the inability to function as political equals, a democratic state has an obligation to provide minimum standards. To do otherwise would violate the democratic, and U.S. constitutional, requirement of equal protection and due process (Michelman 1969; Zietlow 1998).[23]

Rawls's theory is not without its critics (see Daniels 1975; Sandel 1982). At the other end of the liberalism spectrum, Nozick's (1974) entitlement theory of justice emphasizes the achievement of justice through libertarian rights of individual freedom and private property in the tradition of John Locke. However, even libertarian theorists such as Locke and Nozick are troubled by social outcomes that deprive some individuals of enough income to survive (Edelman 1987).[24] In fact, Sterba (1988) argues that libertarian (emphasizing liberty), socialist (emphasizing equality), feminist (emphasizing androgyny), and communitarian (emphasizing the common good) theories of justice all support the liberal egalitarian right to welfare and affirmative action.[25] Sterba's (1988) logic applies equally well to minimum wage and safety standards. As such, various political theories can be argued to support the standard of workplace equity, especially in terms of minimum standards and nondiscrimination. Ideals of political equality, civic engagement, and social cohesion also imply that a balanced distribution of income is desirable (Krueger 2002; Osterman et al. 2001; Sandel 1996).

But what about just-cause dismissal protections? The libertarian argument is that personal freedoms mandate that employers are free to discharge workers at any time just as employees are free to quit at any time (Epstein 1983). Two counterarguments are often made. First, the lack of unjust dismissal protections embedded in the employment-at-will system undermines the ability to achieve other dimensions of the workplace equity standard (Blades 1967; Summers 2000). That an at-will employee can be fired for saying "blacks have rights too" to a coworker begs the question of the reality of equal opportunity laws.[26]

Second, and more strongly, respect for liberty, due process, and human dignity ought to imply the need for unjust dismissal protections in their own right. Examples of abusive discharge have been well-catalogued (Blades 1967; Summers 2000) and include being legally fired for failing to divorce one's wife, refusing to falsify federally required food and drug records, and refusing to illegally smuggle liquor or illegal immigrants for an employer. Workers have been fired for living with someone without being married, smoking, drinking, riding a motorcycle, and other legal activities outside of work (Dworkin 1997). Unjust dismissal protections therefore develop "a greater respect for the individuality of the employee" (Blades 1967, 1414), provide "elemental fairness" (Bellace 1983, 212) and are "an essential element of industrial justice" that "should need no argument in our time" (Summers 1976, 532). In short, how can the employment-at-will doctrine, with its explicit admission that workers can be fired for morally wrong reasons, be morally acceptable?[27]

In sum, equity should be a societal objective of the employment relationship that includes both minimum and fair standards that pertain to material outcomes such as wages and to issues of treatment such as nondiscrimination and just-cause discipline and discharge (see table 1.1). In other words, equity is fairness in distribution and administration. This equity standard stems from ethical and religious theories rooted in the sanctity of human life and dignity, and from political theories of liberty and democracy. It is an instrumental standard because its violation denies individuals the ability to live a full and free (working) life. This equity standard, however, can be fulfilled without the employee's participation—all of the dimensions involve how the employee is treated (unilaterally) by the employer. For a standard of participation or involvement, the voice component is necessary.

Voice

Voice is the ability to have *meaningful* input into decisions. The addition of voice to the pillars of efficiency and equity explicitly adds and emphasizes an element of self-determination in the employment relationship—even if it doesn't enhance efficiency. This conception of voice has two elements: industrial democracy rooted in political theories of self-determination, and employee decision making that stems from the importance of autonomy for human dignity (see table 1.1). As such, although voice is closely related to democracy, there are aspects of voice that go beyond democratic conceptions of voice or participation. Put differently, it is difficult to fulfill the voice standard without some elements of democracy in the workplace (industrial democracy), but there are additional forms of individual decision making and autonomy that can also contribute to this standard. It is therefore better to use the term "voice" than "democracy" even though to a large extent they are closely related.[28]

Before turning to the elements of voice, it is important to note that "voice" has been used in employment research and practice in varied ways. Hirschman (1970, 30) largely established the conception of voice in economics as efforts to "change, rather than escape from [that is, exit], an objectionable state of affairs." This thinking has been very influential in employment research as illustrated by the numerous studies of the determinants and consequences of employee voice versus exit (e.g., Bemmels 1997), and of labor unions as institutions of collective voice (Freeman and Medoff 1984). For Hirschman (1970), Freeman and Medoff (1984), and others in this tradition, the interest in voice focuses on its effect on efficiency. But this is not the only use of the term "voice" in employment research and practice. Over one hundred years ago, a hearing of the United States Industrial Commission (1901, 772, emphasis added) discussed whether "it is a *legitimate purpose* of workingmen, or a set or workingmen, to have some *voice* in fixing the hours of labor and the sanitary conditions under which they work." Foreshadowing Senator Wagner's New Deal vision of promoting collective bargaining as "a voice in industry" (see below), Estey (1928, 208, emphasis added) wrote

> It is a fundamental doctrine of political democracy that one should have some voice in regard to matters that vitally affect him. . . . For unless he has this voice, usually exercised through the vote, then the most important incidents of his life, his wealth, his property, indeed his very life itself are removed from out of his control. . . . If there is an argument for giving [a worker] a vote, even more is there an argument for giving him a *voice* in the conditions of shop and factory.

Osterman et al. (2001, 12, emphasis added) similarly describe labor unionism as, at least partly, "a positive social and economic institution that helps give workers a *voice* in regard to their working conditions." Or witness the AFL-CIO's recent "voice at work" campaign, which similarly highlights unions as vehicles for participating in the workplace determination of wages, hours, and terms and conditions of employment. These conceptions of voice are not narrowly limited to Hirschman's (1970) efficiency-enhancing, alternative-to-exit definition of voice but are rather linked to visions of workers' rights for self-determination in the workplace. This latter conception of voice is what the standard of voice developed in this book extends.[29] The principle of voice articulated here as one of the three objectives of the employment relationship stems from political, moral, religious, psychological, and even property rights foundations.

The first element of voice is industrial democracy. Heckscher (1988, 166–67) articulates four basic rights critical for "an effective system of representation . . . necessary to permit the expression of employee concerns": due process, information, speech, and association.[30] It borders on a truism, but freedom of speech is essential for meaningful voice. But to make this freedom effective, it must be backed up by three other protections. Due process provides for a set of standards so that employees can only be disciplined or discharged for just cause. This includes not only discipline or discharge for valid, job-related reasons, but also standards relating to reasonableness, evidence, and the nature of a hearing (Koven and Smith 1992).[31] Due process is vital if voice is not to be hollow, in both the workplace and the political arena, to prevent reprisals against the expression of complaints and unpopular or critical views (Derber 1970). Information is necessary not only because viable participation and the expression of voice must be based on informed knowledge of situations, but also to foster the accountability of leaders and representatives (Derber 1970). Lastly, the freedom of association or representation is essential (Greenfield and Pleasure 1993; Gross 1999).[32]

In other words, industrial democracy entails having a *meaningful* voice in the determination of working conditions based on the political principles of democracy. Workers should be able to express unpopular views. Workers should be protected from arbitrary treatment and have access to fair dispute resolution procedures when disagreements arise. And either directly or through representatives, workers should be able to participate in workplace decision making. The earliest arguments for voice appear to stem from political thought—hence the term "industrial democracy." As far back as the 1790s, Albert Gallatin, the later Secretary of the Treasury for Presidents Jefferson and Madison, stated "The democratic principle on which this nation was founded should not be restricted to the political process but should be applied to the industrial operation as well" (as quoted in Derber 1970, 6). The arguments behind this idea were diverse (Harris 1993), but a basic undercurrent flows from the concept of liberty.[33] This is apparent in this 1904 Iron Molders editorial: "Political equality is not sufficient and unless the wage-earner possesses an industrial equality that places him upon a par with his employer there can never exist that freedom and liberty of action which is necessary to the maintenance of a republican form of government" (as quoted in Harris 1993, 46–47). Senator Wagner promoted the National Labor Relations Act on this same basis:

> The struggle for a voice in industry through the process of collective bargaining is at the heart of the struggle for the preservation of political as well as economic democracy in America. Let men become the servile pawns of their masters in the factories of the land and there will be destroyed the bone and sinew of resistance to political dictatorship (Keyserling 1945, 14).

These sentiments are often echoed today. Gould (1993, 32) is typical: "democratic values are important in the workplace . . . Real participation in industrial society is critical to a democratic society. Regrettably in the United States the concept of economic democracy has lagged considerably behind political democracy." Weiler (1990, 185) similarly emphasizes the critical objective of employee participation because of the "intrinsic value" in having "employees take the responsibility for defining, asserting, and, if necessary, compromising their concerns." These assertions reinforce the need to distinguish equity from voice, but it is important to explicitly examine why democracy in the workplace is a societal objective of the employment relationship.

The most fundamental reason for industrial democracy is that in a democratic society, there should not be an arbitrary distinction between having a voice in political decisions but not economic ones, especially since economic decisions might impact individuals' lives more directly (Estey 1928). As argued by Gross (1999, 70), "a full human life requires the kind of participation in the political, economic, and social life of the human community that enables people to have an influence on the decisions that affect their lives." These principles should not be checked at the factory gate or office door (Adams 1995; Gross 1999) and a democratic society should seek to "democratize the entire existential space of the world" (Klare 1988, 8), including the workplace.[34]

The rationale for extending political democracy to the workplace is reinforced by the central institutional labor economics belief in an inequality of bargaining power. Without industrial equality, there is little to prevent economic coercion of workers by companies—recall the early twentieth-century labor problem. In addition to failing to provide equity, this coercion can also undermine liberty. A widespread concern in the late nineteenth and early twentieth centuries was that economic power threatened political freedom because the coercive power of employers spilled into the political arena, for example through controls over local government machinery. In fact, unions argued that without collective voice and its derivative power, labor was not effectively free. As such, it is argued that individual and collective employee voice is rooted in the First, Thirteenth, and Fourteenth Amendments to the U.S. Constitution (Forbath 2001; Pope 1997, 2002).[35] These amendments deal with fundamental political freedoms—speech, assembly, freedom from involuntary servitude, and due process—which provide social citizenship or economic and social freedoms.[36] Social citizenship includes industrial democracy: employee voice is necessary for workers to enjoy legitimate political liberty. This continues to be an important issue as witnessed by the protests against the World Trade Organization and the International Monetary Fund based on frustration with decisions being made behind closed doors with only the interests of multinational corporations and financial institutions in mind (Stiglitz 2002; Wallach and Sforza 2000), and as witnessed by concerns that multinational corporations dominate markets and countries (Estes 1996; Flexner 1989; Korten 1995, 1999).

It is also argued that participation in civil and political life is crucial to democracy, but that much of one's life is spent at work, which is often undemocratic (Brest 1988; Estlund 2000; Pateman 1970). Consequently, an additional political argument for industrial democracy is to create citizens who are trained in participatory democracy. In other words, the workplace should be a school or training ground for democracy, both practically and psychologically (Klare 1988; Pateman 1970). This is reminiscent of Senator Wagner's assertion "but let men know the dignity of freedom and self-expression in their daily lives, and they will never bow to tyranny in any quarter of their natural life" (Keyserling 1945, 14). In the political arena, a strong voice for workers is also necessary to protect and advance workplace justice and the goals of workplace equity and voice; in democratic societies this political voice is typically provided by the labor movement (Lichtenstein 2002).

The second element of voice is employee decision making, which is rooted in theology and moral philosophy. These justifications for voice stem from the importance of self-determination and autonomy for human dignity. As such, this aspect of voice is less closely tied to workplace structures that are democratic, and can be achieved by allowing employees to exercise some discretion or to have their opinions considered. Consider first Catholic social teachings. Both as a necessity for moral and spiritual development and because human beings are part of God's ongoing creation, papal social doctrine in the Catholic Church mandates employee participation in decision making (Naughton 1995).[37] In *Laborem Exercens* ("On Human Work," 1981), Pope John Paul II asserts that employees should "be able to take part in the very work process as a sharer in responsibility" (§15.1). While drawing the line at decision making over investments, mergers, and other business decisions such as plant closings—in other words, the "core of entrepreneurial control"—there is a clear papal mandate for employee participation and responsibility in determining how work is done on a day-to-day basis (Naughton 1995).[38]

These arguments are consistent with Kantian moral philosophy. For Kant, the basis of human dignity is autonomy and therefore self-governance, which in turn mandate the ability to reason (Bowie 1999; O'Neill 1989). Fulfillment of autonomy, self-governance, and the ability to reason require workplace voice. According to Kant (1998 [1781], 643, emphasis in original), reason "has no dictatorial authority, but whose claim is never anything more than the agreement of free citizens, each of whom must be permitted to express his reservations, indeed even his *veto,* without holding back" (A739/B767). Therefore, employees are entitled to free speech and to participate in workplace decision making (Bowie 1999). Similarly, Sashkin (1984) asserts that autonomy, meaningful work, and interpersonal contact are basic human needs and therefore workplace participation in decision making (self-governance) is a moral obligation. Solomon (1996) makes a similar argument, using Maslow's famous theory of needs, based on personal growth.[39] And Hodson's (2001, 237) extended analysis of worker dignity is based on the premise that "working with dignity ultimately requires the right to participate actively in all aspects of work life, through both formal and informal means. Dignity rests on the opportunity to exercise agency—to operate purposively and effectively in one's environment."

The stakeholder theory of the corporation also asserts that employees are entitled to workplace voice as stakeholders. Perhaps ironically, this right is argued to stem from property rights (Donaldson and Preston 1995). Once one admits that property rights are not unrestricted because of restrictions against harming others, then multiple interests automatically enter into the equation of rights.[40] It then becomes a question of distributive justice and Donaldson and Preston (1995) assert that employees' interests, whether based on effort in contributing to the development of a company or on employee needs, fit into standard models of distributive justice.[41] Thus, employees have a moral interest, or a "stake," in a company and are entitled to voice.

In sum, political democracies are premised on the ideal that people should have input into decisions that affect their lives—voice (Pateman 1970).[42] For reasons stemming from political theory, religious thought, human dignity, and elsewhere, extending voice into the workplace is a "moral imperative" (Adams 1991; also, Gross 1999). This echoes Dunlop et al.'s (1975, 39) test (among others) for the performance of industrialization: "contributions to opportunities for individuals to participate in the making of decisions affecting them as citizens, as workers, as consumers." But must employee voice be individual or collective? The industrial democracy dimension of voice suggests that a collective voice component is necessary while the self-determination dimension implies that individual voice mechanisms are also important. The traditional industrial relations mechanism for establishing a level playing field between labor and management—and therefore the foundation of democratic practices among equals—is through unionization. Other perspectives, such as the human resource management view, challenge the necessity of unionization to bring democracy into the workplace. In practice, whether workplace voice is individual or collective and whether an independent labor union is required are critical—and often divisive—issues, but these questions are left to future chapters. The key point at this juncture is that the standard of voice—perhaps individual, perhaps collective—is a necessary objective of the employment relationship and it merits equal consideration with efficiency and equity.

Beyond Efficiency, Beyond Equity

To move beyond public discourse, and the dominant research on the employment relationship, which focuses almost exclusively on efficiency, competitive markets, and marginal productivity justice, a careful statement of the employment relationship objectives is needed. As work is a fully human activity, employment outcomes and processes must respect human dignity and therefore the societal objectives of the employment relationship are efficiency, equity, and voice. Moreover, existing paradigms that emphasize efficiency and equity—as in traditional industrial relations thought, but also in some streams in economics, law, and other disciplines—need to broaden their perspectives to also include voice as an equal standard. As with equity, voice is grounded in scholarship on democracy, freedom, and human dignity. The trilogy of efficiency, equity, and voice advances the maxim of efficiency and equity by explicitly distinguishing between the instrumental dimension of equity and the intrinsic standard of voice. The addition of voice to efficiency and equity is also consistent with what U.S. workers want. Most visibly, a survey by Freeman and Rogers (1999) found that 63 percent of American workers want more influence over "company decisions that affect your job or work life." A majority of workers also indicated that they would like representation that is independent of management.

Important historical and recent scholarship has also articulated objectives broader than the standard twin pillars of efficiency and equity. Barbash (1984) sees industrial relations as resolving conflicts between management's drive for cost discipline (efficiency) and labor's objectives of price, equity, effort, and power (PEEP). "Price" is labor's compensation, "equity" is distributive justice or fairness, "effort" is the degree of on-the-job exertion, and "power" is "having a voice in the terms of employment" (Barbash 1984, 40). Price and effort, however, are inextricably linked to equity and efficiency. As such, Barbash's cost discipline and PEEP reduces to efficiency, equity, and voice.

In analyses firmly rooted in the writing of John R. Commons and the Wisconsin School, Kaufman (1993, forthcoming) describes the goals of industrial relations as efficiency, equity, and individual or human well-being or self-actualization.[43] Insight into Kaufman's (1993, 13) definition of the concepts comes in his discussion of the establishment of industrial relations in the 1920s: "greater efficiency in production; greater equity in the distribution of economic rewards, the utilization of labor, and the administration of employment policies in the workplace; and greater individual happiness and opportunities for personal growth and development." These efficiency and equity standards are clearly analogous to those outlined in this book. In terms of individual well-being, Kaufman (1993, 13–18) further cites the early industrial relations beliefs in due process, dignity and respect, and opportunities for skill and leadership development. This moves beyond the standard efficiency and equity pillars, and is consistent with the voice dimension articulated here. It stops short, however, of explicitly articulating voice as a standard. It can be argued that self-actualization requires meaningful or democratic voice (e.g., Klare 1988; McClelland 1990). However, actualization can also be more narrowly interpreted as personal growth in terms of skill and leadership development. In this interpretation, self-actualization is a weaker standard than voice. As such, "voice" is less ambiguous and more clearly articulates the standard of democratic participation than "self-actualization."

Osterman et al. (2001, 11) also explicitly reject an efficiency-only objective of the employment relationship and stress that "an employment system must be judged on its ability to find and maintain a balance between efficiency and a series of other goals." They articulate the following "moral foundations" for the employment relationship: (1) work as a source of dignity; (2) a living wage; (3) diversity and equality of opportunity; (4) solidarity or social cohesion; and (5) voice and participation (Osterman et al. 2001, 11–12).

These thought-provoking principles are consistent with my framework of efficiency, equity, and voice. As emphasized throughout this chapter, work as a source of dignity underlies arguments for both equity and voice. A living wage and equality of opportunity are explicit dimensions of the equity standard articulated in this book. The solidarity or social cohesion value is a "focus on achieving the common good for all workers, not just material gain for the individual," which is also a strong equity ideal (12). And their fifth value explicitly promotes voice and participation—this is the voice standard advocated in this book. Osterman et al.'s (2001) principles for the new workplace are, in essence, efficiency, equity, and voice. Hodson (2001, xiii) similarly emphasizes that "working with dignity is a foundation for a fully realized life" and his requirements for dignity at work essentially reduce to equity and voice. The trilogy of efficiency, equity, and voice therefore advances both previous emphases on only efficiency and also on efficiency and equity while building on important earlier scholarship.

Fully valuing the need for effective use of scarce resources for economic prosperity, the quality of individuals' lives, and human dignity implies that the employment relationship objectives are efficiency, equity, and voice. These are the basis of employment with a human face. These three objectives provide the structure for analyzing contemporary employment outcomes, practices, and institutions—and therefore for constructing future institutions as the na-

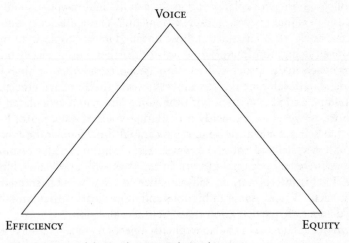

Figure 1.1 The Geometry of the Employment Relationship

ture of work evolves. Particular outcomes, practices, and institutions reflect different combinations of efficiency, equity, and voice. This yields a triangular relationship between these three employment relationship objectives (see figure 1.1).[44] Analysis of workplace and employment relationship outcomes, practices, and institutions is thus the analysis of the geometry of the employment relationship—the determinants of efficiency, equity, and voice and the extent to which they are achieved.

2 The Balancing Imperative:
Human Rights in Conflict

THE SOCIETAL OBJECTIVES of the employment relationship are efficiency, equity, and voice. If there are externalities, public goods, information gaps, or
psychological motivators of behavior, equity and voice can foster efficiency.
For workplace issues that have the possibility of mutual gain, equity and voice
might increase efficiency. But conflicts between efficiency and equity and voice
are likely. The clash between labor and management over workplace issues
that involve distributive rather than integrative interests will reflect an underlying opposition between equity and voice, on the one hand, and efficiency,
on the other.[1] The laissez-faire logic of neoclassical economics and its common-law supports also implies that efficiency is maximized by unfettered marketplace transactions. Almost by definition, the principles of equity and voice
seek to place limits on unrestrained markets, and therefore may undermine efficiency.[2]

A well-known debate over conflicts between efficiency and equity in the employment relationship is the minimum wage (Card and Krueger 1995). Another continuing debate is whether restrictions on employers' ability to lay off
and discharge workers cause higher levels of European unemployment (Blank
1994; Booth 1997; Gregg and Manning 1997). Within labor relations, popular views of labor unions as labor market monopolies emphasize that unions
distort competitive outcomes (Friedman and Friedman 1980; Heldman, Bennett, and Johnson 1981; Epstein 1983). This is a conflict between efficiency
and equity because, for example, there is a potential incongruity between seniority-based layoff or promotion policies and managerial flexibility (Slichter,
Healy, and Livernash 1960). Employee voice can conflict with efficiency by
making decision making more cumbersome. Equity and voice can also clash.
For example, the tendency for labor unions to centralize their power to better achieve equity might make the leadership less responsive to individual
needs and voice. Government regulations that mandate overtime payments

might disagree with the desire of individuals to have input into how they are compensated for working extra hours. The sharpest conflicts, however, are typically between efficiency, on the one hand, and equity and voice, on the other.

Conflicts between efficiency and equity and voice are the fundamental human resources and industrial relations or employment relationship conflicts. These conflicts are ultimately a clash between property rights and labor rights. Efficiency is tightly intertwined with property rights. Shareholders—the owners of corporate property—champion efficiency to maximize profits and the returns on their investments. Economic theory emphasizes that well-defined property rights, and the freedom to use them, are crucial foundations for efficient, market-based economies. To the extent that government regulations and labor unions constrain the freedom to allocate resources to their most economically productive use, these institutions are seen as restrictions on property rights and efficiency. In contrast, equity and voice derive from concerns for the treatment and the rights of employees as human beings. Of particular interest is ensuring that markets do not produce outcomes that undermine the value of human life. Consequently, conflicts between efficiency, on the one hand, and equity and voice, on the other, can be thought of as conflicts between property rights and labor rights.

As noted by Selig Perlman (1928, 155–56) many years ago, "A labor movement must, by its very nature, be an organized campaign against the rights of private property." How should conflicts between property rights and labor rights be resolved? Property rights are widely believed to trump labor rights, but I argue that both property rights and labor rights are human rights. Conflicts between property rights and labor rights are therefore a clash between competing human rights. This implies that efficiency, equity, and voice must be balanced rather than ordered or prioritized.

The drivers of employment—individuals, markets, institutions, organizational strategies, and public policies—should thus support a balance between efficiency, equity, and voice. In this discussion, it is important that the modern employment relationship and corporation are purposeful human constructs. Work of some sort is necessary for survival, but modern employment—working for someone else in a limited-liability corporation—was created by society to serve human and social ends. In that they are created rather than natural institutions, society must determine the desired ends— they are not preordained—and the rights and obligations that must be respected.[3]

Rights

Rights can be categorized along several dimensions. One important, albeit oversimplified, distinction is between positive and negative rights (Gewirth 1996; Cross 2001). A positive right is something that must be provided, whereas a negative right is a protection against something. Property and free speech rights are negative rights because they protect the holders of property and opinions against attempts to seize or limit these possessions. In contrast, if a living wage is a right, it is a positive right: society has an obligation to directly or indirectly provide it.

Rights can also be categorized by their source. Contractual rights are obligations and entitlements that stem from entering into an enforceable contract. Being entitled to a minimum of four hours call-in pay or to being laid off by inverse seniority because they are included in a union contract are examples. Statutory rights are provided through legislative statute. The right of U.S. employers to be free of secondary boycotts and union members' rights to elect officers within certain time periods are statutory rights granted by U.S. labor law, and are also negative and positive rights, respectively. Constitutional rights are granted in a nation's constitution. The right to not be deprived of property without due process is a constitutional right in the United States. International law—both through treaties and the customs of nations in the international arena—might also provide rights, such as through human rights conventions. With some exceptions, conventional analyses of U.S. employment relations focus on these categories of rights. Furthermore, the domestic legal hierarchy is clear: due process and free speech are explicitly mentioned in the Constitution, while the right to form a union and to a minimum wage, to strike, or to receive equal treatment in the workplace are granted by statutes. Thus, property rights and free speech trump labor rights (Gross 1999). Both of these trump contractual rights.[4]

Political and moral philosophy, however, implies that human rights trump constitutional, statutory, and contractual rights (Gewirth 1996; Humphrey 1988; Lauren 1998).[5] This hierarchy is advocated for labor relations (Adams 2001; Gross 1999; Wheeler 2000), occupational safety (Gross 1998), minimum wages (Spectar 2000), and education (Gross 2001). In short, critical elements of equity (such as minimum wages and equal opportunity) and voice (such as freedom of association, speech, and self-determination) are human rights. Property rights, however, also have a central role in human rights discussions. Consequently, although equity and voice need to be elevated above their current, low-priority statutory-right status, the importance of property rights implies that efficiency, equity, and voice must be balanced rather than ordered. This conceptualization of property rights and labor rights as competing human rights that must be balanced rests on two foundations. One, the sanctity of property rights has been weakened through the recognition that property rights have evolved from Lockean natural rights that serve as the fundamental basis for liberty to an economic bundle of rights that serves efficiency, not liberty. Two, modern human rights thought recognizes both first-generation civil and political rights as well as second-generation economic and social rights as human rights. As such, labor rights are human rights.

A Brief History of Human Rights

Standard conceptions of the contemporary basis for human rights are reflected in the opening of the United Nations Universal Declaration of Human Rights: "recognition of the inherent dignity and of the equal and inalienable rights of all members of the human family."[6] To more fully understand the universal aspect of this belief, its scope, and its implications, a brief history is instructive.

Visions of human rights can be traced back twenty-five hundred years to early religious and moral philosophy such as in the Confucian, Hindu, and Buddhist traditions (Lauren 1998; Rosenbaum 1980b). As is also true with the later development of Judaism, Christianity, and Islam, these diverse traditions in religious and spiritual thought "share a universal interest in addressing the integrity, worth, and dignity of all persons, and, consequently, the duty toward other people" (Lauren 1998, 5; also Perry 1998; Rosenbaum 1980a; Shestack 1984). This universal interest lies beneath what is often referred to as the Golden Rule and is the fundamental issue underlying human rights. Similar concerns are echoed in the questions of natural law examined by early Western philosophies (Lauren 1998; Rosenbaum 1980b). Greek philosophers such as Plato and Aristotle asserted that equal respect for all citizens, equality before the law, equality in political power and in suffrage, and equality of civil rights were the basis of a universal law of nature, or natural law.[7] As extended by the Roman Stoic philosophers, these principles gave civic equality to everyone on the basis that they were human (Lauren 1998; Rosenbaum 1980b). The roots of human rights are therefore both religious and moral, Western and non-Western (Donnelly 1989).[8]

Leaping forward a number of centuries, the Magna Carta in 1215 laid the foundation for modern conceptions of personal rights by protecting nobles and their property from arbitrary action by monarchs (Painter 1947). In the seventeenth century, John Locke transformed natural law into natural rights:

> Man being born, as has been proved, with a title to perfect freedom, and an uncontrolled enjoyment of all the rights and privileges of the law of nature, equally with any other man, or number of men in the world, hath by nature a power, not only to preserve his property, that is, his life, liberty and estate, against the injuries and attempts of other men; but to judge of, and punish the breaches of that law in others, as he is persuaded the offence deserves. (Locke 1690, §87, 341–42)

This is the basis for the primacy of protection of property rights through the negative rights of noninterference that are enshrined in U.S. political thought. In the American Revolution, this belief was famously articulated in the Declaration of Independence (1776) as "We hold these truths to be self-evident, that all men are created equal, that they are endowed by their Creator with certain unalienable rights, that among these are life, liberty, and the pursuit of happiness."[9] In the French Revolution, this belief was stated in the Declaration of the Rights of Man and Citizen (1789), which declared "the natural, unalienable, and sacred rights of man" to be "liberty, property, security, and resistance to oppression."[10] These strong expressions of negative rights occurred when the enemy of human rights was absolutist monarchies.

In the nineteenth century, the human rights focus was on the oppression of slaves and their rights as humans, and the push to end slavery then raised questions about the rights of women (Burns and Burns 1991; Lauren 1998). This eventually led to civil and political rights for all races and both genders—not only facilitated by wars, but also by revolutions in transportation and communication, including popular novels such as *Uncle Tom's Cabin* (1852) by Harriet Beecher Stowe and *A Doll's House* (1879) by Henrik Ibsen (Lauren 1998). In the United States, these new rights were embodied in several amendments to the Constitution: the Thirteenth (ending slavery), Fourteenth (guaranteeing due process and equal protection), Fifteenth (ending racial discrimination in voter eligibility), and Nineteenth (ending gender discrimination in voter eligibility). Thus, stemming from a Lockean emphasis on the protection of private property and the nineteenth-century drives for equal rights for all races and both genders, the first generation of human rights are civil and political. These include basic individual liberties, equal protection, the right to vote, due process protections, the right to own property, free speech, and freedom of assembly, association, and religion. For the most part, these are negative rights.

The worldwide attention on slavery provided an opportunity for reformers to expand public awareness of other forms of economic exploitation, such as the sweatshop conditions in the mills and mines of mid-nineteenth century Europe:

> What good were civil rights such as freedom of speech or political rights for voting, asked those who suffered, to people like themselves who had no food, no home, no clothing, no medical care, or no prospect of an education? What were the benefits of freedom from slavery or serfdom if the alternative was destitution? (Lauren 1998, 54)

From this movement grew a second generation of human rights—positive economic and social rights in which governments have a responsibility for ensuring adequate living standards through employment opportunities, income, housing, medical care, safety, and education.[11] Workers' rights received further attention at the end of World War I, partly because of labor's sacrifices during the war and partly as a strategy to further continued peace (Lauren 1998), which led to the creation of the International Labour Organization (ILO) in 1919. The Great Depression in the 1930s further increased calls for economic and social rights. In fact, in January 1944 President Franklin Delano Roosevelt articulated an economic bill of rights that included rights to "a useful and remunerative job," a decent home, adequate medical care, "protection from the economic fears of old age and sickness and accident and unemployment," and "to earn enough to provide adequate food and clothing and recreation" (Burns and Burns 1991, 264). Many of the bases for these economic and social rights in the context of the employment relationship—ranging from religious thought on human sacredness to liberal, egalitarian theories of justice and liberty to moral precepts on human dignity—were outlined in the previous chapter.

Arguments for international standards for both human rights generally and labor rights specifically clashed sharply with deep-seated beliefs about national sovereignty. The Holocaust during World War II, in which Hitler's regime asserted national sovereignty over its right to commit incredible atrocities, however, broke this stalemate (Szabo 1982; Weissbrodt 1988).[12] The United Nations was thus formed in June 1945 "to save succeeding generations from the scourge of war" and to "reaffirm faith in fundamental human rights, in the dignity and worth of the human person, in the equal rights of men and women of nations large and small" (United Nations Charter).

The idea of human rights was central to the founding of the United Nations in 1945, and by the end of 1946 a commission, chaired by Eleanor Roosevelt, had been formed to develop an international bill of human rights. The result was the Universal Declaration of Human Rights, which was adopted and proclaimed by the United Nations General Assembly on December 10, 1948. This declaration continues to be the most important document in modern human rights and in shaping current discussions of human rights. It is based on "the inherent dignity" and "the equal and inalienable rights of all members of the human family" and integrates second-generation economic and social rights with first-generation civil and political rights (Glendon 1998; van Boven 1982).

The universality of these human rights is repeatedly stressed in the declaration. In addition to "universal" appearing in the title, the rights apply to "all members of the human family," and "all peoples and all nations" should strive "to secure their universal and effective recognition and observance." This conflicts with claims of national sovereignty and its cousin, cultural relativism (Perry 1998), but the belief that underlies the declaration is that human rights are so basic and fundamental that they take priority over national sovereignty and cultural relativism.[13]

This crucial feature of universality is grounded in the belief that human rights stem from the basic quality of being human, generally expressed as "inherent dignity." These rights are "essential to the adequate functioning of a human being" (Freeden 1991, 7). Simply by being a human, "certain things ought not to be done to any human being and certain other things ought to be done for every human being" (Perry 1998, 13). Because these rights flow from the "virtue of being human," they do not depend on "varying social circumstances and degrees of merit" (Shestack 1984, 74).[14] In short, human rights are universal (Donnelly 1989).

Common threads of human dignity are found in all of the major religions (Lauren 1998). Judaism (Kaplan 1980), Christianity (Henle 1980), and Islam (Nasr 1980) all trace human rights back to the belief that humans are created in the image of God, though the nature of this linkage can vary.[15] Basic conceptions of dignity or the value of human beings are found in the natural laws of Locke and others and in the moral philosophies of Immanuel Kant and others (Shestack 1984). Thus, although there are differences in beliefs over the details of the nature of human rights, there is a common affirmation that intrinsic human value and inherent dignity endow humans with a set of basic rights.[16]

Implementation, however, has been less than universal, as illustrated by the experience of the United States.[17] To further the cause of human rights and to add greater specificity and legal impact, the United Nations finally opened two covenants for ratification in 1966: the International Covenant on Civil and Political Rights (ICCPR) and the International Covenant on Economic, Social, and Cultural Rights (ICESR).[18] The United States ratified the former (with its negative rights), but not the latter (with its positive rights). Moreover, the United States did not ratify the ICCPR until 1992 and even then only with a set of "RUDs": reservations, understandings, and declarations, including the declaration that the provisions are not self-enforcing (Sloss 1999). The poor record of the United States and other countries notwithstanding, human rights stem from the inherent dignity of human beings and are universal. The next two sections examine both property rights and labor rights as human rights. Of particular import is that the sanctity of property rights has weakened while the importance of labor rights has increased.

The Deflation of Property Rights

This section stakes out a middle ground between those who assert that either property rights or labor rights take precedence over the other right. The Universal Declaration of Human Rights clearly makes property rights and due process human rights: "Everyone has the right to own property alone as well as in association with others" and "No one shall be arbitrarily deprived of his property" (Article 17). Consequently, if the Universal Declaration is used to legitimatize labor rights as human rights, property rights cannot be summarily dismissed as secondary to labor rights. At the same time, a closer examination of property rights reveals that the sanctity of property rights was diminished in the twentieth century—except in U.S. labor law (Estlund 1994) and in its mythical status in U.S. thought (Nedelsky 1990). The history of property rights is essentially a shift from seeing property rights as the root of liberty to seeing them as the basis of economic efficiency. As a result, property rights should not now trump labor rights. Labor rights and property rights should be balanced.

Questions of property—is ownership natural or a product of the state, can others restrict an owner's use of their property, should property be distributed equally, what intangibles are considered property—have a longstanding history in political and moral thought dating back at least to Plato and Aristotle (Schlatter 1951; Ryan 1987; Bethell 1998). The Magna Carta in 1215 established due process rights for individuals faced with deprivation of property (Ely 1998), but most modern treatments of property start with John Locke. With his late-seventeenth century statement that man "hath by nature a power . . . to preserve his property, that is, his life, liberty and estate," Locke (1690, §87, 341) elevated property rights to a natural right of human beings—a right that stems not from laws, but from being human (Schlatter 1951).

The reason property is a Lockean natural right is important—humans have a right to survive and are entitled to their own labor (Schlatter 1951; Horne 1990; Simmons 1992; Lauren 1998). In the words of Locke (1690, §27, 305–6), "Every man has a property in his own person. This nobody has any right to but himself. The labor of his body, and the work of his hands, we may say, are properly his." In the nineteenth and twentieth centuries, this view was rejected by neoclassical economists and utilitarians (Ryan 1987), and ironically it endures today as the labor theory of value in the Marxist tradition. Although Locke elevated the status of property rights, his natural rights justification is not consistent with contemporary conceptions of property rights in modern society (Schlatter 1951).

The influence of the Lockean triad of life, liberty, and estate on U.S. political and legal thought, however, is well known. From the Bill of Rights' protection of life, liberty, and property to *Lochner*-era rulings that many protective labor standards violated economic due process to recent rulings such as *Lechmere* that allow union organizers to be banned from private property, the central importance of property rights is clear.[19] This centrality stems from the belief that property ownership is essential to political liberty (Ely 1998; Forbath 1985).[20] Property rights have been at the heart of the U.S. system of government because they provide the boundaries of or the limits on legitimate government (Nedelsky 1990). Property rights yield autonomy, whether as Jefferson's independent farmers (Burns and Burns 1991) or as a privately owned modern media (Nedelsky 1990), and this autonomy prevents government oppression.

But property rights have rarely been absolute. Locke also asserted that the poor were entitled to take from the rich to survive if they had no other choice (Horne 1990; Simmons 1992). In republicanism, the common good is paramount over private interests (Ely 1998). The common-law doctrines of public necessity and nuisance as well as the generally accepted police power of the states allow justifiable restrictions on, or even the taking of, private property (Ely 1998). The *Lochner*-era Supreme Court was the champion of substantive due process and freedom to contract, but it upheld some legislation when it felt the public interest was truly served (Phillips 1998). For example, in *Muller v. Oregon,* the Court upheld an Oregon law that limited the hours of women in factories and laundries.[21]

Additionally, since the 1880s the definition of property has widened and has also been transformed from a principle of liberty to one of efficiency. In earlier periods, the common (and natural) law view of property was limited to the control of tangible, physical things. In the late 1800s, however, U.S. courts dephysicalized property by expanding property rights to include value as well as physical things (Vandevelde 1980; Forbath 1985, 1991). Intangible property rights now include the right to conduct business, the value of goodwill, intellectual property, and trade secrets.[22] As such, the importance of property has shifted away from being a source of freedom and liberty and toward being an instrument of economic efficiency (Merrill and Smith 2001). In the early 1900s, the Legal Realist school attacked the view that property rights, and common law more generally, are neutral, apolitical orderings that protect individual freedom against government oppression (Alexander 1997; Klare 1988; Nedelsky 1990). Property is seen as a bundle of state-created rights such that property's purpose is economic, not political or civic. In fact, Commons (1924) articulates how the shift to a modern industrial society inverts the classic function of property rights. Before the rise of wage earning on a dominant scale, property rights provided autonomy because individuals could withhold their labor and still survive. This is the classic liberty function. However, the strong tangible and intangible property rights of industrial corporations change property rights from "holding for self" to "withholding from others" the ability to work, and therefore, survive (Commons 1924, 53; Alexander 1997). In other words, "if the capitalist-employer owned the capital, the workers *had* to work for him if they wanted to work at all. Their labor now became a commodity to be bought and sold on the market. This was a far cry from Locke's concept of property, which he perceived to be the product of labor, used and owned *by those who produced it*" (Flexner 1989, 32, emphasis in original). In this view, unrestrained corporate property rights in the modern economic era undermine rather than support individual freedom.

Seminal writings by Coase (1960), Alchian (1965), and Demsetz (1967) helped the modern neoclassical economics and Law and Economics schools further cement the definition of property as a bundle of user rights rather than a natural right to control "things" (Merrill and Smith 2001). A central component of the contemporary view of property is based on laissez-faire, market-oriented principles of achieving economic efficiency (Alexander 1997). This shift toward efficiency concerns is evident in U.S. Supreme Court rulings.[23] If property rights are government created and are for economic efficiency, instead of being natural and fundamental to freedom, then they are no longer sacred. The Court's 1937 upholding of a Washington state minimum wage law in *West Coast Hotel Co. v. Parrish* marked the end of the Court's emphasis on economic due process and the freedom to contract.[24] The Supreme Court has not ruled against any economic or social legislation on these grounds since that time (Ely 1998). Moreover, the doctrine on eminent domain has evolved so that the question is not whether property can be taken, but whether compensation is required (Nedelsky 1990)—though recent rulings might be reversing this trend (Zietlow 1998).

Where does this leave the employment relationship? The fundamental importance of property rights has historically stemmed not from laissez-faire beliefs about economic efficiency, but from a belief that private property is a fundamental freedom and the key to preventing government abuse. The existing dominant economic and legal view, however, is that property rights are bundles of rights that are essential for economic efficiency and development. The continued role of property rights in safeguarding freedom is sharply debated. In the libertarian view, property rights continue to serve economic efficiency *and* the classic principles of liberty and negative rights (Bethell 1998; Epstein 1995; Friedman 1962; Nozick 1974). In other words, property rights are still viewed as "the guardian of every other right" and do not warrant a secondary status (Ely 1998).

On the other hand, Nedelsky (1990, 234) argues that property is "no longer the source of autonomy for most people."[25] In this view, the continued importance of property rights stems from their significant symbolic, mythic, and rhetorical power (Nedelsky 1990; Alexander 1997).[26] One manifestation of this phenomenon is the continued general impression that laissez-faire orderings are natural, apolitical, or free of regulation rather than state-created and enforced (Hartmann 2002; Klare 1988; Nedelsky 1990).[27] For example, whether or not peaceful picketing is viewed as coercion in common law has obvious distributional consequences as does whether or not tort liability rules should extend to the internalization of injury to workers' human as well as physical capital (Klare 1988). And yet, common law and free markets—and property rights within them—are rhetorically viewed as apolitical, which serves to elevate the power of property rights in legal and public policy discourse (Nedelsky 1990).

Public and scholarly discourse about employment needs to break through this myth of property rights, but it can do so without a wholesale rejection of the continued importance of such rights for individual freedom. The employment-relationship concern with property rights is the extent to which property rights should shield employers from limitations on their freedom to contract with employees—in other words, the extent to which the freedom to contract should be tempered by the standards of equity and voice. A corporation's freedom to contract is an efficiency issue to facilitate the productive use of resources; it is not a critical source of individual autonomy against government oppression. Property rights underlie the axiom that "management acts and the union grieves"—management hires, fires, schedules, assigns, and the like because of property rights. These are issues of efficiency, not freedom, and providing a basis for labor to challenge these actions—for example, by specifying just-cause standards for discipline and discharge—does not involve the sanctity of property rights as a protection against government oppression. This does not mean that efficiency is unimportant or that employers and investors are not entitled to the same human rights protections of free speech as are employees. Rather, it means that property rights concerns in the employment relationship are rooted in modern definitions of efficiency-supporting, not in traditional liberty-supporting, property rights. Consequently (and without rejecting the importance of property rights for autonomy), property in employment scholarship and practice should not be treated as "an inviolable and sacred right" that trumps all else.[28]

Labor Rights as Human Rights

Positive economic and social rights were elevated to an equal status with civil and political rights during the twentieth century. For employment, this trend is illustrated by the International Labour Organization's fundamental objective, proclaimed in the 1944 Declaration of Philadelphia: "All human beings, irrespective of race, creed or sex, have the right to pursue both their material well-being and their spiritual development in conditions of freedom and dignity, of economic security and equal opportunity."

These objectives are reinforced by several articles of the Universal Declaration of Human Rights, the eight fundamental ILO conventions, and the ILO Declaration on Fundamental Principles and Rights at Work (1998).[29] In the Universal Declaration, human rights include just and favorable working conditions, including pay sufficient for an existence worthy of human dignity, equal pay for equal work, reasonable working hours, periodic paid holidays, unemployment and disability insurance, and the right to form labor unions. The eight fundamental ILO conventions specify that freedom of association and collective bargaining, the abolition of forced labor, equal opportunity and pay, and the elimination of child labor are "fundamental to the rights of human beings at work." The 1998 declaration reaffirms these fundamental conventions and requires all member countries to promote these rights even if they have not ratified the specific conventions.

In other words, the basic dimensions of workplace equity and voice outlined in the previous chapter are recognized worldwide as human rights—at least as nonspecific principles. Although compliance and enforcement are uneven at best, antidiscrimination is covered explicitly by the ILO fundamental conventions and is an underlying thread throughout the Universal Declaration, not only in the context of employment but in the context of all civil, political, economic, and social rights. Adequate pay ("just and favorable remuneration ensuring for himself and his family an existence worthy of human dignity"), benefits ("medical care and necessary social services, and the right to security in the event of unemployment, sickness, disability, widowhood, old age or other lack of livelihood in circumstances beyond his control" as well as "periodic holidays with pay"), and working conditions ("just and favorable conditions of work" and "reasonable limitation of working hours") are included in the Universal Declaration. Freedom of association generally, and the right to form unions and engage in collective bargaining specifically, are explicitly enumerated in both the Universal Declaration and the ILO fundamental conventions, albeit not universally respected in practice (Human Rights Watch 2000). As an additional dimension of voice, the Universal Declaration also includes freedom of expression.

All of the dimensions of equity and voice are repeated in either the International Covenant on Economic, Social and Cultural Rights or the International Covenant on Civil and Political Rights. In fact, the right to form and join labor unions is enumerated in *both* the ICESR and the ICCPR. This underscores the two critical functions of unions (Weiler 1990): protection, which serves economic rights (equity); and participation, which serves political and civil rights (voice). The difference between principles and practice, however, is emphasized by the reality of union-density decline as a near-global phenomenon.

In spite of difficulties with implementation and enforcement, the human rights history described earlier in this chapter illustrates why these are asserted as human rights: they stem from the basic features of being human and are necessary to fulfill the inherent dignity of human beings. Underlying this inherent dignity are the common beliefs of the major religions that humans are created in the image of God and the common belief in the intrinsic value and equality of human beings in diverse writings on natural law, moral philosophy, and political theory.[30] With respect to employment, therefore, the human rights argument is that equity and voice are human rights because employees are human beings, not simply commodities or production inputs. Human dignity and freedom are undermined if people are not able to maintain a minimal standard of living and are subjected to onerous working hours in dangerous or unhealthy conditions (Edelman 1987; Gross 1998; Spectar 2000). Due-process protections against arbitrary and discriminatory discipline and discharge are essential for human dignity (Wheeler 1994). Denying workers the freedom of association "denies individuals what they need to live a fully human life"—human dignity—and undermines democracy—that is, freedom (Gross 1999, 71; also, R. Adams 2001; Wheeler 2000). Dignity and freedom are undermined if employees do not have freedom of speech (Wheeler 1994).

There are admittedly difficult issues concerning the implementation of these principles and with competing objectives and rights. My goal is not to describe an employment system that delivers these human rights, but to establish the framework within which such analyses should take place.[31] Moreover, for a "labor rights as human rights" argument to be credible, it must focus on the underlying rationale for human rights (Ewing 2002). The history of human rights is marked by the drive to protect human dignity and freedom through civil and political rights, as well as through economic and social rights. Consequently, the rights of employers, especially with respect to property rights, due process, and free speech, must also be considered. An elevation of equity and voice to human rights accords them equal, not superior, status with the rights of employers and investors to property, free speech, and due process.[32]

Balancing Property Rights and Labor Rights

Efficiency, equity, and voice in the employment relationship often conflict with each other. Explicit recognition of this conflict is an essential theme of the employment relationship: the rights of labor to equity and voice clash with the property rights of capital (see figure 2.1). Without an appreciation of the nature of human rights, popular U.S. thought asserts the dominance of property rights (as constitutional rights) over workplace equity and voice rights (as lesser statutory rights).[33] Incorporation of human rights thought alters this deep-seated hierarchy and gives renewed justification to the traditional industrial relations emphasis on balancing competing employment relationship objectives. In other words, the intellectual history of property rights and labor rights provides a richer justification for the traditional industrial relations balancing paradigm. This is not to say that the current system necessarily reflects an appropriate balance, but it does assert that balancing is the correct maxim to pursue.

Property rights and employers' free speech rights are two of a number of important civil, political, economic, and social rights. But, as emphasized by internationally accepted human rights documents, labor rights are also economic and social rights and are, therefore, also human rights. Moreover, there is no accepted consensus as to a hierarchy of human rights (Meron 1986; Wuerffel 1998).[34] Thus, there is no legal hierarchy to fall back on when effi-

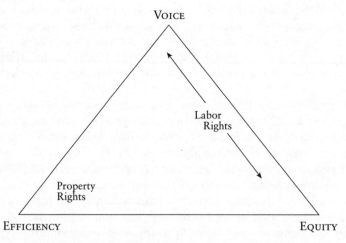

Figure 2.1 Property Rights, Labor Rights, and the Employment Relationship

ciency, equity, and voice conflict. The elevation of labor rights to human rights puts them on an equal footing with property rights; it does not automatically make labor rights dominant. Rather, it is imperative that a balance be struck between these competing human rights—that is, between property rights and labor rights.

The tradition that asserts the superiority of property rights over labor rights focuses on *exclusive* property rights—the extent to which ownership allows the exclusion of others, which has historically served as a foundation of autonomy and liberty. But the function of property rights has evolved from protection of liberty to promotion of economic efficiency. Moreover, classical theories of property rights also have an *inclusive* or common dimension—the right to share, or be included, in the use of property necessary for one's welfare. The goal of the modern, liberal state is to balance exclusive (or negative) and inclusive (or positive or civic) rights (Alexander 1997; Horne 1990). In the context of the employment relationship, this problem translates to balancing efficiency, equity, and voice (see figure 2.1). Put differently, Alexander (1997, 377) distinguishes between the commodity view of property as protecting individuals against material loss and the civic view of property as protecting against ethical and political loss—"the loss of self-respect that is the basis for proper citizenship and, ultimately, the proper social order." Balancing these two is a difficult problem for the liberal state and provides another useful way of characterizing the balance that society should seek to achieve in the employment relationship.

Although I argue for an elevation of labor rights to human rights to emphasize their importance in society, this balancing argument is admittedly reminiscent of Progressive and New Deal-era scholars who wanted both labor and capital to relinquish their claims to fundamental rights and instead focus on balancing the economic outcomes of the employment relationship (Pope 2002). For those troubled by the elevation of too many rights (see Glendon 1991), an alternative interpretation of my analysis is that property rights have weakened sufficiently to be considered property interests (in support of efficiency interests). My conclusion can then be restated by saying that property interests must be balanced with labor interests. In either case, the critical task is seeking a *balance*.

In broader terms, this balancing paradigm for the employment relationship is additionally reminiscent of the old institutional labor economics, or Wisconsin, school's belief in reforming and refining market-oriented capitalism, not discarding it (Kaufman 1997b; Kaufman forthcoming).[35] In contrast to its apparent decline in U.S. discourse, this belief continues to be echoed in international debates on human rights, free trade, economic development, and the role of markets (Flexner 1989; Korten 1999; Stiglitz 2002). For example, in 1999 the United Nations issued a Global Compact challenging world business leaders to respect human rights around the world that explicitly cites labor and environmental concerns. United Nations Secretary-General Kofi Annan told U.S. business that "the United Nations, for its part, would continue to make a strong case for free trade and open global markets. Business could then be left to do what it does best, create jobs and wealth, while giving the global market more of a 'human face.'"[36] This reflects the objective of balancing property rights and labor rights, or efficiency, equity, and voice. A balancing objective provides the measure for evaluating workplace and employment-relationship outcomes, practices, and institutions: they should be judged on the extent to which efficiency, equity, and voice are balanced. What then are the alternatives for achieving this balance, for creating employment with a human face?

3 Balancing Outcomes: The Environment and Human Agents

THE FIRST TWO CHAPTERS demonstrate that the three fundamental objectives of the employment relationship are efficiency, equity, and voice, and that these three objectives should be balanced. Understanding how employment outcomes are produced in actual workplaces is a necessary foundation for analyzing the determinants of efficiency, equity, and voice, and for addressing how to structure the employment relationship to support these desired objectives. What determines employment outcomes? In the framework developed here, employment outcomes are the product of interactions between employees and employers in the sociopolitical, strategic, functional, and workplace tiers of the employment relationship, as shaped by both the environment for and the nature of human decision making, including ethics. The role of the employment-relationship environment has long been an important topic in studies of work, especially within industrial relations and economics. At the same time, the nature of human decision making and behavior—such as social interactions and person-specific needs, feelings, and mental processes—have long been central in employment scholarship in psychology, sociology, and organizational behavior.[1] A full understanding of the employment relationship requires both components—the environment and the human agent—plus ethics.

In the first decades of the twentieth century, John R. Commons and other institutional labor economists emphasized relative bargaining power between labor and management as the determinant of wages, hours, and other terms and conditions of employment (Kaufman 1997b). Bargaining power was analyzed as a product of the environment: labor market competition, the extent of legal regulation and social services, and the macroeconomic environment. John Dunlop's *Industrial Relations Systems* (1958) is the seminal formalization of the role of the environment in employment (Kochan, Katz, and

McKersie 1986). In this model, outcomes—Dunlop's "web of rules"—result from the interactions of actors within the environment—Dunlop's "contexts." The environment consists of the technical context, labor and product markets, and the distribution of power in society. The factors that determine the distribution of power can be thought of as legal, political, and social forces (Kochan, Katz, and McKersie 1986). Kochan, McKersie, and Cappelli (1984) and Kochan, Katz, and McKersie (1986) extend Dunlop's model in two important ways. One, the institutional structure of labor, management, and government is divided into a three-tiered structure: the strategic level, the functional level, and the workplace level. Two, the role of the environment is weakened to be less than fully deterministic; actors can make choices within the environment and, therefore, values are important.

Reinforcing this second point, Kaufman (1989, 1999) emphasizes the need to pair the environment with human decision making, in other words, to move beyond a purely rational, self-interested economic model of the human agent to a model of human decision making and choice that also includes richer behavioral and social foundations.[2] The framework developed here models employment relationship outcomes as a product of both the environment and the internal needs, feelings, and mental processes of individual human agents.

The extension of Dunlop/Kochan, Katz, and McKersie with behavioral and ethical foundations is presented in figure 3.1. Labor-management interactions are conditioned by the environment; by the underlying goals of efficiency, equity, and voice; and by human decision making, including ethics. Interactions between employees and employers can occur at the sociopolitical, strategic, functional, and workplace level. In figure 3.1, strategies for achieving goals are broadly considered as individual choices consistent with an individual's underlying ethical belief system and other personal needs, wants, and characteristics. This includes self-interested utility maximization, making the model general enough to include the traditional neoclassical economics paradigm as one special case, but also allowing for alternatives rooted in psychology and sociology. Note carefully that the human agent in figure 3.1 applies to the employer and employee and is intended to capture the decision making and behavior of both managers and workers. The model captured by figure 3.1 is conceptual and not well specified for empirical testing.[3] The main point at this stage is to emphasize the inclusion of the environment *and* human choice *and* ethics in modeling employment outcomes, and their effect on all stages of the process from decision making to action to outcomes. Tighter specifications that more precisely capture and measure the interplay between the environment, human decision-making processes, ethics, and outcomes is left to future research.

The remainder of this chapter explicates the model of figure 3.1 by reviewing the major dimensions of the environment and the human agent. I categorize the employment relationship environment in seven dimensions: legal, economic, technical, political, social, business, and institutional.[4] Furthermore, the major elements of human decision making are categorized in five

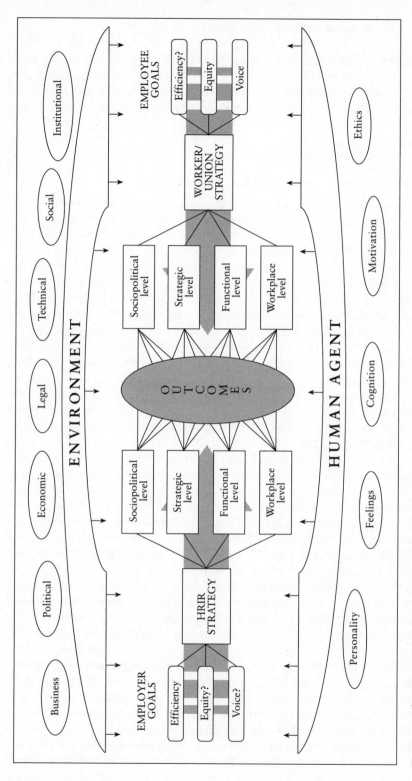

Figure 3.1 The Determinants of Employment Outcomes

dimensions: cognition, motivation, personality, feelings, and ethics. Of these twelve categories, the one that has been overlooked the most, and yet is perhaps the most critical for employment with a human face, is ethics. Ethics is therefore given its own extended treatment in the next chapter.

Dimensions of the Environment

The Legal Environment: Establishing the Framework

The legal system in any country clearly establishes the parameters for employee-employer or labor-management interactions. This is perhaps most obvious in the context of specific employment and labor laws. Employment laws that provide workplace protections or a social safety net shape employment outcomes by mandating certain employer behaviors (such as nondiscrimination) and outcomes (such as a minimum wage) and by affecting relative bargaining power between employees (individually and collectively) and employers. In labor law, the National Labor Relations Act (NLRA) specifies the steps U.S. unions must follow to be recognized as the exclusive bargaining agent of the employees; the bargaining obligations of labor and management (including process and content); the constraints on labor (such as secondary boycotts) and management (such as no discrimination against union supporters); and various other aspects of the framework of labor-management relations. Simply by mandating exclusive representation, the U.S. legal system makes U.S. industrial relations significantly different from European industrial relations (see chapter 7).

Debates over employment and labor law reform reflect frustrations by various parties over perceived imbalances between efficiency, equity, and voice that result from interactions within the current legal framework. Opponents of employment law changes—such as increases in the minimum wage or extensions of the Family and Medical Leave Act's provisions—believe that efficiency would be significantly reduced. Organized labor frequently criticizes the NLRA's lack of penalties, the scope for management delay through legal challenges, restrictions on secondary boycotts, and failure to completely restrict the use of permanent strike replacements (Friedman et al. 1994; Bronfenbrenner et al. 1998). These features are said to favor management and prevent the attainment of an appropriate balance in outcomes—both by reducing the chances of unionization and by weakening labor's power once organized. On the other hand, the probusiness lobby criticizes labor law for impairing efficiency, for example, by allegedly restricting nonunion employee participation through the NLRA's ban on company unions. In Europe, there are longstanding debates over the extent to which mandated severance pay and other legal constraints on workforce reductions increase unemployment (Blank 1994; Booth 1997; Gregg and Manning 1997).

The importance of the legal environment for employment outcomes is not limited to specific employment and labor laws, however. In a voluntarist system, such as in the United States before 1935 or in Great Britain today, common law doctrine determines the extent to which employment is at-will and contracts are enforceable, defines the limits of property rights, specifies objectionable actions that can be remedied through the law of torts, and shapes other critical dimensions of the framework for union organizing, bargaining, and dispute resolution. Common law regulation of so-called free markets determines the balance of power between labor and management and therefore the extent of the balance among efficiency, equity, and voice. For example, whether common law judgments treat employee picketing as coercion or not have obvious implications for the distribution of economic outcomes (Klare 1988). Tax laws can affect business decisions and therefore employment and labor relations outcomes (Stanger 2002). Trucking and airline labor relations and employment outcomes have been significantly affected by deregulation (Belzer 2000; Cappelli 1995). At the same time, although regulations can shape specific manifestations of behavior, they do not necessarily drive the human or economic underpinnings of that behavior. For example, Hebdon and Stern (1998) show that prohibiting strikes increases other forms of industrial conflict rather than removing it.

The Economic Environment: Marshall's Conditions

Within the framework established by common and statutory law, the economic environment is believed to critically determine relative power (again, either individually or collectively) and employment outcomes (Commons 1919; Dunlop 1958; Kochan and Katz 1988). The economic environment includes the labor market, the market for the employer's products or services, markets for other factors of production, and the overall macroeconomy. At a fundamental level, the economic environment includes the extent to which markets are competitive. Much of the economic environment can be captured by the recognition that labor is a derived demand (Marshall 1920), that is, the demand for labor is derived from labor's role in the production process for a product or service that is demanded by customers. Employee bargaining power—formally through labor unions, or informally as individual employees—is greater when labor demand is more inelastic (less responsive to wage changes). This occurs when (1) labor is essential or difficult to replace, (2) demand for the resulting product or service is inelastic (less responsive to price changes), (3) labor accounts for a small fraction of the entire production cost, and (4) the supply of the other factors of production is inelastic (Marshall 1920; Hamermesh 1993).

The state of the labor market is captured in the first dimension of Marshall's conditions. When the labor market is tight, or when workers have specific skills that are difficult to acquire, labor will be hard to replace and labor's bargaining power will be higher. Strike leverage that comes from perishable products or lack of inventories also means that labor is difficult to replace because there is little scope for substitution in the use of labor by the firm. Industry ability to pay, market concentration, and the nature of product market competition work through Marshall's second condition as these dimensions translate into differing degrees of product demand elasticity.

The macroeconomic environment can also affect bargaining power through Marshall's conditions and thereby determine the balance between efficiency, equity, and voice. For example, when the overall economy is strong, product demand might be more inelastic because consumers have greater disposable income. Increased globalization reduces labor's bargaining power by making product demand more elastic with increased imports and by making the supply of other factors more elastic through increased capital mobility.

As employee bargaining power is higher with inelastic labor demand, it is also higher with inelastic labor supply. If the economy is booming and there are ample opportunities for workers and/or their spouses to obtain employment during a strike, labor supply will be more inelastic and bargaining power higher because a larger wage increase will be needed to elicit increased labor supply. When unemployment and layoffs are high, labor supply is likely to be more elastic; employers can generate larger labor supply responses with smaller wage changes and labor's bargaining power will be lower. Changes in labor market demographics, such an increased female labor force participation and increases in average educational levels, can also affect the elasticity of labor supply and employment outcomes.

The Technical Context

The third dimension of the environment is Dunlop's (1958) technical context, the nature of production and the organization of work. The technical context includes whether the workplace is fixed (as in a factory) or variable (as in transportation industries); the degree of workforce and workplace stability; the size and hours of the workforce; and workers' job content and responsibilities (Dunlop 1958). These factors influence employment outcomes not only through their effect on bargaining power but more fundamentally by providing the issues that workplace rules must govern and by establishing workplace-level social relations. The issues facing a fixed-location, stable workforce that does not have any contact with the public will be different than the issues facing a high-turnover workforce with transient locations and a lot of customer contact. Marshall's conditions, and therefore bargaining power, may also be very different between these two groups. In fact, how formal organizational structures, including work structures, serve as methods of control is a central topic in the sociology of work (Cornfield, Campbell, and McCammon 2001; Grenier 1988; Watson 1995). Moreover, some of the biggest challenges for employers, employees, policy makers, and unions are devising new behaviors, policies, and strategies—and, therefore, employment outcomes—as workplaces move from mass manufacturing to flexible specialization (Appelbaum and Batt 1994; Bluestone and Bluestone 1992; Cappelli 1999; Heckscher 1988; Levine 1995).

A critical component of the technical context is technology. The main debate over technology is whether technological change is skill biased or de-skilling. Skill-biased technological change upgrades the skill requirements of technical jobs and results in greater demand for high skills. This phenomenon is generally associated with information technology and is widely argued by economists to be responsible for the increased wage gap between low- and high-skilled workers (Autor, Katz, and Krueger 1998; Berman, Bound, and Machin 1998; Haskel and Slaughter 2002). On the other hand, de-skilling technological change reduces the skills required. Braverman (1974) and Montgomery (1979) argued that managers used scientific management to break down both skilled craft and clerical occupations into simplified, routine, low-skilled jobs in order to gain control over the workplace.

The likely answer to the debate between de-skilling and skill-biased technological change is "it depends on the context, and in some cases on managerial strategies." Automation of information-handling functions in semiconductor manufacturing appears to be skill-biased because it leads to greater demand for engineers and a widening skill gap in the workplace (Brown and Campbell 2001), whereas in grocery stores a rapid increase in the use of scanning technology and changes in meat-processing technology has coincided with declining real wage levels for low- and high-skilled workers alike (Budd and McCall 2001). In retail banking, some banks are using new information technologies to upgrade the bank teller position, whereas others are using it to focus teller responsibilities on simplified data-entry tasks (Hunter et al. 2001). The former use likely makes employees harder to replace and thereby increases employee bargaining power (Marshall's first condition), whereas the latter likely makes employees easier to replace.[5]

The Political Environment

The relationship between employment outcomes and the political environment is captured by longtime UAW President Walter Reuther's statement that "there's a direct relationship between the bread box and the ballot box, and what the union fights for and wins at the bargaining table can be taken away in the legislative halls." Lawmakers determine not only the laws but how they are administered and adjudicated. But the political environment can also be important beyond the operation of the legal system.

This importance is most stark in the public sector where the political environment is perhaps as important as the economic environment. During collective bargaining in the public sector, for example, the extent to which elected officials are dependent on local union endorsements and union-member votes for reelection affects a union's bargaining power. Unions can also strengthen their bargaining power by convincing the public that there is a need for mutually beneficial services such as additional police officers or smaller class sizes (Devinatz 1999). In fact, the perceived weakness of market constraints and the importance of political power have led some to argue that unionization of the public sector should be forbidden because unions would be too strong (Wellington and Winter 1971; but compare Lewin et al. 1988).

The political environment can also shape the behavior of private sector labor unions. At various times in history, labor leaders have felt compelled to pursue a strategy of responsible unionism as a way to prevent antiunion government interference and legislation. During World War II, most unions effectively agreed to a "no strike" pledge for this reason (Lichtenstein 1982). The importance of the political arena is further revealed by the weakening of union power in the postwar period that accompanied depoliticization of labor issues—which removed any political urgency associated with labor conflict—by national union and AFL-CIO leaders (Lichtenstein 2002). It is also common to cite governmental actions such as the firing of the air traffic controllers by President Ronald Reagan during the (illegal) PATCO strike in 1981 and the British government's role in labor's defeat in the 1984–85 National Union of Mineworkers strike as setting the tone or climate for private sector industrial relations, especially in making antiunion activity acceptable (Babson 1999; Ghilarducci 1986; Lichtenstein 2002; Towers 1997; Weiler 1990).

The Social Environment

Many theories in sociology, social psychology, and organizational behavior emphasize the social context of the employment relationship, especially at the work group or workplace level. This aspect of the social context includes both interpersonal group interactions and social norms (Cialdini and Trost 1998; Coleman 1986; Hackman 1992; Pfeffer 1998). Social identification is one component of mobilization theory, and this identity determines whether a worker will seek to redress perceived workplace injustices individually or collectively (Kelly 1998). Hodson (2001, 203) identifies four major functions of the social aspects of work groups: socialization to norms, solidarity in defense against managerial abuse, support of personal space, and affirmation of workplace identities. Social norms—social standards to which conformity is expected—can limit piece-rate output among workers (Barbash 1984; Hodson 2001). Legitimate use of managerial power in the workplace also relies on managers adhering to workplace norms against abuse of authority (Hodson 2001). Societal norms can structure workplace norms and maintain traditional hierarchies and conceptions of disability or gender roles (Harlan and Robert 1998). And Godard (2002, 249) emphasizes the role of the state in shaping "the cognitive and normative rules that undergird employer decision processes" beyond the state's traditional legal rule-making function. Social norms can therefore be important for both worker and managerial decision making. (Social norms as ethics will be addressed in the next chapter.)

The broader social environment can also affect the relative power of employees and employers. For example, Lichtenstein (2002) emphasizes the relationship between organized labor's power and "national consciousness": union power is high when society believes that the labor movement's ideals are central to national problems (such as when strong collective bargaining supported the Keynesian goals of the New Deal) and is low when they are not (such as from the 1960s to the present when strong collective bargaining has been viewed as undermining individual rights and competitiveness). This national consciousness is similar to union legitimacy, and Chaison and Bigelow (2002) emphasize the importance of the public in determining the amount of legitimacy unions command. Taras (1997) argues that the healthier Canadian labor movement can be partially explained by greater social acceptance of collective action and the lack of acceptance of antiunion behavior by management. Similar arguments can be applied to the degree of social acceptability of human resource management.

The Business Context

The fifth dimension of the employment relationship environment is the business context. A central component of this category is strategy (Kochan, Katz, and McKersie 1986; Cappelli and Singh 1992). For example, consider Porter's (1980) cost leadership and differentiation strategies. A cost leadership strategy focuses on gaining a competitive advantage through low costs while a differentiation strategy creates a competitive advantage through unique products and services. Steel minimills with a cost leadership strategy are more likely to have incentive-based pay plans, low benefits, narrow job classifications, and few skilled workers; minimills with a differentiation strategy are more likely to have salaried pay plans with extensive benefits, broad job classifications, and more skilled employees (Arthur 1992). As mentioned above, the use of information technology in retail banking to upgrade the teller position in one corporation and to de-skill the position in another is broadly consistent with these two different business strategies (Hunter et al. 2001). Cappelli (1985) finds that different business strategies among U.S. airlines have significant effects on collective bargaining and on employment outcomes. The Southern strategy of General Motors in trying to open new nonunion plants in the 1970s reflects a different business strategy than its partnership with the UAW at Saturn and, of course, has yielded very different employment outcomes (Kochan, Katz, and McKersie 1986; Rubinstein and Kochan 2001). For individual employees, business strategies and the resulting human resource management practices and policies can affect behavior through rewards, incentives, and controls.

An organization's business strategy is likely to be a product of the organization's external environment and the ethical beliefs of its leaders. As such, the claim that business strategy is part of the employment relationship environment does not mean it is strictly exogenous. For example, Cooke and Meyer (1990) show that companies with fewer unionized plants are more likely to pursue union avoidance strategies. By itself, this does not discount the importance of business strategy to employment outcomes, but it does make empirical analysis more complex.

The business dimension also includes broader questions of corporate governance and the power of corporations in society. Shareholder versus stakeholder models of corporate governance create different environments for the employment relationship (see chapter 5). And corporate power in society clearly establishes important parameters for the employment relationship. If corporations are simply efficient producers of goods and services that are regulated by markets and policy makers, then consideration of the economic and legal environment discussed above suffices. But if corporations, especially huge multinational corporations in a global economy, dominate local and national governments as well as the global economy (Korten 1995; K. Phillips 2002), then the nature of corporate power in society must be explicitly included in discussions of employment relationship outcomes.

The Institutional Context

The institutional context includes nonmarket institutions and forces that are not captured by the other dimensions. This includes community groups that focus on specific groups of workers (such as immigrants), specific issues (such as work-family balance), economic development, or training (Osterman et al. 2001; Wheeler 2002). It also includes church and nongovernmental organizations. The most visible labor market institution, however, has been labor unions. As discussed in chapter 5, the presence of a union drastically changes the employment relationship from individual employee interactions with employers to collective employee dealings. In pluralist industrial relations, this collective feature is critical for countering the power of corporations (as collectives of individual investors) when labor markets are imperfect.

Within the unionized employment relationship, the unionism context—pressures and structures within individual unions and the labor movement—is also important as a significant dimension of the employment environment. Number one is perhaps the overall strength of the labor movement, including cooperation and competition within the labor movement. For example, competition between the Teamsters and other unions drove the aggressiveness of Teamster bargainers in 1940s and 1950s Detroit (Russell 2001). In contrast, the pursuit of a tripartite, corporatist philosophy caused Walter Reuther, Sidney Hillman, and others to follow a strategy of responsible unionism and very different bargaining strategies (Fraser 1983; Russell 2001). Bargaining structures are also important. Reminiscent of Ross's (1948) "orbits of coercive comparison," I have argued (Budd 1995) that the UAW's well-known pattern bargaining strategy across industries results from internal union political pressures stemming from centralization. In a comparative framework, Turner (1991) links international differences in union structures of representation—from being integrated into managerial decision making in Germany to being adversarial and at arm's length in the United States—to international differences in outcomes, especially stable union representation in Germany but declining in the United States. Thus, structural union factors are also an important component of the employment environment.

Demographics and history also matter. Demographic trends affect the composition of union membership (Kochan and Katz 1988), while history can shape structures and agendas. Contemporary union emphasis on contractual, seniority-based protections stems from the abusive use of managerial subjectivity and favoritism extending back to the 1930s and before (Brody 1993;

Gersuny and Kaufman 1985). Bureaucratic forms of representation, a weak shop steward system, and widespread no-strike clauses in contracts can be traced back to the pressures for discipline and military production during World War II (Atleson 1998; Lichtenstein 1982). Moreover, the continuing system of grievance arbitration developed in this same period, and it, in turn, was heavily influenced by the experiences of the Amalgamated Clothing Workers in the 1920s (Fraser 1983; Lichtenstein 1993). The tenor of management resistance to unions, and therefore the shape and state of the U.S. labor movement, has important historical origins in the economics, politics, and ideologies of the early twentieth century (Jacoby 1991). In other words, union strategies and behaviors are path-dependent (Hyman 2001).

As with the business dimension, aspects of this institutional dimension are strategic choices influenced by the environment. The rise of community groups may stem from the economic or political environment; and union decisions about whether to engage in pattern bargaining or industrywide bargaining depend at least in part on the nature of product market competition. Because aspects of this dimension may be endogenous, the research design needed to confidently analyze them is complicated, but this does not mean that they are not important aspects of the environment. For example, Mangum and McNabb (1997) document the strong influence of product and labor markets on the rise and fall of steel industrywide bargaining, as well as the effect of the Experimental Negotiating Agreement (ENA) on wage and benefit outcomes in the 1970s. The economic environment influenced the institutional environment, including industrywide bargaining and the ENA, but once in place, the ENA had an independent effect on bargaining outcomes.

Dimensions of the Human Agent

In the seven dimensions of the employment environment, some elements may be beyond the short-run control of the labor and management participants. Examples include labor law, trade agreements in international treaties, demographic trends, and the capabilities of information technologies. Nevertheless, there are numerous areas in which the participants have choices, such as in individual and collective work behaviors, management and union strategies, forms of work organization, bargaining philosophies, political and social agendas, and the deployment of technology. What determines the course of action chosen? This is the question of how to model the human agent or the human decision-making process. Mainstream neoclassical economics assumes the model of "economic man" in which individuals are rational utility maximizers. In other words, choices are effectively dictated by utility maximization and market constraints. Behavioral scholarship incorporates psychological dimensions, or mental states and processes, into the decision-making process (Kaufman 1989, 1999), while sociology emphasizes the importance of informal and formal social structures (Watson 1995). Still others focus on sociobiology elements, such as natural selection and social dominance (Wheeler 1985). For purposes of exposition, these diverse factors can be parsimoniously categorized into five groups: cognition, motivation, personality, feelings, and ethics (see figure 3.1).[6]

Cognition

The category of cognition includes information-processing techniques and abilities. The standard neoclassical economics vision of cognition is the most straightforward: human agents are assumed to fully process all relevant information in a rational way to maximize their well-defined utility objectives (Kaufman 1989, 1999). In this model, cognitive ability determines the labor market opportunities for selling one's labor only to the extent that ability is related to the value of the person's labor; it does not affect the information-processing capabilities necessary for optimal, rational choice. Though firmly cemented in mainstream economic thought, this rational choice model of the human agent has been widely challenged.[7] A very influential alternative to pure rational choice is bounded rationality (March and Simon 1958; Simon 1982). Bounded rationality posits that human agents seek optimal actions, but human cognitive limitations and time constraints prevent them from processing all of the information and alternatives. Because of bounded rationality, individuals "satisfice" instead of optimize—they find a solution that is deemed "good enough," perhaps aided by heuristics ("rules of thumb"). Wheeler (1985) further argues that strong emotions such as frustration can impede rational calculation, replacing optimization with aggression. Alternatively, social influences that limit rational choice amount to bonded rather than bounded rationality (Halpern 1998). Other models also include instinct (Wheeler 1985), habit (Hodgson 1998), and learning (Bandura 1986) as central features of cognition, making the decision-making process one that is not based purely on rational calculation.

A large literature reveals diverse ways in which observed human behavior diverges from predictions of rational choice. In the context of negotiations, at least four cognitive biases have been well-documented: framing, anchoring, availability, and overconfidence (Neale and Bazerman 1991). "Framing" pertains to how a problem is framed or contextualized, for example, as a gain or a loss. Even when the final outcome would be the same, individuals evaluate negatively framed outcomes (losses) differently than positively framed outcomes (gains). One clear application to the employment relationship is the effect of this bias on collective bargaining (Neale and Bazerman 1985). The bias of "anchoring" occurs when an initial reference point affects subsequent behavior. Negotiations that start with a high opening offer typically settle at a higher point than negotiations that start with a low opening offer. "Availability" means that events that are more easily recalled will be incorrectly judged to occur more frequently, and "overconfidence" results when many individuals overestimate the accuracy of their judgments. Kahneman, Knetsch, and Thaler (1986) further show how fairness is very important in individual decision making. This is more consistent with equity theory (Adams 1965) and "orbits of coercive comparisons" (Ross 1948) than with strict rational choice as foundations for employee judgments about wages and other elements of their job.

In addition to how information is processed, cognition also includes individual differences in the ability to understand complex ideas and to learn from experience—in other words, intelligence (Neisser et al. 1996). The existence of differences in individual intelligence leads to the logical prediction that there will be a wide range of observed outcomes across individuals, employment outcomes included. General cognitive ability captures stable individual differences in information-processing capabilities. It tends to account for so much variance in employment-related outcomes—including decision making and job performance—that researchers in industrial/organizational psychology simply refer to it as g (Murphy 1996). Cognitive ability is related to work goals and motivation (Austin and Klein 1996), leadership (Baron 1996), and earnings (Bowles, Gintis, and Osborne 2001). And hundreds of studies over eighty-five years have shown that cognitive ability predicts job performance and, in fact, is perhaps the single best predictor of job performance (Schmidt and Hunter 1998).

Motivation

Motivation is "variability in behavior *not due solely* to individual differences in ability or to overwhelming environmental demands that coerce or force action" (Kanfer 1992, 78, emphasis in original). In other words, motivation is a drive to do something. In neoclassical economics, motivation is a sole drive to maximize individual utility. Sociobiological models in which natural selection pushes human action (e.g., Wheeler 1985) effectively define motivation as the need to pursue resources for survival. A human agent's concern with conforming to social norms is another motivator. The dominant psychological concept of motivation is rooted in intrinsic and extrinsic psychological needs (Kanfer 1992). In sum, motivation can be broadly defined to include material, biological, social, and psychological wants and needs that drive human behavior.

An early theory of motivation is Maslow's (1943) hierarchy of needs. In this famous conceptualization, humans seek to first satisfy their most basic needs—physiological needs of food, water, and air. Once satisfied, attention is turned to safety needs and then to love, esteem, and finally self-actualization. These contain biological and material needs (physiological and safety), social wants (love), and psychological wants (esteem and self-actualization). Contemporary psychology research on intrinsic motivation reinforces the higher-order psychological needs and wants identified by Maslow. In fact, wide-ranging intrinsic motivators—such as stimulation, competence, mastery, challenge, autonomy, and control—have been posited as significantly affecting work behavior (Kanfer 1992).

Another major group of motivation theories are rooted in organizational justice. J. Stacy Adams's (1965) equity theory emphasizes distributive justice: individuals will alter their behavior to establish fair outcomes (equity) with some comparison group. The classic example is an individual's pay relative to their effort. Theories of procedural justice (e.g., Thibaut and Walker 1975) similarly posit that human needs and wants include fairness, but they focus on the processes, such as how wages are established or layoffs determined. Greenberg (1987) further theorizes that both distributive and procedural justice can have both proactive and reactive variants. Organizational justice is thus an important component of understanding employee behavior (Gilliland and Chan 2001) and of modeling the human agent.[8]

Psychology models of motivation differ from the neoclassical economics approach by emphasizing the significance of intrinsic motivators and concerns for justice. Another approach to enriching the neoclassical economics model of the human agent is to add concern for others as a motivating factor. This includes the power of conforming to social norms (because of a concern for how others perceive you) and also direct concern for the welfare of others (Ben-Ner and Putterman 1998). These concerns may stem from natural selection (Ben-Ner and Putterman 1998) or from a social need to affiliate and belong to groups (Hodson 2001) or from altruism (Dawkins 1976). Concern for others can be an important motivator of workplace behavior and outcomes. The most fundamental descriptions of the extent to which we should care about others are ethics; these are addressed in the next chapter.

Organizational strategies and goals are part of motivation as well as the environment. For workers and managers to keep their jobs, or for union leaders to be reelected, they need to fulfill various organizational objectives and social norms. In the model of figure 3.1 a firm's profit motive is translated into action by individuals pursuing profit-maximizing behaviors motivated by extrinsic desires to retain their jobs and be promoted, by fulfilling social norms of being good employees, and by satisfying intrinsic desires to be successful. At the same time, other motivators may conflict with organizational goals. These conflicts are the source of principal-agent problems, which have received considerable attention in research on organizational theory (Milgrom and Roberts 1992).

Personality

Personality is an enduring dispositional quality or stable mental state (Hogan 1992). The most widely recognized set of personality dimensions in psychology is known as the Big Five: extraversion, agreeableness, neuroticism (emotional stability), conscientiousness, and openness to experience. These factors are believed to be robust and stable across cultures, though with differing degrees of precision (Hough and Ones 2001). Barrick and Mount's (1991) widely cited review found that only conscientiousness was consistently related to job performance. However, subsequent research that looks at other dimensions of personality and finer job behaviors is more supportive of a nontrivial link between personality and job performance (Hough and Ones 2001).

Personality also appears partially linked to job satisfaction; health, safety, and stress on the job; and leadership (Hart and Cooper 2001; Hough and Ones 2001; Judge, Heller, and Mount 2002).

Feelings

To keep the model in figure 3.1 parsimonious, I group several distinct psychological constructs into a category of feelings—attitudes, moods, and emotions.[9] Although personality is fixed, these three sets of feelings can vary over time and with experiences, albeit differently. Attitudes are "mental states developed through experience, which are always ready to exert an active influence on an individual's response to any conditions and circumstances that the attitudes are directed towards" (McKenna 1987, 239). One of the most important attitudes in the employment relationship is job satisfaction—the attitude toward one's job. Job dissatisfaction has been linked to absenteeism, tardiness, employee turnover, early retirement, and propensity to unionize (Judge, Hanisch, and Drankowski 1995; Miller and Rosse 2002; Wheeler and McClendon 1991). Glomb, Steel, and Arvey's (2002) model includes job dissatisfaction as a predictor of some forms of workplace aggression. Organizational commitment and union commitment are two other employee attitudes that can affect employment outcomes (Barling, Fullagar, and Kelloway 1992; Gallagher and Strauss 1991; Meyer and Allen 1997). Attitudes toward unions—such as favorable beliefs about unions in general or about union instrumentality—are related to support for unionization in an individual's workplace (Wheeler and McClendon 1991). Vocational interests predict occupation and job tenure (Hogan and Blake 1996).

Two critical attitudes for individual behavior are attitudes or evaluations about one's self: self-esteem and self-efficacy. Self-esteem measures the degree of positive or negative views that individuals hold about themselves. Positive self-esteem is believed to help individuals "maintain optimism in the face of failure" and thereby perform better; empirically, self-esteem predicts both job satisfaction and job performance (Judge and Bono 2001, 81). Self-efficacy is the extent to which individuals feel they can control themselves and their tasks. It is related to job performance, coping with difficult tasks, career choice, and adaptability to new technology (Gist and Mitchell 1992).

Moods and emotions are often considered together under the term "affect" (Forgas and George 2001). Moods are feelings of a general nature and are not linked to specific triggers. Emotions are similar to moods, but are more intense, short-lived, and linked to specific causal factors (Forgas and George 2001; Weiss 2002). Having a positive outlook is a mood; being angry with a coworker is an emotion. Positive moods are linked with increased work motivation, greater levels of helping coworkers, increased flexibility, improved leadership effectiveness, and reduced absenteeism (Forgas and George 2001). Of particular relevance for unionized outcomes that result from bargaining, positive mood (or positive affect) increases cooperation in bargaining situations. Negotiators with a positive affect are more likely to reach an agreement

and are better at integrative ("win-win") bargaining through creative problem solving (Forgas and George 2001; Isen 2000). Emotions are also linked
with numerous workplace behaviors and decisions (Lord, Klimoski, and Kanfer 2002). As emotions are more closely linked with specific triggers, they can
prompt behaviors directed toward the specific cause, and can momentarily
overwhelm other goals and behavioral patterns (Lowenstein 1996). Wheeler's
(1985) model of industrial conflict features the emotion of frustration as a central component leading to strikes.

Strategy

To produce employment outcomes, the concerns of the human agent and the
constraints of the environment need to be translated into action. In general
terms, this process involves the construction and implementation of a strategy
for achieving goals. "Strategy" is used here quite broadly to capture individual choices and plans of action consistent with an individual's underlying ethical belief system and other personal needs, wants, and characteristics.[10] In
figure 3.1, employers move toward the middle from the left by translating
goals into strategies; strategies become action through interactions with employees and unions at the workplace, and at functional, strategic, and sociopolitical levels. Employees move toward the middle from the right-hand
side of figure 3.1 through similar steps. As developed by Kochan, Katz, and
McKersie (1986), the workplace level is the lowest level of interaction involving individual employees, work groups, union representatives, and managers. The functional level includes the development of human resources
policies and the process of collective bargaining. For emphasis and clarity, I
split Kochan, Katz, and McKersie's (1986) strategic level into an organization-
specific strategic level and a sociopolitical level. Decisions at the strategic level
are focused inward on the employment relationship, employer, and union; sociopolitical activity is focused outward toward the broader social and political environment. A union corporate campaign that seeks to generate public
pressure on a company is an example of a sociopolitical activity.

The model in figure 3.1 captures many theories of action and strategy in the
employment relationship. On the employer side, human resources and industrial relations strategy includes wide-ranging choices of human resource management policies and practices ranging from authoritarian, hierarchical
practices to attempts at creating high-performance work systems (Katz and
Darbishire 2000). Also included are the possible approaches for dealing with
unions, such as union acceptance, substitution, avoidance, or suppression
(Kochan and Katz 1988). On the employee side, possible actions include
unionizing, pursuing individual representation (Troy 1999), or other workplace-level actions to achieve dignity at work (Hodson 2001). To emphasize
the generality of figure 3.1, unionizing, for example, can be approached from
various perspectives—an instrumental calculation (Wheeler and McClendon

1991), a multi-identity movement (Kurtz 2002), or mobilization theory (Kelly 1998), to name just a few. Figure 3.1 also includes various union strategies and philosophies (Hoxie 1917; Wheeler 2002).

The Current State of Efficiency, Equity, and Voice

The role of the environment and the human agent in the employment relationship can be approached from two directions. In academic research, the focus is on analyzing how the environment and human decision-making affects employment outcomes. How does an organization's business strategy affect human resource management practices? Have the decline in labor unions and in the value of the minimum wage, or changes in technology, increased wage inequality? How does cognitive ability affect job performance? To what extent are personality traits related to organizational citizenship behaviors? But the environment and the human agent can be also be approached from the opposite direction. A paradigm of seeking a balance between efficiency, equity, and voice, and between property rights and labor rights, provides the framework for evaluating the extent to which an existing environmental context promotes this balance and for designing new laws, institutions, strategies, and social norms for achieving this balance. In short, one goal of a country's employment system should be to manipulate the controllable dimensions of the environment to balance property rights and labor rights to promote a balance between efficiency, equity, and voice. Similarly, one can analyze existing employment outcomes against the standard of whether these outcomes are supportive of the needs of the human agent.

Except in the neoclassical economics conception of the human agent, individuals are not simply mechanistic, self-interested, utility maximizers. Rather, human agents are believed to have concern for fairness, justice, equity, voice, other people, and social norms. Both extrinsic and intrinsic rewards from working are important motivators of employment-related behaviors. Attitudes, moods, and emotions can also affect decision making and, therefore, employment outcomes. Beyond neoclassical economic thought, all of the models of the human agent specify a richer set of human needs and wants—whether biological, psychological, or social. This richness emphasizes the need to conceptualize work as a fully human activity. And thus, a richer set of employment relationship objectives beyond efficiency is required; decision making with a human face points toward employment with a human face.

Are U.S. employment outcomes consistent with employment with a human face? To many observers, U.S. employment outcomes are out of balance. First, consider efficiency. The U.S. period of economic expansion between 1991 and 2001 was the longest in U.S. history and produced some impressive results. From 1995 to 2000, the growth rate of labor productivity was more than double the rate for 1973 to 1995, real gross domestic product often increased by at least 4 percent annually, and the unemployment rate was at its lowest point in many years (*Economic Report of the President* 2001). Lingering below the surface, however, are nagging concerns with efficiency. Corporations continue to push for flexible work practices and compensation systems. Health care costs continue to grow quickly (*Economic Report of the President* 2002). Workforce development and education is an important issue as technology impacts the skill requirements of many jobs.

Moreover, there are few who would say U.S. employment and (especially) labor law contributed to this recent period of economic growth; rather, most would assert that growth in the 1990s occurred in spite of, not because of, this aspect of the legal environment.[11] As a result, business continues to lobby for changes in labor and employment law. The Labor Policy Association advocates amending the NLRA to promote nonunion employee representation and revising the Fair Labor Standards Act to allow payment of compensatory time, reduce barriers to paying bonuses, and update the exemption provisions (Bartl 2002). The U.S. Chamber of Commerce opposes increases in the minimum wage and supports repeal of the Davis-Bacon Act, which requires paying the prevailing wage for federal construction projects. Others argue for deregulating labor relations (Baird 2000; Epstein 1983; Heldman, Bennett, and Johnson 1981). All of these positions implicitly reflect the belief that the balance between efficiency, equity, and voice can be improved.

Second, consider equity.[12] Although household income grew in the late 1990s (partly because of increased working hours), it grew much slower than between 1947 and 1973, and grew slowest for those in the bottom half of the income distribution. Similarly, although inequality slowed in the 1990s relative to the 1980s, it still increased.[13] The median corporate chief executive officer earns more than one hundred times what the average worker earns; this is a fivefold increase since 1962. After the expansion in the 1990s, the poverty rate of 11.8 percent in 1999 was still about the same as in 1979, and poverty rates for minority groups are nearly twice as high as for whites. Forty million Americans do not have health insurance (*Economic Report of the President* 2001). The U.S. Equal Employment Opportunity Commission receives nearly 30,000 race-related discrimination charges and over 15,000 sexual harassment charges each year.[14] Some companies severely restrict employees' access to restrooms (Linder and Nygaard 1998). And modern sweatshops, such as in the Los Angeles apparel industry (Bonacich and Appelbaum 2000), continue to exist.

Third, consider voice. A survey of over two thousand employees by Freeman and Rogers (1999, 48) revealed that 55 percent of respondents said that "it is very important to have a lot of influence" over workplace issues such as benefits, training, departmental goals, safety standards, and how to do one's job, while 53 percent indicated that they had less influence over or involvement in workplace decision making than they desired. Some people preferred individual voice and some collective, and respondents differed over independent representation versus joint labor-management committees, but the demand for workplace voice is clear. Moreover, drawing on several surveys,

Freeman and Rogers (1993, 1999) found that one-third of nonunion workers would like a union in their workplace. This is often referred to as a representation gap: employees say that they want more representation in the workplace than they have (Freeman and Rogers 1993, 1999; Towers 1997; Weiler 1990). The existence of a representation gap equates to inadequate provision of workplace voice in the employment system.

That the U.S. system has recently performed better along the efficiency dimension than along the equity and voice dimensions is not surprising in light of the employment relationship environment (see figure 3.2). The efficiency dimension is perhaps the envy of businesses in many other developed countries. There are few restrictions on hiring and firing, layoffs and relocations are an accepted part of the American labor market, and many employers have established flexible work systems and pay-for-performance programs. In contrast, the dimension of equity is less well served. Relative to many European countries, for example, U.S. labor policies for minimum labor standards and for social insurance programs are modest. The promotion of employee voice in the current U.S. employment relationship environment is also weak. Union density, especially in the U.S. private sector, is very low, and in the large nonunion sector, very few (if any) formal protections exist in support of employee voice.

Employment relationship outcomes come from the interaction of human agents in the employment environment. Most models of the human agent reinforce the need for the employment relationship objectives of efficiency, equity, and voice. Thus, the environment should be structured so promote these objectives. How to do this is the dominant topic for nearly the remainder of this book. But first, the next chapter explicitly addresses a heretofore-neglected part of both the environment and the human agent—the ethics of the employment relationship.

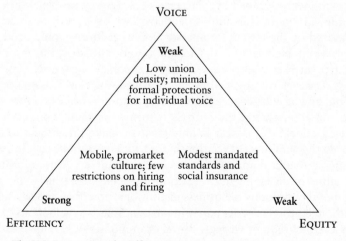

Figure 3.2 The U.S. Environment for Efficiency, Equity, and Voice

4 Balancing Outcomes Revisited: The Ethics of the Employment Relationship

COMPARED TO THE industrial relations scholarship on the environment and the psychology and sociology research on the human agent, the role of ethics in determining employment outcomes is an underdeveloped area.[1] And, in practice, John Ryan's (1912, 5) assertion continues to be as accurate for the early twenty-first century as it was for the early twentieth century:

> In fixing wages, as in other actions, there are men who will not hesitate to gain their ends by deliberate dishonesty and extortion. Others ignore the moral side of the wage-contract merely because it does not attract their attention. The greater number, however, of those who strive to make the best possible bargain, regardless of any formal ethical standard of wages, seem to think that the contract is fair, inasmuch as it is free and made under rule of competition.

This sentiment is echoed by Osterman et al. (2001, 12) when they ascribe the continued "moral vacuum" in employment issues to U.S. society being "mesmerized by the idea that impersonal market forces would produce efficient and equitable results." McClelland (1990, 59) labels this moral equating of free market outcomes with just outcomes "marginal productivity justice." However, whether actions result from a singular focus on profit maximization, or a broader conception of a corporation's social structure and purpose, or an emphasis on the fairness or justice of the action, each reflects underlying ethical theories. It is important to make these theories explicit. Moreover, the employment relationship is ultimately about people and quality of life, and ethical analysis is therefore warranted.[2] A useful foundation for the ethics of the employment relationship is business ethics—the application of moral philosophy to business institutions, practices, and decision making. Although business ethics partly involves normative evaluations of specific actions as either right or wrong—moral or immoral—it also analyzes the underlying bases for decision making (as emphasized in figure 3.1).[3] Ethical analyses in human resources and industrial relations have both normative (prescriptive) and positive (analytical) applications.

The emphasis on strategic choice in contemporary models of employment (Kochan, Katz, and McKersie 1986; Kochan, McKersie, Cappelli 1984), for example, underscores the need for positive analysis of ethical issues. This strategic choice framework emphasizes managerial choices and values. In Kochan, Katz, and McKersie's (1986) analysis, postwar managerial values include a desire to be union free. Managerial emphasis on "union free" is implicitly a utilitarian or libertarian ethical principle. The strategic choice framework can be strengthened by making this connection explicit. Moreover, the strategic choice model implies that if managers possess a different ethical principle, such as Kantian duty or Rawlsian fairness, then employment outcomes will be different.[4] As a second example, an ethical work climate might be related to employee decision making and, therefore, to organizational outcomes (e.g., Barnett and Vaicys 2000). The incorporation of ethical analyses into human resources and industrial relations provides the framework for such analyses.

The normative aspect—the analysis of whether actions should be thought of as right or wrong—of the incorporation of business ethics into human resources and industrial relations provides the needed framework for evaluating existing employment practices. If behaviors or outcomes in the U.S. employment system fail to meet ethical standards, reform is warranted. Business ethics provides these alternative ethical standards. Business ethics can also help make human resources and industrial relations practitioners "more comfortable facing moral complexity" and thus become better professionals (Solomon 1992, 4).[5]

Thus, to further both the understanding of the drivers of the employment relationship—individuals, markets, institutions, organizational strategies, and public policies—through positive research, and the framework for debating what the characteristics of the employment relationship should be (normative research), an explicit ethical foundation should be incorporated into scholarship and debates on employment. Ethical theories are generally divided into two broad categories focusing either on outcomes (teleological ethics) or actions (deontological ethics). Utilitarianism is the central example of the former and Kantian moral philosophy is the dominant example of the latter.[6] There are additional possibilities, however, and for the employment relationship, six categories are instructive: the ethics of utility, the ethics of duty, the ethics of liberty, the ethics of fairness, the ethics of virtue, and the ethics of care. These six frameworks are summarized in table 4.1.

The Ethics of Utility

The ethics of utility is utilitarianism, which focuses on maximizing net social welfare or utility. In utilitarianism, an act is morally good if aggregate welfare

Table 4.1 Six Ethical Frameworks for Human Resources and Industrial Relations

Ethic	Founder	Essence	Balance of Efficiency, Equity, and Voice
Utility	Jeremy Bentham; John Stuart Mill	Welfare maximization through cost-benefit analysis (utilitarianism)	Efficiency is key to maximizing welfare. Equity and voice might be important but only if they are instrumental in increasing aggregate welfare.
Duty	Immanuel Kant	Respect for human dignity through the Kantian categorical imperative	Employment contract yields duty of efficiency, but equity and voice are essential aspects of respecting dignity. Must balance efficiency, equity, and voice.
Liberty	John Locke	Negative right of freedom from noninterference through strong property rights (libertarianism)	Strong property rights yield freedom of contract and efficiency. Property owners are free to provide equity and voice, but compulsion is coercive and therefore a violation of personal freedom.
Fairness	John Rawls	Justice as liberty, equal opportunity, and concern for the least well-off through the veil of ignorance and the difference principle	Efficiency is important but does not trump equal opportunity and the welfare of the least well-off so equity is required. Workplace voice likely implied by liberty and the veil of ignorance. Consistent with balancing efficiency, equity, and voice.
Virtue	Aristotle	Moral character to achieve flourishing through virtues and community	Emphasis on individual excellence includes efficiency but also interpersonal and community-building virtues. Consistent with balancing efficiency, equity, and voice.
Care	Carol Gilligan	Nurturing personal relationships through caring for people	Efficiency is not a concern, but importance of relationships and community is consistent with equity and voice.

(utility) is maximized, defined as producing the greatest benefits with the least costs compared to alternative possible actions (Beauchamp and Bowie 1997; Hausman and McPherson 1996; Velasquez 1998). This requires defining the parameters of welfare: the founders of utilitarianism, Jeremy Bentham and John Stuart Mill, focused on maximizing aggregate pleasure or happiness (hedonistic utilitarianism). Consistent with contemporary neoclassical economic theory, modern utilitarianism focuses on preference satisfaction. In either case, this is a consequentialist moral theory: the judge of an action is the consequences.

Utilitarianism is closely associated with neoclassical economic analysis and, therefore, employment research, in at least two important ways. First, the utilitarian calculation of totaling costs and benefits is the same cost-benefit analysis used in economic policy analysis and business decisions. In effect, cost-benefit analysis puts utilitarianism into practice (Hausman and McPherson 1996). If one equates monetary costs and benefits to utility, then a project or decision in which the economic benefits outweigh the costs is welfare improving and, according to utilitarian principles, should be undertaken. In comparing several alternatives, the one with the greatest net benefit should be chosen. A well-known example in industrial relations is Freeman and Medoff's (1984) calculations of the social costs and benefits of labor unions that stem from the monopoly and voice effects, respectively. If the negative monopoly effects of labor unions, such as union members' supracompetitive wage rates, cost more than the monetary benefits of the voice model, such as reduced turnover costs, then in utilitarian terms labor unions are socially harmful and should not be allowed. Troy (1999, 54) embraces utilitarianism at the company level: "Managerial opposition to unions is pragmatic, and motivated by competitive pressures. . . . They evaluate unionism as a net cost in the cost/benefit ratio of the performance of the company, and that is why they oppose unionization."

The second, and most important, link between utilitarianism and contemporary economics (and business) is efficiency. The first fundamental theorem of welfare economics states that every (perfectly) competitive equilibrium is Pareto optimal, that is, no one can be made better off without making someone else worse off. This is the standard economics definition of efficiency (Hausman and McPherson 1996). No resources can be reallocated to improve welfare. As such, unless one is willing to make interpersonal utility comparisons, "the greatest good for the greatest number" is achieved through competitive markets. And "the greatest good for the greatest number" is the central premise of utilitarianism. Support for free international trade because of the standard economic arguments of increased efficiency is precisely this utilitarian ethic (Garcia 1999). If, however, the standard neoclassical assumptions are not fulfilled (in short, if markets are not competitive), then individual self-interest is simply individual egoism, not utilitarianism, because aggregate welfare is not necessarily maximized (Flexner 1989).

Moreover, in neoclassical marginal economic analysis, competitive outcomes are characterized by each factor of production being compensated at the value of its marginal product. The wage rate for labor, for example, equals the value to the firm generated by hiring the last unit of labor in standard theoretical models. More productive workers will earn a higher wage, less productive workers will earn less. Because of the rudimentary belief held in popular U.S. thought that hard work should receive higher rewards, the analytical predictions of marginal analysis in the neoclassical economics paradigm have become a normative statement: "Factors of production *ought to be paid* the value of their marginal product" (McClelland 1990, 19, emphasis in original).[7] But this "marginal productivity justice" (McClelland 1990) is a utilitarianism ethical philosophy: factors of production (workers included) ought to be rewarded according to the value of their marginal productivity because this is efficient—uses of scarce resources are optimized and the greatest good is produced for the greatest number. If a factor is not being paid optimally, the current situation is inefficient; a price adjustment is necessary to reallocate factors to increase aggregate output and presumably utility. In economic analysis, efficient outcomes result from profit-maximizing behavior in competitive markets. Consequently, "the enterprise of business harbors a fundamentally utilitarian conception of the good society" (Beauchamp and Bowie 1997, 22).

Strategic business decisions to open nonunion plants instead of investing in existing unionized facilities in order to maximize profits (Kochan, Katz, and McKersie 1986) reflect a management philosophy of utilitarianism. Arguments against strike-replacement bans, because such a restriction would increase labor's bargaining power and increase labor costs and hurt competitiveness, are ultimately rooted in a utilitarian belief system. In the human resource management school of thought, provision of workplace equity and voice, which is justified because of its instrumental value in increasing efficiency and competitiveness, is rooted in utilitarianism. In short, economic behaviors predicated on efficiency and profit maximization reflect a utilitarian ethical theory. It is worth emphasizing that such behaviors are not devoid of ethical content; they are premised on a very specific ethical theory.

The logic of the utilitarian-neoclassical economics nexus is powerful: individuals pursuing their self-interests in competitive markets create efficient outcomes in which profits and welfare are maximized and each factor—labor, capital, raw materials, and the like—is rewarded with its value. Outside of economics, business, and conservative political thought, however, the *normative* value of this logic is not well accepted. In addition to problems of measuring utility, making interpersonal comparisons of utility, and violations of the perfect-competition assumptions underlying neoclassical economic theory, utilitarianism can be criticized for allowing the ends to justify the means, irrespective of the rights or virtues that might be violated, for accepting ends (outcomes) that seem unfair or unjust, and for ignoring broader concerns of community and relationships (Bowie 1999; Hausman and McPherson 1996; Sen and Williams 1982; Solomon 1996; Velasquez 1998).[8] These criticisms are similar to familiar industrial relations concerns with reliance on free markets or unilateral managerial control for governing the workplace. The remaining categories of ethical theories address these criticisms in one way or another.

The Ethics of Duty

The ethics of duty is an important foil for the ethics of utility because: in the former, actions are judged on the nature of the action; in the latter, actions are judged on the consequences without regard for the action itself. The most powerful proponent of the ethics of duty is Immanuel Kant. Kantian moral philosophy is based on the categorical imperative "Act only on that maxim by which you can at the same time will that it should become a universal law," which can be expressed as three synonymous formulations (Bowie 1999; Korsgaard 1996; Sullivan 1989):

1. Act only on that maxim by which you can at the same time will that it should become a universal law (Formula of Universal Law).
2. Act in such a way that you always treat humanity, whether in your own person or in the person of any other, never simply as a means, but always at the same time as an end (Formula of the End Itself).
3. So act as if you were through your maxims a law-making member of a kingdom of ends (Formula of the Kingdom of Ends).[9]

The foundation for these principles is that humans are rational beings capable of self-determination and self-governance (Bowie 1999; Sullivan 1989). Every (responsible) person is entitled to dignity and respect. Treating someone only as a means—for example, to increase your own or even aggregate wealth or welfare—violates the intrinsic value and sanctity of human life (Formula of the End Itself). Because everyone has equal intrinsic value, universality is crucial (Formula of the Universal Law). This also implies that you must be willing to be treated as you treat others. And this intrinsic value must be respected in social interactions (Formula of the Kingdom of Ends).

The moral principles embodied in the categorical imperative specify our duties—we have a duty to act such that our actions are universal and never treat individuals as only a means, even at the expense of aggregate utility. A common illustrative example in business ethics is employment discrimination (Bowie and Duska 1990; Velasquez 1998). To refuse to hire someone because of their race or gender, for example, violates the first formulation of the categorical imperative unless we are willing to not be hired because of our race or gender. Discrimination also violates the Formula of the End Itself because discriminatory treatment for arbitrary reasons violates the equal sanctity of all human life. Because union sympathies are irrelevant to job performance, the extension to discrimination on the basis of union support is straightforward.

Employment discrimination is an example of a perfect or negative duty. Discrimination violates the categorical imperative so it is morally unacceptable and forbidden. Individuals have a perfect duty to never act this way. Kant's two examples are committing suicide and making false promises (deception or lying). Kantian moral philosophy also includes imperfect or positive duties (Bowie 1999; Sullivan 1989).[10] A full respect for human dignity and a moral kingdom of ends requires concern for your own development and the welfare of others. Kant's examples of imperfect duties are developing one's own talents and helping others (beneficence). These are imperfect duties because there is not an obligation to always or exhaustively pursue them, but there is an obligation to pursue them sometimes.[11]

An employment relationship based on a Kantian moral philosophy of the ethics of duty would be very different than that based on the ethics of utility. In utilitarianism, workplace equity and voice are required only if they are instrumental—only if they increase aggregate efficiency. Human resource management policies or labor unions are only beneficial if they contribute to welfare or utility. In the pluralist industrial relations school of thought, utilitarian thinking implies that unions are justified if equalized bargaining power between labor and management stabilizes economic activity, as in the justification for the National Labor Relations Act (Kaufman 1996), or improves aggregate welfare by redressing other externality problems. In a Kantian employment system, however, workplace equity and voice stem from the duty to respect the value of human life. It has already been noted how the Formula of the End Itself rules out discriminatory treatment. The same logic applies to unjust dismissal because, by definition, unjust dismissals are for reasons not relevant to job performance or business demand. Failure to pay a living wage also treats workers solely as a means and is therefore also a violation of basic Kantian principles (Bowie 1999).

With respect to voice, "Kantian moral philosophy requires a vast democratization of the workplace" (Bowie 1999, 102). The Formula for the Kingdom of Ends requires that communities—including business organizations—respect the critical autonomy and rationality features of human beings. Denying participation in decision making violates this central principle (Bowie 1999). Moreover, unilateral rule making treats workers as means only, violating the second formulation of the categorical imperative (Pincoffs 1977). The noninstrumental justification for the NLRA as promoting industrial democracy (Forbath 2001; Gross 1999; Pope 2002) is not consistent with utilitarianism but is fully consistent with the Kantian ethics of duty. In contrast, however, the NLRA's emphasis on majority support and exclusive representation seems rooted in utilitarian thought. As such, noninstrumental, industrial democracy reasons for unionism undermine the continuing insistence on majority support and exclusive representation in U.S. labor policy.

Last, Bowie (1999) argues that managers have a Kantian moral obligation to stockholders to pursue profits to increase shareholder wealth. For a manager to disregard profitability would violate an implicit if not explicit contract

between managers and shareholders and thus violate the categorical imperative. But as Bowie (1999) further argues, this is not the same as *maximizing*
shareholder wealth at the expense of all other concerns. Therefore, combined
with the previous Kantian obligations of providing equity and voice, a Kantian employment relationship should provide efficiency *and* equity *and* voice.
In other words, the model of the employment relationship articulated in this
book in which the central premise is balancing efficiency, equity, and voice is
a Kantian employment system.[12]

As with the other ethical systems, however, Kantian moral philosophy can
be criticized. The emphasis on universal, unwavering rules has been attacked
as removing considerations of virtue, or what it means to be a good person in
everyday life (Solomon 1992). Universal rules are also challenged by situations
such as protecting an innocent person by telling a lie. Proponents of negative
rights object to obligations to others embedded in imperfect duties or positive
rights as coercion and violations of individual freedom. Others note that Kantian moral philosophy ignores the development of relationships or the concerns
of distributive justice.[13]

The Ethics of Liberty

The ethics of liberty, or libertarianism, echoes the Kantian emphasis on individual freedom but asserts that freedom means the negative right to noninterference. The only restriction on behavior should be preventing harm to
others—unless your actions harm others, you should be free to do as you
please. This is the essence of liberty in the libertarian view. Moreover, libertarianism has a narrow conception of harm to others: paying less than a living wage or providing unsafe working conditions are not considered harmful
as long as the dangers are not hidden from employees and they freely accept
employment. Going back at least to the writings of John Locke, strong property rights are central to libertarianism. For Locke (1690, §87, p. 341), man
"hath by nature a power . . . to preserve his property, that is, his life, liberty
and estate" and therefore the role of government is to protect the individual
and his or her property. In other words, property is the guardian of every other
right (Ely 1998). Taxation or other forms of redistribution from the wealthy
to the poor that are not purely voluntary are viewed as coercive takings of private property and a violation of the primary right of liberty. As long as the
distribution of wealth in society is achieved through fair acquisition and exchange (not through coercion or fraud, for example), then the distribution is
just, regardless of any degree of inequality, even if extreme (Nozick 1974).

Like utilitarianism, the ethics of liberty is closely associated with free markets, though for different reasons. Utilitarianism supports free markets because of the belief that this is the best way to achieve efficiency and aggregate
welfare maximization; libertarianism supports free markets because of the primacy of liberty—individual autonomy to interact with others without undue

interference.[14] Despite their differences, both views advocate strong property rights, freedom to contract, and free exchange without interference (Ely 1998). The primacy of property rights and the freedom to contract have been very important in the U.S. employment relationship for more than a century. The *Lochner*-era court in the early twentieth century is synonymous with the protection of economic due process, and therefore the legality of yellow dog contracts and the unconstitutionality of many protective labor standards (Ely 1998; Forbath 1985; Phillips 1998). And even though New Deal legislation explicitly established the government as a protector of social welfare, labor law continues to endorse the sanctity of property rights.[15]

Criticism of libertarianism challenges its narrow conception of liberty. In simple terms, are people who are starving truly free? It is not clear why the freedom from harm to private property always overrides other freedoms such as the freedom from hunger (Donnelly 1989; Gewirth 1996). These concerns are reinforced by claims that property rights are no longer a source of autonomy (see chapter 2 and Alexander 1997; Commons 1924; Nedelsky 1990). Libertarianism also relies heavily on the justice of existing patterns of property rights and resources, but fraud, slavery, forced takings, and other actions undermine this justice. The inequality of bargaining power between individuals and corporations (Commons 1919; Flexner 1989; Kaufman 1997b) further calls into question the extent to which unregulated marketplace transactions are free and therefore just.

The Ethics of Fairness

As a fourth ethical framework, consider the ethics of fairness or justice. Rawls (1971) famously developed a theory of distributive justice that augments the Kantian standards of equality and freedom with concern for the distribution of outcomes.[16] Rawlsian justice is based on a veil of ignorance: individuals must determine the principles of justice behind a veil of ignorance in which they do not know their own characteristics (such as race, gender, social status, and abilities). Rawls (1971, 83 and 250) asserted that under such conditions, rational, self-interested, and equal individuals will agree to the following (ignoring intergenerational concerns):

1. Each person is to have an equal right to the most extensive total system of equal basic liberties compatible with a similar system of liberty for all.
2. Social and economic inequalities are to be arranged so that they are both:
   a. to the greatest benefit of the least advantaged, and
   b. attached to offices and positions open to all under conditions of fair equality of opportunity.

Rawls presented these principles in lexical order so that the first principle, the liberty principle, is the highest priority. Unlike in utilitarianism, welfare does not take precedence over individual liberties.[17] Moreover, Rawls (1971, 302) was explicit in stating that justice takes precedence over efficiency. Principle 2a, the difference principle, allows inequalities in utility or welfare, but such inequalities should also benefit the least well-off members of society. Principle 2b emphasizes equality of opportunity—differential outcomes are allowed, but these should reflect legitimate differences in ability and effort, not arbitrary and discriminatory factors.

The importance of this Rawlsian ethics of fairness for the employment relationship is that it highlights the importance of social justice. In very broad terms, this ethical framework is consistent with an employment system in which efficiency is important but does not dominate concerns of distributive justice. This framework also reinforces the importance of equity in the employment relationship, not only in terms of distributive justice but also in terms of nondiscriminatory treatment. As in Kantian moral philosophy, discrimination is unjust and immoral in the ethics of fairness. One can also infer support for workplace voice in this Rawlsian ethics of fairness. First, the primacy of political liberty in Rawls (1971) suggests that democratic principles are of sufficient importance to extend to the workplace. Second, would individuals agree to hierarchical, authoritarian workplaces or workplaces with voice mechanisms from behind the veil of ignorance before their ultimate positions are revealed? Faced with the prospect of being on the subservient end of an autocratic employment relationship once the veil is lifted, I suspect that most would instead create workplaces with a voice mechanism from behind the veil of ignorance.

The Ethics of Virtue

The previous moral theories emphasize outcomes, rights, and/or duties, all which overlook issues of virtue and character (Solomon 1992). When people are described as generous, honest, greedy, or ruthless, it is their moral character, not their actions, that is being described (Velasquez 1998). The ethics of virtue focuses on the type of person each individual ought to be. Virtues are the characteristics that make a person a good human being and are necessary to live a good life—to flourish. Moral behavior flows from virtues—not by the application of rules but from the virtuous moral character of individuals. Virtue ethics can be traced back at least to Plato and Aristotle, and contemporary applications of virtue ethics are sometimes referred to as Aristotelian (e.g., Solomon 1992).

Aristotle viewed virtues as the mean between excess and deficiency (Aristotle 1980). Courage, for example, is the mean between cowardice and foolhardiness. Aristotle's other virtues are listed in Aristotle (1980) and Ross (1923). Either extreme, of excess or deficiency, is a vice. The difficulty is knowing where the mean lies—"to the right person, to the right extent, at the right time, with the right motive, and in the right way" (Aristotle 1109^{a}30, 1980,

p. 45). In contrast to the categorical imperative, for example, virtues are learned by perception, practice, and education, not through reasoning, and it is impossible to construct unambiguous rules for their application (Norman 1998). That virtues are developed and reinforced through education, and that some virtues are social (friendliness, truthfulness, and wittiness), underscores that Aristotelian ethics emphasize community (Solomon 1992). It is not an ethical framework of atomistic individuals.

Contemporary definitions of virtues echo this importance of community and interaction. Pincoffs (1986, 82) defines virtues and vices as "dispositional properties that provide grounds for preference or avoidance of persons." Among these, the moral virtues are those that show a concern for others, such as honesty and reliability, because of "the foundation of ethical thought: the fact that we must live together, we must live with each other in as effective, meaningful, fruitful, and harmonious a way as possible" (Pincoffs 1986, 8). In other words, virtues are the means to bind individuals to society and create holistic, flourishing individuals and communities (Solomon 1992). Thus, virtue ethics "holds that a web of close relationships is essential for the good life" (Boatright 2000, 66).

As applied to business ethics, virtue ethics views corporations as human communities with a vital sense of purpose that contribute to, and have responsibilities in, the larger social community (Solomon 1992). As a human community, a corporation is a collection of mutually dependent individuals, not isolated competitors, in which individual excellence and virtues contribute to the success of the community.[18] The importance of social interaction is critical. As part of a broader community, corporate excellence is defined by service to the broader community. As applied to the employment relationship, actions that undermine a holistic sense of community are unethical. Moreover, if the adjectives for an employer's or a union's character are vices, such as greedy, selfish, dangerous, or wicked, then the employer or the union is acting unethically (Schumann 2001). Rather, employment should be characterized by cooperation, integrity, honesty, fairness, and tolerance; the employment relationship should promote flourishing and social consciousness. Aristotelian justice includes a central industrial relations belief: might does not make right (Solomon 1992). Virtue ethics is consistent with balancing efficiency, equity, and voice. The emphasis on excellence requires a concern for efficiency and productivity, but excellence is a holistic concept and interpersonal and community-building virtues also support the need for workplace equity and voice. Aristotelian business ethics is therefore consistent with the need to balance efficiency, equity, and voice.

The Ethics of Care

With the exception of virtue ethics, the other ethical frameworks do not generally pay special attention to relationships (Velasquez 1998).[19] Gilligan

(1982, 79), however, asserts that the feminine voice consists of "defining the self and proclaiming its worth on the ability to care for and protect others," which therefore implies the need for a moral framework different from universal duties, rights, or utility-maximization. This is the ethics of care. Caring in this sense refers to more than caring *about* something but rather to caring *for* someone and is focused on nurturing their well-being (Noddings 1984; Velasquez 1998). Rather than making moral judgments based on rules or principles, the ethics of care relies on the deeper context, and especially the implications for relationships, of each particular situation (Gilligan 1982; Noddings 1984).

This framework is related to virtue theory, but the central virtues are those that are important to personal relationships such as sympathy, compassion, fidelity, love, and friendship (Beauchamp and Bowie 1997). This framework is also similar to the Aristotelian tradition that emphasizes the importance of community. However, the ethics of care places special emphasis on particular relationships, such as parents, neighbors, coworkers, or friends. As such, it is acceptable, or even encouraged, to treat those people differently. But in developing and nurturing these special relationships, conflicts can arise, such as favoritism in the workplace (Velasquez 1998).

In the employment relationship, the application of the ethics of care is similar to the application of virtue ethics. In particular, the importance of the community has clear implications for managerial attitudes toward employees. Moreover, the ethics of care implies that deceiving employees is unethical because of the lack of care demonstrated (Schumann 2001). Last, this ethical framework legitimizes special treatment. When considering, for example, whether to invest in an existing unionized plant or opening a new nonunion plant in another location, the ethics of care highlights the importance of the existing relationship with the current workers and the local community. Care for others is also consistent with workplace equity and voice—it is difficult to imagine a healthy, respectful relationship among equals that does not include a concern for minimal welfare standards and reciprocal voice.

Positive Analyses

In the strategic choice model of Kochan, Katz, and McKersie (1986), managerial values are posited to moderate the effect of the environment and therefore contribute to employment outcomes. In the expanded model of employment outcomes presented in the previous chapter, ethical beliefs are similarly assigned an influential role in shaping employment outcomes. Ultimately, these are testable hypotheses, and the six ethical systems presented here provide the framework for positive analyses of these models by generating predictions about outcomes. Kochan, Katz, and McKersie (1986) document the effect of managerial values that result in new investment being targeted away from unionized plants. This reflects a utilitarian ethical system, but researchers can also consider how outcomes may be similar or different under Kantian, Rawlsian, or Aristotelian beliefs. Broadening models of the human agent beyond standard neoclassical/utilitarian utility-maximization may also yield fresh insights about individual decisions to engage in organizational citizenship behaviors, quit, be a whistleblower, vote for a union, be a free-rider, go on strike, or cross a picket line.

Empirically, the increasing diversity in employment practices and outcomes (Katz and Darbishire 2000) provides a rich opportunity for empirical analyses. Using both case study and quantitative methodologies, the extent to which ethical beliefs determine employment relationship outcomes should be investigated as an important question for the field and for policy. There are a number of companies with corporate codes of conduct. These codes of conduct can be analyzed to see how strongly they map into specific ethical frameworks and whether they are associated with different employment practices and outcomes. One might also try to identify the importance (or not) of ethical beliefs using a cross-country, comparative methodology.

Moreover, while management receives more attention because of its authority to make strategic decisions, labor leaders should not be overlooked. Do unions leaders have different ethical belief systems and are they related to different strategies and outcomes? For example, consider job control unionism with its emphasis on constructing universal, rational rules: seniority-based layoffs and promotions, tightly specified bumping rules, narrowly defined work rules, wage rates tied to jobs, and grievance procedures that rely on previous precedents (see chapter 8). Frustration with job control unionism undoubtedly reflects changing paradigms of work organization, but it might also be understood as a frustration with an emphasis on unwavering rules without human discretion. This is a critique commonly made against Kantian moral philosophy. Even though this critique of Kantian ethics is not accurate (Herman 1993; Korsgaard 1996), the ethics literature on these critiques can provide insights into this frustration and into alternative options to strict rule making.[20] Also, some collective bargaining agreements have philosophy statements. Do these philosophy statements relate to specific ethical frameworks? Compared to bargaining units without such a statement, are there significant differences in outcomes? The incorporation of ethics into human resources and industrial relations provides the basis for undertaking these important positive analyses.

Existing literature in business ethics, psychology, and related disciplines indicates that ethics are an important component of behavior and also provides a number of methodological developments that employment researchers can adapt. Two important models in psychology are Kohlberg's (1984) stages of moral development and Rest's (1986) four components of moral behavior. The stages of moral development are the strategies that individuals use to make decisions ranging from the first stage of obedience ("do what you are told") to stages five and six that rely on consensus and Rawlsian concepts of social cooperation (Rest 1994). Several hundred studies have analyzed the relationship between these stages and behavior, and the results support a relationship between moral judgment and behavior, albeit with moderators and other influences. Moral judgment is one of Rest's (1986) four components that determine moral behavior; the other three are moral sensitivity, moral motivation, and moral character.

As concrete relevance for the employment relationship, these models have been applied to organizations (e.g., Jones 1991). Loe, Ferrell, and Mansfield (2000) review twenty-one empirical studies and conclude that moral philosophy is generally related to decision making. Constructs have also been developed to measure an ethical work climate (e.g., Victor and Cullen 1988). Barnett and Vaicys (2000) find that the ethical dimensions of an organization's work climate moderate the relationship between ethical judgment and intended behavior, while Wimbush, Shepard, and Markham (1997) find that the ethical climate is related to forms of organizational governance and control.[21]

Research in other areas echoes the claim that ethics matters. Ben-Ner and Putterman (1998, 5) argue that "there is no scientific basis for the assumption that own well-being or command over resources is the exclusive and immutable concern of human individuals." Rather, natural, social, and behavioral research suggests that humans "will be inclined, conditionally, toward cooperation with others, toward concern with how we are viewed by others, toward hostility to those who fail to reciprocate our cooperation, and toward receptivity toward moral reasoning that is consistent with these and other propensities." In economic utility functions, they advocate augmenting the standard self-regarding preferences with other-regarding and process-regarding preferences. This is an assertion that values matter. Reinforcing this claim is the large experimental literature, especially on the ultimatum game, in which participants act with greater concern for fairness than predicted by individual rationality (Ben-Ner and Putterman 1998; Camerer and Thaler 1995; Cameron 1999). In sum, research outside of human resources and industrial relations has shown that ethics are important for behavior. Furthermore, there is scholarship that can be drawn on to tackle the complex methodological issues involved in empirically analyzing this issue.

Normative Evaluations, Subjectivism, and Relativism

In addition to positive analyses, employment relationship ethics can be used to make normative evaluations of the drivers of the employment relationship—individuals, markets, institutions, organizational strategies, and public policies—as well as outcomes. Normative evaluations of employment systems are of course nothing new. But it is not always clear what standards are being used to make evaluations. The six ethical frameworks provide a set of rigorous standards. Proposals to deregulate employment and labor law, for example, because of concerns about loss of efficiency and individual liberties should be placed in their utilitarian and libertarian contexts. The scholarship in moral philosophy and business ethics that analyzes and compares ethical systems can then be directly applied to these proposals. Alternatively, the literature, pro and con, on the ethics of care can be applied to debates over favoritism, nepotism, and the servicing versus organizing models of union representation (Banks and Metzgar 1989; Fletcher and Hurd 1998).

The normative use of ethics, however, must overcome the challenges posed by ethical subjectivism and relativism. For employee advocates to argue that business should adhere to a Kantian moral philosophy or for business advocates to maintain that labor should subscribe to utilitarianism beliefs is for one to assert that their ethical standards are better. Advocates of ethical subjectivism, however, contend that moral judgments are really feelings, not facts (Rachels 1993). Therefore, there are no right and wrong answers and each person is entitled to their own views. Ethical relativism, at least in the extreme version, ends with the same conclusion: no single ethical theory is universal either because of specific historical or cultural factors or because people's reasons for differing ethical beliefs are equally valid (Wong 1993).

Casual support for both the subjectivist and relativist critiques to universalism stem from apparent diversity in moral codes over time and across cultures combined with a desire to be tolerant and respect cultural diversity. However, this is overly simplistic (Rachels 1993; Wong 1993). Diversity of views does not necessarily make them equally valid. Moreover, tolerance is itself an ethical belief—to assert that everyone should be tolerant of all views, as in the extreme versions of subjectivism and relativism, is a universalistic view and therefore contradicts the basis of subjectivism and relativism. And as in the development of human rights (chapter 2), atrocities such as the Holocaust graphically reveal problems with pure subjectivism or relativism—can these atrocities be acceptable because a certain group of individuals believe they are?

Less extreme, and therefore more reasonable, versions of both subjectivism and relativism have been constructed, but they seem to allow some universal judgments. Moreover, in many cases what appear to be cultural differences in ethical standards in reality reflect different implementation of fundamental standards that are, in fact, in agreement (Beauchamp and Bowie 1997; Velasquez 1998).[22] Most philosophers accept the legitimacy of at least some universal moral standards. Of course, there is not agreement on the dominant ethical theory, but it is acceptable to debate moral standards to try to convince others to adopt your beliefs. Labor and management may have different ethical systems, but this does not mean that each is right or that it is futile to try to establish a societal standard. Diverse scholarship challenges the desirability of assorted business, labor union, and public policies. Probusiness and prolabor prescriptions for reform, whether as proposals for new workplace practices, employment and labor law reform, or strategies for revitalizing the labor movement, are ultimately rooted in normative ethical evaluations. The six ethical frameworks presented here provide a rigorous basis for making such evaluations. Explicit recognition of these ethical theories will, of course,

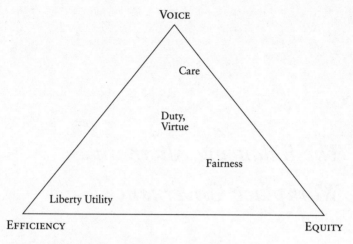

Figure 4.1 Ethical Theory and Efficiency, Equity, and Voice

not resolve debates over labor law reform and other issues, but it provides an important foundation for conducting these debates, and for then designing policies to fulfill those standards.

Finally, Korsgaard (1996, 275, emphasis omitted) writes, "To later generations, much of the moral philosophy of the twentieth century will look like a struggle to escape from utilitarianism." The same might be said of industrial relations, which seeks to move beyond utilitarianism and efficiency by imbuing the employment relationship with a respect for human dignity and justice. Ex· ·cit incorporation of ethical scholarship into employment research and debate—that is, the recognition of the ethics of the employment relationship—provides a rigorous framework for this central feature of industrial relations. In particular, in contrast to the narrow ethical theories of utilitarianism and libertarianism, major ethical theories in the tradition of Aristotle, Kant, and Rawls all support the need for balancing efficiency, equity, and voice (see figure 4.1). There is an ethical imperative for the employment relationship: employment with a human face. The remaining chapters examine alternatives for fulfilling this ethical imperative.

5 The Balancing Alternatives:
Workplace Governance

THE EMPLOYMENT RELATIONSHIP is a web of rules (Dunlop 1958; Clegg 1979; Adams 1995). Rules, probably written in a unionized environment and perhaps unwritten elsewhere, establish policies pertaining to job duties and performance, discipline and discharge, promotion and layoffs, compensation and benefits, and other terms and conditions of employment. But how should the rules be determined so that they promote efficiency, equity, and voice? What should be the rules for establishing rules (Dunlop 1958; Clegg 1979)? In other words, who should govern the workplace (Weiler 1990)? The previous two chapters showed how employment outcomes are determined by human agents interacting in the employment environment. Explicit consideration of the alternatives for workplace governance is important because it provides the analytical framework for understanding how each mechanism yields efficiency, equity, and/or voice. Normatively, it addresses the question of what type of workplace governance mechanisms should be imposed on the environment to promote efficiency, equity, and voice.

The major options for governing the workplace are the invisible hand of competitive labor markets (complemented by common law supports for the freedom to enter into contracts), government regulation, human resource management, human resource management with employee voice, worker control, and bilateral employer-employee negotiations. Which mechanism or mechanisms should govern the workplace is perhaps the most important normative question in human resources and industrial relations and provides the framework for analyzing alternative methods for balancing efficiency, equity, and voice (see figure 5.1). A comprehensive recognition of the alternatives for workplace governance also provides a fuller framework for analyzing the drivers of the employment relationship—individuals, markets, institutions, organizational strategies, and public policies.[1]

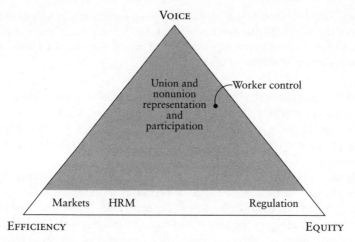

Figure 5.1 The Geometry of Workplace Governance

Historical and Modern Views of Workplace Governance

The question of who should govern the workplace has a rich history (Kaufman 2001b). The father of industrial relations, John R. Commons, captured the range of governance mechanisms in *Industrial Goodwill* in 1919. In his commodity theory of labor, "demand and supply determine wages . . . if labor is scarce, wages will go up. If labor is abundant, wages will go down" (5). In the machinery theory of labor, "each laborer is a machine—its value determined by the quantity of its product" (14). These two theories essentially describe the labor supply and labor demand sides, respectively, of the modern neoclassical economics model of the labor market.

Commons labels his third model "goodwill," and its content foreshadows, or launches (Kaufman 2001b), human resource management: motivating a productive workforce through mutual respect emphasizing "a harmony of interests" (28). The fourth model is the public utility theory of labor in which government regulation of minimum working conditions to prevent worker exploitation is in the public interest. This is, of course, the classic argument for legislative intervention in the labor market. Although not put forth as a significant model for the United States, Commons also mentions the socialist dictatorship of labor, which is worker control—labor, not capital, governs the workplace and makes the rules.

Finally, Commons's fifth model is democracy. This model parallels the historical and current arguments for labor unions. Individual workers are at a significant disadvantage relative to corporations, which are associations of investors, so unions are necessary to equalize bargaining power and to provide "an effective voice" (43). Commons further emphasizes that this is a democratic model because decision making is shared, not unilateral:

> Representative democracy is neither the imagined anarchistic equality of individuals nor the socialistic dictatorship of labor, but it is the equilibrium of capital and labor—the class partnership of organized capital and organized labor in the public interest. (Commons 1919, 43)

Commons (1919) effectively captures the range of alternatives for governing the workplace: markets (the "anarchistic equality of individuals"); human resource management; worker control ("the socialistic dictatorship of labor"); government regulation; and representative industrial democracy—labor unions.

In Dunlop's (1958, 13) seminal work, the question of workplace governance is phrased as the "wide range of procedures possible for the establishment and the administration of the [workplace] rules." In other words, what are the rules for making the rules? In Dunlop's model of the industrial relations system, there are three major actors: managers (and their representatives), workers (and their representatives), and specialized governmental agencies. The possibilities for governing the workplace consist of each of the actors being able to dominate the decision-making process or some combination of pairs, or even all three together, making decisions in a shared manner. As noted by Dunlop (1958, 14), "The procedures and the authority for the making and administration of the rules governing the work place and the work community is a critical and central feature of an industrial-relations system."

This is further echoed in Clegg's (1979, 2) procedural rules, "the rules that settle the ways in which the substantive rules are made, and the ways in which they can be challenged, changed, interpreted, and applied." Clegg (1979) lists five options for procedural rules: collective bargaining, managerialism, trade union regulation, statutory regulation, and joint consultation.[2] In general terms, managerialism and trade union regulation are the two opposite ends of a spectrum from employer to employee control with collective bargaining in the middle. Joint consultation is between collective bargaining and managerialism in that workers are consulted about decisions, but management retains final decision-making authority.

In a thorough and influential analysis, Weiler (1990) presents four alternatives for governing the workplace beyond reliance on free markets: government regulation, management control, worker control, and union representation. Weiler (1990) notes that, in theory, government is the natural neutral party to determine workplace rules, but it has the drawback of being external to the employment relationship. Government can also be politically embedded in the current environment and, therefore, not strictly neutral. The remaining alternatives are internal to the organization, and can presumably better tailor workplace rules to specific needs and constraints. But two of the internal alternatives, management control and worker control, are unilateral. The only mechanism that is both internal to the organization and bilateral is some type of collective bargaining mechanism (broadly considered).

Table 5.1 The Key Dimensions of Workplace Governance

Locus of Decision Making	Decision-Making Authority		
	Market	Unilateral	Multilateral
Internal	n/a	Human resource management	Collective bargaining
			Codetermination
		Worker control	Employee representation in corporate goverernance
External	Free markets with common law supports	Government regulation	Social partnership

Note: The examples of multilateral workplace governance mechanisms all belong to the independent employee representation category.

Building on this literature on workplace governance, I put forth a six-dimensional model of workplace governance: (1) free markets supported by common law, (2) statutory government regulation, (3) human resource management, (4) human resource management with employer-initiated employee voice, (5) worker control, and (6) independent employee representation. These are obviously broad categories and there are many specific possibilities within each category, but the six dimensions capture the major workplace governance alternatives. The major governance options are usefully summarized along two dimensions—decision-making authority (market, unilateral, or multilateral) and locus of decision making (internal or external)—as shown in table 5.1. The six options for governing the workplace are next considered in more detail.

Free Markets with Common Law Supports

Perhaps the dominant or default mechanism in popular U.S. thought is laissez-faire reliance on competitive labor markets, or what Troy (1999) calls individual representation. This governance mechanism has two complementary components: first, neoclassical economic theories of the superior outcomes derived from self-interested, utility-maximizing agents guided by the invisible hand of free markets; and second, legal doctrine supporting the primacy of individuals free to enter into economic relationships of their choosing (generally, "contracts").

The neoclassical economics argument is straightforward: under some assumptions (such as perfect information and no transaction costs), labor market competition among firms and potential workers results in optimal outcomes. No one can be made better off without making someone else worse off, and scarce resources are used as efficiently as possible. Everything is rewarded in terms equal to its contribution, labor included. Sophisticated models that incorporate various complexities such as risk aversion; heterogeneous workers, jobs, and firms; or unobserved features do not change the economic primacy of competitive markets and free transactions by self-interested agents (Boyer and Smith 2001).

With labor market competition, the best protection employees have against their current employer is not the government, a lawyer, or a union, but other employers (Friedman and Friedman 1980, 246; Weiler 1990). Employees are free to choose among many jobs so that substandard employers who are not responsive to workers' preferences will be unable to hire employees. Thus, free markets and competition for labor will govern the workplace. This is an external model of workplace governance (table 5.1): with competitive markets, individual employees and employers must take the resulting outcomes as given; by themselves, they cannot affect competitive market outcomes. Furthermore, if high unemployment, for example, impedes the operation of competitive markets, the appropriate policy response in this governance model is to reduce unemployment, not to create alternative mechanisms for governing the workplace.

In the legal counterpart to the neoclassical economics school, the role of the law is to promote and protect the operation of free markets with voluntary exchange between parties, companies, investors, consumers, and workers.[3] This view manifests itself in an emphasis on common law supports for economic transactions, especially well-defined property rights, liberty of contract, and the law of torts to protect against property damage (Posner 1986).[4] The central feature of the common law supports for economic efficiency in the labor market is the employment-at-will doctrine (Epstein 1984; Feinman 1976).[5] In the absence of legislative, contractual, or judicial restrictions, employees in the United States can generally be discharged at any time for any reason.[6] A classic statement of this doctrine is found in a Tennessee court's ruling that "all may dismiss their employees at will, be they many or few, for good cause, for no cause or even for cause morally wrong, without being thereby guilty of legal wrong."[7] The link between the employment-at-will doctrine and economic efficiency is plainly stated in the seminal work of Epstein (1984).[8] Although parties should not be forced into an at-will relationship (this compulsion would violate the underlying laissez-faire principle of liberty to contract), parties should be able to freely agree to an at-will contract because "freedom of contract tends both to advance individual autonomy and to promote the efficient operation of labor markets" (951). Why? Because "the flexibility afforded by the contract at will permits the ceaseless marginal adjustments that are necessary in any ongoing productive activity" (982). This clearly reflects a neoclassical economics paradigm as does the claim that "the employee can use the contract as a means to control the firm, just as the firm uses it to control the worker" (957). But this is true only if labor markets are competitive so that firms and workers are effectively equal.

One major criticism of relying on laissez-faire economic and legal theories to govern the workplace is that real-world labor markets are not competitive in the ideal sense of the neoclassical theories (Edwards 1997; Flexner 1989;

Kaufman 1997b; Weiler 1990; Yonay 1998). As explained in chapter 1, workplace public goods will be underproduced in a competitive market because of the free-rider problem (Freeman and Medoff 1984; Kaufman and Levine 2000). Also, even if competitive markets achieve long-run efficiency, laissez-faire policies do not compensate workers harmed during short-run adjustments. More significantly, perfect competition depends on employers and employees being economic and legal equals in the labor market.[9] With information asymmetries, mobility costs, or even tilted benefit structures, firms can have monopsony power. More generally, mobility costs and lack of family savings or other resources combined with excess labor supply can cause individual workers to have unequal bargaining power relative to employers. These factors can turn perfect competition into excessive or destructive competition, which drives wages and working conditions down (Kaufman 1997b). Although inequality of bargaining power is difficult to observe, Weiler (1990, 58, emphasis added) has noted that "it is almost unheard of . . . that an *employee* abuses his power to quit at will by using it to coerce his employer to violate its legal obligations or forfeit its statutory rights."[10] The current era of large multinational corporations that have the power to influence, if not dominate, markets and governments in the global economy further undermines the claim that markets are ideally competitive (Korten 1995; Phillips 2002).

Additional questions about relying on free markets and common law to govern the workplace pertain to expertise and information. It has long been recognized that corporations are collectives of investors who hire representatives and experts. In the words of the 1898 annual report of the Ohio State Board of Arbitration:

> Stockholders unite their accumulations of capital and knowledge in a particular line of business and create a simple agency called a corporation. The agency secures the best skill and ability money will command to conduct its affairs. Thus, supplied with a sagacious and powerful representative, they stand back and say to their laborers through this representative: "No representative from you will be heard. You each must speak and act for yourself." (Quoted in U.S. Industrial Commission 1901, 478)

Individual workers without the resources to purchase equivalent expertise will not be the legal equal of expert employers. Concerns over the fairness of mandatory arbitration of employment law and commercial disputes, for example, in large part reflects this asymmetry (Cole 2001; Stone 1996, 1999).[11] The efficacy of the employment-at-will doctrine and other common law supports further requires employers and employees to have complete information (Epstein 1984; Estlund 2002; Kim 1997). But employee ignorance appears common. In a survey of three hundred unemployed workers, Kim (1997) found that job seekers significantly overestimated their protections against arbitrary discharge. Nearly 90 percent incorrectly believed that they could not be discharged because their boss disliked them personally. On the basis of eight simple questions such as this one, less than 10 percent correctly answered more than half of the questions correctly.

Last, the laissez-faire economic and legal model of workplace governance can be attacked on the basis that labor is more than an economic commodity and work is more than an economic transaction. Employees are human beings with political and moral rights in a democratic society. Work is not just an activity tolerated to earn income but is an important vehicle for fulfilling social and psychological needs of interaction, growth, and development. Thus, there are a variety of questions surrounding the assumptions necessary for the effectiveness of the laissez-faire economic and legal theories. These criticisms do not reject the theoretical richness of the neoclassical economics paradigm and its usefulness for partially understanding labor market pressures. But they do question the wisdom of having the lives of human beings controlled by market forces alone and whether markets can provide more than very limited conceptualizations of equity and voice.

Statutory Government Regulation

To correct market deficiencies, either in terms of efficiency or equity and voice, a logical alternative is statutory government regulation. The standard economics approach to government intervention is the public interest theory of regulation. If there are market failures that prevent the attainment of the ideal neoclassical competitive outcomes, perhaps stemming from externalities, asymmetric information, or uncompetitive markets, there may be a role for government intervention to overcome these market failures—if the benefits of government intervention outweigh the costs (Addison and Hirsch 1997; Belman and Belzer 1997; Burton and Chelius 1997). This is the classic efficiency rationale for government regulation.

With efficiency, equity, and voice as the objectives of the employment relationship, however, government regulation to provide equity and voice can be in the public interest for more than just efficiency reasons. The early founders of industrial relations promoted government regulation, even if as a last resort, to establish protective labor standards and social insurance to assure equitable employment outcomes (Kaufman 1997b; Kaufman forthcoming). Major U.S. examples of governing the workplace via government regulation include the National Labor Relations Act (to equalize bargaining power between employees and employers), the Fair Labor Standards Act (to establish a minimum wage and a maximum work hours), Title VII of the Civil Rights Act (to provide equal opportunity), and the Occupational Safety and Health Act (to establish minimum safety standards) (Weil 1997). This workplace governance mechanism has several distinct strengths. This system provides protection to everyone: ideally, all workers are covered, not just workers who enjoy union protection or possess particularly favorable bargaining power.

Ideally, the laws are also equally applied. Unlike competitive markets, equity concerns can be incorporated. Lastly, laws can be determined by reasoned debate and informed research rather than by the invisible hand of free markets or the power struggle of collective bargaining.

On the other hand, direct government regulation of the workplace has some serious weaknesses. First, regulation is removed from those directly involved in the relationship. The specific employer, employees, and union (if present) do not get to decide what the most important issues are in their specific relationship (Levine 1997). In other words, participation, or subsidiarity, is effectively removed from this system. Consequently, it is difficult to shape agreements to fit particular needs and constraints. Second, the U.S. economy is an exceedingly complex entity and it is difficult to craft different laws for narrowly defined groups (Edwards 1997). Thus, regulations end up too broad for some and too narrow for others, and perhaps more costly than no regulation. Third, as a general rule, government regulations tend to be ambiguous. The only way to find out if an action is legal is to do it and pay the consequences if a court finds it illegal. Fourth, determining when market failures exist can be troublesome, and the unintended effects of some policies may be worse than the problem the law intended to correct (Addison and Hirsch 1997). Fifth, laws don't necessarily serve the public interest if they are shaped by special interests and the vagaries of the political process. Finally, there are enforcement and administration problems (Weil 1997).

Given the problems with the two external (to the firm) modes of workplace governance, the free market and government regulation, many argue that the best mechanism for workplace governance relies on internal, not external, operations (see table 5.1).[12] Individuals within an establishment are much better able to identify the problems specific to their situation, and thus, to reach solutions that fit the needs of that particular establishment. However, what internal mechanism should be utilized? There are two basic groups within a firm: shareholders, represented by management, and employees, perhaps (but often not) represented by a union.

Human Resource Management: With and without Employee Voice

The human resource management model for workplace governance is similar to the free market/common law model in that it is marked by an absence of institutional constraints such as statutes or unions. But the human resource management model assumes that management has latitude in setting employment conditions. Although economic markets often establish the broad parameters for decision making, the prime mover of employment conditions, or workplace rules, in this model of workplace governance is management. The major areas of human resource management are well known and include job and organizational design, employee selection and development, performance management, compensation and benefits, and employee relations. Companies with advanced human resource management programs use valid and reliable selection measures to hire and promote employees, provide training and development opportunities, support respectful methods of supervision, promote distributive and procedural justice, compensate employees in a manner that rewards performance and provides more than a living wage, and provide benefits that foster personal growth, security, and work-life balance.

It has also been argued that human resource management strategies should include an employee voice component, or Clegg's (1979) joint consultation. This can include direct employee participation in decision making such as in self-directed work teams or quality circles; indirect participation through some form of committee, employee representation plan, or works council; and dispute resolution procedures that include important due process elements (Hammer 2000).[13] As a result, there are two human resource management governance options: with and without voice.

As part of a human resources strategy, these voice mechanisms are ultimately intended to benefit the organization's bottom line, either directly or indirectly. Direct participation in decision making is believed to directly enhance productivity by harnessing the knowledge and experience of workers to improve work processes. Employee representation can directly improve productivity by improving information sharing and coordination (Freeman and Lazear 1995; Kaufman and Levine 2000). The various employer-promulgated voice mechanisms are also advocated on the basis of their potential to *indirectly* enhance organizational performance. All of the forms of participation can build trust between employees and employers and foster employee loyalty to the company (Hammer 2000; Kaufman and Levine 2000). Direct participation can fulfill individual needs for personal growth and development, which can enhance performance through increased job satisfaction and motivation (Hammer 2000; Solomon 1996). Effective dispute resolution procedures with due process can promote feelings of fairness, through both procedural and distributive justice, which again can improve performance through increased job satisfaction, motivation, and loyalty (Hammer 2000).

Without doubting the good performance, including the respect for employees, of a number of examples of human resource management programs in specific companies, the concern with this workplace governance mechanism is that it is unilateral.[14] Human resource management emphasizes economic performance and competitiveness (Kaufman 2001a; Kleiner, McLean, and Dreher 1988; Wright et al. 1999; Noe et al. 2000).[15] Employment conditions can be weakened and voice mechanisms can be disbanded—unilaterally—if management thinks profitability can be increased through these changes. The fairness of dispute resolution procedures largely relies on managerial goodwill (Colvin 2001). This does not mean that all human resource management or employee voice programs are used underhandedly to undermine employee rights and thwart unionization attempts. There are certainly examples where employee rights and voice are respected (Kaufman and Taras 2000), but even progressive managers and firms appear to tightly control some aspects of employee participation and voice. It is significantly easier to identify examples of nonunion employee participation in work design and flow decisions (for example, scheduling the rotation of tasks) than in reward decisions.[16]

The concerns with human resource management as a workplace governance mechanism are similar to those with the laissez-faire markets mechanism. These governance mechanisms can work for some, and those situations are perhaps models for others to learn from and emulate, but is it wise public policy to place sole reliance on these mechanisms? What are the checks on the marginal employers? As human resource management serves a company's business strategy, and ultimately bottom-line profitability, through unilateral control of employment conditions, what protections exist against the potential for abuse? How can equity and voice be guaranteed?

Worker Control

In terms of authority, the polar opposite of human resource management is worker control. Instead of management unilaterally establishing workplace rules, workers unilaterally control their establishment. Note that this is more than employee participation, it is employee control over organizational objectives and rule making (Ben-Ner and Jones 1995). This is also more than many employee stock-ownership plans, in which employees have a financial stake but not control rights (Godard 2000). Examples include producer cooperatives (Jones 1980), including the Mondragon cooperatives (Whyte 1999), and models of worker control and ownership under socialism. Perhaps the leading U.S. example of worker self-governance was the craft union model of the early twentieth-century American Federation of Labor craft unions, before the dominance of mass manufacturing. These unions established work rules, often unilaterally, and enforced them through refusing to work on any other terms and through fining or expelling members who undermined these standards (Montgomery 1979). This was the original use of the term "job control"—union control over jobs through closed shops, apprenticeship programs, and union members with hiring and firing authority as foremen (Perlman 1928).[17]

Note carefully, however, that the unilateral authority of capital over labor has simply been replaced by the unilateral authority of labor over capital. And as noted by Weiler (1990, 180), "Whenever the exercise of authority in the firm is directly accountable to only one of its constituencies, whichever it might be, there is a risk that the dominant group's decisions will downplay the needs and concerns of the other groups with a comparable stake in the enterprise." On the other hand, the human resource management options, with and without voice, as well as the worker-control option, have the advantage of addressing problems within the enterprise. So to keep this positive aspect while addressing the problems stemming from a governance mechanism that has unilateral authority, the logical alternative is a governance mechanism internal to the firm that includes shared control (Weiler 1990) (see table 5.1).

Independent Employee Representation

The governance mechanism that replaces unilateral authority with shared, bilateral authority focused on a specific enterprise is independent employee representation. Independent means that the representation vehicle is organizationally distinct from management. The dominant (and by some accounts, only) example of independent employee representation is a labor union. Thus, the traditional example of the workplace governance mechanism of shared control has been collective bargaining. More than one hundred years ago, Sidney and Beatrice Webb (1897, 173–74) wrote:

> In unorganised trades, the individual workman, applying for a job, accepts or refuses the terms offered by the employer, without communication with his fellow-workmen, and without any other consideration than the exigencies of his own position. For the sale of his labor he makes, with the employer, a strictly individual bargain. But if a group of workmen concert together, and send representatives to conduct the bargaining on behalf of the whole body, the position is at once changed. Instead of the employer making a series of separate contracts with isolated individuals, he meets with a collective will, and settles, in a single agreement, the principles upon which, for the time being, all workmen of a particular group, or class, or grade, will be engaged . . . By the Method of Collective Bargaining, the foreman is prevented from taking advantage of the competition [between workers] to beat down the earnings of the other workmen.

This description still rings true today for one of the primary roles of unions and collective bargaining: economic protection against abuse by the market, corporations, and managers (Weiler 1990).

Recall from the section of this chapter on the laissez-faire economic and legal model that there are a number of reasons why employers and individual employees might not be equals in the labor market and the legal arena. Unionization can overcome these market failures so that employers and collective employees are more like equals in the labor market and legal arena. In other words, the traditional argument in support of labor unions is that collective employee action can equalize bargaining power between labor and management (Webb and Webb 1897; Commons 1919; Perlman 1928; Estey 1928; Weiler 1990; Kaufman 1993, 1997b). A labor union—a group of represented workers—more closely mimics the corporate organization—a group of represented investors—than individual workers acting alone. This is captured in the preamble to the Wagner Act (1935) promoting unionization among U.S. employees:

> The inequality of bargaining power between employees who do not possess full freedom of association or actual liberty of contract, and employers who are organized in the corporate or other forms of ownership association substantially burdens and affects the flow of commerce, and tends to aggravate recurrent business depressions, by depressing wage rates and the purchasing power of wage earners in industry and by preventing the stabilization of competitive wage rates and working conditions within and between industries.

As in the passages from Webb and Webb (1897) and the Wagner Act, unions can prevent destructive competition among workers and serve as a check on management power and abuse. But in addition to this important protection role, unions can also provide employee voice (Webb and Webb 1897; Commons 1919; Estey 1928; Derber 1970; Freeman and Medoff 1984; Weiler 1990; Greenfield and Pleasure 1993).[18] Although this may enhance efficiency (Freeman and Medoff 1984; Eaton and Voos 1994; Rubinstein 2000), the underlying rationale for voice is more fundamentally rooted in political, moral, and religious thought (see chapter 1). For these reasons, and not to improve economic performance, it has been asserted that the right to form unions is a fundamental human right (see chapter 2).

Therefore, for both efficiency and noneconomic reasons, unions have been advocated as important vehicles for workplace governance to protect workers against economic forces and managerial self-interest. But unlike the government regulation model, decisions are made within the enterprise and employees also have a voice. Consistent with U.S. political theory, a workplace governance model that includes independent employee representation provides a system of checks and balances as well as representation and voice.

On the other hand, to those who believe that employers and employees are equals interacting in competitive markets and the legal arena, unions are monopolies that distort labor markets, reduce overall economic welfare, and violate the liberty of corporations and individuals to freely enter into contracts (Epstein 1983; Friedman and Friedman 1980; Heldman, Bennett, and Johnson 1981; Troy 1999). To advocates of the human resource management approach, unions are adversarial, outside organizations that add detrimental conflict and bureaucracy to the employment relationship (Mahoney and Watson 1993). Moreover, some argue that in practice the current U.S. mode of unionism is not well-suited for the future. Even beyond the fact that U.S. unions currently represent only a fraction of the workforce (Farber 2001; Farber and Krueger 1993), contemporary U.S. collective bargaining is argued to be adversarial and rigid with legalistic, formalized, and detailed contracts (Kochan, Katz, and McKersie 1986; Heckscher 1988; Bluestone and Bluestone 1992). But independent employee representation can take many forms, including not only traditional U.S. unionism but also works councils, enterprise unions, professional associations, activist or militant local unions, joint governance arrangements, employee representation on corporate boards of directors, and other possibilities for future institutions in which the representation/participation mechanism is independent of managerial authority.[19] Although not without strengths and weaknesses, all of these options are part of the independent employee representation model of workplace governance.

Corporate Governance

The question of workplace governance is intimately connected to questions of corporate governance—that is, how rules and decisions regarding resource allocation (such as investment) within corporations are made. The various alternatives for workplace governance largely represent alternative arrangements for corporate governance. A workplace governance model of free markets implies that corporate governance is checked only by market competition and social norms. A model of government regulation places constraints on corporate governance by requiring companies to fulfill certain legal obligations (such as paying a minimum wage). A workplace governance model of collective bargaining is a model of corporate governance in which some corporate actions must be negotiated rather than taken unilaterally. In other words, corporate governance and workplace governance are partially opposite sides of the same coin. However, the traditional options for workplace governance largely leave the strategic aspects of corporate governance—such as decisions over mergers, acquisitions, divestitures, new investment, financing arrangements, and executive compensation—untouched. As a result, corporate governance is an important issue for the employment relationship in its own right.

The dominant U.S. model of corporate governance is the shareholder model (Blair 1995; O'Sullivan 2000). The shareholders—the owners of a company through the ownership of stock—are viewed as the focal group in the corporation because they bear the risk of making a profit or loss. Other groups or stakeholders within the organization are seen as always receiving a fixed payment for their services that was agreed on in advance, such as wage and salary payments for employees. It is therefore argued that only shareholders have the incentive to see that a corporation's resources are used more productively, and economic performance will be best when corporate decisions seek to maximize shareholder value. Corporate governance arrangements in the United States—such as election of the board of directors by the shareholders—support this emphasis on shareholder value. In terms of the employment relationship, a strong shareholder value model of corporate governance establishes a corporate preoccupation with short-term financial results and also usually denies employees or unions meaningful participation in corporate governance and decisions over investments, mergers, and other major business activities.

An alternative model of corporate governance is stakeholder theory. In one version, employees are also residual claimants because employees invest their own human capital in a corporation, and just like shareholders they face risky returns (Blair 1995). A second version relies on property rights: because of restrictions against harming others, property rights are not unlimited, and thus a corporation must take multiple interests into account (Donaldson and Preston 1995). Various groups—the stakeholders: owners, employees, suppliers, customers, and the community—have a moral interest, a "stake," in a company and should be entitled to participate in corporate governance. Stakeholder theory is consistent with the central argument of this book that efficiency should be balanced with equity and voice, because corporate governance structures should not allow unchecked corporate decision making. Stakeholder theory is institutionalized in Europe through employee representation on corporate boards of directors (Jacoby 2001), reinforcing the important connections between models of corporate governance and workplace governance. Furthermore, the contemporary importance, or even dominance, of corporations makes it necessary to incorporate issues of corporate governance into the question of workplace governance. Put differently, the traditional models of workplace governance—such as government regulation or collective bargaining—may no longer be effective without complementary modifications to the strict shareholder model of corporate governance.

The Fundamental Questions of Human Resources and Industrial Relations

The six options for workplace governance—the invisible hand of competitive labor markets (complemented by common law supports for the freedom to enter into contracts), government regulation, human resource management, human resource management with employee voice, worker control, and independent employee representation—are the alternative methods for establishing workplace rules. But which are best for balancing efficiency, equity, and voice? The answer depends on beliefs about four critical questions that underlie human resources and industrial relations:[20]

1. Is labor a commodity?
2. Are employers and employees equals in self-regulating, competitive labor markets?
3. Is there an inherent conflict of interest between employers and employees?
4. Is employee voice important?

The first and third questions are standard in industrial relations (Lester 1941; Kochan, Katz, and McKersie 1986; Kochan and Katz 1988; Kaufman 2001a). The addition of the other two, however, allows the four questions to parsimoniously distinguish the six alternative workplace governance mechanisms (see figure 5.2).

First, what is the nature of labor? One view is that labor is just another

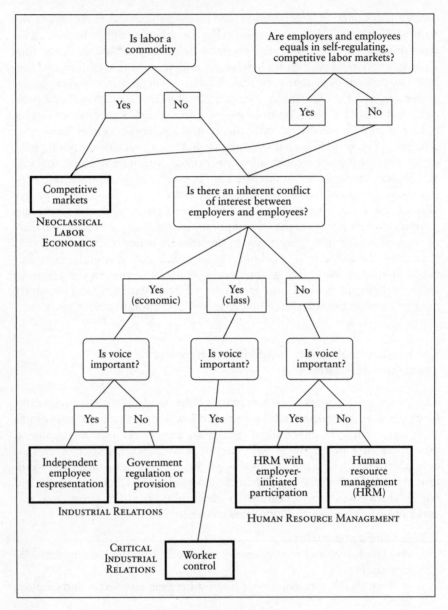

Figure 5.2 The Intellectual Foundations of Workplace Governance

commodity in the production process, and work is only endured to earn income. It is then logical to consider the invisible hand of the free market as the
workplace governance mechanism that sets employment conditions—if employers and employees are equal in the labor market and the legal arena. Thus,
this is the second question. If the parties are equals, competitive markets can

regulate behavior and provide checks and balances against abuses. Affirmative answers to the first two questions point to free markets as a workplace governance mechanism. This is the standard neoclassical economics school of thought and generally defines the scope of its analysis of the employment relationship (Kaufman 1988; Boyer and Smith 2001).

But what about negative responses? An alternative view of labor is that it is composed of human beings with aspirations and feelings (Bloomfield 1923; Tannenbaum 1951).[21] Moreover, work fulfills important psychological and social needs and provides more than extrinsic, monetary rewards. In this view, human dignity and personal growth are not respected by placing total reliance on economic markets, and there is a need for alternative governance mechanisms. Moreover, if employers and employees are not equals, unequal power between employers and employees may cause competition among employees that leads to, rather than prevents, substandard working conditions, and to the erosion of democracy. For both economic and noneconomic reasons, negative responses to the first two questions lead to a search for governance mechanisms beyond competitive markets.

The third question provides a critical distinction between the nonmarket (or market-supplementing) workplace governance models: Is there an inherent conflict of interest in the employment relationship? Human resource management is associated with a rejection of a pervasive or insurmountable inherent conflict of interest in the employment relationship. This is a unitarist view of employment relationship conflict in which effective policies and practices can align the interests of employees and employers (Fox 1974). Conflictual employment relationships at specific organizations may exist, but this stems from poor management rather than any universal nature of the employment relationship. Because it is in the firm's best interest to treat employees well, there is no need for an outside check on managerial authority. The preferred mechanism for workplace governance is human resource management. Labor unions and government regulations are unnecessary constraints; rather, the emphasis is on effective staffing, compensation, performance management, and work design practices. If employee voice is important (question 4), then the workplace can be governed by human resource management with some type of employee involvement or participation vehicle.

On the other hand, the mainstream U.S. industrial relations belief is that there is an inherent economic conflict of interest between employers and employees.[22] Employees' desires for higher wages, better benefits, increased security, and favorable working conditions clash with employers' pressures for lower labor costs, flexibility, and high output.[23] This is a pluralist view of employment relationship conflict (Clegg 1975; Fox 1974; Kochan 1982).[24] Consequently, in the industrial relations school there are two important governance mechanisms for balancing this conflict: statutory government regulation and labor unions. Government regulation can protect workers by specifying labor standards that all employers must fulfill, such as minimum wages or nondiscriminatory hiring. But is voice important (question 4)?

Should the democratic rights of voice and participation be extended to the workplace? Government laws by themselves cannot provide voice in the workplace.[25] If there is an inherent conflict of interest, and employee voice is also important, a system of independent employee representation is needed. Labor unions can counter corporate bargaining power and also provide voice that is independent of managerial authority. Designing public policies and organizational strategies and competencies to support the best form of labor unionism is therefore an important topic within industrial relations.

However, there are three possible answers to the question about the nature of employment relationship conflict (Legge 1995). Employment relationship conflict can also be viewed as class based or social rather than a limited economic conflict over the distribution of wages and profits between an individual employee and employer. In this perspective, conflict is not limited to higher wages or better benefits—it is a social conflict of unequal power relations (Giles and Murray 1997; Godard 1994; Kelly 1998; Littler 1993). This is a political economy conception of conflict, and the group with greater power is able to structure institutions to perpetuate the dominance of its ideology.[26] In this critical industrial relations school of thought, the ideal workplace governance mechanism is replacing capitalism with worker control under socialism (Hyman 1975).

In sum, the most appropriate workplace governance mechanism to achieve efficiency, equity, and voice depends on fundamental views of the nature of work, how labor markets work, the nature of employment relationship conflict, and the importance of workplace voice. Proponents of laissez-faire markets might argue that equity is provided by competitive markets rewarding inputs, including labor, with their value—McClelland's (1990) marginal productivity justice—and that voice is provided through worker entry and exit into desirable jobs and out of undesirable ones (Troy 1999). Human resource management advocates might assert that voice can be provided through nonunion employee representation plans. If employment relationship conflict is social or class based, then balancing property rights and labor rights is a smokescreen for maintenance of the domination of capital over labor. In contrast, the need for *nonmarket institutions* to balance efficiency, equity, and voice reflects the pluralist industrial relations conception of employment relationship conflict combined with an inequality in bargaining power between labor and management in imperfect markets and a belief that workers are entitled to workplace voice in a democratic society.

The Centrality of Employee Representation

An important issue with workplace governance is whether the governance options are complements or substitutes. Jacoby (1997), for example, argues that the primary objective of welfare capitalism, or human resource management, is keeping corporations free of union and government regulation. This implies that the human resource management perspective views the workplace governance mechanisms as alternatives, not complements to each other.[27] Laissez-faire proponents also see unions and government regulation as undermining rather than complementing the market-based governance mechanism. On the other hand, the industrial relations perspective is generally more complementary.[28] Unions can increase the effectiveness of productivity-enhancing voice mechanisms in the human resource management model (Eaton and Voos 1994; Rubinstein 2000). Unions clearly aid enforcement of government regulation (Weil 1996, 1997; Budd and McCall1997). Even many supporters of independent employee representation do not advocate unions as the sole governance mechanism (Weiler 1990; Kochan 2000).[29] In fact, John R. Commons supported government regulation and collective bargaining for protection against exploitative employers and destructive competition, but he also embraced human resource management practices, including nonunion employee representation, among progressive employers (Kaufman forthcoming).[30]

Nevertheless, the intellectual foundations of industrial relations reveal the central importance of employee representation (see figures 5.1 and 5.2). In terms of equity—because of a belief in imperfect markets, inequality of bargaining power, and destructive competition—unions are important in industrial relations, because the bargaining power that comes from collective action can achieve negotiated labor standards and redistribute income from profits to wages. Unions are also seen as a vehicle for using this bargaining power to bring a system of industrial jurisprudence to the workplace (Slichter 1941). Just cause discipline and discharge provisions are now nearly universal in U.S. union contracts (Feuille and Hildebrand 1995).[31] Independent employee representation also suffers less than government regulation from difficulties of trying to establish universal standards for diverse workplaces (Weiler 1990; Levine 1997). Workplace employee representation allows standards and policies to be tailored to specific contexts and is more responsive to individual needs, constraints, and preferences.[32] In sum, unions are important industrial relations institutions of protection that promote equitable distribution and administration in the employment relationship.

Unions are also central in industrial relations because of voice. As emphasized in chapter 1, the voice objective in the employment relationship is rooted in political, moral, religious, and psychological theories, all of which emphasize the importance of human dignity. Employee voice is an intrinsic standard and important in its own right. To the extent that equal power is necessary for *effective* voice (Commons 1919; Greenfield and Pleasure 1993), unions or works councils that are independent of management are seen as critical vehicles for providing meaningful collective voice. Kaufman (forthcoming, 39) states that Commons and the Wisconsin school believed that nonunion employee representation could provide meaningful voice "as long as it is established on an equality of bargaining power, is not an overt union avoidance device, and incorporates a form of constitutional government for voice and due process." Skepticism toward how equality and due process can be established without an independent labor union or a statutorily protected works council underlies the attention that industrial relations gives to independent employee representation (Godard and Delaney 2002; Greenfield and Pleasure 1993; Weiler 1990).

The goal of balancing efficiency, equity, and voice means that efficiency is also important, and employee representation can improve efficiency as well. One rationale for encouraging unionization by the passage of the Wagner Act during the Great Depression was to stimulate the economy through the increased purchasing power of labor that would result from increased bargaining power (Kaufman 1996).[33] Increased labor power also has the potential to make employee participation efforts more successful by protecting employee interests (Eaton and Voos 1994). And Freeman and Medoff (1984) describe various ways in which the exercise of collective employee voice can increase productivity. On the other hand, many view increased labor power as distortionary, undermining rather than enhancing efficiency (see Addison and Hirsch 1997). The bottom line, however, is that because of equity and voice, employee representation is more than a productivity-enhancing mechanism:

> For trade unions have given to the average isolated wage earner lost in the struggling crowd of exploited workers a feeling of independence, of dignity, of self-reliance, of self-respect. Without unions he becomes a sort of commodity, bought and sold in the market, dominated by formidable and very impersonal economic forces, a person of no importance, hardly a person at all. In his group, and through his group, he can do something to impose his will on his surroundings, he can bargain in dignified fashion with his employer. He can make himself felt; and in doing so he has recovered his personality that was being lost in the maze of economic forces. (Estey 1928, 114)

The question of workplace governance provides the framework for considering the broad options for striking a balance between efficiency, equity, and voice, and for constructing an environment, or employment system, to serve this goal. When labor is more than a commodity (that is, when work is more than simply an economic transaction), when employers and employees are not equals, when employment relationship conflict is not entirely unitarist so that there are employer-employee conflicts of interest, and when voice is important, *independent employee representation* is a *critical* element of a system of workplace governance that yields employment with a human face. The best form of unionism to achieve this objective in the twenty-first-century employment relationship, however, is still an unsettled question.

6 The New Deal Industrial Relations System

In the U.S. employment system, the leading attempt by policy makers to promote efficiency, equity, *and voice* are the public policies toward the employment relationship that emerged out of the Great Depression and President Roosevelt's New Deal in the 1930s. The centerpiece of this New Deal industrial relations system is the National Labor Relations Act, or Wagner Act, passed in 1935 to protect workers' efforts at forming unions and engaging in collective bargaining. The NLRA is complemented by other pieces of New Deal legislation, especially the Social Security Act (1935) and the Fair Labor Standards Act (FLSA) (1938). The Social Security Act established what has grown into OASDHI: old age, survivors, disability, and health insurance, which provides monetary assistance and health care coverage from the federal government to retirees, the disabled, and their dependents. This legislation also established a system of state unemployment insurance benefits programs administered under the Federal Unemployment Tax Act. The FLSA created a national minimum wage, a mandatory overtime premium for covered workers for hours worked in excess of a weekly standard (now forty hours), and restrictions on child labor.[1]

The New Deal industrial relations system is an explicit endorsement of governing the workplace through a combination of collective bargaining and mandated employment standards, especially for wages, hours, and insurance against unemployment resulting from layoffs, retirement, and disability (recall figure 5.2). This is rooted in practical and ethical desires to balance efficiency, equity, and voice, as well as property rights and labor rights, in the context of specific environmental factors and perceptions. Continuing debates about this system, such as those over employee involvement, flexible work practices, and nonunion employee representation, reflect differing perspectives on how to balance these conflicting rights and achieve efficiency, equity, and voice in a new environment. An emphasis on all three of these objectives of the employment relationship and the alternatives for their achievement provides a productive framework for understanding and analyzing the public policy aspects of the New Deal industrial relations system.

The Labor Problem and New Deal Legislation

The New Deal industrial relations system and the field of industrial relations in the United States were responses to the conditions of wage labor in the early twentieth century—conditions that were often inequitable and contentious, and sometimes oppressive and exploitative. This "labor problem" was the critical human resources and industrial relations problem of the day.[2] Working hours were often long, wages were often low, conditions were often dangerous, and insecurity—from business cycles, seasonal labor demand, accidents or disease, old age, and discriminatory or arbitrary firings—was widespread. Government surveys around 1910 found that only 15 percent of wage earners had a standard workweek of fewer than fifty-four hours. Over 20 percent of southern workers had standard workweeks of more than sixty hours. Among iron and steel workers, over 40 percent worked more than seventy-two hours per week, and about 20 percent worked more than eighty-four hours per week (Lauck and Sydenstricker 1917; Interchurch World Movement of North America 1920). During the same time period, at least half of working class families had annual incomes below the $800 that was estimated "as a reasonable minimum for healthful, efficient, and decent living" (Lauck and Sydenstricker 1917, 376; Harris 2000; Cummins 1932).

In terms of safety and health, the scientific management emphasis on breaking work into specialized tasks caused what was labeled "new strain," the kind of injuries that now are known as repetitive stress and carpal tunnel injuries (Lauck and Sydenstricker 1917, 327).[3] It was also estimated that during World War I, industrial accidents—resulting in 25,000 deaths, 25,000 permanent disability cases, and 2 million temporary disability cases per year—resulted in more U.S. causalities in the workplace than on the battlefield (Downey 1924). Additionally, fear of unemployment was pervasive. Companies might hire workers on a short-term basis, perhaps for only one day at a time with foreman selecting the day's work crew each morning from among those massed outside the factory gate (Jacoby 1985). A 1909 government investigation of nearly thirty thousand male workers found that only 37 percent did not have any time lost from work over the course of a full year; half of the workers were unemployed for four or more months (Lauck and Sydenstricker 1917). The fear of arbitrary dismissal was inherent in the foreman's empire system of complete management control (Cohen 1990; Gabin 1990; Jacoby 1985; Lichtenstein 1989). Workers could be fired for any reason, including simply to demonstrate the foreman's absolute power.

The problems were viewed as more than simply a lack of minimum standards of treatment (equity), but also a lack of industrial democracy (voice):

> For a workman perhaps the most important facts of life are his wages, his working hours, the conditions under which he labors. The quality of his life, his happiness, his prosperity, the kind of education he can give his family, his very life as affected by accident and disease, depend much more upon factory hours, wages, and conditions than upon taxes, justice, police, or the occasional possibility of war. His life is a factory life; and it is the incidents of factory life over which he needs some control. If there is an argument for giving him a vote, even more is there an argument for giving him a voice in the conditions of shop and factory. (Estey 1928, 208)

Or as Senator Wagner, the clear champion and prime mover of the NLRA, put it:

> There can no more be democratic self-government in industry without workers participating therein, than there could be democratic government in politics without workers having the right to vote. . . . That is why the right to bargain collectively is at the bottom of social justice for the worker, as well as the sensible conduct of business affairs. The denial or observance of this right means the difference between despotism and democracy. (Quoted in Keyserling 1945, 13)

The labor problem was more than long hours, low wages, dangerous conditions, great insecurity, and arbitrary supervision, it was also a lack of voice in a democratic society.

Moreover, there were also problems with efficiency. Absenteeism and turnover were very costly. At Ford, the absenteeism rate in 1913 was 10 percent and the annual turnover rate was 370 percent, which prompted Henry Ford's famous five-dollar-a-day plan (Meyer 1981). Poverty-level wages were believed to yield insufficient aggregate consumer purchasing power. Prior to the five-dollar-a-day plan, Ford workers couldn't afford to buy the cars they were producing. Last, the economy was frequently disrupted and weakened by strikes and other forms of industrial conflict that resulted from the labor problem.

As described in chapter 5, the neoclassical economics school, the (unitarist) human resource management school, the (pluralist) industrial relations school, and the critical industrial relations school have different views on the nature of work, labor markets, employment relationship conflict, and voice. Consequently, they differ as to their solutions to the labor problem. Neoclassical economics looks to free markets to maximize efficiency and provide marginal productivity justice (McClelland 1990). Its solution to the labor problem emphasizes competitive markets and the freedom to contract. Human resource management emphasizes managerial policies and sees the solution to the labor problem as managerial reform. Critical industrial relations views the labor problem as inherent in capitalism and seeks to replace it with worker ownership and socialism. The depths of the Great Depression shook popular faith in the laissez-faire reliance of the neoclassical economics and human resource management views, though not enough to generate sufficient political support for socialism. Consequently, pluralist industrial relations beliefs shaped New Deal public policy.

The intellectual foundations of the New Deal industrial relations system reflect the fundamental industrial relations assumptions outlined in chapter 5 (recall figure 5.2; see also Kochan, Katz, and McKersie 1986): (1) labor is more than a commodity; (2) labor and management are not economic or legal equals (in other words, there is an imbalance of bargaining power); (3) there is at least some conflict of interest that cannot be resolved by unitarist management policies, but this is pluralist employment relationship conflict, not class-based or societal conflict; and (4) employee voice is important. Note carefully that this perspective stance reflects underlying ethical beliefs.[4] That labor is more than a commodity rejects utilitarianism in which utility-maximization justifies treating labor as a commodity. It also rejects libertarianism in which individual freedom justifies every private action short of coercion or physical harm of others. Rather, the view that labor is made up of humans with rights to both minimum material standards and workplace voice is consistent with the ethics of duty (Kantian moral philosophy), Rawlsian fairness, and the ethics of virtue and relationships—and the closely intertwined views on human dignity of the world's major religions.[5]

These ethical beliefs were combined with a certain perspective on the environment. The (essentially libertarian) legal environment was viewed as favoring employers as evidenced by the *Lochner* Court's emphasis on economic due process, which invalidated many (though not all) pieces of protective labor legislation (Forbath 1991; Phillips 1998). Moreover, before 1932, common law doctrines regarding property and contracts were used to end strikes and boycotts via court injunctions, but these same doctrines "often failed in business-against-business cases" (Forbath 2001, 184). This legal environment was viewed as unfavorable toward labor because of the economic environment. Excess labor supply, little worker savings or social safety nets, and labor market imperfections gave companies a significant advantage in bargaining power over individual employees (Kaufman 1997b). This labor market inequality underlies the frustration with the legal rulings that sought to balance individual freedoms among equals. In the words of John R. Commons (1919, 47):

> The court starts with a fiction that a corporation is a "person" and then holds that an individual worker and an individual corporation are exactly equal, in that the right of one person to quit work is exactly equal to the right of the other person to discharge him. It thereupon declares unconstitutional all the laws in which the legislature tries to protect, against employers, the worker's right to belong to a union, by prohibiting employers from discharging them solely on account of union membership.

Commons characterized such rulings as "absurd." Additionally, Senator Wagner believed that this legal and economic inequality between labor and management depressed consumer purchasing power and prevented macroeconomic stabilization (Huthmacher 1968; Kaufman 1996).[6]

The New Deal industrial relations legislation sought to solve the labor problem by establishing a social safety net and labor standards, and by equalizing bargaining power between labor and management. The safety net was established by the Social Security Act—insurance for the unemployed, disabled, and elderly. Labor standards were enacted by the FLSA's creation of a national minimum wage, a standard for weekly hours of work, and child labor restrictions. Employees' abilities to unionize are protected by the NLRA as enshrined in its famous section 7:

> Employees shall have the right to self-organization, to form, join, or assist labor organizations, to bargain collectively through representatives of their own choosing, and to engage in other concerted activities for the purpose of collective bargaining or other mutual aid or protection.

Building from earlier legislative failures and shortcomings, the NLRA prohibits employer interference, restraint, or coercion of employees pursuing these rights, specifies a certification procedure for establishing whether a majority of workers want union representation, grants a certified, majority-status union the right to be the exclusive representative of the relevant employees, and obligates the employer to bargain with a certified union.[7] This is a framework for equalizing bargaining power between employees and employers and for providing employee voice.

The New Deal industrial relations system seeks to solve the labor problem by balancing efficiency, equity, and voice. Efficiency is pursued through macroeconomic stabilization via equalizing bargaining power, both through encouragement of unionization and through social safety nets, which can increase purchasing power and also reduce industrial conflict. Efficiency was also promoted through the preservation of property rights and the freedom to contract. Strong laissez-faire proponents saw the New Deal interventions as unwarranted and distortionary interference, but the New Deal reformers viewed the basic standards as leveling the playing field while maintaining the overall structure of private property and economic exchange. As noted by Kochan, Katz, and McKersie (1986, 24), "The NLRA did not dictate the terms and conditions of employment, but rather endorsed a process by which the parties could shape their own substantive contract terms." The NLRA protects worker choice regarding unionization and provides an affirmative obligation for employers to bargain with a majority union, but it does not require specific outcomes.

Equity is fostered through the protective, redistributive functions of unionization, social safety nets, and mandated labor standards. Industrial democracy—voice—is pursued through unionization. The NLRA limits the arbitrary and unilateral exercise of managerial power and authority over terms and conditions of employment. This serves equity by providing checks and balances on corporate actions and provides voice by making the determination of working conditions shared rather than unilateral. One can debate which of these various functions was most important—Kaufman (1996) provides quotes from Senator Wagner regarding macroeconomic stabilization; President Roosevelt and Secretary of Labor Frances Perkins were concerned with social justice and equity (Bernstein 1950; Forbath 1999); and Becker (1993) provides quotes from the NLRA's legislative history emphasizing industrial democracy. But the key point here is that the New Deal industrial relations system can be analyzed in terms of efficiency, equity, and voice. As Senator Wagner later said, "The spirit and purpose of the law is to create a free and dignified workingman who had the economic strength to bargain collectively with a free and dignified employer in accordance with the methods of democracy" (Keyserling 1945, 31). Moreover, the New Deal legislation reflects the desire to balance efficiency, equity, and voice to satisfy underlying ethical beliefs in the context of a specific legal, economic, political, and social environment.[8]

To be clear, this is not intended as an apologist defense of the NLRA. The New Deal leaders could have chosen alternative models of unionism to support through legislation. For example, it has been argued that the New Deal system cemented the institutionalization of pluralist visions of stable collective bargaining by rejecting the early twentieth century model of worker self-governance pursued by the American Federation of Labor's (AFL) craft unions. This self-governance model is different from the 1920s strategy of the Amalgamated Clothing Workers union, for example, to bring stability to the clothing industry by replacing spontaneous job actions of small work groups with negotiated standards through regularized collective bargaining (Fraser 1983). Tomlins (1985a, 1985b) argues that an undue emphasis by key individuals in the New Deal period on stability and this type of orderly resolution of industrial disputes ended the AFL's self-governance model by giving unions legitimacy only as the elected representatives of workers as certified by the state, not as self-governing organizations that can unilaterally determine work rules for its members.[9] Rather, the major point is that the appropriate framework for considering and debating the NLRA is that of balancing efficiency, equity, and voice.

Balancing Property Rights and Labor Rights

Balancing efficiency, equity, and voice in the NLRA requires balancing property rights and labor rights. This remains a central, yet vexing, issue. The union-organizing process under the NLRA is a vivid illustration of the conflict between property rights and labor rights. The arguments cited in chapter 2 imply that it is a human right for employees to form unions, but do property and free speech rights also give employers the right to participate in the union organizing process? Although not without critics, the answer is well established in contemporary U.S. legal thought: employers can express views and opinions as long as their speech "contains no threat of reprisal or force or promise of benefit." Moreover, the fundamental power of property rights is apparent: an employer can force employees to listen to its views in captive audience speeches, while using exclusionary property rights to prevent union organizers and supporters from doing the same.[10] Labor law in the United States attempts to balance property rights and labor rights by providing union organizers with employee names and addresses so that unions can contact employees, in support of their human right to form unions, while allowing employers to express views and restrict access, in support of their rights to free speech and property.[11] Whether this is an appropriate balance can be questioned (Estlund 1994; Gross 1995, 1999; Weiler 1983), but the important point here is that the crux of the legal environment's task is balancing property rights and labor rights.

The bargaining process further illustrates the property rights versus labor rights theme. Employers must bargain in good faith with a duly certified union over wages, hours, and other terms and conditions of employment. This is the labor rights portion: employees can have a voice in the determination of the conditions of employment. But this is balanced with property rights by limiting the duty to bargain to conditions of employment (the scope consistent with human rights) and by limiting the employer's obligation to bargaining—the employer cannot be forced by law to accept specific contractual terms (property rights).[12] Property rights and labor rights are further balanced by allowing the employer to unilaterally implement specific provisions (property rights), but only after their good-faith bargaining obligation over those specific terms has been fulfilled (labor rights).[13] In cases of impasse, U.S. labor law further tries to balance the employer's property rights to conduct business with the employees' rights to strike by allowing the employer to hire strike replacements while granting reinstatement rights (as jobs become available) to striking workers.[14]

Property rights versus labor rights conflicts are also reflected in contractual outcomes and in the contract administration process. As part of due process in the context of employee discipline, U.S. courts in *NLRB v. J. Weingarten* and its successors have attempted to carve out a balance (Morris 1989; Ostmann 2001).[15] On the employee rights side, if the employer directs an employee to participate in an investigatory interview, the employee has the right to have a union representative present if the employee thinks discipline may result. On the employer's side, *Weingarten* rights cannot interfere with employer prerogatives: employers can choose not to interview the employee, the employee cannot delay the meeting by insisting on a specific representative, and the representative cannot coach the employee to be uncooperative.

Or consider the "obey now, grieve later" doctrine commonly applied by arbitrators. With narrow exceptions, an employee must obey a managerial directive, even if the worker believes that the order violates the collective bargaining agreement. Failure to obey is insubordination. In essence, an employer's property rights provide the authority to require employees to obey their orders. Employees' rights grant them the right to due process, including representation and third-party determination if needed, but these rights do not trump the power of property rights to compel immediate compliance. However, if employees feel that obeying the order will place them in imminent danger, their rights are elevated and they can refuse the order.

These examples are from contemporary U.S. industrial relations, but the fundamental conflict of property rights versus labor rights is a general phenomenon not limited to the New Deal industrial relations system. The Americans with Disabilities Act tries to balance property rights and labor rights by prohibiting discrimination against disabled workers only up to the point of reasonable accommodations. Prior to the passage of the NLRA, labor asserted its right to organize and strike on the basis of First Amendment rights of freedom of speech and assembly, the Thirteenth Amendment's prohibition of involuntary servitude, and the Fourteenth Amendment's prohibition on denials of life and liberty (Forbath 2001; Pope 2002). In fact, this Thirteenth Amendment view seems to be endorsed in the preamble to the Norris–LaGuardia Act (1932), which states that "the individual unorganized worker is commonly helpless to exercise actual liberty of contract and to protect his freedom of labor, and thereby to obtain acceptable terms and conditions of employment" (Pope 2002). These rights, however, clashed with employers' property rights, especially freedom to contract and due process protections. The *Lochner*-era Court often sided with property over labor (Forbath 1985; Phillips 1998). One can debate how balanced the decisions were, but, nevertheless, the underlying conflict is one of property rights versus labor rights.

Nonunion Employee Representation

In the New Deal industrial relations system, legally protected employee voice is limited to collective voice that is independent of management authority and pertains to wages, hours, and terms and conditions of employment. This is usually equated to representation by majority-status, exclusive-representative labor unions, but section 7 also protects informal *concerted*—that is, group—activity. Employees cannot be fired for acting together to protest or improve their compensation and working conditions even if the activity is spontaneous and the employees are not unionized. Employee voice on an individual basis, however, is not protected.[16] The New Deal industrial relations system's protection of collective over individual voice reflects the bargaining power focus of labor law and the corollary view that without collective power, voice is meaningless (Greenfield and Pleasure 1993). Moreover, nonunion or employer-promulgated collective voice—company unions—for terms and conditions of employment is expressly prohibited. These nonunion employee representation plans rarely grant employees authority independent of management. Management, not the employees, typically controls how these groups are structured, when they meet, what topics are covered, whether employment conditions are changed, and even whether they continue to exist. This is an important contrast with labor unions as envisioned by the NLRA: independent organizations in which workers control the structures, leaders, bargaining agendas, acceptability of tentatively reached agreements, and the right to strike. The tension between union and nonunion representation reflects differing views on power and voice (Kaufman and Kleiner 1993; Kaufman and Taras 2000).

In the 1910s, the early management consultant John Leitch advocated a nonunion industrial democracy plan modeled after the U.S. government that included a council of supervisors (the Senate) and elected employee representatives (the House of Representatives). The Leitch Plan was based on "the innate spirit of democracy—of the desire which is in almost every man to have a voice in his own destiny and a means for self-expression," which then leads to cooperation and reduced production and labor turnover costs (Leitch 1919, 137). More widespread was the Rockefeller Plan popularized by John D. Rockefeller Jr. as he sought to counter negative publicity after twenty-four miners and family members were killed in 1914 in the Ludlow Massacre by the Colorado militia during a strike against a Rockefeller-owned mine. This plan included a committee with managers and elected employee representatives in equal numbers (Gitelman 1988; Kaufman 2000a; Rockefeller 1923). In the 1920s, nonunion employee representation plans were an important part of the welfare capitalism model of human resource management, and leading industrial relations scholars such as John R. Commons and William Leiserson believed they favorably served both employee and employer interests (Kaufman 2000b).

By 1935, however, nonunion employee representation plans were explicitly prohibited by both the NLRA and the Railway Labor Act. The question of nonunion employee representation split industrial relations in the 1930s and it continues to split industrial relations in the twenty-first century (Kaufman forthcoming). These divisions reflect competing visions for the delivery of efficiency, equity, and voice. As documented by Kaufman (2000b), the dominant wisdom is that nonunion employee representation plans are company-dominated sham unions used as management tools to prevent workers from forming independent, more powerful unions. In this view, they perhaps serve efficiency by providing productivity-enhancing suggestions to management, but genuine employee equity and voice are lacking. In this view, nonunion employee representation plans fail to deliver equity and voice and do not accomplish the goals of the New Deal industrial relations system.

In contrast, Kaufman (2000b; forthcoming) emphasizes the importance of macroeconomic stability in the 1930s debates over nonunion representation plans. In this view, employee representation plans provide genuine workplace voice but lack bargaining power to raise wages. Nonunion employee representation plans—company unions—therefore could not serve Senator Wagner's goal of stimulating the fragile 1930s U.S. economy by increasing the purchasing power of workers/consumers.[17] Kaufman (2000b) therefore argues that the NLRA ban on nonunion representation was a reaction to the proliferation of representation plans under the National Industrial Recovery Act—often to avoid unionization—and the vicious destructive competition that drove wages down in the early 1930s, not from the accomplishments of welfare-capitalism representation plans in the 1920s.

This represents a split in industrial relations thought in the 1930s as Commons believed that employee representation plans were appropriate for progressive, cutting-edge employers, whereas Leiserson supported the NLRA's complete ban on all nonunion plans (Kaufman forthcoming).[18] Commons's view was that efficiency, equity, and voice could be legitimately balanced by nonunion employee representation in some companies, while government legislation and labor unions are needed to prod other companies along and provide equity and voice in those instances. Commons relied on representation plans with shared decision making and due process protections to achieve workplace voice, but he thought that this could be accomplished both by progressive employers and labor unions.

The debate over nonunion employee representation is therefore about efficiency, equity, and voice. Is such a plan an effective method of providing legitimate equity and voice while enhancing efficiency, as Commons believed, or is it a tool for preventing legitimate equity and voice (in the form of an independent union)? In other words, can workers join together to effectively share with management the task of setting employment conditions and policies in the absence of independent unions? This debate highlights the importance of employee voice and collective representation, and it continues to divide human resources and industrial relations today. And the New Deal industrial relations system ban on company-dominated representation plans underscores this system's support of a specific system of workplace governance: government regulation and collective bargaining based on independent employee representation.

From Taft-Hartley to Heartily Daft

Although the NLRA grew out of the experience of earlier laws and executive orders, it nevertheless represented a major shift in government intervention in economic and social affairs and was immediately controversial. "Scarcely had the ink dried on the President's signature establishing the NLRA as part of our national policy when bills to repeal or amend the Act began pouring into the congressional mills" (Millis and Brown 1950, 332). The resulting Taft-Hartley Act revisions to the NLRA in 1947 represent another visible employment relationship focus on balancing.

The standard story is well known: in the decade after the NLRA, union membership increased significantly and many believed that unions were too strong, lacked a sense of public responsibility, and should be bound by the same responsibilities and restrictions that employers faced under the NLRA.[19] The questions regarding organized labor, and the underlying NLRA, were cemented by the great strike wave of 1946, and on the opening day of Congress in 1947, seventeen bills were introduced to amend the NLRA (Millis and Brown 1950). The Taft-Hartley Act passed later in 1947. Its purpose is often explained using a pendulum metaphor (for example, Hartley 1948): the NLRA sought to bring the pendulum representing the balance of power between labor and management from the earlier position favoring management to a middle balanced point, but by omitting unfair labor practices by unions and other things, the NLRA overcorrected and the pendulum had swung too far in favor of labor. The Taft-Hartley Act—with its addition of union unfair labor practices, provisions allowing individuals to refrain from union activity, inclusion of a free speech clause for management, allowance for states to pass right-to-work laws, exclusion of supervisors from the Act's protections, and other provisions—was then viewed as an attempt to restore a balance and move the pendulum back toward the middle of the bargaining power spectrum.[20] Organized labor, on the other hand, termed it the Slave Labor Act.

With some modifications in the Landrum-Griffin Act in 1959, the Taft-Hartley Act–amended NLRA remains today as the legislative framework for the employee representation component of the New Deal industrial relations system. The important themes continue to be workplace governance, property rights versus labor rights, and striking a balance among efficiency, equity, and voice. Though with hindsight we now know better, it was widely believed in the 1950s and 1960s that management had accepted collective bargaining (Kochan, Katz, and McKersie 1986; Troy 1999). This perception reinforced the New Deal industrial relations system's governance strategy: government regulation of minimum standards to provide equity paired with collective bargaining to provide additional protection and also voice. Since that time, the emphasis has been on direct government provision of standards, such as the Civil Rights Act (1964), the Occupational Safety and Health Act (1970), the Americans with Disabilities Act (1990), and the Family and Medical Leave Act (1993). Meanwhile, private sector union density has declined from over 30 percent of the labor force in the 1950s to less than 10 percent today.

The reasons for this union density decline are varied and not universally accepted. The decline appears related to structural changes such as industry, occupational, demographic, and regional trends in the economy, including the decline in traditionally unionized manufacturing industries and the increase in traditionally nonunion southern employment (Chaison and Rose 1991). By itself, however, this is an incomplete explanation because it begs important questions about why certain industries, occupations, regions, or workers are more or less receptive to unionization. A second possibility is that demand for union services has declined (Farber and Krueger 1993)—or that demand for individual representation has increased (Troy 1999). This may be a function of unresponsive unions (Hurd 1998), the use of human resource management practices to substitute for union protection (Jacoby 1997), and the substitution of increased government legislation for union protection (Bennett and Taylor 2001).

The third, and most controversial, explanation for the decline in U.S. union density is employer resistance or opposition. Relative to their peers in other industrialized countries, it is argued that American managers are exceptionally hostile toward unions and have significantly stronger traditions of using union avoidance tactics (Jacoby 1991; Taras 1997). Rather than invest in unionized plants or workplaces, U.S. companies often invest in their nonunion operations (Kochan, Katz, and McKersie 1986).[21] Moreover, it is argued that many companies actively fight union organizing drives by illegally firing union supporters, interrogating workers about their support for a union, making threats and promises, hiring antiunion consultants, manipulating the legal system to frustrate and delay organizing campaigns, and, in unionized companies, forcing strikes and then hiring replacement workers to bust unions (Freeman and Medoff 1984; Gross 1995; Lawler 1990; Weiler 1990).

A fourth possible reason for the decline in U.S. unionization is that U.S. labor law—either the legislative statutes or their subsequent application by the courts, and either directly or indirectly—supports only a proscribed vision of industrial democracy that has weakened the vitality of the labor movement. As noted above, Tomlins (1985a, 1985b) critiques the NLRA's support of stable, shared rule-making forms of unionism over more confrontational republican forms of worker self-government. Klare (1978, 268) argues that the early court interpretations of the NLRA laid the "intellectual groundwork" for defining the nature of appropriate unionism in the United States, one that was ultimately based on unions as a valuable institution of stability in a capitalist economic system. This philosophy served to incorporate the working class, and especially their labor leaders—indirectly and not maliciously—into the economic system and gradually smothered grassroots activism. Stone (1981) further criticizes the postwar philosophy of industrial pluralism embraced by postwar liberals supportive of labor unions (see also Atleson 1993). This postwar industrial pluralism emphasized the private nature of labor-management affairs and the achievement of industrial justice and efficiency through written workplace rules and contracts and private arbitration.[22] But the emphasis on rules and stability ultimately suppressed worker activism and, in the view of critical scholars, failed to challenge the fundamental power structure of the property rights of capital.

The increase in legislated government standards combined with the steady decline in private sector union density undermines the New Deal industrial relations system's governance model that relies on collective bargaining to provide protection and voice. The reason for the union decline, however, is critical. If low levels of unionization represent limited demand for union representation, then perhaps employees are satisfied with the current balance of efficiency, equity, and voice. Purely structural explanations point in this same direction by implicitly assuming that workers in traditionally nonunion sectors do not desire union representation. In sharp contrast, if management opposition or a legal stifling of worker activism underlies the decline in union density, then efficiency, equity, and voice are likely out of balance and labor law reform is warranted.

Organized labor and proponents of industrial democracy believe that management manipulation of weaknesses in the NLRA is at least partly responsible for this current weak state of U.S. collective bargaining (Friedman et al. 1994). As a result, the labor movement and others view the current NLRA framework as heartily daft with many weaknesses and that in order for the United States to "reconfirm the congressional objectives underlying the original Wagner Act," both remedial and substantive changes are needed (Craver 1993, 140). Remedial changes include increasing the penalties for violating the NLRA—including both monetary penalties and stronger remedial directives such as bargaining orders—and reducing delays in the organizing process as a result of legal challenges. Substantive changes include expanding the coverage of the NLRA to close the independent contractors loophole and to include low-level supervisors, removing restrictions on secondary labor activities such as boycotts and hot cargo agreements, and widening the scope of bargaining items.

The most important issues (at least from the pluralist perspective), however, pertain to the representation election process and the issue of strike replacements.[23] Several aspects of the NLRA's representation election process are often attacked. One, it is argued that management should not be a party to this process. Weiler (1990) emphasizes that this process is to determine the employees' wishes, and, thus, management should be excluded from all proceedings, even from campaigning. Two, without going so far as proposing complete managerial exclusion from the process, others assert that labor and management's access to employees is unbalanced. Employers can force employees to listen to their views in captive-audience speeches while preventing equal access for union organizers and supporters by invoking property rights (Craver 1993). Three, as a party to the proceedings, management can file legal challenges and, therefore, delay and frustrate the organizing process (Estreicher 1993; Gould 1993). Four, Weiler (1990, 240) calculates that one-third of representation elections involve one or more workers being fired for supporting a union, but the penalties for such tactics are recognized as minimal—reinstatement with back pay, but with no punitive damages. Five, a significant fraction of newly unionized employee groups fail to successfully negotiate a first contract, often because of management tactics to frustrate the process (Weiler 1984).

Commonly proposed reforms, therefore, include instant or card check elections, which avoid a long and contentious campaigning period; restrictions on management campaigning and/or equal access for union organizers; punitive damages and immediate reinstatement for illegally discharged union supporters; and first contract arbitration if an agreement cannot be reached. All of these proposed changes reflect tension between property rights and labor rights. Perhaps most tangibly, increased union access to employees on the employer's premises conflicts with traditional conceptions of private property. Restrictions on management campaigning is alleged to violate free speech rights, while remedial changes might be viewed as infringing on the due process rights of the property owners. First-contract arbitration can be viewed similarly. The question, therefore, is how to balance property rights with labor rights.

This question is echoed in debates over the use of strike replacements. It is well established in U.S. labor law that management is allowed to replace striking employees with new employees.[24] This is a clear conflict between the employees' right to strike and the employer's property right to conduct business. The conclusion of a strike brings about a new conflict between property rights and labor rights: Are the replaced employees entitled to return to their jobs (human rights in support of collective bargaining and voice)? Or can the employer retain the replacement workers (property rights to conduct business as they see fit)? The 1938 *Mackay* doctrine essentially sided with property—absent any employer unfair labor practices, replacements are allowed to be permanent, that is, they do not have to be discharged at the conclusion of a strike to make room for returning workers. So that striking workers are not technically fired for legally striking—a clear violation of the NLRA—they are granted reinstatement rights as jobs become available, which may take several years.[25] Many commentators view the *Mackay* doctrine as destructive of the right to collective bargaining, and many proposals for reform have been articulated (Craver 1993; Estreicher 1994b; Gould 1993; Weiler 1990). At its core, debates over strike replacements are debates over property rights versus labor rights.

Beyond the dissatisfaction with some components of U.S. labor law, there is a more general sense, among both friends and foes of independent employee representation, that the New Deal industrial relations system no longer matches the global, competitive environment of the twenty-first century—and has therefore progressed from Taft-Hartley to heartily daft.[26] Two broad examples are concerns with adversarialism and employee involvement. Adversarialism is a culture of conflict (Adams 1995), and in U.S. industrial relations this is typically associated with traditional, distributive negotiations that revolve around a power struggle. Every labor-management interaction is a contest of strength, and each side assumes the other is trying to gain the upper hand. Adams (1995) and Heckscher (1988) both argue that adversarialism is embedded in the provisions of the New Deal industrial relations system because of the centrality of exclusive representation and majority support.[27] Because a union must garner the support of a majority of workers to have any workplace rights, the representation process becomes a battle for support between labor and management. The need for a union is presented as protection against abusive or unresponsive management, creating an us vs. them adversarial culture. And because existing unions must maintain majority support, this adversarial culture is perpetuated indefinitely.

It is also argued that adversarialism is established in the New Deal industrial relations system because labor law draws sharp distinctions between labor and management, including the FLSA's distinction between exempt and nonexempt employees, thereby reinforcing the us vs. them mentality (Potter and Youngman 1995). As supporters of employee rights and collective voice, Adams (1995) and Heckscher (1988) believe that adversarialism harms organized labor and individual employees by making effective representation more difficult in today's environment, but business similarly attacks adversarialism as inimical to developing the level of cooperation needed in a competitive environment (Potter and Youngman 1995).

The second argument that the New Deal industrial relations system no longer matches the global, competitive environment of the twenty-first century is the accusation that section 8(a)(2) of the NLRA prevents nonunion employee involvement and participation.[28] Competitive pressures for quality goods and services in quickly changing markets have undermined both the once-dominant scientific management model of work organization and the hierarchical, bureaucratic corporate structure (Applebaum and Batt 1994; Bluestone and Bluestone 1992; Kochan, Katz, and McKersie 1986). As a result, many organizations—union and nonunion—have experimented with different methods of restructuring work, supervision, compensation, information sharing, and employee involvement in workplace decisions. The latter ranges from simple employee suggestion systems to joint labor-management meetings such as quality circles to high-performance work teams (Applebaum and Batt 1994).

Section 8(a)(2) of the NLRA, however, bans company-dominated representation plans wherein employees deal with management over wages, hours, and terms and conditions of employment. This is not an issue for employee involvement at either end of the spectrum. Suggestion systems that involve one-way communication from workers to management and high-performance work teams in which employees have decision-making authority do not deal with management—in both cases, there is not a bilateral relationship. It is the middle area of the spectrum—joint labor-management forums—that is controversial. The flash point for this controversy is the National Labor Relations Board's 1992 ruling in *Electromation* that several joint labor-management committees that were established unilaterally by this nonunion employer and which involved discussion of terms and conditions of employment were illegal, company-dominated representation plans.[29] Business uses this ruling as evidence that the NLRA is outdated in that it prohibits employer efforts to establish legitimate employee-representation systems that benefit workers by giving them voice, and benefit companies by increasing quality and productivity (Potter and Youngman 1995).

This ongoing controversy parallels the split within industrial relations during the New Deal. Organized labor sees nonunion committees such as those used by Electromation as the same sham unions used by employers under the National Industrial Recovery Act in the early 1930s to prevent the formation of legitimate, independent unions—exactly the type of company-dominated unions the writers of the NLRA targeted with section 8(a)(2). The business perspective on these modern employee involvement programs echoes the positive contributions of the 1920s welfare-capitalism representation plans described by Kaufman (2000b). This controversy rests on a particular dimension of employee voice: the ability to freely select one's representatives. In the presence of true free choice, employees can opt for an independent labor union if equity and voice are underserved by a nonunion representation plan. Moreover, the threat of this option can bolster the employees' power in a nonunion plan (Kaufman 2000b; Taras 2000). In contrast, critics of nonunion representation plans believe that it is impossible to construct a policy regime that effectively prevents managerial manipulation and establishes employee free choice of representatives. Academic reform proposals are frequently in the middle of these two perspectives and pair a weakening of section 8(a)(2) to allow more nonunion committees with reforms of the representation election procedure to bolster employee free choice of their representatives (Estreicher 1994a; Gould 1993; LeRoy 1999).[30]

The current dissatisfaction with the New Deal industrial relations system can be graphically captured by the geometry of the employment relationship (figure 6.1). Before the Taft-Hartley amendments, union density was increasing, and equity and voice were provided through collective bargaining. The Taft-Hartley amendments shifted the balance of the system in the direction of efficiency, away from voice and equity, by exempting supervisors, outlawing secondary activities, and other changes described above. Moreover, as globalization and pressures for cooperation became widespread in the last two decades, the popular view that the New Deal industrial relations system no longer serves the economic system implies that it has moved away from efficiency in the geometry of the employment relationship. And to the extent that legal rulings implementing the industrial pluralism philosophy have limited employee voice to bureaucratic, service-model representation (Klare 1978; Stone 1981), the system has moved away from the voice dimension as well. In fact, if one factors in the low level of union density, one might argue that the New Deal industrial relations system has nearly faded entirely from the geometry of the employment relationship in figure 6.1.

In sum, in the postwar period the public policy portion of the New Deal industrial relations system has gone from Taft-Hartley to heartily daft. Although often for different reasons, both labor and management find serious faults with the NLRA in the twenty-first century. Wide-ranging scholarship articulates myriad reform proposals, including complete deregulation, substantive and remedial changes to the NLRA, and rewriting U.S. labor law from a clean slate. Debates over employee involvement provide clear illustrations of the centrality of efficiency, equity, and voice in these debates. Are nonunion labor-

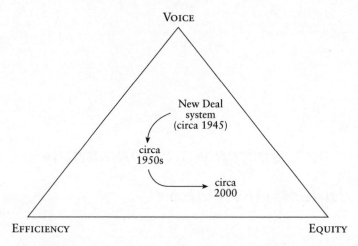

Figure 6.1 The Geometry of the Employment Relationship: The New Deal Industrial Relations System

management committees sham unions that are manipulated to prevent the establishment of a legitimate voice mechanism? Or, in contrast, do employee involvement plans produce win-win situations that serve employers and employees? Do labor-management committees provide legitimate voice while also enhancing efficiency? There are no easy answers to these questions, but a paradigm of balancing efficiency, equity, and voice through workplace governance mechanisms that balance property rights and labor rights is the best framework for analyzing such critical questions.

7 The Geometry of Comparative Industrial Relations

ALTHOUGH THE PARADIGM of balancing efficiency, equity, and voice through institutions reflects the normative foundations of pluralist industrial relations thought, it is not limited to the U.S. institutional context. Moreover, setting aside the normative prescription of balance, the trilogy of efficiency, equity, and voice provides a useful analytical framework for analyzing employment systems around the globe. The New Deal industrial relations system is but one possible institutional structure for pursuing efficiency, equity, and voice in the employment relationship. Consider the commonly discussed features of industrial relations systems in industrialized market economies.[1] From most centralized to most decentralized, the major features are social partnerships, sectoral bargaining, centralized awards, enterprise unionism, exclusive representation with majority support, codetermination, and voluntarism.[2] Each of these institutional arrangements can be analyzed using the standards of efficiency, equity, and voice. For example, sectoral bargaining that establishes minimum terms of employment for an entire industry is biased toward equity—establishment-level efficiency and grassroots-level employee voice are sacrificed for uniform conditions across the industry. In contrast, codetermination can better serve employee voice and workplace efficiency, but as works councils commonly are prohibited from striking, equity is less well served.

The framework of efficiency, equity, and voice therefore provides a common focus for comparative industrial relations analyses. Undertaking such comparative analyses in the context of the geometry of the employment relationship reveals the trade-offs involved in different industrial relations institutional arrangements (see figure 7.1). It also highlights the difficulty of industrial relations reform—the common features of industrial relations systems are often biased toward one or two employment relationship objectives. A system that balances efficiency, equity, and voice likely needs complementary features rather than sole reliance on a single component.

Figure 7.1 The Geometry of Comparative Industrial Relations

Social Partnerships

A social partnership is a neocorporatist (or bargained corporatist) arrangement in which peak-level representatives of labor, business, government, and perhaps others collaborate to achieve consensus on a national framework for economic and social development.[3] To the extent that some social partnership agreements contain wage and pay guidelines, a social partnership model of industrial relations contains a system of centralized bargaining. For example, the series of three-year agreements negotiated by the Irish Congress of Trade Unions, the Irish Business and Employers' Confederation, and the Irish government beginning in 1987 contain explicit wage-increase guidelines, and compliance has been very high (Gunnigle, McMahon, and Fitzgerald 1999; Ó'Móráin 2000). But a social partnership model is more than just centralized collective bargaining. Economic items not normally addressed in collective bargaining are often included in social partnership agreements, such as monetary and fiscal policies, exchange rate management, tax reform, and government debt reduction. Moreover, social issues can also be addressed. The Irish Programme for Prosperity and Fairness agreement for 2001–4, for example, includes provisions regarding discrimination, training, health care, public transportation, housing, and child care.

Various forms of social partnerships or corporatism have been prevalent, albeit not continuously or uniformly, in smaller European countries such as Austria, Belgium, Denmark, Ireland, the Netherlands, Norway, and Switzerland (Ferner and Hyman 1998). The most exceptional and stable example is Austria and its system of Sozialpartnerschaft, which is often traced to a desire to replace class conflict—which was at least partly responsible for the Nazi occupation in 1938—with cooperation at the end of World War II (Traxler

1998). The Austrian social partnership arrangement provides both advisory and regulatory functions for economic and social policy. Wage policies are no longer directly established through the partnership, but a high degree of macroeconomic coordination results from strong pattern-following within sectoral bargaining. Workplace issues are handled by works councils. In contrast, Ireland's current experience with social partnership dates back to 1987 and was implemented to create a fiscal and monetary climate that was conducive to economic growth and to reduce government debt in response to a growing economic crisis in the 1980s. At the workplace level, Irish industrial relations is voluntaristic.

Debates over social partnerships can be interpreted as debates over balancing efficiency, equity, and voice. On the positive side, social partnership arrangements are often associated with stability, predictability, coordination, and consensus. Stabilization of government spending and debt, tax rates, interest rates, wage growth, and inflation as well as industrial conflict are argued to be conducive to investment and economic growth (Ó'Móráin 2000). Equity can be served by building social concerns into the social partnership agreements. In addition to the social issues mentioned above, the Irish Programme for Prosperity and Fairness agreement for 2001–4 also includes consensus on a national minimum wage. With respect to voice, organized labor has a clear, institutionalized voice in the peak-level negotiations and discussions. This can provide enhanced economic and social relevance for unions and provide a voice for all workers in the determination of national economic and social policies. A favorable interpretation of social partnerships is, therefore, that they enhance efficiency, equity, and voice (see figure 7.1).

The drawbacks of a social partnership system of industrial relations also revolve around efficiency, equity, and voice. Centralized, peak-level policies can conflict with managerial drives for flexibility, pay-for-performance, and other enterprise-level efficiency-enhancing mechanisms. For example, as firms in Finland look to employee participation and other "bottom-up" sources of competitive advantage, there is growing pressure on the "top-down" nature of social partnerships (Lilja 1998). These pressures are heightened by the increasing diversity of Finnish firms, which means that employers no longer face uniform market and competitive conditions. With respect to labor, there are questions regarding whether social partnerships are equal collaborations or cooption (Hyman 2001). In the Irish context, some believe that the extent of wage restraint has been excessive and that the partnership agreements overemphasize an efficiency agenda (Ó'Móráin 2000). If the labor movement is complicit in a pure efficiency agenda, it loses its legitimacy (Hyman 2001), and an overly centralized focus can also weaken the legitimacy of workplace voice. Moreover, the extent to which a macrolevel spirit of partnership and shared decision making extends to the workplace can be questioned (Gunnigle 1997). This is in essence a questioning of the presence of workplace employee voice instead of unilateral management control. In general, a peak-level social partnership only provides voice at a macro level; workplace voice depends on the nature of establishment-level industrial relations. Nevertheless, efficiency, equity, and voice provide the dimensions for evaluating social partnerships.

Sectoral Bargaining

A social partnership of peak-level institutions is a very centralized feature of an industrial relations system. The next level down the centralization scale is sectoral bargaining—industrywide collective bargaining that produces a contract for an entire sector. A system of sectoral bargaining, however, is more than voluntary industrywide bargaining (as in the case of the steel industry in the United States until the 1980s). It is an institutional framework in which sectoral bargaining is a widespread, critical feature of an industrial relations system, often because of legal support, especially the legal power to extend agreements to entire industries. Significant examples of sectoral bargaining with legal-based extension procedures are in Belgium, France, Germany, and Portugal. In fact, extension procedures are found throughout Europe with only three exceptions—Britain, Norway, and Sweden (European Industrial Relations Observatory 2002b). Unlike the United States, in these sectoral bargaining systems union coverage (being covered by collective bargaining) is divorced from union membership (being a union member). As many as 80 or 90 percent of workers might be covered, even if only a minority of employees are union members.

In Germany, each major industry or sector has a dominant union and employer association. Sectoral bargaining generally occurs between the regional branches of each union and employers' association, but it is tightly coordinated by the national organizations. The first regional agreement usually sets a strong pattern for the other regions (Jacobi, Keller, and Müller-Jentsch 1998). Wage agreements specify minimum standards for hourly wages and piece-rate pay; framework agreements outline wage and salary grades; and umbrella agreements specify working-time, holidays, overtime, and other working conditions. All members of the employers' association are bound by the terms of the sectoral-level agreements. When the signatories to an agreement employ at least 50 percent of the industry's employees within that region, if the minister for labor thinks that employment conditions will otherwise fall below the prevailing conditions, the terms of an agreement can be extended by an order for imposing extension (Allgemeinverbindlichkeitserklärung) to the remaining employers. Although this procedure is rarely used, especially outside of construction and retail trade, the potential for extension encourages membership in the relevant employers' association (Katz and Darbishire 2000). Approximately 80 percent of German employees are therefore covered by collective bargaining agreements (Jacobi, Keller, and

Müller-Jentsch 1998). Some companies—Volkswagen being the notable example—have negotiated company-level agreements instead of participating in sectoral bargaining, but sectoral bargaining continues to be the most influential type of bargaining in German industrial relations. Implementation of the collective bargaining agreements is often handled through the workplace-level system of works councils (see the section on codetermination below).

Sectoral bargaining is similarly a major feature of industrial relations in Portugal. In 1993, 83 percent of private and public sector employees in legal employment were covered by sector-level collective bargaining agreements (Barreto and Naumann 1998). Once a sectoral agreement is registered with the Ministry of Employment, an extension directive (*portaria de extensão*) can extend the terms of the agreement to other employers in the same region and industry who are not members of the employers' association and also to other employers in other regions (but the same industry) that do not have an employers' association. Approximately 30 percent of agreements are extended in this way (European Industrial Relations Observatory 1998). French industrial relations law includes similar provisions for extending sectoral agreements to others within the same area and industry (*procédure d'extension*) or others in the same industry but different geographical area (*procédure d'élargissement*) (Goetschy 1998). French industrial relations involves greater inter-union competition than in Germany and collective bargaining is therefore weaker, but sectoral bargaining in France nevertheless has an important impact on pay levels for lower-paid workers (Goetschy 1998).

As with other features of national industrial relations systems, a sectoral bargaining system can be analyzed in the geometry of the employment relationship. A sectoral bargaining system best serves the equity dimension of the employment relationship objectives. In countries with this institutional feature, contract coverage is very high—often over 80 percent and sometimes over 90 percent of the workforce, even if union membership is low. Moreover, these contracts provide uniform minimum standards for a range of employment terms and conditions. Thus, equity is well served. The voice standard is fulfilled to some degree because terms and conditions of employment are established through collective bargaining, not unilateral management action. But this fulfillment is limited because collective bargaining is very centralized and largely removed from rank-and-file participation.[4] Contract ratification votes are rare and bargaining is even more removed from individual employees than in the New Deal industrial relations system's decentralized bargaining, though coverage is much greater under sectoral bargaining. Last, sectoral bargaining is consistent with efficiency when stability is valued, but contemporary corporate industrial relations strategies emphasize decentralized relationships to enhance competitiveness and efficiency (Katz and Darbishire 2000). As such, sectoral bargaining serves efficiency and voice to a limited degree, but it is weighted toward equity in the geometry of the employment relationship (see figure 7.1).

Centralized Awards

In a centralized awards system, a government arbitration commission (or tribunal) issues a binding arbitration award that specifies minimum standards for pay and working conditions. To the extent that these awards often cover employees across establishments, this system is similar to sectoral bargaining because a centralized process produces minimum standards for numerous workers beyond a single establishment. In the two main examples of centralized awards systems, however, occupations rather than industries have been the focal point. These two main examples are from Australia and New Zealand, at least before the 1990s. The New Zealand arbitration system was established in 1894 and Australia's in 1904 and both were intended to prevent strikes (Dannin 1997; Davis and Lansbury 1998).

Until the 1990s, both systems worked in a similar fashion and the (pre-1990) Australian system is briefly described here. For many years, an annual basic federal award established a minimum wage for unskilled workers to fulfill "the normal needs of an average employee, regarded as a human being living in a civilized community" based on a family of five (Davis and Lansbury 1998, 124). From this basic award, a series of wage differentials for skilled occupations was further established. The federal awards established the pattern for state and industry-specific occupational awards. Although unions in Germany and Sweden, for example, are organized by industry, unions in Australia and New Zealand were traditionally more craft- or occupation-based and the awards specified minimum terms for occupations. In periods of labor market tightness, unions were successful in negotiating more generous terms ("over-award" pay) through collective bargaining with individual employers (Katz and Darbishire 2000).[5]

The intent of the creators of this system arguably was that arbitration would be a final impediment to destructive strikes, not the centerpiece of a centralized system for determining terms and conditions of employment (Creighton 1999; Stewart 1989). The authority for the federal arbitration commission was Article 51 of the Australian Constitution, which authorizes Parliament to make laws for "conciliation and arbitration for the prevention and settlement of industrial disputes extending beyond the limits of any one State." Arbitration requires a dispute, but the courts broadly interpreted "dispute" to include paper disagreements and have not required more explicit forms of industrial conflict. A simple managerial rejection of a union's "log of claims" creates a sufficient dispute for the arbitration process (Creighton 1999; Stewart 1989). Because the arbitration process only requires a minimal dispute, the ability of unions to create a dispute, and thereby obtain an award, encourages employers to negotiate or join as a party to an award (Creighton 1999). This explains the development of arbitration awards as the dominant feature of Australian industrial relations and also the resulting high coverage rates—estimated to be around 80 percent before the 1990s (Creighton 1999; Stewart 1989).[6]

The content of Australian arbitration awards in different time periods reveals a struggle to balance efficiency, equity, and voice. Most explicitly, the living wage standard based on supporting a family of five is a clear equity standard. Unions attempted to extend these conceptions further, especially in the 1970s and 1980s when parental leave, equal pay for equal work, and severance pay were added to awards (Creighton 1999). On the other hand, large over-award settlements during the early 1970s were popularly associated with inflation and unemployment (Davis and Lansbury 1998). As a result, in the late 1970s the arbitration commission reasserted its centralized control and implemented partial wage-indexation awards (Dabscheck 1989). Pressures from both the government (because of macroeconomic problems, such as an exchange-rate crisis) and employers (to improve labor-management cooperation, flexibility, and responsiveness to firm-specific conditions) for decentralization in the 1980s led to a 1988 national award that established a "structural efficiency principle." Although respecting the minimum rates established by the awards system, this principle allowed for the modification of awards by local bargaining to enhance skill-related career paths and flexible working patterns and to eliminate barriers to multiskilling (Dabscheck 1995).

Although a strong centralized awards system no longer exists in either Australia or New Zealand, its traditional operation can be evaluated using the geometry of the employment relationship.[7] Equity, especially with uniform minimum standards for a living wage applicable to large numbers of workers, is well served by this centralized system. This is reinforced by the nature of arbitration rather than bargaining—ideally, the outcome reflects neutral consideration of objective materials submitted by all parties. In determining the basic award, for example, the commission traditionally received submissions from the Australian Council of Trade Unions, various employers' associations, the federal and state governments, and other interested parties. Employee voice is also served by this process, but not as well as by some other systems. As with sectoral bargaining, voice is well served by high coverage rates, but it is not well served by such a high degree of centralization. Moreover, that arbitration ultimately imposes a settlement on the parties is another question mark for the provision of employee (and employer) voice under a centralized awards system. In terms of efficiency, if efficiency is promoted by standardization across workplaces, then a centralized awards system contributes toward this objective of the employment relationship. But this is a big "if" because over the last two decades, the centralized awards system has been heavily criticized for interfering with efficiency, especially with decentralization and the promotion of workplace cooperation and flexibility (and hence, it no longer exists in New Zealand and exists only in a weakened version in Australia). In conclusion, a centralized awards system is biased toward equity in the geometry of the employment relationship (see figure 7.1.).

Enterprise Unionism

In contrast to the industry and occupation-wide scope of sectoral bargaining and centralized awards, enterprise unionism is a system of industrial relations focused at the company level. The best-known example is the Japanese industrial relations system in which the vast majority of unions are confined within a single enterprise, hence the label "enterprise unionism." This differs from the industrial unionism of the United States in which unions often represent workers at different companies (for example, the UAW represents workers at Ford, General Motors, and many others). Furthermore, most unions in Japan represent all of the workers in "their" single company, though there are some instances of competing unions within the same company (Kawanishi 1992). Venezuela is a second example—the majority of unions are organized at a single company, and although there can be more than one union in the same establishment, management must bargain with the union that represents the majority of the employees (Lucena 1992). Even though enterprise unionism isn't necessarily mandated by law, these systems are distinguished from the United States and other countries with isolated examples of enterprise unions (Jacoby and Verma 1992), because in an enterprise unionism system an enterprise focus dominates the nature of labor relations in that country.[8]

The Japanese system of enterprise unionism is embedded in the context of lifetime employment, seniority and firm-based wages, and broad job classifications (Araki 1994; Kuwahara 1998). These features might not even cover a majority of the total workforce, but they have traditionally been central for core employees in large firms. Because this is where unionism is most prevalent, these features are closely intertwined with the general nature of Japanese unionism. Lifetime employment is an implicit, not legal, practice such that employees are normally never laid off; rather, they are able to work for a single firm for their entire working life. Cyclical and seasonal burdens are borne by temporary workers who are not covered by either lifetime employment practices or unions. Wages for regular employees are based largely on seniority, not jobs. Moreover, a large annual bonus is an important component of worker pay and this bonus partly fluctuates with a company's ability to pay (Katz and Darbishire 2000). Japanese firms often utilize broad job classifications in combination with job rotation.

All of these features mean that employees identify with an enterprise—its internal labor market and financial performance—not a specific job. This strong sense of enterprise identification provides the context for a system of enterprise unionism in which labor relations are often characterized as cooperative or consensual (Araki 1994; Kuwahara 1998). With the exception of the annual spring offensive (*shunto*) for wage bargaining, labor-management interactions are nearly always at the level of the enterprise. With a union's entire membership contained within a single company, enterprise unions are responsive to company economic performance; union demands and the resulting agreements are tailored accordingly. It has also been argued that this system effectively includes employee interests in corporate governance, albeit informally. Insulation from outside shareholder pressures, the need for high levels of worker cooperation, and the inclusion in corporate governance of high-level managers who have risen through the ranks (as a result of lifetime employment)—including perhaps a stint as a labor union leader—can allow employee interests to be considered when corporate boards make strategic decisions (Charny 1999).

Three-quarters of unionized companies also have joint labor-management consultation bodies that are established voluntarily, not because of any legal mandate (Araki 1994). About 60 percent report dealing with managerial issues, though most frequently by simply providing information. Working conditions are dealt with by over 80 percent of joint committees and are most frequently handled in the spirit of joint consultation rather than information sharing or codetermination. Araki (1994) argues that because this consultation process is divorced from the (allegedly) inherent adversarial nature of collective bargaining, better relationships and communication are developed through joint consultation. It is further argued that because consultation precedes collective bargaining, subjects for which agreements are reached through consultation do not need to be negotiated; therefore, consultation is becoming more important than collective bargaining in Japanese industrial relations.

On the other hand, others argue that these cooperative enterprise unions are in fact management-dominated sham unions. In contrast to the claim that enterprise unions are dominant because of their responsiveness to workers' concerns for an efficient enterprise, critics assert that the prevalence of enterprise unions resulted from management suppression of industrial unions in the 1950s (Kawanishi 1992; Turner 1991). Kawanishi (1992, 52) in particular argues that many enterprise unions have "become a kind of extra-managerial body which assists management in the implementation of its personnel policies." Moreover, in a system of enterprise unionism, existing unions have little incentive to organize new unions at other establishments and overall labor movement solidarity is low.

A system of enterprise unionism represents another set of trade-offs between efficiency, equity, and voice. There seems to be little debate that efficiency is well served. Enterprise unionism in Japan is congruent with other dimensions of human resource management strategies, such as lifetime employment, company loyalty, and worker participation. Critiques of the Japanese system of enterprise unionism on the basis of impairing efficiency or quality are therefore rare. However, the extent to which equity is fulfilled is questionable. Responsiveness to firm profitability and the lack of interfirm labor solidarity undermines the establishment of minimum work standards (Kawanishi 1992). Moreover, the exclusion of large numbers of noncore employees within the enterprise is not consistent with the provision of equity. Evaluating the ability of enterprise unions to provide employee voice is more difficult. The extent of employee involvement and joint consultation provides employee input into a wide range of topics—in most cases much broader than in the New Deal industrial relations system. Moreover, enterprise unions are legally distinct from the companies and have the right to strike to back up the exercise of employee voice. On the other hand, the extent to which consultation over managerial topics is voluntary and the extent to which enterprise unions are dependent on a single company potentially detracts from the legitimacy of employee voice in this system.[9] It is beyond the scope of this book to resolve this important debate, but analyzing the trade-offs between efficiency, equity, and voice provides the framework for pursuing this debate, and for understanding enterprise unionism.

Exclusive Representation with Majority Rule

Exclusive representation with majority rule is the central feature of the industrial relations systems of the United States and Canada. Workers in an explicitly defined bargaining unit—which may be defined by occupation, work group, or employer—can only be represented by a single union. This union is the exclusive representative of the workers in this bargaining unit when there is majority support. Employers are required to bargain with a union only when majority support among the employees can be demonstrated. Union representation is therefore closely linked with union membership. These features are in sharp contrast to sectoral bargaining in which many employees and workplaces are covered by collective bargaining based on their industry, not because of individual union membership choices. These features are also significantly different from other systems in which multiple unions exist side by side in single workplaces and compete for representation of similar employees. Bargaining in a system of exclusive representation can range from centralized (as in the case of past industrywide negotiations in the U.S. steel industry) to decentralized, including company-based, workplace level, or work group level bargaining. In the United States and Canada, bargaining has typically been decentralized.

Because of the varied nature of exclusive representation, such as centralized or decentralized bargaining, the relationship with efficiency is similarly varied and depends on union and management strategies within this system (see chapter 8). When exclusive representation is paired with majority support, equity is determined democratically, such as through voting to ratify contracts. Legal doctrine in the United States requires exclusive-representative unions to fairly represent all workers in the bargaining unit, which promotes equal and comprehensive treatment and, therefore, equity and voice. A difficulty with the majority support system of exclusive representation is that equity and voice through labor unions is critically dependent on a majority of workers favoring a specific union.[10] This begs very important questions about the pursuit of equity and voice for workers who want a union while a majority of their co-workers do not, or vice versa. As with other issues raised in this chapter, it is beyond the scope of this book to resolve these questions. The main point is that debates over these questions are at their heart debates over equity and voice.

Codetermination

Codetermination is an institutionalized system of employee voice in which employees are entitled to participate in workplace decision making. Codetermination is an important component of many national industrial relations systems in Europe, and although the specifics vary, national laws generally support works councils (as in Germany and Spain), or something similar (enterprise committees in France, joint councils or local unions in Sweden), as well as board-level employee representation (as in France, Germany, and Sweden, but not Spain). A works council is a workplace-level committee of employees elected to represent all of the workers (except senior executives)—skilled and unskilled, blue and white collar, union and nonunion—in dealings with management. In some cases, this workplace representation is intimately connected to unionism (for example, Spain and Sweden), while in others workplace committees receive assistance from unions but are legally independent from them (for example, France and Germany). But a common focus is on workplace issues, and thus codetermination is a decentralized aspect of industrial relations systems. Among workplaces with at least fifty employees, it is estimated that 80 percent have enterprise committees in France and 70 percent have works councils in Spain (Escobar 1995; Tchobanian 1995). In Germany, 35 percent of establishments have a works council, but those without works councils are predominately small firms, so it is estimated that 70 percent of eligible workers are covered by works councils (Müller-Jentsch 1995).

German codetermination is perhaps the most well known and involves both works councils and employee representation on corporate supervisory boards. The Works Constitution Act entitles all workers in companies with at least five employees to form a works council (Betriebsrat) if at least three employees wish to do so. The works council must meet with an employer at least once a month, and the company pays for a works council's expenses. The law mandates that "the employer and the works councils shall work together in a spirit of mutual trust . . . for the good of the employees and of the establishment." A works council therefore cannot strike, but it can sue if an employer does not fulfill its legal obligations. German works councils are legally distinct from unions—their existence does not depend on a local union presence—but in practice union members are likely to be active in the works councils and unions help provide training and expertise (Müller-Jentsch 1995). Companies with multiple establishments must also establish companywide works councils.

German works councils have codetermination, consultation, and information rights regarding various workplace issues. With respect to codetermination, the company and the works council must jointly determine issues pertaining to work rules and discipline, daily working hours, leave schedules, performance-based pay and bonuses, overtime, safety and health, training, and personnel selection methods. In terms of consultation rights, the employer must notify the works council and consider its suggestions and objections before implementing changes pertaining to the nature of work and the physical plant. Last, employers must share with works councils financial information pertaining to the firm's balance sheet, investment and marketing plans, and other corporate plans. Complementing the system of sectoral bargaining in Germany, works councils negotiate the details for implementing the broad initiatives contained in industrywide collective bargaining agreements (Müller-Jentsch 1995). Moreover, when labor markets are tight, works councils are sometimes able to negotiate extra wage increases (somewhat illegally); when labor markets or a specific firm's competitive position are weak, some works councils engage in wildcat cooperation—agreeing to concessions below the collective bargaining agreement's standards (Jacobi, Keller, and Müller-Jentsch 1998). German companies are introducing the same types of flexible work systems as in other countries, but the legal rights of works councils gives them the power to represent employee interests when these changes are implemented (Katz and Darbishire 2000).

The second component of German codetermination is employee-representation on corporate supervisory boards (Aufsichtsrat).[11] Employees are entitled to minority representation (one-third of representatives) on the supervisory boards of companies with more than five hundred employees and to nominally equal parity (one-half of the representatives) in companies with more than two thousand employees.[12] German supervisory boards are less powerful than U.S. boards of directors, but employee representation nevertheless provides workers with a voice when strategic decisions are being considered (Wever 1995). This representation also provides an important complement to the operation of the works councils, especially by increasing the quality of information received regarding both financial issues and strategic plans (Müller-Jentsch 1995; Turner 1991). In fact, employees are incorporated into corporate governance mechanisms in various ways in many European countries (European Industrial Relations Observatory 2002a). Corporate governance issues should not be overlooked in discussions of employee representation (Jacoby 2001).

French codetermination is linked to guarantees of workers' right of expression giving them the right to voice opinions regarding the nature of their work (*droit d'expression*) (Goetschy 1998). Companies with fifty or more employees are required to have an elected enterprise committee (*comités d'enterprise*) and a health and safety committee (*comités d'hygiène*). The enterprise committee has rights to information and consultation regarding "the firm's organization, management, and general functioning" and can also negotiate profit-sharing arrangements (Tchobanian 1995, 117). As in Germany, the employer pays the expenses and a group committee is required for multi-establishment companies. This form of codetermination is complemented by personnel delegates (*délégués du personnel*) (required in firms with more than ten employees), which handle grievances, and also by the right of several enterprise committee members to attend corporate board meetings. The trend toward decentralized industrial relations in France has increased the importance of the enterprise committees, though there is wide variation in their operation across firms, which results from differing attitudes of both managers and unions toward these committees (Tchobanian 1995).[13] In Spain, works councils (*comités de empresa*) are mandatory in firms with more than ten employees and have the right to information (production, sales, employment, safety, discipline); consultation (changes in work organization or job evaluation, layoffs); legal action (if employment laws are broken); and negotiation (wages and hours) (Escobar 1995). Unlike works councils in many countries, Spanish works councils have the right to strike. Although this makes Spanish works councils more like local unions, legally and functionally they are distinct (Escobar 1995). Employees in Spain have board-level representation only in the public sector.

In the geometry of the employment relationship, the strength of codetermination is in delivering efficiency and voice (see figure 7.1). It is common for works councils to be required to cooperate with management, and such councils are intended to benefit companies as well as employees. For traditional management rights issues, works councils often have rights of consultation or information but not negotiation, so managerial prerogatives are preserved in the pursuit of efficiency. Additionally, codetermination is a clear vehicle for workplace voice. Employees can negotiate issues pertaining to working conditions, and even though limited to consultation on managerial issues, they can provide input. Board-level representation further provides voice in a different forum. And employee voice is well served by the ease of establishing works councils in many countries—there are no drawn-out campaigns or requirements to garner majority status as in the U.S. New Deal industrial relations system—and the coverage rate is often quite high. Equity is served by the grievance processing capacity of works councils (or French personnel delegates), but more generally, codetermination provides efficiency and voice, not equity. Works councils are generally limited in the issues they can codetermine—wages, in particular, are often excluded—and they usually lack the right to strike so that the redistribution activities of works councils are limited. Equity is generally pursued through collective bargaining, not codetermination and works councils.

Voluntarism

In a voluntarist industrial relations system, labor and management voluntarily agree (or not) to enter into individual or collective bargaining and to abide by (or not) whatever agreements are reached. Union recognition and bargaining are not backed by the force of law. Contracts may or may not be enforceable; if they are, enforceability is governed by common law under the same conditions as other business contracts. The term voluntary, therefore, refers to the absence of direct legal regulation of industrial relations; behaviors and outcomes are compelled by economic power, common law, and perhaps goodwill, but not through industrial relations laws. A voluntarist system, however, is not completely unregulated—in the absence of statutory regulations, the parties are bound by common law rulings, which might not be neutral (Klare 1988). In practice, voluntarist systems often have some industrial relations legislation so voluntarism is better conceived as a relative rather than absolute concept.

The British industrial relations system is a major example of a voluntarist system.[14] Collective bargaining agreements are not legally enforceable, and until very recently, union recognition was voluntary. British voluntarism can be traced back to the late nineteenth century and a strong system of craft-based production in which workers developed workplace practices. Fear among both labor and management of unfavorable, restrictive government regulation caused their support for a laissez-faire, voluntarist approach to industrial relations, and in 1906 the Trade Disputes Act provided immunity for unions and their leaders from common law liability for industrial disputes. Out of this framework developed a pattern of centralized negotiations, which established industry-level standards, complemented with informal workplace bargaining led by shop stewards. Although their power may have resulted more from tight labor markets than militant ideology, the shop stewards were viewed as causing high levels of unauthorized strike activity, often over grievances (recall that contracts are not legally enforceable). The Donovan Commission in the mid-1960s, although endorsing voluntarism, advocated formalizing establishment-level collective bargaining to address the perceived shop steward problem. Since that time, industrywide bargaining has generally been abandoned.

Britain is also a good example of why voluntarism is not an absolute term.[15] The Conservative Thatcher government introduced a number of acts in the 1980s. One result of this legislation is to narrow the scope of the 1906 industrial disputes immunities by limiting secondary action and picketing and by requiring strike votes. These acts also outlawed the closed shop by protecting nonmembers against dismissal. Regulation of internal union democracy also increased: election requirements for union officers were specified and rights were granted to individual union members. More recently, the Employment Relations Act (1999), while still encouraging voluntary recognition of unions, provides for statutory recognition of a union under specified majority demonstration provisions (Gall 2003). These laws, which would fall under the umbrella of labor law in U.S. terminology, are supplemented by provisions similar to U.S. employment laws (sometimes prompted by Britain's membership in the European Union): an equal pay act, safety and health standards, an antidiscrimination act, and various family-friendly leave policies.

The regional wage councils that had traditionally established minimum wages were abolished in 1993 as part of the Conservative government's deregulation effort, but a minimum wage was reestablished in 1999. Indirect regulation of industrial relations also serves to make voluntarism a relative rather than absolute concept. Pencavel (1999), for example, argues that prevailing wage arrangements and anticompetitive product market interventions, such as privatization, favored unionization.

As in the United States (and many other countries), a significant issue in Britain is a steep decline in union representation. The British decline began in 1979—much later than the mid-1950s turning point in the United States—and since that time, union membership has fallen by more than five million and the fraction covered by collective bargaining agreements has plummeted from 70 percent to 36 percent (Katz and Darbishire 2000). As restrictions on secondary labor activity have been added to the already decentralized, or fragmented, bargaining structure that focuses on local bargaining, unions are unable to standardize conditions across firms. As a result, competitive pressures have increased diversity in employment practices and outcomes: greater workplace flexibility, increased individual differences in work and rewards, and increased income inequality (Katz and Darbishire 2000). Moreover, the voluntaristic lack of legal standards on union representation has allowed—because of their economic leverage—the Japanese auto plants in Britain to concede union recognition on the condition that broad managerial prerogatives remain in management's unilateral control. Wages and terms and conditions of employment are established not through bargaining but through a joint employee-management company council in which the union has no formal role, strikes are not allowed, and the company retains final decision-making authority. Katz and Darbishire (2000, 97) label this "quasi-nonunionism" and note that it would be illegal in both the United States and Germany. But voluntarism allows any arrangement that is mutually acceptable, where "acceptable" is determined only by bargaining power.

Although illegal in the United States and Germany, this quasi-nonunionism is probably legal in New Zealand after passage of the Employment Contracts Act (ECA) in 1991. The ECA is essentially a common-law-based industrial relations system (Dannin 1997). Employers and employees can agree to either individual or collective employment contracts, and unions are free to negotiate collective contracts if they have explicit authorization from each worker and if the employer wants to bargain. But in a voluntaristic spirit, the law does not compel bargaining of any type. Between 1991 and 1994, union membership declined from 600,000 to 376,000 (Dannin 1997). In 1991, an advertisement in Australia touted "Right now there are many good reasons to consider relocating your manufacturing base in New Zealand. The recent Employment Contract Act abolishes industrial awards, leaving employers free to negotiate terms of employment for a labour cost saving of up to 25%" (as quoted in Dannin 1997, 175).

The struggle with balancing efficiency, equity, and voice within a voluntaristic industrial relations system is clear. As discussed in chapter 5, when employers and employees are economic and legal equals, efficiency, equity, and a narrow conception of voice might be balanced. This is a utilitarian perspective on industrial relations. Voluntarism is also consistent with a libertarian method of balancing property rights with labor rights—as long as outcomes are produced by free interaction without coercion, the results are, by definition, balanced and just.[16] In frameworks beside utilitarianism and libertarianism, the balance between efficiency, equity, and voice depends on the vagaries of markets and public policies. When labor markets are tight, as in Britain in the 1960s, labor in a voluntaristic system has sufficient power to compel a higher standard of equity and voice ("strong voluntarism" in figure 7.1). But this leads to concerns with efficiency, as illustrated by the reform agenda of the Conservative British government targeting union power as a perceived roadblock to efficiency and competitiveness (Towers 1997). When labor markets are loose, as in Britain and New Zealand in the 1980s and 1990s, the evidence suggests that employers' leverage translates, as expected, into the domination of efficiency over equity and voice, as illustrated by the quasi-nonunionism at the Japanese auto plants in Britain ("weak voluntarism" in figure 7.1).

Comparative Analyses and U.S. Reform Proposals

Efficiency, equity, and voice and the geometry of the employment relationship provide a useful framework for comparative industrial relations analyses— "the geometry of comparative industrial relations." As shown in figure 7.1, the components of national industrial relations systems embody trade-offs between the three goals of the employment relationship and, therefore, occupy different locations in the geometry of the employment relationship. In figure 7.1, social partnership arrangements are at the middle of the triangle because voice is provided for all workers on both economic and social issues, which in turn raises the visibility of equity concerns as well. Efficiency is also served through macroeconomic stability. An important caveat, however, is that these dimensions are fulfilled by social partnerships only at a macro or national level. Workplace-level voice and efficiency must be sought elsewhere. In contrast, codetermination and enterprise unionism also provide voice and efficiency, but equity is not as well served because of the lack of power to establish minimum labor standards. In figure 7.1, codetermination is above enterprise unionism in the voice dimension because of greater coverage and legal support. Sectoral bargaining and centralized awards are effective in establishing minimum standards, but because of their centralized nature, workplace-level efficiency is not aided. Sectoral bargaining is stronger than centralized awards in the voice dimension because agreements are negotiated rather than imposed. These two systems are also rated above the New Deal industrial relations system because of high coverage rates, but one could also argue that for those who are covered, U.S. patterns of collective bargaining provide better employee voice because negotiations are more decentralized and less removed from the rank and file. The current U.S. system can also better provide equity than a system of codetermination or enterprise unionism, but at the expense of efficiency and voice.

Three additional points are important. One, the features discussed in this chapter and mapped in figure 7.1 are *elements* of industrial relations systems, not an entire system. Social partnerships are combined with voluntarism in Ireland and codetermination in Austria. Many other European systems involve both sectoral bargaining and codetermination. The Japanese industrial relations system is dominated by enterprise unionism, but it also includes pay bargaining via *shunto*. Each country's system can therefore also be mapped in figure 7.1 as some function of the location of its components. Two, that the relative locations of various elements in figure 7.1 are subject to debate reinforces the utility of the framework for analysis. And three, the geometry of comparative industrial relations can also be used to consider proposals for reforming industrial relations systems.

Comparative industrial relations is, of course, important in its own right to increase our understanding of industrial relations, but comparative analyses are also used to generate reform proposal for the United States (and elsewhere). Such proposals implicitly reflect dissatisfaction with the lack of current balance between efficiency, equity, and voice. In other words, U.S. reform proposals stem from discontent over the location of the New Deal industrial relations system in the geometry of the employment relationship, and each proposal seeks to move the U.S. system elsewhere within figure 7.1. One major reform proposal for U.S. industrial relations based on comparative research is Weiler's (1990) employee participation committees. Explicitly modeled after German works councils, this proposal calls for mandated committees in every workplace above a minimum size. The committees would be elected by the employees to represent all workers. Management would be required to "inform and consult with" the committee on issues pertaining to terms and conditions of employment as well as workforce adjustments including layoffs, plant closings, and technological change (Weiler 1990, 285). The committee would also be responsible for implementing U.S. employment laws regarding workplace safety, equal opportunity, and wrongful dismissal. For unionized employees, local union officials could serve as their committee representatives. In contrast to the German model, Weiler (1990) would grant U.S. employee participation committees the right to strike.

Freeman and Rogers (1993) similarly propose the addition of employee participation committees to the U.S. system of industrial relations. The form and function of these committees parallel Weiler's (1990) proposal, but Freeman and Rogers (1993) would not mandate committees (at least not initially) but rather seek to encourage their formation through tax incentives and also would only allow employee-initiated formation after a significant demonstration of support through a card-check procedure. Adams (1995) advocates the adoption of mandatory works councils with codetermination rights over safety and health, technological change, and training. Summers (1993) proposes a modification to the National Labor Relations Act's section 8(a)(2) ban on company-dominated labor organizations, and his proposal is also explicitly based on the German works councils model. In particular, employers would be allowed to establish a representation plan only if it can be modified by the employees; it can be discontinued only by the employees; representatives are elected and protected against discrimination and discharge; and employers must "confer with the employee representatives on all matters which substantially affect the employees' working lives" (Summers 1993, 143). Employers would not be able to limit the subjects, but would only have an obligation to confer or consult, not to bargain.[17]

The proposals that seek to import modified forms of codetermination into U.S. industrial relations are an effort to augment the New Deal industrial relations system to improve both efficiency and employee voice. In other words, these proposals seek to move the U.S. system more toward codetermination in figure 7.1. In contrast, Harper (2001) is critical of these works council-type proposals. Instead, his reform framework is partly based on the bargaining power generated by sectoral bargaining and seeks to develop a strong labor movement rather than workplace representation. The difference between Harper's (2001) proposal and the works council-type proposals is that while the latter are in pursuit of efficiency and voice, the former emphasizes equity: "The problem is that American workers have lost power—power to extract a larger share of the returns of American enterprise and power to protect individual employees from arbitrary, unjust or discriminatory treatment" (104). Harper's (2001) proposal is more concerned with moving the New Deal industrial relations system toward sectoral bargaining than toward codetermination.

Japanese enterprise unionism has also motivated U.S. reform proposals.[18] For example, Gifford (1997) advocates the enterprise focus of Japanese unions and wage-setting policies as a model for the United States to follow. The emphasis here is on moving the New Deal system toward improved efficiency: "Increased identification between workers and their enterprises" causes "enhanced productivity and responsiveness to changes in market conditions, thus maintaining scale economies, sustaining profits, employment, and progress down learning curves" (155). Oft-heard critiques of U.S. industrial relations as being overly adversarial frequently point to the Japanese model of cooperative labor relations. The underlying, if unstated, basis for such critiques is a desire to improve economic efficiency.

Comparative analyses should be an important component of studying the employment relationship. Explicit recognition of efficiency, equity, and voice fosters the understanding not only of the elements of comparative industrial relations systems but also of diverse reform proposals, which are often rooted in comparative research. Moreover, the geometry of the employment relationship provides a unifying framework for analyzing the extent to which elements of comparative industrial relations systems contribute to a balancing of efficiency, equity, and voice. This analysis reveals the difficulty of industrial relations reform—the common features of industrial relations systems are often biased toward one or two of the employment relationship objectives. To construct a system that balances efficiency, equity, and voice most likely requires multiple, complementary components.

8 Alternatives to Job Control Unionism

THE PRIMARY MECHANISM of collective employee voice in many countries is a labor union. The dominant philosophy of U.S. unions is business unionism, which fully embraces capitalism and the need for employers to make a profit (Hoxie 1917).[1] In the context of either occupation-focused craft unions or industry-focused industrial unions, unions emphasize collective bargaining to win a fair share of the profits and decent working conditions. In the New Deal industrial relations system, a business unionism philosophy in an environment of mass manufacturing and corporate insistence on maintaining the right to manage has resulted in a dominant paradigm of job control unionism (Kochan, Katz, and McKersie 1986) or workplace contractualism (Brody 1993). Detailed contracts, enforced by formal grievance procedures, tie employee rights to narrowly defined jobs with predictable compensation and seniority-based procedures. The New Deal industrial relations system is under fire from all angles, and so too are business unionism and job control unionism. Though its roots lie in management-driven work systems, job control unionism is criticized for its workplace inflexibility (Heckscher 1988) and removal of employee decision making in business and work issues (Bluestone and Bluestone 1992; Golden and Ruttenberg 1942). Business unionism more generally is criticized for its narrow focus on servicing current members and for stifling rank-and-file participation in union decision making (Tillman and Cummings 1999). Hyman (2001) further argues that purely market-focused business unionism is futile because of the inherently political nature of market regulation, even under common law, and the need to pursue nonmarket strategies when labor markets favor employers rather than employees. Strategies for revitalizing the U.S. labor movement therefore abound.[2]

Within the workplace focus of business unionism, one alternative to job control unionism is what I label "employee empowerment unionism." Rather than negotiating restrictive job control provisions that determine outcomes, unions can negotiate frameworks of procedures in which workers are then empowered to determine their own outcomes. This is consistent with an organizing rather than servicing model of business unionism. Greater employee empowerment can also be interpreted as a rejection of the bureaucratic tradition of industrial pluralism (Stone 1981) in favor of an empowered vision of workplace pluralism.[3] On a broader level, the major alternative to business unionism is social unionism, which is frequently found outside of the United States. In its most general form, social unionism replaces a singular focus on collective bargaining of workplace issues with a broader political and social agenda. Many conceptions of social unionism also include active grassroots participation. In this social movement unionism, unions are part of a broader social movement of community, social, and political activist groups, and the emphasis is on social mobilization. Radical versions of social unionism are oppositional and seek to replace capitalism with worker control. This chapter analyzes business unionism, job control unionism, and the alternatives of employee empowerment unionism and social unionism in the context of balancing efficiency, equity, and voice.

Job Control Unionism

Job control unionism consists of very detailed and legalistic union contracts, enforced by a quasi-judicial grievance procedure, that tie employee rights to very narrowly defined jobs while removing labor from decision making (Katz 1985; Kochan, Katz, and McKersie 1986).[4] This system represents a negotiated compromise between employers' property rights and labor's interest in employee rights. On the management side, exclusive property rights allow companies to unilaterally structure work, and before the 1980s, employers chose Taylorist or Fordist production systems involving very detailed job classifications. Moreover, employers are adamant about maintaining their property rights authority over what they consider managerial prerogatives—discipline, production, scheduling, marketing, pricing, investment, and other managerial functions—and in limiting union involvement as much as possible (Harris 1982).

Unions embraced a strong business unionism philosophy and a desire to replace the abuses of managerial subjectivity and favoritism (Brody 1993; Gersuny and Kaufman 1985). Faced with these goals and the constraints of managerial-driven work systems, starting in the 1930s unions pursued employee rights by winning seniority systems, grievance procedures, and predictable wage increases that cemented the importance of job rights.[5] Within the context of scientific management and business unionism, job control unionism represents a compromise between management's insistence on its right to manage and labor's goal of objectivity—employment conditions are determined by seniority and job classifications, employment disputes are resolved consistent with standards of justice. But the "encroachment" (in management terms) of labor is limited to terms and conditions of employment. Job control unionism further served the mass manufacturing need for stable and predictable production (Heckscher 1988), union leaders' needs for countering managerial authority without needing to resort to wildcat strikes and risking their own leadership positions (Lichtenstein 1993), and the goals of industrial pluralist reformers who sought industrial justice and efficiency through the peaceful, quasi-legal application of workplace rules and contracts (Atleson 1993; Stone 1981). In other words, job control unionism reflects a tension between property rights and labor rights that occurred in a specific environmental context. Any expansion of employee involvement was viewed by management as an infringement on property rights and efficiency; any weakening of seniority systems, job rights, and steady wage and benefit improvements was viewed by labor as undermining labor rights.

The problem with job control unionism is well-known: although it fit with the immediate postwar environment, the environment has changed (Heckscher 1988)—though the task still remains to balance property rights and labor rights. By the 1970s, the U.S. economy was "the mass-production economy in crisis": supply shocks such as the oil crises launched inflationary episodes, which triggered a demand crisis that ended the era of mass markets for standardized products (Piore and Sabel 1984, chap. 7). Global competition, deregulation, and slow productivity growth further erased monopoly profits for U.S. business (Bluestone and Bluestone 1992). For unionized establishments, these pressures were exacerbated by the rise of a large domestic nonunion sector (Kochan, Katz, and McKersie 1986). Starting in the 1980s, companies responded by trying to cut costs, improve quality and innovation, and move toward flexible specialization and various forms of employee involvement.

In fact, the goal of flexibility is ubiquitous in discussions of contemporary business, employment, and public policies—employment flexibility, wage flexibility, functional flexibility, and procedural flexibility (Ozaki 1999; Wailes and Lansbury 1999).[6] Employment flexibility is promoted to allow business to be able to adjust to quickly changing levels of demand for products (Ozaki 1999). Wage flexibility as it pertains to the ability to make downward wage adjustments—or the willingness of employees to make concessions—is advocated on the same basis. Wage flexibility in terms of pay for performance, profit sharing, and other forms of incentive pay is an important component of human resource management strategies for motivating workers (Fossum and McCall 1997). Functional and procedural flexibility are imperative to be able to react quickly to changing market opportunities and embrace emerging forms of technology and work organization in a world of flexible specialization (Piore and Sabel 1984) as a nimble organization (Connor 1998).

In contrast, job control unionism is the antithesis of these four forms of flexibility.[7] Consequently, since the 1980s the major parameters of job control unionism have been attacked as obsolete (Bluestone and Bluestone 1992;

Heckscher 1988; Katz 1985).[8] Restrictive work rules and detailed, lengthy, and legalistic union contracts (only renegotiated every few years) inhibit employment, functional, and procedural flexibility. Seniority-based procedures make it difficult to switch workers around on the basis of skills. Extensive bumping rights make frequent changes in deploying labor very cumbersome. Continued reliance on a legalistic interpretation of the law of the shop lengthens adjustment times and prevents innovation. Detailed job classification systems also prevent functional flexibility. Moreover, sharp divisions between labor, which provides the brawn, and management, which provides the brains, are breaking down. Standardized wages tied to jobs that are independent of both individual productivity and company ability to pay are inimical to wage flexibility. And job control unionism's limitation of employee voice to the bargaining table deprives both companies and workers of the benefits of increased employee involvement in workplace decision making (Golden and Ruttenberg 1942).

The mismatch between employers' visions of flexibility and traditional job control unionism is clear. The obsolescence of job control unionism is compounded by the breakdown in internal labor markets and stable lifetime career patterns (Cappelli 1999; K. Stone 2001). Job control unionism's emphasis on advancing through a firm's internal labor market based on seniority is useless for temporary workers and provides limited benefits to the increasing number of regular employees who are expected to be more mobile, both within and across firms, during their careers. Contingent and mobile workers are also not well served by fringe benefits such as health insurance and pensions that are traditionally tied to a specific employer. And a traditional focus on seniority rather than skills fails to provide training and other developmental opportunities that appear increasingly necessary in the employment relationship of the twenty-first century.

Even labor advocates—who are frequently critical and skeptical of employer flexibility initiatives because of their use as management tools for weakening labor and increasing work effort—are critical of the servicing mindset that has resulted from the system of job control unionism. The servicing model of representation derives its name from the fact that union members are serviced by shop stewards and union leaders (Banks and Metzgar 1989). Union staff negotiate contracts and handle grievances; consistent with job control unionism, there is little scope for an employee's participation in his or her representation. Problems are solved *for* the workers, not *by* the workers. The foil to the servicing model is the organizing model in which active rank-and-file members serve as internal organizers to create strong, dynamic unions. Moving away from a servicing model provides the opportunity for reconceptualizing unions as institutions of empowerment and mobilization (Fletcher and Hurd 1998; Nissen 1997; Tillman and Cummings 1999).

Because of the close connections between job control unionism, business unionism, and the servicing model, rejection of any of the three in favor of some form of social unionism is common. It is important, however, to clearly distinguish between the soul and scope of employee representation. The servicing and organizing models represent different *souls* of representation—the focal point of how representation is delivered or pursued is union officials in the servicing model, but is rank-and- file union members in the organizing model. In contrast, business unionism and social unionism differ in the *scope* of representation—whether representation is concentrated in the workplace or in the broader social arena. Job control unionism is a major example of a union leader soul of representation (servicing model) in the context of a business unionism (or workplace) scope. Traditional U.S. craft unionism, in which business agents handle negotiations and grievances, and European works councils, in which council members handle representation, are also examples of the servicing model with a workplace focus. As shown in table 8.1, it is possible to reject the servicing model while maintaining a workplace scope—this is what I label "employee empowerment unionism." It is also possible to have social unionism with minimal rank-and-file participation, as in the servicing model—European social partnerships are an example. Debates over job control unionism, business unionism, and the servicing model are important for both understanding and improving labor unions, but care should be taken to distinguish between the soul and scope of employee representation.

In sum, as the environment changes—as systems of work organization shift from scientific management to flexible specialization and, to a lesser extent, employee involvement, as stable internal labor markets break down, and as the desirability of passive methods of employee representation wanes—job control unionism, and perhaps business unionism more generally, becomes an anachronism that poorly serves employees, firms, and society. On this account, there is widespread agreement. There is less agreement on a replacement model, or models, of unionism for the twenty-first century. Two broad alternatives are employee empowerment unionism and social unionism.

Table 8.1 The Soul and Scope of Independent Employee Representation

	Scope of Representation	
Soul of Representation	Workplace (business unionism)	Social Arena (social unionism)
Union officials (passive servicing model)	Job control unionism, traditional craft unionism, works councils	European social partnerships
Union members (active organizing model)	Employee empowerment unionism	Social movement unionism

Employee Empowerment Unionism

Employee empowerment unionism is a model of independent employee representation in which unions negotiate the parameters for future individual or group decision-making processes. In contrast to job control unionism's specification of outcomes, employee empowerment unionism specifies a framework and employees are empowered to pursue their own actions and outcomes within this framework.[9] This model of unionism is still business unionism—the scope is focused on representation in the workplace, rather than in the social arena, and gains are achieved through collective bargaining (recall table 8.1). But the soul of employee empowerment unionism is active rank-and-file participation consistent with the organizing model rather than the servicing model. Bargaining does not determine all work rules or outcomes. Rather, for some topics, collective bargaining establishes processes for individual employee empowerment that incorporate minimum standards and procedural safeguards. These last features are critical: the difference between employee empowerment unionism and a reliance on free markets or human resource management or Troy's (1999) individual representation is that the collective power of a union is used to establish processes in which employees are truly empowered by providing minimum standards, protection against reprisal, and other support as needed (such as legal expertise or training). At the same time, employee empowerment unionism supports Freeman and Rogers's (1999) finding that workers would like a combination of collective and individual voice.

The previous section described three trends underlying the obsolescence of job control unionism: a shift toward flexible forms of work organization (sometimes including employee involvement), increased employee mobility, and the declining attractiveness of the servicing model of union representation. Based on these three trends, I distinguish between two types of employee empowerment unionism. First, there is the *employee discretion* variant. This applies to workplaces with stable employees, flexible forms of work organization, and employee involvement. The high-performance work system at Saturn is a leading example. This form of representation can also exist in (more commonly found) workplaces with less extensive systems of high-performance work practices that include employee discretion in decision making.

Second, there is the *self-representation* variant. This version includes both traditional workplaces in which employees are looking for greater involvement in their own representation (rejecting the servicing model) and nontraditional workplaces, or boundaryless workplaces (K. Stone 2001), in which there is high employee mobility across workplaces or episodic employment patterns. Two examples of the former are professional baseball players and Harvard University clerical employees represented by the Harvard Union of Clerical and Technical Workers (HUCTW) in which individual employees are involved in self-representation over wages and grievances, respectively. An example of the latter is the below-the-line crafts occupations in the television and film industry represented by the International Alliance of Theatrical and Stage Employees (IATSE) who negotiate some of their own terms and conditions for their short-term spells of employment.

The employee discretion and self-representation forms of employee empowerment unionism stem from various factors—the use of high-performance work systems, unique individual skills, episodic employment patterns, and a desire to avoid a paternalistic, passive servicing model of representation—and can be applied to diverse settings and to various aspects of traditional union contracts. The extent to which companies have fully embraced high-performance work systems is questionable (Babson 1995), and it is important to emphasize that these work systems are only one possible application of employee empowerment unionism. And employee empowerment unionism does not require employee discretion in all aspects of work. The examples below pertain to different issues that can be opened up to employee empowerment (such as wages, work hours, grievances, or day-to-day decision making) while retaining the traditional determination of the remaining issues through collective bargaining. Yet the forms of employee empowerment unionism share the common feature of establishing the parameters for empowered employees to pursue their own actions and decision making within a system that includes minimum standards, procedural safeguards, and institutional support. The two variations of the employee empowerment model of unionism are summarized in table 8.2 and discussed in greater detail in the remainder of this section.

Employee Discretion Empowerment Unionism

The most extensive examples of the employee discretion variant of employment empowerment unionism are found in workplaces with high-perfor-

Table 8.2 Employee Empowerment Unionism

Variants	Examples
Employee Discretion	
Individual employees or teams are empowered to make business or employment decisions within a framework established through collective bargaining. Unions provide support and protection, but employees have significant day-to-day discretion and autonomy.	Saturn, Shell-Sarnia plant, Minneapolis nurses
Self-Representation	
Individual employees represent themselves in negotiations and/or dispute resolution over terms and conditions of employment within a framework established through collective bargaining. Unions provide minimum standards, support, and protection, but employees are actively involved in aspects of their own representation.	Unique skills: Major League Baseball players; Episodic employment: theatrical crafts workers (IATSE); Antipaternalism: Harvard clericals (HUCTW)

mance work systems and self-directed work teams. A frequently cited example is the Spring Hill, Tennessee, plant of the Saturn subsidiary of General Motors.[10] Saturn developed in the mid-1980s out of a joint General Motors-UAW benchmarking investigation of worldwide best auto manufacturing practices. The decision was made to create a new partnership that embraced team-based production and decision making that would be comanaged by the company and the union. A 1985 memorandum of agreement between General Motors and the UAW specified the principles of the partnership and the team-based decision-making structure. A new factory was built in Spring Hill, Tennessee, and production started in 1990.

The roughly seven hundred self-directed work teams of six to fifteen employees are the building blocks of the organization. In addition to being responsible for their part of the production process, the teams are empowered to make decisions regarding work pace, planning and scheduling, vacation approvals, and training, and they are responsible for safety and health, inventory, quality and scrap control, repair, maintenance, and other issues. Above the teams are a series of joint labor-management "decision rings"—committees that meet weekly to share information, wrestle with problem solving, and make higher-level decisions. Employees are involved not only in day-to-day production decisions but have been a part of far-ranging decisions regarding product design, marketing, and supplier selection. As an example of the extent of partnership and comanagement, teams are grouped into modules of approximately one hundred employees and each module is comanaged by one union leader and one manager. These two partners work together on a daily basis comanaging the modules. This partnership arrangement has also been extended to staff functions such as engineering, quality, marketing, training, and organizational development.

Saturn is not a typical management-run high-performance work system; it is comanaged by the UAW and Saturn management, and individual employees have the backing of the UAW. Employees are empowered as part of their work teams to make numerous decisions on a daily basis, but within a framework that was negotiated between the UAW and General Motors, and later Saturn. As such, protections are built into the structure, and the union can ensure that employees receive support and due process. Although low-level, informal problem solving is encouraged, formal grievances are also allowed. The union can also make sure that employee interests are represented when making changes, such as when new absenteeism policy guidelines were developed in 1994. The union, of course, also has the right to strike during contract negotiations. In 1998, the membership authorized a strike if contract negotiations failed to resolve concerns with decision making and with production and quality bonuses. Although a strike was averted, this source of collective power independent from the company is a critical underpinning of the employee empowerment unionism model and distinguishes the employee discretion form of this model from managerial-controlled high-performance work systems.

Extensive levels of employee empowerment as well as union comanagement of business operations admittedly present numerous challenges for the local union (Rubinstein 2001; Rubinstein and Kochan 2001). A traditional servicing model of union representation clashes sharply with the Saturn model of employee discretion. The local union consequently created a number of participatory structures such as town hall meetings, rap sessions, and a twice-a-month congress meeting involving 450 union leaders. These are supplemented by an extensive annual membership survey. Membership referendums on specific policy issues have also been used. Nevertheless, a conflict persists between the union's dual functions of comanagement and representation. This is reflected, for example, in debates over whether the module leaders (the union half of the partnership arrangement) should be jointly appointed, consistent with comanagement and consensus, or elected by the membership, consistent with representation and a traditional shop steward system. Managing these tensions—which can also be conceptualized as individual discretion versus collective power and standards—is an ongoing task for the local union at Saturn, and it is a critical issue for the employee discretion variant of employment empowerment unionism.

Although Saturn is probably the most extensive U.S. example of the employee discretion variant of employment empowerment unionism, other examples exist. Before Saturn, a chemical plant in Sarnia, Ontario, was designed jointly by Shell Canada and the Energy and Chemical Workers Union, using sociotechnical, team-based work organization principles (Rankin 1990).[11] Six self-directed work teams are empowered to make business and employment decisions and, in fact, run the entire plant, within the parameters of a framework negotiated by Shell and the local union.[12] The plant is governed by three negotiated agreements: a collective bargaining agreement, a "Good Works Practices" handbook, and a philosophy statement. The philosophy statement defines the basic principles of the plant, such as extensive communication, commitment, employee discretion, and collaborative problem solving. The collective bargaining agreement, which is less than twenty pages long, outlines basic issues, such as shift premiums and the number of vacation days. Administration of these items, however, is not pursued through the contract, as is typical in job control unionism, but is rather handled through the Good Works Practices handbook. This handbook contains some explicit rules, but primarily provides general guidelines for the teams to follow when making decisions. Changes are jointly handled by labor and management, but because administrative issues, which often involve integrative rather than distributive conflict, are not in the collective bargaining agreement, they can be addressed without reopening the agreement and, therefore, can be handled in a more flexible and participative manner.

The three documents provide the framework within which employees are empowered to make decisions pertaining to plant operations and employment issues. Within these parameters, the teams assign work, select new team members, handle overtime, and approve vacations. Because the framework is subject to negotiations rather than unilateral management control, it contains minimum entitlements and protections. The resolution of grievances is similar. Employees are encouraged to solve their own problems, so grievances are first tackled by the relevant team and then, if unsuccessful, by the joint Team Norm Review Board. In these two steps, employees generally handle their own cases—it is not simply passed to a steward for servicing. At the same time, the process provides procedural safeguards, including due process, and the final step is arbitration.

Employee empowerment unionism can also be found in Sweden. The traditional goal of the Swedish labor movement was a solidaristic wage policy that consisted of equal pay for equal work across companies (so that company ability to pay is unimportant) and wage compression within establishments. Managerial pressures for decentralization and flexibility, however, have greatly strained this centralized system. As Swedish firms have pushed for more high-performance work practices, the Swedish labor movement has advocated a solidaristic work policy.[13] In broad terms, the goal of the solidaristic work policy is to ensure that workers are truly empowered in, and benefit from, high-performance work practices. This includes self-directed work teams in which each team, according to the dominant blue-collar union federation Landsorganisation i Sverige (LO), "has the right to decide on everything related to the internal work of the group" and is also "the best source on what volumes can be produced, when the goods can be produced and the resources required by production" (as translated and quoted in Mahon 1991, 308). The solidaristic work policy also calls for training, job development, and wages tied to skills and responsibilities (Sandberg 1994). In short, the Swedish labor movement's solidaristic work policy advocates employee empowerment within a negotiated framework that includes union representation.[14]

Last, the employee discretion variant of employee empowerment unionism is not limited to workplaces with high performance work systems. During contract negotiations for nine thousand nurses represented by the Minnesota Nurses Association at thirteen hospitals in the Minneapolis–St. Paul metropolitan area in 2001, one of the critical issues was staffing shortages. Six of the hospitals, three of them after a twenty-three–day strike, agreed to a contractual provision that allowed nurses to temporarily close units to new patient admissions if they are understaffed and cannot handle any additional patients. Within a framework negotiated through collective bargaining—that provides nurses with certain rights and protections—individual employees are empowered with the discretion to make business decisions. This is a limited example of employee empowerment unionism because it is confined to a single issue, but it illustrates the possibilities of moving away from a narrow model of job control unionism.[15]

Self-Representation Empowerment Unionism

The second variant of employee empowerment unionism is self-representation. Although the employee discretion model arises from the context of employee involvement in business decision making, the self-representation model stems from a desire to involve workers in their own representation regarding terms and conditions of employment. This desire, in turn, arises from various underlying factors. Workers in some occupations, especially those that emphasize unique individual skills, might want the opportunity to strike a better bargain for themselves, while also benefiting from union-negotiated minimum standards and procedural guidelines. Episodic employment might reinforce the desire for minimum standards and continuity of some benefits. Alternatively, a self-representation model might arise from a desire to move away from a passive servicing model of representation—*in any type of workplace.*

A visible example is the representation of professional baseball players by the Major League Baseball Players Association. In baseball, individual skills are fundamental to the employment relationship. There is a long tradition of individual negotiations between players and team owners to establish unique salaries and bonuses for each player. However, for one hundred years between the 1870s and 1970s, the owners employed a reserve system in which a player was owned by a single team until that team assigned the contract to another team. Owners, therefore, generally controlled salaries (Abrams 2000). The first union agreement in 1966 established a pension plan, and in 1968 a minimum salary of $10,000 and a grievance procedure were negotiated (Jennings 1997). Arbitration of salary disputes was added in 1973. Following an unsuccessful lawsuit, a grievance ended the reserve system in 1975 via an arbitrator's ruling that the standard player contract implied a one-year renewal, not an indefinite reserve system. In response, the players' union and owners negotiated a system of free agency in 1976 (Abrams 2000). These agreements provide the basis for the current system, which includes a minimum salary level, salary arbitration for players with between three and six years of service, and free agency—the ability to negotiate with any team—for players with at least six years of service. This is a system of self-representation: a framework established by collective bargaining delineates the procedures and minimum standards, in this case a minimum salary for all players, and within this framework individual players conduct their own negotiations/representation.

Although baseball players and other professional athletes may seem like a unique situation, this model of self-representation can be sensibly applied elsewhere. A similar structure of minimum standards and procedural safeguards for individual negotiations could be appropriate for college professors, doctors, and other professionals. Moreover, this type of structure is widely used in the entertainment industry. Collective bargaining agreements for the Screen Actors Guild, the American Federation of Television and Radio Artists, the Writers Guild of America, and the Directors Guild of America all specify minimum compensation levels, and individuals are free to negotiate higher levels on their own.[16] Lest one may think this model only applies to superstar markets, it must be added that this same model is also used by the International Alliance of Theatrical and Stage Employees for below-the-line craft employees in the television and film industry who handle cameras, sound, lighting, and other production aspects (K. Stone 2001).[17]

Through typical collective bargaining, IATSE negotiates Basic Agreements with various associations of producers, such as the Alliance of Motion Picture Television Producers or the Association of Independent Commercial Producers, and with production companies, such as Walt Disney or Twentieth Century Fox. The Basic Agreements are similar to typical union contracts and include union recognition and security clauses, benefits, standards for rest and meal periods, overtime provisions, no-strike clauses, and a grievance procedure. The critical differences between these Basic Agreements and a typical U.S. union contract, however, are that there are no just cause provisions and the wage rates are minimums. Individual IATSE members are explicitly allowed to negotiate higher rates—often referred to as "better conditions"—on their own. In other words, "IATSE's collective bargaining agreement is simply an umbrella that contains and defines the parameters of embedded individual bargains" (K. Stone 2001, 635). The embedded bargaining fits well with IATSE's membership because of their episodic employment patterns. Specific jobs, such as making a commercial or a movie, only last a few days or months, so the self-representation aspect provides producers and employees the opportunity to tailor wages and hours for each project. At the same time, the umbrella collective bargaining agreement provides a set of minimum standards and also a continuity of benefits.

These examples from professional sports and entertainment primarily involve self-representation for compensation and hours and are rooted in a combination of unique individual skills and episodic employment patterns. But the most widely applicable rationale for developing features of a self-representation model is to move away from the passive servicing model of representation—*in any workplace*. The experience of clerical and technical workers at Harvard University is instructive (Eaton 1996; Hoerr 1997). After unsuccessful grassroots organizing drives in the 1970s, the UAW became active in trying to organize Harvard University's clerical and technical workers.[18] The traditional UAW tactics, such as using mass leafleting to sell the need for protection from an abusive employer, clashed with the grassroots organizers' strategy of developing one-on-one relationships with the largely female workforce. This grassroots strategy was consistent with, and inspired by, Gilligan's (1982) feminine voice that underlies the ethics of care described in chapter 4. In other words, the local Harvard organizers rejected the paternalistic servicing model of representation in favor of an empowering organizing model of representation. The local organizers ultimately split from the UAW and formed the independent Harvard Union of Clerical and Technical Workers. In 1988, the HUCTW was victorious and won representation rights.[19]

In the HUCTW's own words, "We organized our Union around a single idea: that every employee should have the opportunity to participate in making the decisions that affect her or his working life" (as quoted in Eaton 1996, 291). The collective bargaining agreement and underlying model of representation reflects this philosophy (Eaton 1996; Hoerr 1997). In contrast to traditional negotiations, sixty-five employees served on various bargaining committees. The resulting contract replaces the traditional grievance procedure with a decentralized problem-solving system. Although the last step of this system is traditional arbitration, the initial steps are structured to foster the worker's involvement in resolving their own issue. There is no management rights clause or seniority protections; rather, joint councils (labor-management committees) were established for each area of the university. The main intent of the problem-solving system and the joint councils is to allow workers to represent themselves—within a framework of support and protection by the union, as needed. This is another example of a self-representation model of employee empowerment unionism—employees are empowered not to negotiate their own wages, as in the sports and entertainment industries, but to solve their own problems and to be more involved in the bargaining process and union governance.

In sum, the nature of employee empowerment unionism varies. It might involve employee discretion in business and employment decisions, or it might involve self-representation. Individuals with unique skills might prefer self-representation for compensation, whereas others might benefit from self-representation in problem solving or grievance resolution. Skill-based pay is another example of self-representation: labor and management negotiate the parameters of the system and workers are empowered to be responsible for upgrading their skills and reaping the rewards. But all of these systems share the essential element of employee empowerment over decision making within a framework negotiated and supported by an independent labor union. Contemporary trends toward increased use of high-performance work systems, episodic employment patterns, and an organizing rather than servicing model of representation (in any type of workplace) magnify the significance of this employee empowerment unionism model.

Employee empowerment unionism is also consistent with the capabilities approach within the literatures on human rights, ethics, and human welfare. To understand the capabilities approach, consider the measurement of human welfare and justice. Standard economic theory equates welfare to preference satisfaction, so justice is pursued by individual utility maximization (Hausman and McPherson 1996). A common critique is that this utilitarian perspective ignores distributive justice—Rawls (1971), for example, argues that justice depends on primary goods such as income, education, liberty, and other means for a good life. Institutions should therefore promote the realization of primary goods. Sen (1980, 1993) and Nussbaum (2000), however, argue that welfare or well-being should be measured as capabilities—"a person being able to do certain things" (Sen 1980, 218). Rather than limiting concern to external means, such as income, well-being must also account for individual abilities (Hausman and McPherson 1996). As such, institutions must promote capabilities (Nusssbaum 2000).[20] These arguments can be applied to debates over the nature of unionism. The neoclassical economics emphasis on maximizing preference satisfaction supports employment relationships governed by free markets, while the distributive justice critique leads to an important role for unions. However, in very broad terms, job control unionism is a focus on primary goods in the employment relationship: wages, job rights, due process, and other external means for achieving basic satisfactions in the workplace. An emphasis on primary goods, as in job control unionism, ignores internal means (capabilities). As applied to the workplace, the Sen-Nussbaum capabilities approach implies that unions and other workplace institutions should develop individual capabilities. Employee empowerment unionism is consistent with this standard.[21]

Social Unionism

Social unionism broadens the narrow workplace focus of business unionism to include a larger social and political agenda. Labor's influence comes less from strong bargaining power in the workplace and more from being an active participant in a country's political and social arenas. Social unionism is therefore a form of representation with a broader scope than the workplace focus of business unionism. Like business unionism, however, the soul of social unionism can be passive rank-and-file participation—consistent with a servicing model of representation—or active participation—consistent with an organizing model of representation (see table 8.1). The European social partnership arrangements described in the previous chapter in which national, peak-level organizations negotiate agreements on broad social and economic issues are examples of social unionism with passive rank-and-file participation. Active lobbying by U.S. unions for minimum wage increases, civil rights legislation, or other broad reforms without grassroots participation is another example.

In contrast, social *movement* unionism embraces labor unions as part of a broader social movement of community, social, and political activist groups that relies on active grassroots participation and mobilization. Advocates of a greater social unionism orientation for the U.S. labor movement are generally reacting against the passive servicing model and focus on social unionism with widespread rank-and-file participation—social movement unionism.[22] Social movement unionism in the United States is often advocated as a basis for revitalizing the labor movement by providing the means to increase organizing, especially among traditionally overlooked groups such as immigrant workers, and to resist management demands for concessions (Tillman and Cummings 1999).

With respect to organizing immigrant workers, the most prominent U.S. example is the Service Employees International Union's (SEIU) Justice for Janitors Campaign in Los Angeles (Waldinger et al. 1998), Washington, D.C. (Williams 1999), and other cities. Organizing janitors in the building services industry is challenging because of the high fraction of immigrant workers, who bring language barriers and fears of reprisal. Moreover, janitorial services are provided to commercial buildings by cleaning service contractors, not the building owners, which introduces complexities and restrictions in terms of labor law. To be successful, the campaign has to organize the entire building service industry in a city because of the ease of switching to nonunion contractors. Consequently, the Justice for Janitors campaigns have been aggressive, public, and broad-based. To pressure building owners outside of the traditional National Labor Relations Board election procedures, these campaigns have included aggressive public demonstrations to bring widespread attention to the situation. This publicity is complemented by intense efforts to form community and political alliances and to create grassroots participation by the janitors. The efforts transform the campaign into a form of social movement unionism by making justice for janitors a community issue, not just a workplace or employee issue. In Washington, for example, low pay for janitors was tied into the larger issue of tax breaks for the real estate industry and the decline in public education and other services resulting from the city's financial crisis. Civil rights, immigrant rights, and sexual harassment were other issues raised during the campaign that resonate with the broader community.

Social issues and linkages with other groups have also been emphasized in other instances. Cesar Chavez and the United Farm Workers in the 1960s famously linked organizing of California field workers with religious groups and community activists through nationwide grape and lettuce boycotts, thereby creating a social movement ("La Causa") (Ferriss and Sandoval 1997). As part of an effort to organize the Los Angeles garment industry, the Coalition of Garment Workers was formed in the late 1990s to provide legal services and education. It includes not only the local garment workers union but immigrant rights and legal aid groups (Bonacich 2000). Organizing concession workers at O'Hare airport in Chicago was facilitated by alliances with the Chicago Catholic archdiocese and the Interfaith Committee on Worker Issues (Peters and Merrill 1998). The Harvard Union of Clerical and Technical Workers grew out of the ideas of the women's movement in the 1970s (Hoerr 1997).

U.S. social movement unionism to fight concessions and erosion in working conditions is similarly rooted in a combination of broader alliances and grassroots rank-and-file participation (Moody 1988). The success of the Teamsters' strike against UPS in 1997 is widely credited to the mobilization of public support as well of the rank and file for the national, not UPS-specific, problem of part-time workers (Witt and Wilson 1999). In the Pittston coal strike by the United Mine Workers in 1989–90, civil rights tactics and broad-based community support and solidarity, especially in support of health insurance, led to mass demonstrations and ultimately a victory by the union. Though not successful, the Hormel strike in Minnesota in 1985–86 is notable for the grassroots, not national union leadership, support across the country among other union members (Rachleff 1993). The call for social movement unionism to increase labor's militancy and power is also closely intertwined with questions of internal union democracy. The New Directions Movement within the UAW, for example, is pushing for democratic reforms within the UAW to complement its emphasis on militant workplace confrontation and international solidarity with workers in the same industry (Tillman 1999). The Teamsters for a Democratic Union similarly emphasizes increased decentralization of the Teamsters, greater grassroots participation in both union governance and workplace representation, and the development of networks with other community groups (Tillman 1999).

The emphasis on community is echoed in a recent proposal for citizen unionism (K. Stone 2001). Citizen unions have a geographical focus rather than the occupational focus of craft unions or the industry focus of industrial unions. They seek to organize all employees in a specific area and to use a combination of bargaining, public pressure (including both negative publicity and boycotts), and political power to ensure that all companies in a labor market are good employers and social citizens. With a geographical focus, unions can also provide portable benefits and other services such as training, child care, and legal assistance that help contingent workers and other frequent job changers. A union that includes all employees in a locality regardless of occupation or industry could also be a strong advocate for community programs: "By reconceptualizing workers as citizens of a locale who collectively have an interest in the health, education, well-being, and employability of the entire local population, narrow labor issues are transformed into issues of general concern" (K. Stone 2001, 644).

Rejection of business unionism in favor of the broader orientation of social unionism pervades European labor unions and labor movements. This includes both social democratic unionism and radical/oppositional unionism (Hyman 2001; Slomp 1996). Hyman (2001, 55) defines social democratic unionism as "a synthesis between pragmatic collective bargaining and a politics of state-directed social reform and economic management." In this model, unions pursue workplace-level representation as part of a larger social and political agenda. Collective bargaining, organizing, political activity, alliances with other advocacy groups, and education on social issues are used in pursuit of social justice and a broadly defined social wage (Godard 2000). Radical/oppositional unionism is a more militant version of social democratic unionism in which unions represent class interests in opposition to the capitalist class (Hyman 2001). Historically, this revolutionary form of unionism sought the overthrow of capitalism, but in the modern industrialized democracies this goal has largely moderated into social democratic goals of reform and social justice. But the issue of class continues to be an important component of labor unionism in numerous countries (Godard 2000; Hyman 2001). Depending on the extent of grassroots participation, forms of European social unionism range between the active and passive representational souls in table 8.1.

The French labor movement is illustrative of European social unionism. Unlike the traditional U.S. emphasis on business unionism, the French union federations have distinct political or ideological perspectives (Daley 1999;

Goetschy 1998). The Confédération générale du travail (CGT, General Confederation of Labor) traditionally had a radical, syndicalist orientation focused on class conflict and close alignment with the Communist Party.[23] The Force ouvrière (FO, Workers' Strength) split from the CGT and has informal links with the Socialist Party, though the strongest ideological commitment is anticommunism. The Confédération français des travailleurs chrétiens (CFTC, French Confederation of Christian Workers) embraces an anti-class struggle, pro-collective bargaining Catholic unionism, while its now-larger progeny, the Confédération français democratique du travail (CFDT, French Democratic Confederation of Labor), supported a more militant and socialist Catholic unionism when it broke away in the 1960s. The CFDT has advocated a more moderate focus on union adaptation to economic change and integration into the European Union in recent years.

In addition to ideological unions, workplace-level representation by unions is fragmented and weak (Daley 1999; Goetschy 1998). Although many workers are covered by sectoral collective bargaining agreements and works councils, less than 10 percent of the workforce belongs to unions. French unions are highly dependent on political activity, interactions with the government, and their ability to mobilize strikes and demonstrations against the government. Moreover, the radical/oppositional unions such as the CGT have not always supported collective bargaining, because signing a contract limits worker freedom and legitimizes capitalism (Hyman 2001). In short, political mobilization and political strikes—motivated by each union's ideological focus—have been as important, if not more important, than collective bargaining in French labor relations. In recent years, such actions have included protests against subminimum wages, changes in public sector pensions, and reductions in French social programs. The role of organized labor as more than a workplace voice is also underscored by union participation in the joint administration of social security, health insurance, and unemployment funds. In sum, social unionism in France is characterized by ideological unions, significant political activity, and periodic mobilization of the rank and file (and allied groups).

Beyond Job Control Unionism

Dissatisfaction with the U.S. tradition of job control unionism stems from both its passive soul of representation and its narrow workplace-focused scope. Separate consideration of the soul and scope of employee representation is analytically important, and the alternatives of employee empowerment unionism and social unionism address each of these dimensions, respectively. The complementarities between employee empowerment unionism and social movement unionism, however, should not be overlooked. As revealed by table 8.1, the commonality between these two models is active rank-and-file participation. U.S. social movement unionism that harnesses grassroots participation to organize new workers, especially women, immigrants, and other workers traditionally outside of the mainstream U.S. labor movement, must confront questions of workplace representation when organizing drives are successful. The Harvard Union of Clerical and Technical Workers was successful in establishing a framework of participation in both union affairs and grievance resolution consistent with both employee empowerment unionism in the workplace and social movement unionism outside of it. In contrast, the Justice for Janitors campaign was successful in organizing janitors in Los Angeles through active grassroots participation, but once organized, the soul of workplace representation reverted to a traditional servicing model. Newly organized members felt that they were locked out—sometimes literally—of participation in union governance (La Luz and Finn 1998). One dissident leader was quoted as saying, "We built this union. We want to be able to make the decisions. I want to improve the lot of the workers. We must be respected as much by the companies we work for as by the union we pay dues to" (as quoted in Williams 1999, 215).[24]

The comparative experiences of the U.S. and French labor movements further reveal the importance of both the soul and scope dimensions of employee representation. In France, the social and political orientation of the labor movement is associated with weak workplace-level representation. In the United States, the opposite is true: the business unionism focus of most labor unions yields weak social and political representation. Moreover, the lack of active grassroots participation in union activity in France, excepting the occasional demonstration, makes it difficult to develop stronger workplace-level representation. The U.S. servicing model, and its low levels of grassroots activity, similarly denies the U.S. labor movement the strong foundation needed to develop into vibrant social movement unionism.

Two central analytical questions emerge from this consideration of the soul and scope of employee representation: What determines the soul and scope of a labor movement? And what are the effects of different souls and scopes? The former is a longstanding question in industrial relations. For example, the Sturmthal-Scoville theory of the labor movement focuses on the interaction of political and social conditions with collaborating groups in shaping the initial form of the labor movement, followed by the influence of the labor market on the development of collective bargaining (Sturmthal 1966; Sturmthal and Scoville 1973; Scoville 1995). Environmental factors provide alternatives, but choice should not be overlooked. In the words of Hyman (2001, 169–70), "Union action is not simply determined externally but is also the outcome of internal discussion, debate and often conflict." The dual reliance on environment and choice is consistent with the framework developed earlier in chapters 3 and 4 for employment outcomes.

The geometry of the employment relationship provides a framework for analyzing the second question—how do different souls and scopes affect efficiency, equity, and voice. Figure 8.1 summarizes this approach. Job control unionism is biased toward equity: wages, benefits, just cause provisions, and

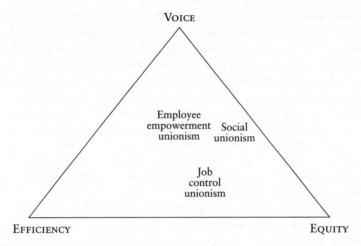

Figure 8.1 Alternative Union Strategies

protective work rules are all explicitly contained in a legally enforceable contract backed by a quasi-judicial grievance procedure. Seniority-based job rights provide a large degree of procedural justice. In contrast, efficiency and voice are less well served. Job control unionism is a barrier to many forms of flexibility and, therefore, impairs efficiency, while voice is bureaucratic with generally passive rank-and-file participation.[25] In other words, criticism of job control unionism stems from its failure to strike a desired balance between efficiency, equity, and voice.

In most forms of social unionism, efficiency is not a leading concern, and social unionism is generally biased toward equity and voice. Moreover, social movement unionism, with its emphasis on grassroots participation, contains a stronger employee voice component than social democratic or social partnership forms of social unionism, in which rank-and-file participation is more sporadic or passive. Equity and voice are achieved to a greater level than in job control unionism because of a broader focus on social issues that affect the entire working population. A social partnership arrangement can contribute to macroeconomic stability and therefore this form of social unionism may balance efficiency, equity, and voice at a macro level. In short, the geometry of the employment relationship is a useful framework for analyzing different forms of social unionism.

Although limited to unionized employees and workplace issues, employee empowerment unionism can balance efficiency, equity, and voice and be at the center of the geometry of the employment relationship (see figure 8.1). The negotiated processes for individual or team decision making and representation that are central to employee empowerment unionism provide greater flexibility and responsiveness to changing conditions, which can promote efficiency. Moreover, the employee discretion form is intimately related to high-performance work systems and is therefore consistent with the pursuit of employee involvement, efficiency, and quality. At the same time, because the processes for employee discretion or self-representation are negotiated, collective bargaining provides an equity component: minimum standards can be specified, procedural safeguards and protections can be incorporated, and institutional support can be supplied as needed to individual employees. This is what separates employee empowerment unionism from the free market and human resource management models of workplace governance. Last, employee voice in employee empowerment unionism is achieved both through collective bargaining and through individual decision making. Employee empowerment unionism balances the core objectives of the employment relationship—efficiency, equity, and voice.

A movement from job control unionism to forms of employee empowerment unionism can also be analyzed using the theories of the ethics of the employment relationship developed in chapter 4. Common, if oversimplified and inaccurate (Herman 1993; Korsgaard 1996), criticisms of Kantian ethics attack the emphasis on universal, unwavering, rational rules for ignoring considerations of virtues and relationships. Consequently, frustration with the perceived inflexibility and lack of human vitality of Kantian rules underlies, at least partially, the resurgence of the Aristotelian ethics of virtue tradition and the development of the ethics of care (for example, Gilligan 1982; Solomon 1992). This frustration parallels the tension between job control unionism and its alternatives, such as employee empowerment unionism. Seniority-based layoffs and promotions, tightly specified bumping rules, narrowly defined work rules, wage rates tied to jobs, and grievance procedures that rely on previous precedents are inflexible rules. Like the movement to seek alternatives to Kantian rules, alternatives to job control unionism are sought that incorporate greater levels of human discretion and an emphasis on interpersonal relationships.

The possibilities and pitfalls of alternatives to Kantian ethics, especially the ethics of virtue and care, can therefore help reveal the possibilities and pitfalls of alternatives to job control unionism. For example, the Harvard Union of Clerical and Technical Workers clearly emphasizes relationships. Consistent with the ethics of care (Gilligan 1982; Noddings 1984), the HUCTW does not represent employees through unwavering application of contractual rules but relies on representation that respects the specifics and interpersonal relationships of each situation. To foster healthy working relationships, the problem-solving procedure facilitates direct resolution of conflicts by the parties involved, especially individual employees and their supervisors. At the same time, in the ethics of care one needs to be vigilant against an emphasis on relationships that leads to favoritism or abuse. The HUCTW model of representation needs to guard against these same pitfalls.

In less philosophical terms, voice was defined in earlier chapters as something workers participate in. In fact, this is the distinction between equity and voice. Models of employee representation, and other ways of providing em-

ployee voice, must bear this definition in mind. The frustration with bureaucratic modes of voice are captured by this union representative in the early
1960s:

> When the men settled things on the floor . . . it was something they did them-
> selves. They directly participated in determining their working conditions. When
> things are settled legalistically, through the grievance procedure, it's something
> foreign. (Quoted in Strauss 1962, 90)[26]

The nature of unionism is often central to the provision of voice in the employment relationship, and union strategies must therefore pay particular attention to how employee voice is achieved. The intellectual framework
developed in this book—designing workplace governance mechanisms to balance the societal goals of efficiency, equity, and voice—provides the means for
analyzing and understanding alternative forms of unionism. These analyses
point to employee empowerment unionism as an important model for employee representation as the U.S. employment system seeks to move beyond
job control unionism.

9 Balancing the Global Workplace

ONE OF THE MOST IMPORTANT pressures on the employment relationship of the twenty-first century is globalization. Globalization is the increased international integration of countries and regions. It is useful to divide globalization into four components: international trade, foreign direct investment (FDI), international investment portfolios, and immigration (Scheve and Slaughter 2001). In other words, globalization arises from the cross-border flow of goods and services, multinational corporate capital investment, investment securities, and people. Although the current relative level of trade is roughly similar to the late nineteenth century, the current degree of international integration is a sharp departure from earlier in the postwar period, and the integration of international product and financial markets is also broader and deeper today than it was one hundred years ago (Bordo, Eichengreen, and Irwin 1999).[1]

Increased globalization is a significant change in the postwar employment environment. For a relatively high-skill, high-wage country such as the United States, increased integration of product markets puts particular pressure on lower-skilled workers as labor-intensive, low-skilled goods can be purchased from low-cost foreign competitors. Increased outward FDI has the same effect, and globalization is predicted to reduce demand for unskilled U.S. workers. A second feature has received less attention: increased integration, even with other high-skill, high-wage countries, reduces labor's bargaining power by making it easier to find alternative sources of labor (Rodrik 1997). This occurs because FDI makes domestic employees easier to replace by investing abroad, and trade makes it easier to replace domestic employees with outsourcing. This is often phrased as a concern with social dumping (Erickson and Kuruvila 1994)—the ability of a foreign competitor to unfairly sell at a lower price because of lower labor or environmental standards, such as no minimum wage floors, lack of safety regulations, or absence of pollution standards. Immigration of low-skilled workers further changes the employment environment. The increasing supply of low-skilled workers puts downward pressure on low-skilled wages (Borjas 1999) and creates challenges for union organizing (Milkman 2000).

Globalization is thus a critical issue for the contemporary employment relationship. Empirical research should continue to analyze the effects of globalization on employment outcomes.[2] But the larger question is how to seek a balance between efficiency, equity, and voice in the global workplace. In other words, who should govern the global workplace? The major alternatives parallel the options for governing the workplace presented in chapter 5: free markets, human resource management, worker control, government regulation, and independent employee representation. In the international context, a reliance on free markets is the pursuit of free trade and the reduction of trade barriers, such as through the World Trade Organization (WTO) or the North American Free Trade Agreement (NAFTA). Human resource management entails corporate self-monitoring or self-policing: a prominent example of this in the international arena is the use of corporate codes of conduct. The global form of government regulation includes the incorporation of labor standards into trade agreements, such as the side agreement to NAFTA, or the enforcement of international labor standards, such as through the International Labour Organization (ILO). Examples of independent employee representation (or potential representation) in the global context include European Works Councils, instances of transnational union cooperation and solidarity, and the possibility of collective bargaining on an international scale. The intellectual foundations of global workplace governance are summarized in figure 9.1 and parallel the intellectual foundations of domestic workplace governance (recall figure 5.2).

Globalization: The Good, the Bad, and the Unequal

A review of the debates over globalization will set the stage for a discussion of governing and balancing the global workplace. The economic theory of increased economic integration is straightforward and applies equally to all four dimensions: international trade, foreign direct investment, international investment portfolios, and immigration. The benefits of international trade were clearly articulated in the writings of Adam Smith, David Ricardo, and other early classical economists two hundred years ago (Irwin 2002). In short, free trade across countries allows consumers and producers to benefit from specialization and to take advantage of differences in comparative advantage. FDI, international investment portfolios, and immigration further allow productive resources to find their optimal use. Thus, the removal of trade barriers and other impediments to economic integration leads to more efficient use of scarce resources. Productivity is higher, greater income is produced, economic growth is enhanced, and better jobs are created.

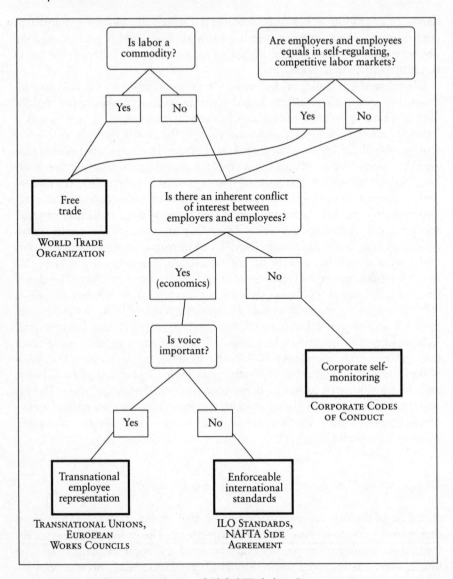

Figure 9.1 The Intellectual Foundations of Global Workplace Governance

Free trade also increases the size of markets, allowing companies to exploit economies of scale (Irwin 2002). The monopoly power of domestic companies is also reduced and consumers benefit from lower prices and greater choices. Increased wealth can also be used to conserve the environment, promote public health, and improve education. FDI can benefit countries by bringing jobs and new technology, providing the base for economic development and growth. Foreign subsidiaries of multinational companies pay higher wages than local domestic companies and share in the profits of their multinational parents (Aitken, Harrison, and Lipsey 1996; Budd, Konings, and Slaughter 2002). International portfolio investment provides working capital for local companies, financing (and discipline) for foreign government spending, and opportunities for improved risk-sharing across borders (Obstfeld 1998). In short, international portfolio flows allow investment capital to find its most productive use. And as FDI and international portfolio flows provide the opportunity for capital to seek its highest rate of return, immigration provides labor with the same opportunity. In short, overall economic welfare is improved through economic integration, because scarce resources are free to find their most efficient and productive uses.

This textbook economic model of economic integration has been criticized in several ways. One, there are winners and losers as an economy adjusts to increased international trade and integration. Removing trade barriers that were protecting an inefficient industry will likely cause job losses in that industry. Increased outsourcing and outward FDI further shifts production elsewhere. In fact, such restructurings are the source of the gains from integration—with no restructuring, improvements in efficiency are unlikely (Rodrik 1997). In the standard economic model, however, job losses and other negative consequences of restructuring are more than compensated for by increases in other sectors that benefit from trade (Irwin 2002). The question for this theory is how the losers are compensated by the winners. Although possible in theory, in practice it is, at best, a thorny issue (Rodrik 1997; Summers 2001).

Two, there are short-run versus long-run concerns. Kuznets (1955) argued that initial economic development or industrialization widens income inequality before later stages narrow inequality. With respect to globalization, it has similarly been hypothesized that pollution and environmental degradation follow an inverted-U Kuznets curve—in the short run, pollution increases with added production, but in the long run increased levels of income can be used to reduce pollution and environmentally harmful production processes (Esty 2001; Grossman and Krueger 1995). Similar logic might apply to workplace safety and other employment issues. Another negative short-run component of globalization is the great volatility of international investment portfolios into and out of developing countries (Stiglitz 2002). During the East Asia crisis in 1997, international financial flows to Thailand went from inflows equal to 15 percent of its gross domestic product to outflows equal to 20 percent in just one year (United Nations Development Programme 1999, 41). This volatility greatly destabilized the banking system and also spilled over into employment and working conditions. For example, in Indonesia, average annual real wage growth in manufacturing went from 5.6 percent in the boom period of 1990–96 to -25.1 percent in the bust of 1997–98 (United Nations 2000, 64).

Three, standard economic models are predicated on assumptions of perfect competition and information. Market imperfections can cause the benefits of

international trade to be distributed unevenly. The fundamental industrial relations assumption of unequal bargaining power between corporations and
individual employees (especially those lacking savings, education, and a social
safety net) is typically ignored in standard trade models (for an exception, see
Rodrik 1997). But if true, the nature of globalization looks quite different. In
particular, the traditional industrial relations analysis of the U.S. labor problem of worker exploitation in the early twentieth century (see chapter 6) can
be applied to the developing countries' labor problem of the early twenty-first
century. With unequal bargaining power, the benefits of globalization flow
disproportionately to shareholders; employees are left with low wages, long
hours, and dangerous working conditions.[3]

Consequently, proponents of fair trade distinguish between legitimate and
illegitimate, or socially unacceptable, sources of comparative advantage (Rodrik 1997; Summers 2001). An abundance of natural resources or differences
in worker productivity are legitimate; slavery is not. Proponents further argue
that violations of other core labor standards—child labor, discrimination, and
suppression of the freedom of association—are not legitimate sources of comparative advantage.[4] These problems are thought to be especially acute with
export processing zones (Gordon 2000a). These areas of developing countries
explicitly target multinational FDI by providing incentives such as duty-free
importing and exporting, reduced taxes, and publicly provided infrastructure.
It is also argued that some countries provide additional inducements such as
lax enforcement of labor laws and government assistance in keeping out independent unions, such as in Mexico's *maquiladora* sector (Cravey 1998). Under these circumstances, globalization looks more like corporations searching
for ways to increase their labor market bargaining power and less like the free
trade model with perfect competition in labor markets. This is the root of concerns with social dumping, which can undermine labor standards elsewhere.[5]
Moreover, more Americans than not believe that globalization destroys jobs
and lowers wages (Scheve and Slaughter 2001). Rather than being ill-informed
about standard economic models, these beliefs may reflect skepticism with the
assumptions of perfect labor market competition.

Reinforcing this skepticism are the statistics on the inequalities of globalization (United Nations Development Programme 1999). Income in the countries with the richest 20 percent of the global population was eleven times that
of the poorest 20 percent in 1913; today it is nearly 75 times greater. The richest 20 percent account for 86 percent of the world's gross domestic product
(GDP); the poorest 20 percent account for only 1 percent. The assets of the
world's three richest people exceed the combined GDP of the forty-three least
developed countries, which have a population of six hundred million, and
more than a billion people live on less than $1 a day. Worldwide sales for the
very largest corporations exceed the GDP of countries such as Israel, Norway,
the Philippines, Poland, and Thailand, while over 80 percent of patents in developing countries are held by residents of developed countries. Of the 110
million primary school age children who do not attend school, over 95 per-

cent are in developing countries. By themselves, these statistics do not prove that there are labor market imperfections and a resulting inequality in bargaining power between employers and employees, but they suggest that may be so.

Free Trade

Free trade has not always been the goal of U.S. economic policy, and many trade barriers around the world exist. Historically, tariffs have been an important component of economic policy because of the revenue collected and because they protect and foster certain industries. In fact, with the passage of the Smoot-Hawley Tariff Act in 1930, average U.S. tariff rates exceeded 50 percent (Irwin 2002; Rothgeb 2001). Nontariff trade barriers include quotas, subsidies, discriminatory government procurement policies, and regulations such as import licensing and product standards. Transportation costs, language barriers, and exchange rate risk also affect international trade (Frankel 2001). To try to open up foreign markets to U.S. producers during the Great Depression, the Reciprocal Trade Agreements Act of 1934 authorized the president to negotiate tariff reductions with other countries on a product-by-product basis. This act laid the foundation for today's multilateral trading system, now under the umbrella of the World Trade Organization, which has reduced average tariff levels on manufactured goods to less than 4 percent (Irwin 2002; Porter 2001). Regional trading and economic integration agreements seek to further remove barriers to trade. The regional examples of the European Union and the North American Free Trade Agreement will be discussed in later sections because labor issues are handled differently than under the WTO.

The premier mechanism for pursuing free trade and reducing trade barriers on a global scale is the World Trade Organization. The WTO is an organization of 144 member countries that serves as a forum for negotiating international trade agreements and as the monitoring and regulating body for enforcing trade agreements. This latter function includes handling trade disputes. The WTO was created in the Uruguay round (1986–93) of the General Agreement on Tariffs and Trade (GATT) and came into existence on January 1, 1995. It inherited the GATT multilateral trading system framework. The GATT is an international agreement among signatory countries to reduce tariffs on specific products and was negotiated in several major rounds beginning with twenty-three countries in 1947.[6] It is a multilateral treaty for reducing trade barriers; it is not an organization. The GATT embodies four principles: nondiscrimination (so all participants receive most-favored-nation status from one another); transparency (no hidden trade barriers or agreements); consultation (differences resolved through negotiation); and reciprocity (equal concessions by all) (Rothgeb 2001).

With the complexity of the Uruguay round agreement—containing 22,000 pages and weighing 385 pounds—came renewed calls for the creation of a permanent organization, resulting in the WTO to administer the GATT provisions and to handle future negotiations. The WTO is a permanent organization with headquarters (in Geneva), a director, and a permanent staff. Members negotiate continuously rather than during formal rounds, as was the case with the GATT, and the WTO has the authority to resolve trade disputes. More specifically, the dispute resolution procedure consists of three steps: consultation, a ruling by a three-person panel of experts, and the possibility of appeal to an appellate body. Violating countries must change their trade policies or pay damages. Refusal to do so can result in trade sanctions. The trade ministers of each member country must meet every two years. The third ministerial conference took place in 1999 in Seattle and was accompanied by intense protests against the WTO and its approach to free trade.

The WTO promotes free trade through the reduction of trade barriers, especially tariffs, quotas, and regulations. As noted above, average tariff levels on manufactured goods are less than 4 percent and quotas are illegal except in limited circumstances. Regulations in the form of product standards must be supported by scientific evidence. Equal market access must be provided to all member countries (the most favored nation principle) and domestic and foreign products must be treated equally (the national treatment principle). These provisions are significant, but from the perspective of pure free trade, the WTO system is incomplete (Schott 2000). Within manufactured goods, there are some remaining sectors with high tariff levels or quotas, such as in textiles and clothing. Outside of manufacturing, many trade barriers remain in agriculture and services. There is also a lack of uniformity of intellectual property rights and competitive (or antitrust) policies across countries.

Nevertheless, the WTO exemplifies the free trade model of global workplace governance. Labor standards—as well as environmental and other standards—are evaluated against the test of trade barriers: if a labor regulation interferes with free trade, it is a trade barrier and therefore illegal. For example, consider a requirement that all imports are produced subject to some set of core labor standards. GATT Article 20 states:

> Subject to the requirement that such measures are not applied in a manner which would constitute a means of arbitrary or unjustifiable discrimination between countries where the same conditions prevail, or a disguised restriction on international trade, nothing in this Agreement shall be construed to prevent the adoption or enforcement by any members of measures: (a) necessary to protect public morals; (b) necessary to protect human, animal or plant life or health . . . ; (e) relating to the products of prison labor; . . . (g) relating to the conservation of exhaustible natural resources if such measures are made effective in conjunction with restrictions on domestic production or consumption.

Although these provisions can be read to allow protection of core labor standards (Bal 2001; Howse 1999), existing rulings are instead consistent with the priority of free trade.[7] There are no explicit WTO rulings on labor standards or human rights, but environmental standards also fall under Article 20 and involve substantially the same issues.[8]

The GATT and WTO rulings in such cases narrowly construe the provisions of Article 20 and have ruled against environmental standards (Dailey 2000; Gaines 2001; Wallach and Sforza 2000).[9] In Article 20(b), "necessary" has been interpreted to mean "least trade restrictive," and U.S. requirements on tuna nets have been struck down on the grounds of not being the least trade-restrictive option for saving dolphins. In a recent high-profile case, a U.S. requirement that all shrimp—domestic and imported—be caught with nets safe for endangered sea turtles was ruled to violate Article 20. The WTO ruled that by not taking national differences into account, the U.S. standard was discriminatory and, therefore, protectionist.[10] With respect to food safety regulations, there is only scope for challenging standards that are too high, not too low (Kennedy 2000).[11]

Such rulings are reminiscent of early twentieth- century U.S. court decisions in which legislative labor standards were declared illegal on the basis that they interfered with the freedom to contract. In the WTO context, freedom to contract has been replaced by freedom to trade, but the underlying intellectual foundations are the same: economic efficiency is maximized by laissez-faire policies that promote free exchange. If individuals and companies within and across countries are equals, then this free trade model of workplace governance balances the global workplace. In other words, free trade arrangements are based on the belief that "the social caboose [is] pulled by the economic locomotive" (Blanpain 1999, 91). This is the free market model of workplace governance (see chapter 5) in an international economy. If labor markets are not perfectly competitive, however, other models of global workplace governance should be considered to supplement the sole reliance on free trade and more securely hitch the social caboose to the economic locomotive.

Corporate Codes of Conduct

A corporate code of conduct is a written statement of standards that a company voluntarily pledges to follow in its business activities. The codes can be created by transnational governmental organizations, national and local governments, labor unions and other nongovernmental organizations, and individual corporations. There is tremendous diversity in the content of different codes, but generally they address fair business practices, labor standards, environmental concerns, corporate citizenship and ethics, and respect for relevant laws (Hepple 1999). With respect to labor practices, the common concerns are child labor, discrimination, health and safety, and to a lesser extent freedom of association and perhaps collective bargaining (Tsogas 2001).

It is common to trace the use of corporate codes of conduct back to the Organization for Economic Cooperation and Development's (OECD) Guidelines for Multinational Enterprises in 1976. Revised in 2000, the guidelines specify standards for environmental protection, prevention of bribery, disclosure of information, payment of taxes, consumer safety, fair competition, and labor practices. The latter includes all of the workers' rights specified in the International Labour Organization's Declaration on Principles on Fundamental Rights at Work (1998): freedom of association and collective bargaining, the abolition of forced labor, the elimination of child labor, and equal opportunity and pay. The employment standards further include providing training, promoting consultation, providing information to employee representatives, refraining from threats to move production to prevent union organizing or influence collective bargaining, and providing advance notice of layoffs. Compliance, however, is voluntary. Each OECD country is supposed to have a "national contact point" to promote the guidelines, resolve conflicts, and make recommendations to specific companies (Hepple 1999). In 1977, the ILO issued its own code, the ILO Tripartite Declaration of Principles Concerning Multinational Enterprises and Social Policy, which extends the OECD guidelines to also include the avoidance of arbitrary dismissal, promotion of job stability and income protection, and, in developing countries, payment of a living wage.[12] Compliance is voluntary. The United Nations is also working on a statement of responsibilities of multinational businesses with respect to human rights (Weissbrodt 2000).

More recent corporate conduct codes have been developed outside of the government sphere, especially by nongovernmental organizations and multinational companies.[13] These can be traced back to the Sullivan Principles in 1977, which targeted the apartheid regime in South Africa by having U.S. multinationals agree to desegregate their South African workplaces and to promote advancement opportunities for black South Africans (Baker 2001; Compa and Darricarrère 1996; Liubicic 1998). The MacBride Principles in 1984 took the same approach to fighting discrimination against the Catholic minority in Northern Ireland. The AFL-CIO and environmental, community, and religious groups developed a code for U.S. companies in Mexico's *maquiladora* sector that promotes the freedom to bargain collectively, adequate living standards, and workplace practices that are safe for workers and the environment (Compa and Darricarrère 1996).

In what appears to be the first U.S. example of a joint effort between business, human rights groups, and, at least initially, organized labor is the Apparel Industry Partnership (now, Fair Labor Association) (Liubicic 1998; Tsogas 2001). Twelve apparel and footwear companies agreed to abide by a Workplace Code of Conduct in partnership with human rights groups.[14] The code of conduct forbids forced labor, child labor, harassment or abuse, discrimination, dangerous working conditions, and excessive daily and weekly working hours. The code of conduct also states that the companies will respect rights of freedom of association and collective bargaining and will pay at least the legal minimum wage or prevailing wage. There is also a monitoring system in which employees are informed of these standards and provided with opportunities to report noncompliance. Accredited external monitors also have access to review records and facilities. Companies that are in compliance can use a product label advertising their compliance.[15]

There are also a myriad of individual company codes (Compa and Darricarrère 1996; Hepple 1999; Liubicic 1998). Reebok has one of the most extensive. Their code emphasizes that it also applies to contractors, subcontractors, suppliers, and other business partners. The standards pertain to nondiscrimination, working hours and overtime (including a sixty-hour, six-day maximum work week), no forced or child labor, fair wages and benefits (at least a legal minimum or prevailing wage), freedom of association and the right to bargain collectively, no harassment, and workplace safety and health. Reebok's corporate code of conduct also includes a nonretaliation policy that states "Factories must publicize and enforce a non-retaliation policy that permits factory workers to express their concerns about workplace conditions without fear of retribution or losing their jobs. Workers should be able to speak without fear directly to factory management or Reebok representatives."[16] Reebok has also been involved in various promotions for human rights (Compa and Darricarrère 1996), so their code of conduct should not be taken as representative.

These examples illustrate the second alternative for global workplace governance—voluntary corporate compliance with a published set of standards for behavior and rights. This mechanism is analogous to the human resource management model of workplace governance in chapter 5. Unlike the free markets governance mechanism, a corporate code of conduct model reflects the view that employment conditions are not entirely dictated by market forces; rather, companies have choices. Establishing conditions more favorable to workers than the market minimums might be mutually beneficial for both the company and workers. As stated in Reebok's code, "We believe that the incorporation of internationally recognized human rights standards into our business practice improves worker morale and results in a higher quality working environment and higher quality products." This is similar to the human resource management philosophy that treating workers with respect will increase commitment and effectiveness. In other words, a corporate code of conduct governance mechanism rejects the market-oriented conception of labor as a commodity and the assumption that employees and employers are labor-market equals; it is based on the unitarist belief of shared interests (see figure 9.1). Moreover, as the human resource management model relies on educating firms and managers about best practices so does the corporate code of conduct model in the international context.

But as is also true in the human resource management model, the corporate code of conduct model of global workplace governance is ultimately a unilateral governance mechanism that lacks an external enforcement mechanism. This is the most important problem with corporate codes of conduct (Baker 2001; Compa and Darricarrère 1996; Hepple 1999; Liubicic 1998; Tsogas 2001). By definition, these codes are voluntary, so enforcement is "a matter of private consultation or public embarrassment" (Compa and Darricarrère

1996, 185). Some codes are monitored by human rights groups or other outsiders, including professional social auditors (Tsogas 2001), but even this is controversial. The Union of Needletrades, Industrial, and Textile Employees (UNITE) refused to agree to the Apparel Industry Partnership partly because the inspection process allowed significant company involvement.[17] Companies are often the creator of their own codes and define, or exclude, standards to serve their self-interest. Some codes promote freedom of association but are silent on the issue of collective bargaining (Tsogas 2001), whereas others promote individual representation (Hepple 1999). Another reason that UNITE withdrew from the Apparel Industry Partnership was that the code contains weak language on minimum or prevailing wages rather than stronger language on a living wage.

Corporate codes of conduct as a global workplace governance mechanism can help create publicity on global working conditions, but without more effective monitoring and enforcement this is a weak governance vehicle.[18] Coverage of these codes is low as they are primarily confined to "image-conscious [multinationals], or the subcontractors, contractors and suppliers associated with them, in the formal export sectors of developing economies" (Liubicic 1998, 158). Last, among workers' rights advocates there is debate as to whether these codes do more harm than good. UNITE expressed reservations about the Apparel Industry Partnership because of fears that union endorsement of the code of conduct would legitimize it as a substitute for both national laws and collective bargaining. On the other hand, the International Confederation of Free Trade Unions (ICFTU) has issued a model code of conduct and advocates that unions use such a code to initiate dialogue with companies on globalization and labor rights (ICFTU 2001). In 2002, Volkswagen signed an agreement with the International Metalworkers' Federation to follow the ILO's core labor standards in its worldwide operations.

International Labor Standards

One way to address the lack of enforceable minimum standards in corporate codes of conduct is to mandate standards by treaty or law. This is effectively a government regulation model of global workplace governance, though in the international context it might be undertaken by supranational authorities. Moreover, the implementation of legally enforceable standards can be pursued on a global or regional basis. On a global basis, one option is to add a social clause to the World Trade Organization trading system. Because of the expertise of the International Labour Organization in this area, discussion of global labor standards inevitably involves the ILO. As a regional example, the labor side agreement to the North American Free Trade Agreement also seeks to enforce a minimum set of labor standards. The NAFTA system is an instructive contrast to the ILO system because of the emphasis on enforcing national laws rather than establishing uniform standards.

The International Labour Organization and Core Labor Standards

The ILO is a specialized agency of the United Nations that promotes internationally recognized human and labor rights.[19] Nearly every country is a member and consequently, the ILO is the undisputed chief international authority on labor standards. Through the adoption of conventions (nearly two hundred to date), the ILO formulates international labor standards pertaining to a wide range of employment issues. In 1998, the ILO member countries reaffirmed their commitment to the ILO's basic principles and enumerated the fundamental workers' rights through the ILO Declaration on Fundamental Principles and Rights at Work. These fundamental rights are freedom of association and collective bargaining, the abolition of forced and child labor, and the elimination of discrimination. To underscore the critical nature of these rights, even member countries that have not ratified the eight conventions pertaining to these fundamental rights have an obligation "to promote and to realize" them.

Consequently, these fundamental workers' rights, or core labor standards, are the most frequently cited components of proposed social clauses for the global economic system (for example, Blackett 1999; Elliot 2000; Howse 1999; Summers 2001).[20] The core labor standards are not currently enforceable minimum standards, however. The ILO relies on publicity, diplomacy, and technical assistance, not legal or economic punishment, to encourage compliance with its labor standards (Ehrenberg 1996). Monitoring of compliance is also limited (Cooney 1999). The way to make these labor standards enforceable is to marry the expertise of the ILO with the power of the WTO (Ehrenberg 1996; Elliot 2000; Howse 1999; Leary 1996). By adding a social clause to the WTO system of global trade, a violation of the social clause—a violation of one or more of the core labor standards—could trigger economic sanctions if a country did not redress its violations, just as is the case currently for illegal trade barriers. The ILO would be responsible for determining violations, and the WTO would be responsible for remedies.

It is perhaps an understatement to say that this type of proposal is controversial. This is graphically illustrated by the sometimes violent protests in the "Battle of Seattle" that accompanied the WTO ministerial meeting in 1999. The battle in the streets involved labor, environmental, and other groups demonstrating for fair trade—the addition of an enforceable social clause to the WTO system. The battle inside the ministerial meeting involved, inter alia, the same debate—the United States proposed a working group to study the issue of core labor standards and the developing countries objected on the basis of disguised protectionism against their low-cost exports (Elliot 2000; Summers 2001).[21] This was not a problem unique to the Seattle ministerial meeting, and similar disputes have occurred at earlier trade meetings and as far back as 150 years ago (Ehrenberg 1996; Leary 1996). Several times in the 1990s, the WTO member countries, led by the developing countries, explicitly endorsed the ILO rather than the WTO as the sole authority on labor issues—though perhaps because of the ILO's weak enforcement powers rather than a sincere concern with labor standards (Summers 2001). At the same time, developing countries in the ILO have rejected ILO initiatives to be involved in trade matters (Blackett 1999; Leary 1996).[22] And free trade economists typically see labor standards as disguised protectionism or as an issue unrelated to international trade; in either case, a trade-labor standards linkage is rejected (Brown 2001; Irwin 2002). Enforceable minimum labor standards on a global basis are a possibility, but they are not currently a reality.[23]

The North American Agreement on Labor Cooperation

Enforceable labor standards in the international economy can also be pursued on a regional level. The North American Free Trade Agreement, and especially its North American Agreement on Labor Cooperation (NAALC) component, is a regional example for the United States, Canada, and Mexico. The NAFTA/NAALC example is also constructive because it illustrates a different approach than the WTO/ILO scenario. In particular, the NAALC emphasizes enforcement of existing domestic legal standards rather than common transnational labor standards.

The NAALC is one of two side agreements to NAFTA that were added to address labor and environmental issues as pledged by President Clinton during the presidential election campaign in 1992. By itself, NAFTA eliminates tariff and nontariff trade barriers over a 10–15-year period; allows companies of any of the three countries to invest, sell services, and bid on government contracts in all three countries; protects intellectual property rights; and specifies detailed rules of origin (Weintraub 1997).[24] Labor, however, feared that low Mexican wages would undercut U.S. competitiveness and put downward pressure on U.S. wages and working conditions and cause widespread plant closings—as expressed by independent presidential candidate Ross Perot's "giant sucking sound" of jobs moving to Mexico. Similar concerns were heard regarding environmental standards. The Clinton administration therefore first proposed the enforcement of core labor standards through trade sanctions, as in the WTO/ILO model described above (Mazey 2001). This was rejected by Canada and Mexico, and it was also opposed by U.S. business—the NAALC side agreement was agreed on instead. NAFTA and the labor and environmental side agreements went into effect on January 1, 1994.

The explicit emphasis in the NAALC is cooperation to promote compliance with existing domestic labor laws. No new laws are required nor are there restrictions on future laws; rather, education and cooperation are used to develop mutual understanding of laws and institutions, to pursue mutually beneficial activities, and to promote enforcement of existing labor laws. The NAALC outlines eleven "guiding principles" for labor that the three countries are committed to promote, but the text explicitly emphasizes that these are not common minimum standards. These principles are to be pursed through domestic laws as each country sees fit. Each country must also establish a National Administrative Office (NAO) to collect and disseminate information on domestic labor laws. The NAO is also the focus of the NAALC's dispute resolution procedure if there are allegations of a lack of enforcement of domestic laws. In such a case, a complaint can be filed with one of the NAOs. If the NAO finds that enforcement or compliance is lacking, it can recommend ministerial consultations. For the most part, the dispute resolution procedure ends here.[25]

Lacking enforcement powers or penalties, compliance is dependent on the "sunshine factor" of adverse publicity that results from the public nature of the NAALC proceedings (Bognanno and Lu 2003)—in other words, the "naming and shaming" of violators (Tsogas 2001, 164). Although adverse publicity may have been instrumental in a few cases, evaluation of the existing NAALC cases fails to undercover a strong pattern of victories for organized labor and workers' rights advocates (Bognanno and Lu 2003; Summers 1999). In cases involving freedom of association and collective bargaining, violations have not been remedied. Workers fired for union activity have not been reinstated, and in Mexico independent unions that challenge state-dominated unions have yet to gain recognition. Rather, workshops, seminars, and studies are the usual result of ministerial consultations.[26] Bognanno and Lu (2003) cite additional pieces of evidence that further question the effectiveness of the NAALC's sole reliance on adverse publicity for compliance. Although the number of NAALC submissions has never been high, the filing rate appears to be declining, which suggests that labor unions and workers' rights organization do not think that the process is effective. This conclusion is reinforced by a survey of union and other workers' rights advocate organizations with experience under the NAALC procedures. The responses clearly reject the contention that adverse publicity is sufficient to cause the three NAFTA countries to improve enforcement of their labor laws.

In spite of this poor track record, some remain optimistic that the NAALC can promote its eleven labor principles (Adams and Singh 1997; Tsogas 2001). This optimism results from at least three factors. One, the NAALC partners have been successful in educational activities and in increasing cross-border understanding. This has the potential to serve as the foundation for greater protection of rights in the future. Two, the sunshine aspect of the NAALC procedures provides the opportunity to focus public attention on trade and labor issues. Although the existing process has not worked effectively, it can serve as a starting point for building stronger public forums for addressing trade-labor linkages. Three, the submission process provides opportunities for greater cross-border cooperation among unions. More aggressive coordinated action may generate broader negative publicity for labor law violators and the failings of local enforcement and, thereby, increase the effectiveness of the NAALC procedures.

In sum, a third option for governing the global workplace is the use of international labor standards. Proposals to combine ILO core labor standards with WTO-enforceable trade sanctions on a global scale and the experiences of striving for increased enforcement of existing domestic labor laws under NAFTA's NAALC illustrate two alternative ways to pursue international labor standards on either a global or regional basis. Governing the global workplace through enforceable international labor standards is essentially a government regulation model of workplace governance. The advantages and disadvantages of international labor standards parallel those typically associated with government regulation. On the positive side, protection—for example, against employment discrimination and unsafe working conditions—can be provided without relying on potentially imperfect labor markets, corporate goodwill, or the uneven coverage of labor unions. On the negative side, the examples discussed here clearly reveal thorny issues pertaining to disagreements over the content of standards, to difficulties with a lack of flexibility with uniform standards or laws across diverse situations, and to standard economic concerns with efficiency losses resulting from government intervention in economic markets. In any case, with both potential and pitfalls, the use of enforceable international labor standards is another alternative for trying to balance efficiency, equity, and voice in the global workplace.

Transnational Employee Representation

The standard intellectual framework of pluralist industrial relations includes the rejection of labor as simply a commodity and as equal to employers in self-regulating, competitive labor markets, while embracing the belief that there is an inherent conflict of interest in the employment relationship. As illustrated in figure 9.1, if employee voice is not important, then in the global context the appropriate workplace governance mechanism is the use of international labor standards. However, voice *is* important both for intrinsic reasons of democracy and practical reasons of tailoring workplace rules and representation to local conditions (the principle of subsidiarity). In the global context, employee voice can be provided through various forms of transnational employee representation. Two important examples are European Works Councils and transnational collective bargaining.

European Works Councils

A European Works Council (EWC) is a transnational, company-level committee of employee representatives from multiple European Union (EU) countries. Like typical national- or workplace-level works councils found in various continental European countries (see chapter 7), EWCs are technically independent of unions. The 1994 EU directive "on the establishment of a European Works Council or a procedure in Community-scale undertakings and Community-scale groups of undertakings for the purposes of informing and consulting employees" (generally referred to as the "European Works Council directive") requires all companies with at least one thousand employees in the EU and at least 150 employees in each of two EU countries to establish an

EWC or another procedure "for the purposes of informing and consulting employees."[27]

On issues that affect workers in more than one country, EWCs have consultation and information rights but not codetermination rights. Because EU directives allow individual countries to handle the details of implementation and practice, the European Works Council directive specifies minimum standards: councils must meet with management at least once a year and must be informed and consulted with regard to the "progress of the business." Furthermore:

> The meeting shall relate in particular to the structure, economic and financial situation, the probable development of the business and of production and sales, the situation and probable trend of employment, investments, and substantial changes concerning organization, introduction of new working methods or production processes, transfers of production, mergers, cut-backs or closures of undertakings, establishments or important parts thereof, and collective redundancies (Annex 2).[28]

A company's EWC can also request a meeting with management when there are exceptional circumstances, such as layoffs or plant closings. Consultation is defined as "the exchange of views and establishment of a dialogue" (Article 2). Expenses are paid by the company. Additional details such as the council's size, allocation of members, location and duration of meetings, and procedures for consultation are left up to individual companies and their employees. The national law of the country in which the company is headquartered determines the requirements for what information must be provided and whether employee representatives are elected by the employees or appointed by unions.

Lecher et al. (2001) categorize EWCs as symbolic, service, project-oriented, or participative. Symbolic EWCs are passive and fulfill the minimum requirements of the directive by a single annual meeting in which management provides limited information. Representatives do not make an effort to engage in a dialogue or build the internal capabilities of the council. The McDonald's EWC is illustrative (Royle 1999). Although 90 percent of McDonald's employees are hourly, a majority of the EWC representatives are salaried managers. Preconsultation meetings among EWC representatives do not occur, management dominates the meeting agenda, and little information gets back to employees. Wills (2000) provides another case study of an ineffective EWC.

A service EWC has a more active information flow than a symbolic EWC, but its primary function is servicing national or local unions. In the European auto industry, Hancké (2000) finds that although management has been effective at using the transnational EWC structure to facilitate corporate restructurings, the EWCs are only used narrowly by union leaders to strengthen local union activity. EWCs can pass along the European-level information received by the council that is not provided by the company at a local level. EWCs can also provide networking opportunities for union leaders from different countries. At BMW, the direct activities of the EWC have been modest, but British and German union leaders have been able to develop communication and trust. This networking helped the British union leaders during later negotiations with BMW management (Whittall 2000). In a service EWC, therefore, the internal capabilities of the EWC are not developed and activities are confined to information and networking among EWC members.

In contrast, project-oriented EWCs build their own internal capabilities and pursue projects—such as a comparison of employment conditions across plants in the company—beyond the scope of the required meetings with management. Successful endeavors can transform the EWC into the most advanced form: a participative EWC that embraces active consultation and perhaps joint projects with management. The EWCs at Nestlé and Unilever are examples of participative councils (Lecher et al. 2001). At Nestlé, the EWC and management established a consultation procedure for discussing plant closures and for implementing equal opportunity policies. At Unilever, the EWC has actively pursued activities outside of the annual meeting with management, and the top two EWC officials meet monthly. This EWC developed an information system to integrate the information received by the European-level council and the workplace-level works councils in each country. A handbook of guidelines for corporate restructuring has also been developed and the EWC has been actively involved with management in implementing Unilever's restructuring initiatives.

These four types of EWCs illustrate the reasons for both the pessimism and optimism that are attached to EWCs. Streeck (1997) argues that EWCs are neither European nor works councils. By adding a layer of (weak) participation on top of existing national systems—such as German codetermination or British voluntarism—and by leaving many details to the vagaries of national legislation, EWCs are argued to be extensions of national systems, not integrated European institutions. And by not having codetermination rights, EWCs are not really works councils. Their ability to make a strong contribution to employee rights in a global economy is evaluated pessimistically. On the other hand, while admitting that symbolic EWCs contribute little to employee representation, Lecher et al. (2001) optimistically view the other types of EWCs as enhancing employee representation. The EWC at BMW ultimately strengthened the British union's resources during collective bargaining, while the Nestlé and Unilever EWCs have participated in restructuring decisions. The General Motors EWC negotiated a framework agreement that established basic principles for a major corporate restructuring in 2001.

It is apparent, however, that a common denominator of many EWC studies is the strength or weakness of unions at each company. At BMW, General Motors, Nestlé, Unilever, and other companies, the EWC members include union leaders. Consequently, the EWCs can benefit from union experience, expertise, and resources. In return, the unions can take advantage of the information and networking opportunities of the EWC. On the other hand, McDonald's was successful in marginalizing the union presence in its symbolic EWC. As currently constituted, EWCs appear to have the best chance of aiding employee representation in a global economy when accompanied by strong labor unions.

Transnational Collective Bargaining

The second category of transnational employee representation is transnational labor union collaboration. This transnational collaboration ranges from simple messages of solidarity to sympathy strikes, from sharing of information to conducting coordinated lobbying or public pressure campaigns, from helping establish unions in developing countries to coordinated collective bargaining (Gordon and Turner 2000). However, as unions strive to match the global activity of multinational corporations—activity often facilitated by free trade agreements such as GATT and NAFTA—laws restricting sympathy strikes, secondary boycotts, and the affiliation of labor unions with international federations (at least in some developing countries) all hamper transnational collaboration (Atleson 2002; Servais 2000).[29] Additional barriers to transnational labor collaboration include language barriers; cultural, religious, and ideological differences; fears of losing domestic autonomy; differences in union structures and goals; and employer resistance (Gordon and Turner 2000).

Consequently, true transnational collective bargaining with unions in more than one country negotiating jointly is rare (Bendiner 1987). U.S. and Canadian Chrysler workers were covered by a single UAW contract in the 1970s, ratified by a combined vote, which included a cost-of-living allowance formula based on a weighted average of the U.S. and Canadian consumer price indexes (Budd 1998). Given the integration of the U.S. and Canadian auto industries, however, one can question whether this was truly international—and neither the single U.S.-Canadian contract nor the international UAW survived the concession-bargaining period of the 1980s intact.[30] In Europe, an international union federation has negotiated framework agreements with the French food company Danone that specify standards pertaining to access to information, training, and other items. Implementation, however, is left to unions in each country (ICFTU 2001).

Perhaps the best, though still incomplete, example is transnational collective bargaining in flag-of-convenience shipping (Donn and Phelan 1991; Koch-Baumgarten 1998). This involves shipping companies who are granted flags from developing countries (for a small fee) but have no real attachment to the country and are essentially unregulated by national laws. Although the national maritime unions were not willing to cede representation rights to their international federation, the International Transport Workers' Federation (ITF), the ITF has successfully established minimum standards for collective bargaining agreements negotiated by individual unions in this sector. The ITF also bargains on behalf of workers not covered by a national union, which has resulted in roughly 150 contracts. These are enforced by national unions at their local ports.

Although true transnational bargaining is rare, global alliances and federations are increasingly being used to overcome the barriers to other forms of transnational labor collaboration and employee representation. The peak-level international labor organization is the International Confederation of Free Trade Unions—a worldwide federation of national union federations such as the AFL-CIO (Gordon 2000b). The ICFTU includes 225 affiliated organizations that represent 157 million union members from 148 countries. Its main objective is to facilitate consultation, communication, and cooperation among unions. The ICFTU collects and publishes information and research to keep unions abreast of developments in other countries. Education and training for union leaders as well as financial assistance for emerging labor movements are also provided. The ICFTU is a vocal advocate for organized labor in the international arena, by lobbying transnational organizations such as the WTO and campaigning for multinational corporations to adopt codes of conduct that respect basic workers' rights.

In the pursuit of international solidarity actions, the ICFTU also cooperates closely with ten international trade secretariats—"international associations of national trade unions representing workers in specific industries, industry groups, occupations, professions, or other sectors of employment such as the public services" (Windmuller 2000, 102). The international trade secretariats promote transnational collaboration through information exchange, publicity, education, and various solidarity actions. Although stopping short of true transnational collective bargaining, the international trade secretariats have been instrumental in promoting transnational employee representation through international solidarity in support of bargaining disputes in one country.

The International Transport Workers' Federation aggressively supported the Australian dockworkers in their intense strike in 1998 (ICFTU 2001). This included leading demonstrations in the United States, Japan, Korea, India, the Philippines, and Russia. Unionized longshore workers in Los Angeles refused to unload a ship that had been loaded by the struck Australian facilities, and ships were reportedly turned away in India and Japan. Workers in the United States, Canada, and Japan also refused to unload a ship loaded during a 1997 English dockworkers strike (Atleson 2002). The ITF was also involved in supporting the U.S. UPS strike in 1997 (Banks and Russo 1999). Solidarity among worldwide UPS unions was initially developed through the ITF World Council of UPS Unions. During the 1997 strike, British workers engaged in a sick-out (because of their uniforms, a "brown flu" rather than a blue flu), workers in Belgium launched a wildcat strike to resolve outstanding health and safety issues, and demonstrations in Spain and the Philippines temporarily disrupted package deliveries. Workers in France, Germany, and the Netherlands also voted to authorize sympathy strikes, but the U.S. strike ended before the sympathy strike dates. Banks and Russo (1999) credit these actions with creating additional pressures on UPS to settle the U.S. strike, as well as generating increased vitality among the non-U.S. UPS unions.

As additional examples of transnational labor solidarity, during a United Mine Workers of America coal strike, unions in Australia, Colombia, and South Africa conducted twenty-four–hour sympathy strikes at mines and factories owned by the same multinational parent corporation (Zinn 2000). To promote organizing, the United Electrical, Radio, and Machine Workers of America has a strategic alliance with the Mexican union Frente Autentico del Trabajo (Authentic Labor Front) (Alexander and Gilmore 1999). Joint actions have included filing complaints under the NAALC, education, financial assistance, rallies, and public pressure campaigns. The Communications Workers of America has been involved in similar joint activities with the Mexican labor movement (Cohen and Early 2000). Even without true transnational collective bargaining, these examples illustrate the possibilities of using independent employee representation in a transnational context to govern the global workplace.

Governing the Global Workplace

Globalization—increased international integration—is one of the most contentious contemporary economic policy debates and is a critical issue in the twenty-first-century employment relationship. Although research on the effects of globalization on employment outcomes is important, the larger issue is designing governance mechanisms for workplaces in a global economy. A focus on the objectives of the employment relationship is again essential, and the geometry of the employment relationship provides a framework for tackling this issue (see figure 9.2). Free trade, whether through the WTO or regional arrangements such as NAFTA, emphasizes efficiency. Advocates of fair trade essentially object to this narrow focus on efficiency and press for the additional inclusion of equity and/or voice as important goals. Corporate codes of conduct and international labor standards attempt to augment efficiency with the provision of equity. The mechanisms can also lay a foundation for employee voice through protecting freedom of association, but by themselves they do not provide voice. These mechanisms should not be interpreted as disguised protectionism—they simply seek to augment free trade with a set of internationally relevant checks and balances, as is widely accepted for national-level institutions.

Institutions for providing employee voice in the international arena include European Works Councils and transnational labor union activity. Where each of these voice mechanisms is located in the geometry of global workplace governance in figure 9.2 depends on the details of each situation. The rationale for the European Works Council directive is to enhance employees' rights to consultation and information as it pertains to their company and employment situation. The consultation mechanism provides employee voice, albeit

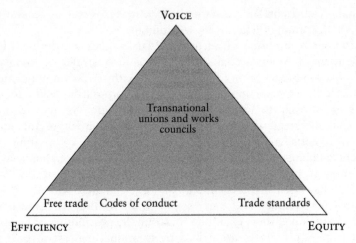

Figure 9.2 The Geometry of Global Workplace Governance

weakly because there is no right to bargain. Moreover, consultation is restricted to narrow issues such as new working methods. The directive also asserts the belief that "harmonious" development of economic activities will be fostered by informing and consulting with employees. In other words, European Works Councils have voice and efficiency components, but no redistributive or equity function. Other forms of transnational labor solidarity are intended to boost labor's bargaining power and therefore deliver greater levels of equity and voice for employees in multinational corporations.

Grounding employment research in the objectives of the employment relationship provides the framework for human resources and industrial relations to contribute to the debates over globalization. Moreover, a renewed emphasis on normative foundations and the explicit development of the ethics of the employment relationship can further advance the globalization debates. The push for fair rather than free trade arises from two distinct beliefs that need to be made explicit. The traditional industrial relations belief in an inequality of bargaining power between labor and management is one source. Reminiscent of the early twentieth-century labor problem in the United States, it is reasonable to question the reliance on free trade for improving welfare if labor markets are imperfect. Expanding on Blanpain's (1999) metaphor, unequal bargaining power between employers and employees makes the coupling between the economic locomotive and the social caboose tenuous. Consideration of additional mechanisms for governing the global workplace can strengthen this coupling so the benefits of global market-based activity can be more broadly shared.

The second source of contention between fair trade and free trade is ethics. Relying on free trade to improve welfare reflects a utilitarian ethical framework (Garcia 1999).[31] Only the resulting consequences of efficiency and utility-maximization are important. That exceptionally low wages in developing countries are justified on the basis of low productivity (for example, Irwin 2002) is the concept of marginal productivity justice criticized by McClelland (1990). Distributional issues, minimum standards, and how outcomes are produced are irrelevant. But as emphasized in earlier chapters and elsewhere (for example, Garcia 1999; Summers 2001), significant scholarship rejects a purely utilitarian or consequentialist ethical approach. Rawlsian principles of justice, Kantian duties, and Aristotelian virtues all rely on the inherent and equal dignity of humans, making distributional and procedural issues important. Governing the global workplace consistent with these normative principles to strike a balance among the efficiency, equity, and voice objectives of the employment relationship is a critical topic for the employment relationship in the twenty-first century, and for creating employment with a human face.

Conclusion

Consider what the employment relationship looks like if viewed as a purely economic transaction. Labor markets and corporate policies mechanically equate productivity and compensation. Hiring and firing constantly adjust to equalize labor supply and labor demand. Work is a burden that is endured only to earn income, and companies must devise incentive and control mechanisms to counter shirking. The rights and obligations of employers and employees narrowly serve efficiency—the freedom to engage in economic relationships ("contract") and the obligation to not undermine this contracting process. But if employment is not simply an economic transaction—if it is an economic *and* social activity with material *and* psychological rewards undertaken by human beings in a democratic society—is the purely transactional view accurate?

The premise of this book is that because work is a fully human activity, employees are entitled to fair treatment and opportunities to have input into decisions that affect their daily lives. In other words, equity and voice should be added to efficiency as the fundamental objectives of the employment relationship. Efficiency, equity, and voice are therefore the key analytical dimensions for studying the employment relationship. The study of employment—human resources and industrial relations—is the analysis of the contributions of individuals, markets, institutions, organizational strategies, and public policies toward the employment relationship objectives of efficiency, equity, and voice in the workplace, as influenced by the environment and individual decision making, including ethics. Such analyses can be captured by the geometry of the employment relationship—a triangular representation of possible outcomes with efficiency, equity, and voice at each corner. Workplace and corporate governance models, industrial relations systems, union strategies, and global workplace governance mechanisms can all be studied by their location in the geometry of the employment relationship—the extent to which they provide each of the three dimensions.

Moreover, as employment is an economic and social activity with material and psychological rewards undertaken by human beings in a democratic society, what are the societal standards for the employment relationship? The modern employment relationship and the corporation are purposeful human constructs. Humans have always had to work to survive, but modern employment—working for someone else in a limited-liability corporation—is a creation of society. In that corporations are created rather than natural institutions, society must determine their ends and the rights and obligations that accompany the modern employment relationship—they are not preordained, natural, or beyond control. Achievement of economic prosperity, respect for human dignity, and equal appreciation for the competing human rights of property rights and labor rights require that efficiency, equity, and voice be *balanced*. The question for research, policy, and practice is therefore how to structure the employment relationship—how to govern the workplace—to achieve this balance. In the framework of the geometry of the employment relationship, workplace and corporate governance models, industrial relations systems, union strategies, and global workplace governance mechanisms are evaluated against the extent to which they approach the center of the triangle and thereby promote a balance.

This triangular analysis also reinforces the need to explicitly consider the critical assumptions of the employment relationship: the nature of work, the operation of labor markets, conflict and power in the employment relationship, and the importance of voice. Important schools of thought are divided by differing perspectives on these assumptions and, therefore, differ on their evaluations of employment systems, practices, and outcomes. In mainstream neoclassical economics, work is an economic transaction and the parties to the employment relationship are equals in competitive markets. Efficiency is achieved, but mandated forms of equity and voice to serve human dignity are viewed as distortionary interferences that impair efficiency. The points on the triangle of the geometry of the employment relationship are in sharp conflict with each other.

Breaking from the shackles of this purely economic view of employment weakens these conflicts. Human resource management, traditional industrial relations, and critical industrial relations all embrace work as much more than an economic transaction and reject the assumption that employers and employees are equals in competitive markets. Under these assumptions, not only is it easier to value the importance of balancing efficiency, equity, and voice, it is also easier to achieve. Though for different reasons, in these schools of thought equitable employment practices and employee voice can enhance efficiency. Moreover, the institutions of equity and voice are often closely related, if not the same, as in the case of labor unions that provide protection (equity) and industrial democracy (voice). The sharpest conflicts between efficiency, equity, and voice are in narrowly conceived neoclassical economic models of human agents and markets. The other three intellectual perspectives on the employment relationship in effect shrink the triangle because the conflicts are not as sharp.

Nevertheless, these three intellectual perspectives also share a fundamental difference with one another—their views on the nature of conflict and power in the employment relationship. The preferred models for governing the workplace are therefore distinct. Human resource management rests on unitarist conflict—effective management policies can align the interests of employees and employers and thereby remove conflicts of interest. The resulting model of workplace governance relies on employer-determined human resource management policies. Mainstream U.S. industrial relations subscribes to the pluralist belief in an inherent conflict of interest in the employment relationship; not all conflict can be resolved by unitarist policies. Governing the workplace, therefore, relies on unions and government regulation to equalize power between labor and management. Last, the critical industrial relations school views employment relationship conflict as class-based or social rather than limited to either a pluralist or unitarist view of conflict confined to the employment relationship. Conflict cannot be solved within the existing capitalist system, and a worker control model of workplace governance is advocated.

This book is ultimately about the objectives of the employment relationship and how to achieve them. To this end, the previous chapters develop both an analytical framework for studying the employment relationship—evaluating practices, systems, institutions, and outcomes against efficiency, equity, and voice—and a normative prescription—that efficiency, equity, and voice should be balanced. These chapters reveal the importance of incorporating all three employment relationship objectives into analyses of employment. These analyses have largely focused on the role of unions in providing equity and voice. But it should be emphasized that unions are not necessarily the only mechanism for delivering these critical objectives of the employment relationship. Many European countries use works councils to provide voice and some also use peak-level social partnerships. Nonunion employee representation plans were used to provide employee voice in the United States in the 1920s and can still be found in Canada and within the domain of the U.S. Railway Labor Act. Equity and voice might also be fostered through employee free speech protections backed by unjust dismissal laws or through employee participation in corporate governance. The intent of this book is not to answer how equity and voice should be provided, but to provide a rich intellectual justification for the importance of this question and a useful framework for analysis. This analytical framework further reveals the significant shortcomings that exist in practice relative to the standard of balancing all three employment relationship objectives. Employment reform is warranted.

Reforming Employment

The goal of public policy should be to design employment systems and shape institutions to promote a balance between efficiency, equity, and voice. In the geometry of the employment relationship, this entails creating policies that move toward the middle of the triangle, and perhaps shrink it as well. However, lack of consensus on reforming U.S. labor policy is longstanding (Dunlop 1961; Brown and Myers 1962). One thing that is needed to break this political gridlock is a return to basic principles. This starts with explicit discussion of the objectives of the employment relationship and the alternatives for their achievement. The intellectual foundations of the employment relationship and whether employment relationship objectives should be balanced or prioritized must also be explicitly discussed. The argument here, of course, is for a balance.

It is beyond the scope of this book to present detailed reform proposals. Rather, the contribution here is to provide an underlying framework for thinking about what we want to achieve and for exploring broad alternatives for achieving them.[1] It is imperative to include efficiency *and* equity *and* voice in any policy discussion. A narrow focus on efficiency omits the critical human dimension; a broader recognition of efficiency and equity still ignores the essential element of voice. The past thirty years of U.S. employment policy have focused exclusively on establishing labor standards through government mandate—the Civil Rights Act, the Occupational Safety and Health Act, and the Family and Medical Leave Act, to name just three major laws. This approach has failed to include voice as an equal objective to equity. The geometry of the employment relationship further reveals the broad need for reform. The U.S. system emphasizes free markets (chapter 5) and free trade (chapter 9), which focus exclusively on efficiency. The New Deal industrial relations system is intended to provide equity and voice, but it is roundly criticized by labor and management for failing to deliver (chapter 6). With very low private sector union density, the New Deal industrial relations system has effectively faded from the geometry of the employment relationship. In workplaces with unions, the traditional (if somewhat exaggerated) model of job control unionism and associated bureaucratic models of representation are at odds with both flexibility (efficiency) and active worker voice (chapter 8). Or consider the criminal penalties for violating property rights or labor rights. Defrauding shareholders has a maximum penalty of twenty-five years imprisonment; willful violation of safety standards that results in a worker's death has a maximum penalty of six months imprisonment (even less than the one year maximum sentence for harassing a wild burro). In short, the U.S. employment system is out of balance.

These analyses further reveal important directions for reform discussions. Individual features of the world's industrial relations systems rarely serve efficiency and equity and voice equally (chapter 7). German works councils operating in isolation would fail to promote the equity standard; sectoral bargaining alone would raise significant questions about workplace efficiency and voice. In combination, these two features are perhaps stronger than the sum of the individual parts and can balance efficiency, equity, and voice as a complementary system. In other words, wholesale rather than piecemeal reform of the U.S. system is warranted.[2] And reform proposals must also consider global arrangements as alternatives for governing the workplace in a global economy (chapter 9). Detailed reform proposals await subsequent research, but the framework developed in this book provides the needed intellectual foundations.

Reforming employment requires more than new public policies on employment issues. New forms of unionism are needed that are consistent with contemporary workplace and workforce trends (chapter 8). Making explicit distinctions between the soul and scope of representation reveals that it is possible to craft new forms of unionism that are consistent with the traditional U.S. scope—the workplace rather than society—while changing from a passive model in which union staff are the drivers of the representation process to an active model in which workers are the soul of the process. Employee empowerment unionism fulfills this need. Individual workers are empowered to determine their own outcomes within a union-negotiated framework of procedures that include minimum standards and procedural safeguards. Employee empowerment unionism can be applied in various ways in diverse workplaces. Blending greater individual discretion—moving beyond the rules-based focus of postwar industrial pluralism—with a framework of safeguards and standards can help balance efficiency, equity, and voice.

On the employer side, a critical examination of the linkages between corporate governance, employees, and employee representation is needed (Blair and Roe 1999; Jacoby 2001). And a new social norm emphasizing employment with a human face needs to be established. As emphasized by Hodson (2001, 267), working with dignity requires the "creation of a workplace with norms for management behavior that include respect for employees' rights and facilitate the maintenance of a coherent and viable system of production." In other words, balancing efficiency, equity, and voice needs to be the social and organizational norm of the twenty-first century.

Last, proposals for reform are ultimately rooted in underlying ethical foundations. The dialogue of reform can be improved by making these ethical foundations explicit. Using specific ethical frameworks is not a magic bullet— it does not erase the differing views of competing groups in society. However, the use of explicit ethical theories can reveal the underlying foundations of these differences (chapter 4). Distinguishing between dissatisfaction that arises from economic inefficiencies, treating people as a means, unequal outcomes, or failing to foster personal relationships is crucial for identifying appropriate reform proposals. In other words, the ethical frameworks can help guide the balance of efficiency, equity, and voice—utilitarianism implies one set of reforms, the ethics of fairness another, and the ethics of care yet another. Explicit incorporation of ethics into employment issues can help society to determine its desired moral standards and then to design policies and governance mechanisms that will promote efficiency, equity, and voice consistent with those standards.

Markets with a Human Face, Employment with a Human Face

Employment with a human face—a productive and efficient employment relationship that also fulfills the standards of human rights—is an essential component of broader calls for markets with a human face, or for harnessing economic markets to serve human needs, not vice versa. With respect to globalization, Stiglitz (2002, 218) advocates moving away from a sole preoccupation with efficiency toward a partnership between regulation and markets to make the global economy "function efficiently—and humanely."[3] Stiglitz (2002, 22) further criticizes the narrow market focus of the World Bank and the International Monetary Fund:

> Globalization can be reshaped, and when it is, when it is properly, fairly run, with all countries having a voice in policies affecting them, there is a possibility that it will help create a new global economy in which growth is not only more sustainable and less volatile but the fruits of this growth are more equitably shared.

In other words, in addition to efficiency concerns, equity and voice are critical aspects of globalization. And sometimes markets need help—the International Monetary Fund, for example, "was founded on the belief that there was a need for collective action at the global level for economic stability" (Stiglitz 2002, 12, emphasis omitted).

Or consider corporate governance. The collapse of Adelphia, Arthur Andersen, Enron, and WorldCom in 2001–2 underscores the power and potential for abuse of unchecked individual self-interest in corporations.[4] Moreover, according to *Business Week,* an "astounding" number of companies had to restate their reported earnings between 1997 and 2001, as companies succumbed to the pressure to produce earnings growth by resorting to misleading accounting techniques.[5] As a result, a number of proposals have been generated to increase transparency and accountability and reduce opportunities for unrestrained self-interest. The pressures of globalization and the power of international financial markets and global corporations magnify the concerns with allowing economic and business transactions to dominate social, political, and human concerns.[6] In other words, a set of reforms is needed to help markets work better and more fairly, and to prevent abuse. Reforms that include incorporating employees into corporate governance can serve both these public concerns and the need to have corporate governance mechanisms support, rather than undermine, workplace governance mechanisms.

The nature of global and national economic systems, corporate governance, and the employment relationship are fundamentally ethical questions (chapter 4). Utilitarianism bolsters the dominant efficiency discourse and conventional economic thinking that individual and corporate self-interest combined with laissez-faire policies to foster free exchange in competitive markets will create the greatest good for the greatest number. If, however, markets are not competitive—if local communities or employees do not have the same resources and mobility as corporations—then individual self-interest is simply individual egoism, not utilitarianism. Moreover, ethical theories in the Aristotelian, Kantian, and Rawlsian traditions are rooted in the importance of human dignity and equal human worth. These theories reject the utilitarian ends-justifies-the-means logic and instead support the principles of balancing competing interests and of creating economic markets with a human face through a system of checks and balances.

Debates over the important contemporary economic and social questions—including the nature of the employment relationship—are also debates over freedom and justice. Supporters of freedom emphasize the power of free market solutions, while advocates of justice question whether this power serves everyone fairly. This is a central issue for the employment relationship, but employment is not divorced from contemporary social and political debates that are rooted in the same competing visions of justice and freedom. In short, are checks and balances needed to provide justice, or are they unwarranted interferences with freedom? The fundamental views are summarized by Mangum and Philips (1988, 18):

> The neoclassicist inevitably advocates market competition as the solution to most ills. The institutionalist insists that knowledgeable tinkering can improve the functions of a generally satisfactory system. The radical is convinced more fundamental interventions and reforms are essential.

This "knowledgeable tinkering" is a system of checks and balances that seeks to harness the power of markets and freedom for human needs and justice.

In the employment relationship, market competition and the resulting economic prosperity through efficiency is important, but work is a fully human activity so equity and voice are also important. Employment should be productive, provide fair standards of treatment, and allow for employee input. The International Labour Organization (1999) calls this simply "decent work." These standards are important for both research and practice. Employment research often studies the operation of employment processes and how outcomes are determined. Knowledge of how processes work is incomplete without an understanding of what the processes are trying to accomplish. And the outcomes that are studied are defined by the objectives that are important. Research that focuses exclusively on whether outcomes are efficient, or whether practices and institutions improve productivity, embodies a normative judgment that efficiency concerns are paramount. Giving equity and voice equal importance with efficiency implies the need for a broader research agenda. In practice, for the decline in union density, or the increase in income inequality, or a lack of true participation or democracy in some employee involvement initiatives, to be of concern (or not) requires a set of standards for judging employment relationship outcomes. These standards are balancing efficiency, equity, and voice and balancing the conflicting human rights of property rights and labor rights.

Public discourse that emphasizes competitive markets, efficiency, and marginal productivity justice; the frequent lack of appreciation for employee voice; the continued turbulence of the twenty-first century workplace; the focus of employment research on the operation of existing processes (often solely with efficiency in mind); and the need for "explicitly recognizing the role of moral choices in the labor market" (Osterman et al. 2001, 12) all make it imperative to ground the study of employment in the objectives of the employment relationship—efficiency, equity, and voice. This grounding provides the basis for a fuller understanding of all aspects of the employment relationship, including the alternative behaviors, strategies, institutions, and public policies for balancing efficiency, equity, and voice. From such analyses can come workplace governance practices and systems that fulfill the economic and human needs of a democratic society and foster broadly shared prosperity.

Epilogue: The Late Middle Ages
of Industrial Relations

INDUSTRIAL RELATIONS is important. The condition of workplace employee-management relations affects productivity, quality, customer service, competitiveness, and economic performance. Terms and conditions of employment —not only pay and benefits, but also how work is organized and managed— determine the quality of life for workers, their families, and their communities. And industrial relations affects society. Airline strikes obstruct travel and business and strikes by nurses disrupt health care delivery. Poor labor-management relations are arguably partly responsible for the decline of the U.S. auto and steel industries. More vividly, defective Firestone tires that were responsible for over 250 deaths were more likely to have been produced during two critical periods of labor-management conflict.[1] Minimum employment standards are central to discussions of fundamental human rights, and to sometimes violent clashes at summit meetings on globalization. Worldwide, the 175 member nations of the International Labour Organization share "the conviction that social justice is essential to universal and lasting peace," and therefore pursue improvements in industrial relations.

And yet, the academic field of industrial relations is at a crossroads forty years removed from its golden age.[2] This arises not from the quality of industrial relations research, which has rebounded over the last two decades, but from questions about the definition and direction of the field. This is partly an issue of nomenclature. Up to the golden age, the label "industrial relations" clearly included questions of labor (markets, law, and unions) *and* today's human resource management, at least in the United States (Kaufman 1993, 2001a). Some still use this broad definition, but many more use a much narrower definition that equates industrial relations with labor unions, collective bargaining, and perhaps labor markets. For some, industrial relations is part of human resource management; for others, they are distinct entities.

Underlying this problem of nomenclature are significant theoretical issues.[3]

These are most clearly captured by the differing views on conflict in the employment relationship. Human resource management embodies a unitarist perspective on conflict: effective policies can align the interests of employers and employees, and thereby create a unity of interests (Fox 1974). In contrast, mainstream U.S. industrial relations assumes a pluralist perspective: employment relationship conflict is "mixed motive," so at least some issues involve an inherent conflict of interest (Clegg 1975; Fox 1974; Kochan 1982). Mutual gains can be pursued in some areas, but others involve distributive conflict and divergent interests. Mainstream industrial relations in Great Britain—a critical or political economy school of industrial relations—generally embraces a third perspective: employment relationship conflict is class-based or social; it is not purely economic and confined to the employment relationship, as in the pluralist and unitarist views (Giles and Murray 1997; Godard 1994; Hyman 1975). These three perspectives yield very different conceptions of the roles of unions, management, and government in the employment relationship. These differences become magnified when research is applied to reform and practice and gets caught in the ideological cross-fire between organized labor and business.

Furthermore, the questions surrounding the future of industrial relations are heightened by the waning influence of the labor movement. Industrial relations is characterized by normative support for independent employee representation and by collective bargaining as a central research area. But union density in the United States has been on the decline since the 1950s, and has also declined more recently in many other countries. Can industrial relations be viable if union density is less than 10 percent and if labor unions are popularly viewed as narrow special interest groups that harm competitiveness? In other words, is the decline of organized labor a sword of Damocles hanging over the head of the field of industrial relations?[4]

Thus, shifting nomenclature, theoretical differences—especially with respect to employment relationship conflict and therefore the value of labor unions—and declining union density have all driven the field of industrial relations to a crossroads. The recent exchange between Godard and Delaney (2000, 2002) and Kochan (2000) demonstrates that these issues are both important and unsettled. The field of industrial relations has moved from the stability of the golden age to the current uncertainty, conflict, and turbulence of what can be labeled the "late middle ages of industrial relations." The field's participants will determine whether this is followed by a renaissance or a reformation.[5]

This book develops an intellectual agenda for pluralist industrial relations rooted in the objectives of the employment relationship. The implications for scholarship in industrial relations and other disciplines that study work and for policy and practice have been described elsewhere in the book. But this renewed focus on the objectives of the employment relationship also has broader implications for revitalizing the academic field of industrial relations by defining an inclusive field of human resources and industrial relations that includes all perspectives on work, by refining the teaching of industrial relations and by establishing new multidisciplinary links.

IR Theory or HRIR Vision?

The centrality of analyses of efficiency, equity, and voice and alternative mechanisms for their achievement defines an inclusive academic field of "human resources and industrial relations" (HRIR) that includes pluralist industrial relations, human resource management, and critical industrial relations.[6] Contrary to long-standing beliefs, HRIR does not need a *single* theory.[7] What is needed is a common vision of the unique domain of the field. In other words, HRIR needs a unifying symbol (Adams 1993) or an axis of cohesion (Abbott 2001). This common vision is the analysis of the objectives of the employment relationship. Although sometimes normative and sometimes positive, researchers in the field of HRIR analyze the dimensions, determinants, and effects of efficiency, equity, and voice in alternative employment relationship models. This is the intellectually distinguishing feature of the field that sets it apart from all others. Alternative employment relationship models include, at a minimum, all of the alternatives discussed in chapters 5–9: legal regulation, human resource management, worker control, works councils, and numerous forms of unionism including business unionism and social unionism. This definition of HRIR is intended to be quite broad. That knowledge of this common core is advanced from diverse theoretical and methodological perspectives should be an enriching feature of HRIR as a single field, not a barrier to it (Kochan 1998).

It is common to cite the need for a single theory to define the field of industrial relations, which I now refer to as HRIR.[8] Although he does not subscribe to this need, Kaufman (1993, 150) characterizes the emphasis on an integrative theoretical framework as "the holy grail of industrial relations." The exemplary example is Dunlop's (1958) assertion that his industrial relations systems model is a general theory of industrial relations.[9] But social science disciplines are usually not characterized by a single theory.[10] Rather, academic disciplines are commonly defined by both content and social standards (Abbott 2001; Becher 1989; Nissani 1995; Toulmin 1972; Whitley 2000). The social aspect involves a community of scholars with shared goals and communication networks. The focus herein is the content dimension.[11] In particular, the content standard for an academic field of study does not require a single discipline-defining theory. Moreover, the content standard for a discipline does not require a lack of overlap with other disciplines nor unique theories or methodologies (Abbott 2001; Becher 1989; Ritzer 1980; Rosenberg 1995; Whitley 2000).[12]

Instead, for HRIR to be an academic field of study, it needs a strong common vision, an axis of cohesion, or a unifying symbol, of the core topics of the field that is inclusive, not exclusive. Hodgson's (1998, 190) assertion that economics "should be defined, as in other sciences, in terms of its object of analysis, rather than by any set of particular tenets" is equally valid for HRIR. HRIR does not need a paradigm, it needs a metaparadigm—an organizing map that defines the parameters of a field (Masterman 1970; Ritzer 1980). My metaparadigm—not theory—for an inclusive field of HRIR begins with the objectives of the employment relationship: efficiency, equity, and voice.

These objectives provide not only a common set of core topics for HRIR scholars from diverse perspectives, but also distinguish HRIR from other disciplines. Mainstream economics is generally concerned only with narrow conceptions of efficiency. When equity and voice are considered, it is almost always instrumental equity and voice—Does inequality provide incentives for improvement or for harmful externalities? How does voice help economic relationships work more effectively?[13] With its supposedly value-free perspective, mainstream neoclassical economics pays little attention to moral, religious, and political aspects of equity and voice. Sociology and psychology are often focused on equity, such as workers' reactions to inequitable situations (Adams 1965; Hodson 2001), but efficiency is not an important concern. Political science concentrates on voice, but not on efficiency and equity. Only HRIR analyzes all three (see figure E.1).[14] With that said, it should be emphasized that this discussion applies to disciplines, not individuals. Individuals studying work from all disciplines should be considered part of the academic field of HRIR; the point of the present discussion is to articulate how the academic field of HRIR is distinct from these other fields, not to exclude scholars from these disciplines who are not formally housed in HRIR units (many of whom fit naturally into the three schools within HRIR as defined here).

The three schools that comprise the field of HRIR—pluralistic industrial relations, human resource management, and critical industrial relations—differ in at least one important respect. Each school has a significantly different view of the nature of employment relationship conflict—pluralist, unitarist, or class-based, respectively. But at the same time, these three schools are bound together by a focus on the employment relationship; the study of efficiency, equity, and voice; an applied problem-solving orientation (which is not the same thing as being atheoretical); and shared foundations about labor as more than a commodity and as being unequal in labor market interactions with employers. These shared foundations are captured in figure 5.2. Excepting neoclassical labor economics, figure 5.2 is an inclusive map of the field of HRIR. It reveals the differences among the three schools, but also the commonalities. Figure 3.1, which models employment outcomes as a function of the environment and the human agent, further reveals the important commonalities of diverse scholarship on employment relationship outcomes. Although different schools emphasize different components of the environment and the human agent in figure 3.1, the subject of analysis is the same—the determination of work behaviors and employment outcomes.

This discussion is not intended to gloss over the differences among these

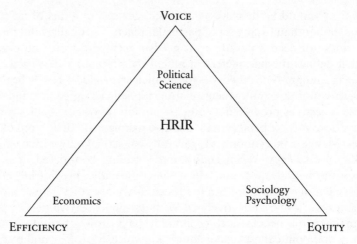

Figure E.1 Academic Disciplines on Work

three schools. The differing views of employment relationship conflict are very significant. As discussed in chapter 5 and above, these contrasting views of conflict underlie vastly different interpretations of the roles of labor unions, human resource management, and government regulation in the employment relationship. The three schools also differ in their relative emphases on efficiency, equity, and voice.[15] With the assumption of unitarist conflict, equity and voice can be harnessed to enhance efficiency; the typical human resource management research perspective analyzes the effects of equity and voice on different elements of efficiency. With the assumption of pluralist or class-based conflict, efficiency clashes more frequently with equity and voice. Research in industrial relations therefore more often analyzes the provision of equity and voice as a function of employee concerns rather than efficiency concerns. Industrial relations research also focuses more (but not exclusively) on the external determinants of employment outcomes, such as markets, laws, and institutions, while human resource management research focuses more (but not exclusively) on internal determinants, such as attitudes, motivators, and managerial policies (Kaufman 1993, 2001a).

Like other disciplines, the scope of HRIR research clearly has positive and normative aspects. Positive research should analyze all workplace governance mechanisms—traditional collective bargaining, proposed models of employee representation, human resource management, free markets, government regulation, and worker control. However, normative beliefs shape positive research agendas—human resource management research focuses on management policies, industrial relations research focuses on unions—so normative and positive issues blend together. The power of figure 5.2 as a map of the field of HRIR is in helping to distinguish positive from normative statements. Recognition of the assumptions outlined in figure 5.2 will not erase the normative differences within HRIR—in fact, this is an "unresolvable debate" (Kochan 1998, 39)—but it can promote constructive dialogue (Kaufman 2001a).

Moreover, positive and normative disagreements over the relative effectiveness of different governance mechanisms, the explanatory power of differing methodologies (Whitfield and Strauss 1998), or even fundamental questions about the wisdom of the dominant logical empiricism research methodology (Godard 1993, 1994) should not prevent the existence of a single field in which researchers with different points of view regularly interact.[16] An inclusive approach to HRIR has an important precedent. The graduate degree programs at Cornell, Minnesota, Illinois, and elsewhere are based on coursework in both human resource management and industrial relations.[17] When graduating master's students enter the professional field of human resources as practitioners, they have knowledge of both human resource management and industrial relations to draw on.

The academic field should follow this model in terms of boundaries, interaction, and discourse. The quality and status of scholarship in all areas of the employment relationship can benefit from being part of an inclusive field of HRIR. Using efficiency, equity, and voice to map the field of HRIR can help broaden the scope of high-performance work systems research, which has tended to focus narrowly on efficiency issues (Godard and Delaney 2000). The value of interaction between industrial relations and human resource management is also revealed by the improved understanding of unions that has resulted from research on union commitment using the behavioral science techniques that dominate the human resource management literature (Barling, Fullagar, and Kelloway 1992; Gallagher and Strauss 1991). Although critical industrial relations is often quite critical of human resource management (e.g., Legge 1995), the two areas share common research interests. For example, Pinder and Harlos (2001) analyze the behavioral and organizational elements of employee silence, while Kelly (1998) analyzes collective determinants of nonsilence through mobilization theory.

Many academic disciplines study work, labor, and the employment relationship, but these are the core topics only in pluralist and critical industrial relations and human resource management. The intellectual perspectives, research agendas, and practical applications of scholars in these areas should comprise the singular academic field of "human resources and industrial relations" (HRIR). This is not to say that some perspectives should be subordinated to others; rather, differing intellectual and methodological approaches to the study of the employment relationship should be brought together to pursue a richer understanding of "all aspects of people at work" (Kochan 1980, 1; Adams 1993). A renewed focus on the objectives of the employment relationship and ways to achieve them provide the needed common vision, symbol, metaparadigm, or axis of cohesion for the field of HRIR. HRIR—the study of employment—is the analysis of the contributions of individuals, markets, institutions, organizational strategies, and public policies to the employment relationship objectives of efficiency, equity, and voice in the workplace as influenced by the environment and individual decision making, including ethics.

Teaching Industrial Relations: The Thematic Imperative

U.S. industrial relations teaching—usually as a course in labor relations—has a dominant process-based focus. This is most visibly illustrated by the numerous textbooks that focus uncritically on the labor relations *processes*— how unions are organized, how contracts are negotiated, and how grievances are resolved.[18] This process-based approach fits with the golden age of industrial relations in which collective bargaining was viewed by industrial relations scholars and others as "self-evidently good" (Reynolds 1988, 123). But it is the golden age no longer. In the late middle ages of industrial relations at the start of the twenty-first century, the existing processes of collective bargaining, which arise from the New Deal industrial relations system, are not *self-evidently* good.

Osterman et al. (2001, 5) summarize the feelings of many:

> The policies that emerged from the New Deal and postwar periods were built around a set of assumptions so fundamental that they were hardly ever recognized explicitly when introduced. Many of the assumptions, however, have been called into question by the subsequent evolution of the economy and society. The result is a basic mismatch between the institutional structure and the reality of today's world of work.

There is a thriving academic literature on this critical topic, but today's textbooks continue to present students with a narrow focus on the existing labor relations processes—organizing, bargaining, and administering contracts in the New Deal industrial relations system. During a period in which the assumptions of the New Deal industrial relations system are widely questioned and in which the resulting processes are under attack from both labor and management, a process-based focus has significant failings.[19] In particular, when the presentation of the labor relations processes is divorced from their underlying reasons, it is difficult to develop a complete understanding. And lacking a discussion of the underlying objectives of the industrial relations system, there are no metrics for evaluating both the current system and reform proposals.

A renewed focus on the objectives of the employment relationship and the options for their achievement fills these critical gaps in industrial relations instruction. The goal of balancing efficiency, equity, and voice illuminates the rationale for existing labor law and the current labor relations processes. Consideration of questions of workplace governance provides the opportunity to address alternatives to labor unionism and therefore to explicitly reveal the important assumptions that underlie industrial relations—such as unitarist versus pluralist conflict and perfect versus imperfect labor markets. Students may or may not agree with these assumptions, but they should confront them to debate them and to better understand the foundations of the existing system. Property rights versus labor rights is a recurring theme in many areas of labor law and industrial relations so that this tension provides a common thread across many topics. Explicit development of this theme reinforces the central problems in industrial relations; otherwise, students tend to see labor law decisions as episodic and unrelated. And in the final analysis, the extent to which efficiency, equity, and voice are balanced, and to which property rights and labor rights are balanced, provide the metrics for evaluating whether the current system needs reforming and for analyzing alternative reform proposals (see chapters 6–8).

Independent employee representation is one of several possible vehicles for achieving the fundamental objectives of equity, efficiency, and voice. The New Deal industrial relations system's processes are one of many alternative arrangements. So while the existing labor relations processes are important, they are more completely understood in a thematic framework that emphasizes the objectives of the employment relationship, alternatives for workplace governance and labor relations, and property rights versus labor rights. As such, there is a thematic imperative for teaching industrial relations.[20] "Collective bargaining, after all, is a means and not an end. The objective is the betterment of the individual working person" (St. Antoine 1988, 70). Contrary to the explicit emphasis in the popular textbook by Holley, Jennings, and Wolters (2001), labor relations is not about contractual work rules.[21] Labor relations is about the objectives of the employment relationship—achieving efficiency, equity, and voice, likely in conjunction with other workplace governance mechanisms, while balancing property rights and labor rights. Work rules are a means, not an end. Process-based approaches that focus solely on how the processes work assume that the value of employee representation is self-evident and elevate work rules to ends in themselves. The true end is lost in the process. And with it, an effective understanding of labor relations is lost as well.

A Renewed Deal for the Academic Field of Industrial Relations

A renewed deal—or a renaissance—for the academic field of industrial relations to increase its viability in the twenty-first century includes forming an inclusive field of human resources and industrial relations (HRIR) with critical industrial relations and human resource management, and also moving toward a theme-based teaching paradigm. Both of these actions are rooted in a renewed focus on the fundamental objectives of the employment relationship and the alternatives for achieving them. Additionally, a more fundamental conception of industrial relations that moves beyond the existing processes to a set of core foundations can provide a stronger basis for academic linkages into disciplines with which there have not been strong ties.

Support for the principle of labor unionism, and employee voice more generally, flows directly from the intellectual foundations of industrial relations—the importance of human dignity and democratic rights combined with imperfect labor markets and an inherent conflict of interest in the employment relationship (recall figure 5.2). But industrial relations is about more than a particular form of unionism. Independent employee representation is one important component of a broader industrial relations emphasis on creating a market-based employment relationship with a human face; in other words, an employment relationship that balances efficiency, equity, and voice. The general perspective of creating markets with a human face, or in the words of John R. Commons (1934, 143), to "save capitalism by making it good," has been a central theme in industrial relations since its founding (Kaufman 1997b, forthcoming). This perspective can form the basis for shared intellectual synergies outside of industrial relations. Scholars who focus on business ethics (Bowie 1999), human rights (Lauren 1998), theology (Alford and Naughton 2001; Naughton 1995), the natural environment (Esty 2001), and governance of international organizations (Stiglitz 2002), all embrace the underlying industrial relations principles of adding checks and balances to economic markets. The decline in union density should not be interpreted as the disappearance of support for the industrial relations philosophy of replacing "might makes right" in imperfect markets with capitalist institutions that are responsive to principles of human dignity and democracy. Multidisciplinary scholarship has long been a hallmark of industrial relations scholarship, and expanding these linkages farther afield can help increase the field's vitality.[22]

Industrial relations and modern institutional economics share a founding figure—John R. Commons—and the contemporary intellectual frameworks of these two fields continue to be quite similar.[23] Like industrial relations, institutional economics emphasizes the importance of power, webs of rules, ethics, and social values that go beyond efficiency (Klein 1993; Ramstad 1993). And yet the lack of synergies between the two fields is reflected by the fact that dual labor market theory is very institutional, but lacks institutional economics references (Ramstad 1993). While also lacking rigorous grounding in contemporary institutional economics scholarship, the employment with a human face paradigm developed in this book is also consistent with the tenets of this school of thought. In behavioral economics, Altman (2001) has recently theorized that labor rights can be welfare enhancing; the parallel with industrial relations is obvious.

Or consider the case of business ethics. This field has very important commonalities with industrial relations, but few linkages between the disciplines exist. Much of business ethics involves employee issues such as discrimination, harassment, unjust dismissal, whistleblowers, privacy, diversity, and leadership. Moreover, both industrial relations and business ethics, and moral philosophy more generally (Korsgaard 1996), seek to move beyond utilitarianism. As industrial relations rejects a narrow focus on utilitarianism and efficiency by imbuing the employment relationship with respect for human dignity and justice, business ethics often has the same thrust with respect to corporate behavior and responsibility more generally. Bowie's (1999) description of a Kantian business firm is to a large extent an industrial relations description of the desired employment relationship: a respect for the need to make a profit balanced with employee dignity and autonomy, including employee participation, a living wage, and just cause dismissal protections. Solomon's (1992) application of the Aristotelian tradition to business ethics similarly emphasizes both employee excellence and respect for employees as people and members of the corporate community. The emphasis on interpersonal relationships in the ethics of care was put into practice in the drive to organize a union for Harvard University clerical workers. Core industrial relations beliefs are alive and well and living in other disciplines. Another avenue for a renaissance is to develop closer multidisciplinary linkages with those disciplines.

In the meantime, industrial relations as an academic field is at a crossroads. Its disciplinary status is unclear. Its influence on public policy and globalization is questionable. Its primary institutions of unions and government regulation are seen as products of a bygone era and therefore as anachronistic in an information-rich, flexible, global economy. The current late middle ages of industrial relations is one of uncertainty, conflict, and turbulence. What follows will likely be either a renaissance—with increased social and academic relevance—or a reformation—with deepening schisms and increased marginalization. A renewed industrial relations focus on the objectives of the employment relationship, the critical need for balance, and the alternatives for achieving this balance provides the foundations of a possible renaissance.

Notes

INTRODUCTION

1. For example, see Applebaum and Batt (1994), Cappelli (1999), Heckscher (1988), Kochan, Katz, and McKersie (1986), Mishel, Bernstein, and Schmitt (2001), Osterman et al. (2001), Potter and Youngman (1995), and Towers (1997).

2. Institutions are broadly defined to include laws, labor unions, and customs consistent with Commons's (1934, 69) definition of an institution as "collective action in control of individual action" (see also Kaufman 1988; Ramstad 1993; Yonay 1998).

3. The need to add checks and balances to economic markets is discussed by Flexner (1989), Hartmann (2002), Kelly (2001), Korten (1995, 1999), Phillips (2002), Soros (2000), and Stiglitz (2002). While not fully grounded in modern institutional economic theory, the analyses developed here are also consistent with the institutional economics emphasis on power, webs of rules, ethics, and social values that go beyond the neoclassical economics emphasis on efficiency (Tool 1993).

4. "Address by Mr. Kofi Annan to the Chamber of Commerce of the United States of America," Washington, D.C., June 8, 1999 (www.un.org/partners/business/sgstat1.htm, accessed August 7, 2002). Also see www.unglobalcompact.org.

5. *Centesimus Annus* is reprinted in John Paul II (2000). Many encyclicals are available online at www.vatican.va/holy_father/.

6. One of the best-selling labor relations textbooks is simply titled *The Labor Relations Process* (Holley, Jennings, and Wolters 2001).

7. This is the product of the postwar U.S. vision of industrial pluralism emphasizing written contracts and rules created through collective bargaining and administered through private grievance arbitration (Stone 1981). As there are other possible institutional structures and strategies for achieving a balance in the workplace beyond a narrow rules-based process, industrial pluralism is a narrow special case of pluralism.

8. More specifically, a central economic principle is marginal productivity theory. Self-interested individuals consume items up to the point that the additional cost of one more unit just equals the additional benefit (in other words, so that the marginal cost equals the marginal benefit). Profit-maximizing companies similarly use inputs, including labor, up to the point that the marginal cost (such as increased wage costs to attract one more employee) equals the marginal benefit (the value of the additional employee's productivity, which is called the value of their marginal product). As such, the basic textbook result is that prices and wages in competitive markets reflect the marginal benefit or productivity of goods, services, and inputs. Marginal productivity

justice turns this economic theory into a normative or ethical theory that says workers (and all other commodities) *ought* to receive the value of their marginal product (McClelland, 1990). In other words, whatever the market determines must be fair.

9. For example, see Baird (2000), Epstein (1983), Heldman, Bennett, and Johnson (1981), Reynolds (1996), and Troy (1999). When the public encounters labor relations through the media, it is likely that it will see it through narrow lenses (Puette 1992).

10. In particular, the Commission on the Future of Worker-Management Relations (the Dunlop Commission) was created in 1993, by the Democratic presidential administration of Bill Clinton, to address three questions:

1. What (if any) new methods or institutions should be encouraged, or required, to enhance workplace productivity through labor-management cooperation and employee participation?
2. What (if any) changes should be made in the present legal framework and practices of collective bargaining to enhance cooperative behavior, improve productivity, and reduce conflict and delay?
3. What (if anything) should be done to increase the extent to which workplace problems are directly resolved by the parties themselves, rather than through recourse to state and federal courts and governmental bodies?

The commission's final report was issued in 1994.

11. Klare (1985), St. Antoine (1988), and Gall (2003) similarly make the point that unionization and collective bargaining are not simply ends in themselves. In this same vein, Kelly (1998) grounds his mobilization theory in workers' interests and objectives.

12. For more details and references on the history of industrial relations, see Barbash (1993) and especially Kaufman (1993, 1997b, 2001a).

13. This framework is more in the mainstream in Great Britain than in the United States and is rooted in Marxist traditions.

14. A triangular representation of efficiency, equity, and voice and the phrase "geometry of the employment relationship" are inspired by Hyman's (2001, 4) "geometry of trade unionism"—a triangle of market, society, and class.

15. The "thundering silence" that followed the Dunlop Commission's report in 1994 is one recent example (Estreicher 1996, 827).

1. The Objectives of the Employment Relationship

1. For example, note the distributive justice focus of equity in economics (Baldwin 1966; Bolton and Ockenfels 2000; Okun 1975; Porter 2001), law (Swygert and Yanes 1998), policy analysis (McMahon and Abreu 1998; D. Stone 2001), and psychology (Adams 1965; O'Neill and Mone 1998).

2. My definition of equity includes distributive justice while procedural justice overlaps with both equity and voice. The distinction between equity and voice is that the former is how you are treated and the latter is whether you can participate. Some elements of procedural justice are therefore part of equity (such as using consistent standards and objective information in pay raise decisions; Folger and Konovsky 1989) while other elements of procedural justice are part of voice (such as providing employees the opportunity to express their side). The distinction between equity and voice more closely parallels Greenberg's (1987) distinction between reactive and proactive organizational justice theories (each of which have outcome and process dimensions).

3. Hausman and McPherson (1996) further note that this standard definition reveals how closely economists equate well-being with the satisfaction of preferences. Precise statements of Pareto optimality should be based on preference satisfaction.

4. Efficiency therefore implies that goods and services are produced and consumed up to the point where marginal benefit equals marginal cost. More formally, there are three conditions for a Pareto optimal equilibrium: 1) efficiency in consumption in which marginal rates of substitution between goods are equal across consumers; 2) efficiency in production in which marginal rates of technical substitution are equal across products; and 3) efficiency in product mix in which the marginal rate of substitution between two products equals the marginal rate of transforma-

tion for the two products. If these conditions are not satisfied, then trades or an altered product mix can increase someone's utility without harming others.

5. Problems of moral hazard and adverse selection are examples of unintended negative consequences that can arise when trying to address market failures through public policy. Addison and Hirsch (1997) further note that concerns about correcting market failures are magnified if public policies are determined more by political lobbying than economic analysis (see also Heldman, Bennett, and Johnson 1981). Finally, there is the problem of administration of government regulation (Weil 1997). As noted by Befort (2002), current U.S. employment and labor regulation is a "patchwork" and a "mess."

6. For an early statement of this idea, see the discussion of "industrial parasitism" in Webb and Webb (1897, 766–67). More recently, see Krueger (2002) for a discussion of the negative economic effects of too much income inequality. The analogous common law concept to an externality is the doctrine of nuisance. If the public is harmed by a private action, such as pollution, such activity can be legally limited (Ely 1998).

7. This is not to say that rational, self-interested parties cannot find efficient outcomes when faced with market imperfections.

8. This is the central belief of the old institutional labor economists such as John R. Commons (Kaufman 1997b).

9. In situations of poverty, there can also be nutrition-based efficiency wages (Bliss and Stern 1978). Samuel Gompers articulated this phenomenon over one hundred years ago. When asked how two mills can have different output levels, Gompers responded, "Well, there are a number of causes, I should say. First, perhaps poorer pay to the workers in one mill who can not secure for themselves sufficient nourishing food, comforts, and surroundings, so as that they might become comparatively enfeebled and unable to keep up with the velocity of the machine" (U.S. Industrial Commission 1901, 651).

10. This literature is vast, but see Appelbaum and Batt (1994), Becker and Huselid (1998), Cappelli and Neumark (2001), and Hammer (2000).

11. The effects of employee perceptions of distributive and procedural justice is a popular research question in human resource management and organizational behavior, but this generally reflects an efficiency standard. For example, if distributive or procedural justice increases employee loyalty, then organizational outcomes can improve. Thus, distributive and procedural justice are advocated in human resource management not because of a concern for employee rights, but because of the potential for organizational improvement. Improved employee welfare is a positive derivative benefit, but the defining objective is organizational improvement.

12. As noted above, some aspects of procedural justice also overlap with voice. But the elements of procedural justice that are unilateral (but fair) treatment by managers toward workers without any worker input are a part of equity rather than voice.

13. This can also be thought of as absolute and relative fairness.

14. This treatment differs from, for example, Cropanzano et al.'s (2001) review of organizational justice theories because the task herein is to support why equity should be an objective of the employment relationship (independent of its potentially positive effects on efficiency) whereas their review analyzes theories of why workers respond to just or unjust treatment.

15. Major ethical theories are surveyed and applied to the employment relationship in more detail in chapter 4.

16. Moses has even been labeled "history's greatest labor leader" for freeing the Israelite workers from Egyptian exploitation (Husslein 1924).

17. *Rerum Novarum* is reprinted in Catholic Church (1943).

18. *Centesimus Annus* is reprinted in John Paul II (2000). Other relevant papal encyclicals include *Quadragesimo Anno* ("Reconstruction of the Social Order," 1931) by Pope Pius XI, *Octogesima Adveniens* ("A Call to Action," 1971) by Pope Paul VI, and *Laborem Exercens* ("On Human Work," 1981) by Pope John Paul II. Many of the encyclicals are available online at www.vatican.va/holy_father/.

19. Ogle (1994) and Ogle and Wheeler (2001) discuss workers' rights in the Protestant faith, Perry (1993) in Judaism, and Khalil-ur-Rehman (1995) in Islam. The sometimes mixed and ambivalent record of major religions on human rights is reviewed by Witte (1996).

20. Like Nussbaum's (2000) human capabilities, Maslow's (1968) concept of self-actualization can be traced back to Aristotle's idea of flourishing (Hill 1997).

21. Note that this is significantly different than the typical application of Maslow's (1968) hierarchy of needs in human resource management. The typical application concludes that companies can motivate employees by being attentive to their hierarchy of needs. This is an efficiency rationale for providing workplace equity, not a moral or political one.

22. Rawls's famous veil of ignorance also supports workplace equity because the veil of ignorance, and therefore justice, is blind to arbitrary factors such as race, gender, or nationality.

23. Contemporary U.S. judicial thought, however, emphasizes procedural rather than distributive justice (Zietlow 1998).

24. Like libertarianism (but for very different reasons), utilitarianism is generally conceived of as being irrespective of distributional consequences, but John Stuart Mill admitted that the state has an obligation to provide minimum standards (West 2001).

25. For example, in the libertarian view welfare boils down to a conflict between "the rich should have the liberty not to be interfered with when using their surplus resources for luxury purposes, or that the poor should have the liberty to not be interfered with when taking from the rich what they require to meet their basic needs" (Sterba 1988, 86). In the libertarian view, both of these liberties should be equally valid, but since they are in conflict some other standard is needed to determine which one takes precedence. Sterba (1988) asserts that the right to welfare is morally superior because people are not morally required to do things which involve an unreasonable sacrifice—in this case, the poor's sacrifice of their liberty because they will starve.

26. *Bigelow v. Bullard*, 901 P.2d 630 (Nev. 1995).

27. The classic statement of the employment-at-will doctrine is found in a Tennessee court's ruling that "all may dismiss their employees at will, be they many or few, for good cause, for no cause or even for cause morally wrong, without being thereby guilty of legal wrong" (*Payne v. Western and Atlantic R. R. Co.*, 81 Tenn. 507, 519–520 [1884], *overruled on other grounds*, Hutton v. Watters, 179 S.W. 134, 138 [Tenn. 1915]).

28. I further hesitate to use voice and democracy as synonyms because, as described in the previous section, democratic principles of equality also underlie the equity standard.

29. Greenfield and Pleasure (1993) similarly reject a narrow definition of voice that focuses exclusively on efficiency and argue for a return to the longer-standing political conception of voice. With that said, my usage of "voice" is not inconsistent with Hirschman (1970). One, "voice" as used in this book can be efficiency enhancing, but is not limited to it. Two, the present analysis examines a more fundamental question than Hirschman (1970). The point of this section is that workers should be entitled to voice. Research on the exit-voice trade-off (e.g., Bemmels 1997; Freeman and Medoff 1984) doesn't address whether workers *should* have voice, but rather addresses how is it used when they do have it and what are the effects of its use. These usages are complementary, not conflicting.

30. Similarly, from the standards of political democracy, Derber (1970) specifies nine principles of industrial democracy: representation, participation, equal rights and opportunities, right of dissent, due process, responsibility, minimum standards, information, and personal dignity. For a discussion of the definition of democracy in political terms, see Dahl (1998). For additional discussions of industrial democracy, see Webb and Webb (1897), Derber (1970), Klare (1988), Greenfield and Pleasure (1993), Lichtenstein and Harris (1993), and Towers (1997).

31. Non-job-related reasons can sometimes be valid, too, such as in the case of an off-duty police officer that commits a crime. More generally, these protections are not unlimited. For example, employee voice does not require that particularly hateful or offensive speech be protected. Rather, competing objectives and interests in the employment relationship should be balanced (see chapter 2).

32. A basic right of association is well accepted in liberal democracy, but there are also difficult questions pertaining to compulsory membership, freedom to disassociate, undemocratic associations, and protections of associations that harm another party (Gutmann 1998; Rosenblum 1998). These issues are of obvious importance in industrial relations, but should not undermine the basic—albeit not unlimited—freedom of association that supports industrial democracy (Leader 1992; White 1998).

33. A more self-interested early argument for industrial democracy is presented by Fink (1987): as the Knights of Labor and then the American Federation of Labor fought for legitimacy at the end of the nineteenth century, they couched their actions in terms of the fundamental political principle of democracy to gain acceptance.

34. For a recent example of the counterargument that this violates property rights and individual liberties, see Bainbridge (1998). This is the same logic used from the 1880s to the 1920s by many judges to make minimum wage, maximum hours, and other labor standards laws unconstitutional (Forbath 1985; Phillips 1998).

35. See also Forbath (2001) and Pope (1997, 2002) for a discussion of how the constitutionality of the Wagner Act could have rested on these amendments rather than the U.S. Constitution's commerce clause. Violations of the Fourteenth Amendment's guarantee of due process are suggested by the Wagner Act's finding that individual workers "do not possess . . . actual liberty of contract." Pope (1997, 942) argues that these amendments gave workers "the ability not only to influence the conditions of working life, but to do so consciously, in combination with one's co-workers."

36. More specifically, the First Amendment protects freedom of speech and assembly. The Thirteenth and Fourteenth Amendments are the post–Civil War reconstruction amendments that outlaw slavery and involuntary servitude and guarantee that the government will not "deprive any person of life, liberty, or property, without due process of law; nor deny to any person within its jurisdiction the equal protection of the laws."

37. The ongoing creation thesis is not universally accepted (Hauerwas 1983). Moreover, Bainbridge (1998, 781) argues that in the Protestant tradition, work should be approached with "an attitude of service," not as a method of fulfilling self-realization. For discussions of other religions outside of the Catholic tradition that are supportive of employee rights, see Perry (1993), Khalil-ur-Rehman (1995), Ogle (1994), and Ogle and Wheeler (2001).

38. To foreshadow the next chapter, papal distinctions between participation in business decisions and employment decisions reflect an attempt to balance property rights with labor rights (Naughton 1995). The "core of entrepreneurial control" in U.S. labor law stems from *Fibreboard Paper Products Corp. v. NLRB,* 379 U.S. 203 (1964).

39. For an objection to both Sashkin (1984) and Solomon (1996), see Bainbridge (1998). Much of Bainbridge's (1998) critique is based on empirical evidence that many employees do not prefer participation/voice (e.g., Witte 1980; but compare Freeman and Rogers 1999). This argument confuses the distinction between the *right* to have a voice and the *requirement* to participate in decision making. Most people do not speak publicly and many do not vote, but this doesn't mean that these fundamental freedoms should be removed.

40. In addition to the fact that no state corporation code specifies that a corporate director's sole fiduciary duty is to the shareholders, thirty-two states have adopted constituency statutes in which directors are explicitly allowed to consider interests beyond those of the shareholders (Adams and Matheson 2000).

41. As an interesting parallel, Khalil-ur-Rehman (1995, 18) indicates that in Islam, workers can acquire ownership rights by contributing skill and labor.

42. Though compare Pateman (1970) with Schumpeter (1947) in which the latter asserts that competition for votes is the key to democracy.

43. In this definition, equity is instrumental and well-being or self-actualization is intrinsic, which provides further support for the need to divide equity into separate instrumental and intrinsic components, as in equity and voice.

44. As noted in the introduction, a triangular representation of efficiency, equity, and voice and the phrase "geometry of the employment relationship" are inspired by Hyman's (2001, 4) "geometry of trade unionism."

2. The Balancing Imperative: Human Rights in Conflict

1. Distributive conflicts involve strict conflicts of interest such that one side's gain is the other's side loss. The standard example is splitting a fixed amount of revenue (a fixed economic pie) between wages and profits. Integrative issues involve the potential for joint gain—increasing the size of the economic pie so that both wages and profits, for example, can increase.

2. This is "almost" by definition for several reasons. One, free market advocates might argue that competitive outcomes are equitable because each product is rewarded with its relative economic value. Two, socially unacceptable behaviors such as discrimination should be driven out by competitive market forces. Three, externalities such as those discussed in the previous

chapter leave open the possibility that equity and voice-enhancing mechanisms might improve efficiency.

3. In particular, the purpose of a corporation is not only to seek profits and maximize shareholder wealth. As articulated by Solomon (1996, 110), the purpose of a corporation is "to serve society's demands and the public good and be rewarded for doing so" and not simply "to make money." This view is consistent with stakeholder theory (e.g., Donaldson and Preston 1995). For additional references on the debate over corporate responsibilities, see Dunfee (1999).

4. Whether contractual agreements can waive statutory rights continues to be an unsettled issue (R. Turner 2000).

5. The legal status of international law in the U.S. legal hierarchy is controversial (compare Bradley and Goldsmith 1997; Stephens 2001).

6. The Universal Declaration of Human Rights is accessible on the United Nations Web site (www.un.org) and is reprinted in numerous books (e.g., Lauren 1998).

7. The "citizen" distinction is important. These rights applied only to citizens, who were a fraction of the entire population (Burns and Burns 1991).

8. Perry (1998), however, argues that human rights are inescapably religious. "Religious" in its broadest sense implies a belief that the world is "ultimately meaningful (in a way hospitable to our deepest yearnings)" (16). This is similar to Tillich's (1959, 40) influential definition: "Religion is being ultimately concerned about that which is and should be our ultimate concern." Using this general conception, Perry (1998) challenges others to develop a sensible basis for inherent human dignity that does not require a belief that the world is ultimately meaningful—that is, a basis that is *not* religious.

9. The U.S. Bill of Rights further defines these negative rights (Cross 2001). Moreover, Thomas Jefferson's use of "happiness" in the Declaration of Independence has been equated with property (Ely 1998; but compare Burns and Burns 1991).

10. This declaration further defined liberty in explicitly negative terms:

> Liberty consists in the freedom to do everything which injures no one else; hence the exercise of the natural rights of each man has no limits except those which assure to the other members of the society the enjoyment of the same rights. These limits can only be determined by law.

11. With the decolonization of Africa and Asia in the postwar period, a third generation of human rights focusing on collective rights of self-determination and development has emerged (Lauren 1998). The typology of first-, second-, and third-generation human rights is common, but not without its detractors (e.g., Donnelly 1989). Note carefully that the generations of human rights are useful for understanding the development of human rights over time, but they are not intended to indicate a hierarchy of rights. First-generation rights, for example, were recognized first, but they are not more or less important than second- or third-generation rights.

12. Other important factors during World War II were the issuing of the Atlantic Charter by Roosevelt and Churchill in which they heralded universal freedoms as the basis for fighting the Axis powers, Roosevelt's call for an economic Bill of Rights, China's drive for equal rights for East and West, and the end of the myth of Western superiority (Lauren 1998; Szabo 1982). The atrocities of the Soviet regime under Stalin, such as the "premeditated famine" (Conquest 1991, 164) in 1932–33 in which more than five million Russian peasants slowly starved to death and the execution of hundreds of thousands of dissidents, were only partially visible to the human rights community, so these atrocities did not attract as much attention as the Nazi atrocities—even though they were later revealed to have resulted in more deaths than the Holocaust.

13. Cultural relativism is the belief that human rights are specific to a certain culture and lack universality (Donnelly 1989). In this vein, it is argued that the Universal Declaration is the product of "moral chauvinism and ethnocentric bias" (Pollis and Schwab 1979, 14; compare Donnelly 1989).

14. This view contrasts with the resistance of the World Trade Organization to mixing labor standards (human rights) with free trade (efficiency). Rather, labor issues are referred to the International Labour Organization (see chapter 9).

15. For example, human rights stem from the belief that humans are created in the image of God in Judaism because this means that humans must be treated with the same respect and reverence as God (Kaplan 1980), while in Islam it is because this means that humans have special obligations to fulfill toward God (Nasr 1980).

16. The widespread nature of this common affirmation is underscored by the history of the Universal Declaration. In seeking comments during the development of the declaration, the basic responses were surprisingly similar even though they came from East and West, Communist and capitalist countries, and religious and secular viewpoints (Glendon 1998). Moreover, the resulting declaration was acceptable to 80 percent of the world's population and fifty-eight countries spanning every continent and representing Christian, Jewish, Islamic, Hindu, and Buddhist traditions (Glendon 1998). This broad support has not translated into consensus on enforcement, however.

17. In the international trade arena, there is a clear divide between developed and developing countries in which the latter resist the efforts of the former to add basic human rights standards to trade agreements. Developing countries see these efforts as disguised protectionism (see chapter 9). Within the United Nations, however, a similar divide is not as transparent; rather, objections to enforcement of human rights come from many countries for various reasons.

18. Interestingly, it was the addition of a number of new member states resulting from decolonization in Asia and Africa—spurred by the Universal Declaration on Human Rights—that provided the numerical support for such actions (Lauren 1998).

19. In *Lochner v. New York*, 198 U.S. 45 (1905), the U.S. Supreme Court ruled that a New York law limiting working hours in bakeries to ten hours per day was unconstitutional because it violated economic or substantive due process. This case is commonly viewed as the symbol of the Supreme Court's emphasis on, but not blind devotion to, property rights in the late nineteenth and early twentieth centuries (Ely 1998; Forbath 1985; M. Phillips 1998). For a discussion of *Lechmere, Inc. v. NLRB*, 502 U.S. 527 (1992), see Estlund (1994).

20. As the Supreme Court wrote in *Lynch v. Household Finance Corp.*, 405 U.S. 538, 552 (1972), "A fundamental interdependence exists between the personal right to liberty and the personal right in property. Neither could have meaning without the other. That rights in property are basic civil rights has long been recognized." Similar quotes for different eras are reported in Ely (1998). Forbath (1985) emphasizes that Gilded Age judges sincerely believed in the importance of *workers'* liberty of contract as the root of personal rights. Freedom, therefore, "was not, to them, mere window dressing, lending a formal symmetry to the 'real' task of protecting capitalist property rights" (Forbath 1985, 799–800).

21. 208 U.S. 412 (1908).

22. Intangible property rights have been important in U.S. labor history because they served as the basis for injunctions against strikes and other labor activity between 1880 and 1930 (Forbath 1991). John R. Commons was an important figure in the debate over the nature of property rights and viewed the dephysicalization of property as a move from "use-value" to "exchange-value" (Alexander 1997; Commons 1924).

23. The status of property rights in international human rights discussions also appears to have declined. As mentioned above, the right to own property was explicitly included in the 1948 Universal Declaration of Human Rights. However, the enforcing covenant, the International Covenant on Civil and Political Rights, does not mention property rights. This is taken as an indication of lack of international consensus on the central importance of property rights (Lillich 1984).

24. 300 U.S. 379 (1937).

25. Moreover, if property is at the root of autonomy and therefore liberty because it provides resources for survival, it is difficult to make this the sole foundation of liberty. The right to food serves this same objective (Donnelly 1989).

26. Solomon (1992) similarly describes and attacks the mythical power of the rhetoric of competition, individualism, and the profit motive.

27. Related to this, the idea that the U.S. Constitution, and therefore judicial review, is neutral has been criticized as helping to preserve the nonneutral status quo (Zietlow 1998).

28. Property as "an inviolable and sacred right" comes from the final article of the Declaration of the Rights of Man and Citizen (1789). Protests against the World Trade Organization and free trade agreements stem from concerns that property rights, such as intellectual property rights, have been elevated above social and economic rights, including labor and environmental rights (Cohn 2001).

29. For additional discussion of the ILO, see Bartolomei de la Cruz, von Potobsky, and Swepston (1996), Lorenz (2001), and Valticos (1982).

30. Note that these theories are similar to those described in the previous chapter in support of equity and voice.

31. Discussions of human rights in the context of the U.S. labor relations system include R. Adams (2001, 2002), Brody (2001), Compa (2002), Gross (1998, 1999), Human Rights Watch (2000), and Wheeler (2000).

32. A renewed emphasis on the objectives of equity and voice can also expand analyses of labor rights as human rights. In particular, the existing literature is dominated by discussions of the freedom of association (Adams 2001; Gross 1998, 1999; Human Rights Watch 2000). Freedom of association, however, is especially thorny because it raises questions of compulsory membership, freedom to disassociate, undemocratic associations, state sponsorship, and associations that harm another party (Gutmann 1998; Rosenblum 1998). In fact, the Universal Declaration affirmatively proclaims not only the right to association but also that "No one may be compelled to belong to an association" (Article 20). The equity-voice framework broadens the human rights foundation of labor rights, beyond a sole focus on freedom of association, to include other human rights, such as just working conditions, due process protections, and free speech.

33. Similarly, Kochan, Katz, and McKersie (1986) assert that managerial acceptance of collective bargaining in the immediate postwar period reflected a strategic choice based on the expected costs of resisting unionization at that time, not an ideological acceptance of collective bargaining. Thus, this acceptance of collective bargaining should not be interpreted as an endorsement by corporate America of the need to balance efficiency, equity, and voice.

34. Some human rights instruments refer to "nonderogable rights," which many view as more important or fundamental than other human rights. But these nonderogable rights do not include property and labor rights. For example, such rights under the ICCPR include the right to life, to freedom from torture and slavery, and freedom of religion. Even if one accepts a hierarchy between nonderogable and derogable rights, there is still no accepted hierarchy between the elements of human rights relevant for the current discussion.

35. Striving for balance is also consistent with Commons's views on property rights. As described above, Commons (1924) shows how property rights no longer serve a traditional liberty or autonomy purpose; nevertheless, in his institutional theory, property rights are critical for understanding economic transactions (Commons 1934, 1950; Kaufman 2003). This is consistent with my assertion that property rights must be respected, but should not by default trump other concerns.

36. "Address by Mr. Kofi Annan to the Chamber of Commerce of the United States of America," Washington, D.C., June 8, 1999 (www.un.org/partners/business/sgstat1.htm, accessed August 7, 2002). See also www.unglobalcompact.org.

3. BALANCING OUTCOMES: THE ENVIRONMENT AND HUMAN AGENTS

1. Dunlop (1993) distinguishes industrial relations from human resource management by criticizing the lack of attention paid to the external environment in human resource management analyses; industrial relations and economics can similarly be criticized for undervaluing models of the human agent (Kaufman 1989, 1999). The distinction between these two perspectives is further reinforced by Kaufman's (1993) labels of "externalists" and "internalists" for scholars in the two groups.

2. The incorporation of choice into Dunlop's (1958) framework does not displace the importance of the environment. Rather, it models actions as not entirely determined by a mechanistic response to the environment—and therefore also harkens back to earlier generations of institutional labor economists (Kaufman 1993).

3. Taken literally, figure 3.1 presents a static model of employment outcomes. A dynamic model should incorporate feedback loops from outcomes to the environment and the human agent.

4. Industrial relations scholars typically equate the environment with the external environment, especially external to a labor-management bargaining pair (essentially, external to the firm). Environment in the framework developed here is broader and captures the environment for human decision makers. Traditional external elements such as laws or the state of the economy are included, but so are "internal" (to the firm) elements such as human resource policies and workplace social norms. These features clearly raise issues of endogeneity, but the model in figure 3.1 is intended to capture the wide range of scholarship on the employment relationship and is not intended as a well-specified theory ready for empirical testing.

5. The effects of technological change extend far beyond changes in bargaining power and wages; for example, see Bognanno and Kearney (1994).

6. This categorization is not intended to portray these dimensions as independent; rather, there are numerous interactions between various components.

7. For example, see Cohen, March, and Olsen (1972), Commons (1934), Halpern and Stern (1998), Kaufman (1989, 1999), Kahneman, Knetsch, and Thaler (1986), and Simon (1982).

8. On an institutional level, unions have long been modeled with a political component that involves managing divergent expectations (Ashenfelter and Johnson 1969; Ross 1948), that is, differing individual views of organizational justice.

9. This category is perhaps more accurately labeled "affect," but "feelings" may reach a broader audience. Affect has come to be more closely associated with moods and emotions, but attitudes also have an affective component (Eagly and Chaiken 1993).

10. The publication of *The Transformation of American Industrial Relations* by Kochan, Katz, and McKersie in 1986 created significant debate within industrial relations (Chelius and Dworkin 1990). The relevant aspect of this debate for the present discussion is the questioning of *strategic* choice versus environmental determinism (Katz, Kochan, and McKersie 1990; Lewin 1987). Lewin (1987) raises valid concerns regarding the definition of strategy and important method- ological problems. However, the incorporation of behavioral and social decision making as well as ethics into human resources and industrial relations decision-making developed in figure 3.1 does not rely on a *strategic* choice framework; it simply posits that actors make choices. Ques- tions of whether the resulting actions are appropriately considered "strategic" are left for future research.

11. Evaluations of earlier periods, such as the 1950s, might be different.

12. Unless otherwise indicated, all of the statistics in this paragraph are from Mishel, Bern- stein, and Schmitt (2001).

13. Research reveals a link between declining industrial relations institutions, especially min- imum wage standards and labor union density and strength, and increasing wage inequality (Budd and McCall 2001; Card 2001; DiNardo, Fortin, and Lemieux 1996).

14. Accessed June 17, 2002 from www.eeoc.gov/stats/race.html and www.eeoc.gov/stats/ harass.html.

4. Balancing Outcomes Revisited: The Ethics of the Employment Relationship

1. In Dunlop's (1958) model of industrial relations systems, ideology or shared understand- ing holds the system together and makes it stable, but the environment rather than ideology is the focus of attention.

2. Solomon (1992, 16) notes that the need for business ethics stems from the fact that busi- ness is a "fully human activity." The same is true for employment. In addition to Osterman et al. (2001), Gross (1995) also emphasizes the need for a moral foundation for industrial relations and labor law. For explicit applications of ethics in human resource management, see Legge (1998) and Schumann (2001).

3. For example, Solomon (1992, 6) writes that business ethics "is not the superimposing of foreign values on business but the understanding of the foundations of business itself."

4. Recall from the previous chapter that the term "strategic" is not critical for the model ar- ticulated in this and the previous chapter. The key feature is that the actions of employees, man- agers, labor leaders, and others are not completed determined by the environment so that they have choices. The model here does not assert that those choices are necessarily strategic, though it does posit that choices will reflect an underlying ethical belief system.

5. This goal is likely not being served through classroom instruction. Little has changed since Scoville (1993, 205) found that "the typical textbook contains no explicit material on ethical is- sues or ethical reasoning (though some case studies will pose ethical problems)." The one excep- tion is a narrowly focused chapter on ethical bargaining conduct in Herman (1998), which contains little discussion of ethical theories. Also see Provis (2000). This is not to be confused with a discussion of ideology.

6. Though see Herman (1993, chap. 10) for a critique of the deontological-teleological dis-

tinction, especially as it reinforces the (mis)conception that Kantian duties are divorced from values.

7. Similarly, the fundamental economic assumption of rationality has become a normative statement: "one *ought* to be rational" (Hausman and McPherson 1996, 41, emphasis in original).

8. In response to some of these criticisms, a rule-utilitarianism variant has been developed in which rules rather than actions are designed to maximize utility (Beuachamp and Bowie 1997; Velasquez 1998). The debate over rule-utilitarianism is whether utility-maximizing (and therefore, moral) rules allow exceptions. If they do, the difference between rule- and act-utilitarianism is quite thin.

9. The categorical imperative was developed by Kant in *Groundwork of the Metaphysics of Morals* (1785).

10. The use of negative and positive duties parallels the standard conception of negative rights (protection against something) and positive rights (something that must be provided).

11. In other words, it is forbidden to never develop one's own talents or help others. Kant's distinction between perfect and imperfect duties stems from contradictions. Perfect duties are those in which the universal application of an action is inconceivable because it always yields a contradiction. If everyone broke promises or contracts there could be no promises or contracts. Living up to promises and contractual obligations are therefore perfect duties. In contrast, it is possible to conceive of no one helping anyone else. But Kant argued that no rational person would *will* (recall the wording of the Formula of Universal Law) this situation, because eventually there would be a contradiction when you needed the help of others (Sullivan 1989). Thus, helping others is an imperfect duty. Korsgaard (1996) labels the first case a logical contradiction and the second case a practical contradiction.

12. This is further supported by Bowie's (1999, 90) third principle of a Kantian moral firm: "It should not be the case that for all decisions, the interests of one stakeholder take priority."

13. Herman (1993), Korsgaard (1996), and O'Neill (1989) address many of these challenges to Kantian ethics.

14. It is sometimes difficult to separate the two. See Baird (2000), Bethell (1998), Epstein (1995), and Friedman (1962).

15. For example, see *Lechmere, Inc. v. NLRB,* 502 U.S. 527 (1992), which upholds the banishment of union organizers from private property (Estlund 1994).

16. Velasquez (1998) describes several additional definitions of justice: based on contributions (capitalism), needs (socialism), equality (egalitarianism), and freedom (libertarianism). The two most relevant here are capitalist justice (ethics of utility) and libertarianism (ethics of liberty).

17. Rawls (1971, 61) listed the following basic liberties: the right to vote and hold political office; freedom of speech, assembly, and thought; freedom from physical and psychological oppression; the right to hold private property; and freedom from arbitrary arrest and seizure.

18. This Aristotelian emphasis on social purpose and interdependence, in contrast to the neoclassical economics emphasis on profits and individual self-interest, is reminiscent of John R. Commons's institutional critique of neoclassical economics. Commons emphasized forbearance instead of unchecked self-interest, which implies that individuals' utility functions are interdependent (Kaufman, 2003). Forbearance is essentially an amalgamation of Aristotelian virtues.

19. Though see Herman (1993, chap. 9) for a discussion of relationships in Kantian ethics.

20. Frustration with the perceived inflexibility and lack of human vitality of the Kantian rules appears to be at least partly responsible for the resurgence of the Aristotelian tradition and the development of the ethics of care (e.g., Gilligan 1982; Solomon 1992).

21. Although traditional industrial relations research in this vein is nearly nonexistent, Godard (1997) is an exception. This study measures managerial ideology relating to unions, participation rights, and employee involvement and concludes that managerial ideology is of secondary importance relative to the environment. Managerial ideology is not measured in terms of the ethical theories presented here.

22. Autocratic and high-performance human resource management systems might be an example of this phenomenon. On the surface, autocratic and high-performance human resource management practices appear to reflect different ethical foundations, with the former not showing any concern for employee equity or voice and the latter embracing it. However, both systems might reflect an underlying utilitarian ethical framework, in which case the differences are not

ethical but instrumental. Both systems seek to maximize organizational performance. If a high-performance work system includes employee equity and voice only to increase organizational performance, then the two systems differ only in their implementation of the same underlying ethical premise.

5. The Balancing Alternatives: Workplace Governance

1. For example, important questions such as whether unions reduce productivity or increase social justice are relative, not absolute, questions. When someone claims that unions increase social justice, it is a claim that unions more effectively provide social justice than an alternative governance mechanism such as laissez-faire competitive markets or human resource management. The epilogue will show how the question of workplace governance provides an organizing map for the field of human resources and industrial relations.

2. Clegg (1979) also includes custom, but immediately notes that this is a way that rules emerge rather than being explicitly made. Consideration of how customs are changed or enforced leads back to the five options noted in the text.

3. Note carefully that "free markets" are not actually free in the sense of having no regulation. "Free" markets are regulated by common law supports, which are not necessarily value or outcome neutral (Klare 1988).

4. This legal viewpoint is usually associated with the law and economics approach, though the law and economics approach is broader than the simple statement in the text (Schwab 1997).

5. In the area of workplace safety, the important common law feature is tort law under which injured employees can sue negligent employers for damages (Burton and Chelius 1997). This system was replaced with workers' compensation laws in the early 1900s.

6. Legislative restrictions on the employment-at-will doctrine include antidiscrimination laws and the National Labor Relations Act, which forbids discrimination on the basis of union activity or support. The major example of a contractual restriction is union contracts that require just cause for discipline and discharge. An example of a judicial exception to the employment-at-will doctrine is a ruling that firing a worker for filing a valid workers' compensation claim illegally subverts public policy.

7. *Payne v. Western and Atlantic R.R. Co.,* 81 Tenn. 507, 519–520 (1884), *overruled on other grounds,* Hutton v. Watters, 179 S.W. 134, 138 (Tenn. 1915).

8. Although there is disagreement about the details of the historical development of the employment-at-will doctrine, the influence of economic activity is not denied (compare Feinman 1976 with Ballam 1995).

9. Institutional economics rejects the neoclassical economics view of the primacy of the market; rather, the importance of institutions—households, companies, unions, social groups, and the like—and their rules, cultures, histories, values, and norms for guiding economic and noneconomic activity are emphasized (Ramstad 1993). Habits, rather than self-interested, utility-maximizing calculations, are also viewed as the key decision-making trait (Hodgson 1998).

10. In contrast, employees have been legally fired for refusing to comply with their employer's order to falsify medical records or federal food and drug records, and reporting misuse of funds or a dangerous product to superiors or legal authorities (Squire 1990; Summers 2000).

11. If individual employees cannot afford to sue in court, this is another example of employers and employees not being equals, which undermines the theoretical benefits of a laissez-faire system.

12. Government, however, might need to be a catalyst for change to happen (Osterman et al. 2001).

13. Note, however, that Ben-Ner and Jones (1995) caution against ignoring financial participation when devising mechanisms for employees to participate in decision making.

14. The statement that human resource management is unilateral is definitional. Employee voice mechanisms, for example, that move beyond standard nonunion employee participation programs by vesting the workers or their representatives with governance authority (see Verma and Cutcher-Gershenfeld 1993) are considered a form of independent employee representation or worker control in the present analysis, depending on the extent of the worker authority.

15. This emphasis is not new. In 1938, Dale Yoder wrote that "the basic purpose of person-

nel administration is that of securing maximum productive efficiency from the man power involved" (Yoder 1938, 3).

16. These two categories are from Mahoney and Watson (1993). They provide alleged examples of employee participation in reward decisions—deciding personal benefit allocations in a cafeteria-style benefits plan, scheduling pretax deductions for health and family care reimbursement accounts, and investing in deferred compensation. These decisions may *reallocate* the compensation package to suit each employee's needs, but they stop short of meaningful participation in the determination of the level of rewards, or more generally in the terms and conditions of employment.

17. As detailed in chapter 8, the term "job control unionism" has a significantly different meaning in the postwar period.

18. Though beyond the scope of this workplace-focused treatment, an additional important voice role of labor unions is as a voice for workers in the political arena (Greenstone 1969; Delaney and Schwochau 1993; Dark 2001; Lichtenstein 2002). Along similar lines, labor unions can be important organizations in civil society where individuals gather to socialize, discuss issues, pursue charitable goals, and form a sense of community (Levine 2001).

19. See chapters 7 and 8. Also, Heckscher (1988), Kaufman and Kleiner (1993), Rogers and Streeck (1995), Towers (1997), Turner (1991), Turner, Katz, and Hurd (2001), Verma and Cutcher-Gershenfeld (1993), and Weiler (1990).

20. Note that I am using the term "human resources and industrial relations" as a singular term capturing the broad field that includes both the human resource management and institutional paradigms, or Kaufman's (1993) internalists and externalists. See the epilogue for additional discussion.

21. Kantian moral philosophy (e.g., Bowie 1999) and religious thought (e.g., Pope John Paul II 1981, 2000) reject the view that labor is a commodity as being unethical and contrary to spiritual development and fulfillment. On the other hand, Heldman, Bennett, and Johnson (1981) emphasize that labor is a commodity because labor services are controlled by market forces. This establishes a false dichotomy: the old institutional labor economists, for example, did not deny market forces but rather questioned the wisdom of placing sole reliance on them (Kaufman 1997b).

22. This pluralist definition of "industrial relations" is admittedly narrower than the historical definition, which also included human resource management, but this narrow definition is more consistent with popular, contemporary usage or stereotypes. I use the term "human resources and industrial relations" to refer to the old, inclusive field of industrial relations (see the epilogue).

23. This pluralist perspective does not imply that all workplace issues involve conflict. Rather, at least some issues involve distributive conflict so that, in general, employment relationship conflict is "mixed motive" (Kochan 2000; Walton and McKersie 1965). Or put differently, the human resource management view is that it is possible to make *all* conflict integrative through appropriate management policies and strategies, while the industrial relations view is that there are at least some issues for which this is not possible.

24. This pluralist view should not be equated with "industrial pluralism" as defined in Stone (1981), which views unions and companies as equals in a private democracy, with arbitration (rather than government involvement) resolving disputes over written rules. Pluralism and industrial pluralism share the view that it is possible to create a balance within a capitalist society, but my usage of "pluralism" does not necessarily focus narrowly on union contracts and arbitration with no government intervention as the way to achieve this balance. The model of employee empowerment unionism in chapter 8, for example, reflects a pluralist perspective but seeks to move beyond the written rules focus of industrial pluralism, and may very well require greater government involvement to be successful.

25. The U.S. experience has shown that legal protection of employee voice is important, but laws cannot provide voice in the same way that they can provide a minimum wage. Ultimately, workers have to participate in the voice mechanism.

26. In Marxist industrial relations, for example, employers structure work organization, human resource management practices, and labor law to serve the class interests of capital at the expense of labor (Klare 1978; Montgomery 1979; Legge 1995). In Europe, anarcho-syndicalist

unions with strong Communist or Socialist orientations do not support collective bargaining because signing a contract limits worker freedom and legitimizes capitalism (Hyman 2001).

27. See also Kochan, Katz, and McKersie (1986) for the prominence of union avoidance strategies in U.S. industrial relations, and see Katz and Darbishire's (2000) human resource management employment pattern (which includes a union substitution strategy).

28. This is not universally true to the extent that human resource management is sometimes viewed suspiciously, for example, as rhetoric to propagate a managerial ideology and weaken unions (Legge 1995).

29. See also Katz and Darbishire's (2000) Japanese-oriented and joint team-based employment system patterns in which human resource management elements such as performance appraisals and career development are combined with forms of employee representation.

30. Similarly, complementarities are possible across workplace issues. Suppose there is a conflict of interest between employers and employees over wages, but not productivity or product quality. Furthermore, suppose voice is not important for wages but is for productivity and quality. The decision tree in figure 5.2 yields two preferred governance arrangements: government regulation of wage issues (such as a minimum wage law) and human resource management with an employee participation voice mechanism for productivity and quality. Last, analyses of workplace governance should not assume that one size fits all—diverse workers in diverse occupations and industries may be best served by different governance mechanisms (Kochan 2000).

31. On the other hand, organized labor's track record on facilitating equality of opportunity is mixed (Gould 1977; Honey 1999).

32. Osterman et al. (2001, 13) label this the principle of subsidiarity: "Those closest to the problem possess the best information about the problem and the best idea of how to proceed toward a solution." This need for diversity and responsiveness to specific situations rather than universal rules is also echoed in debates over social justice and ethics. In terms of social justice, McClelland (1990, 290) argues that "if (a) we honor many values, (b) these can and do conflict, and (c) rules for resolving such conflicts generally cannot be specified independent of the context of the clash, then the search for a universal decision rule for resolving clashes is a vain search." If the employment relationship values are efficiency, equity, and voice, this logic supports the need for workplace decision making rather than universal government regulations. In ethics, the advocacy of the "priority of the particular" (Nussbaum 1993, 257) in Aristotelian virtue ethics reflects, at least partially, frustration with the universal rules in the Kantian traditions.

33. The validity of this logic can be questioned (Kaufman 1996). One can also question the true intent of the Wagner Act. Compare Kaufman (1996), Pope (1997, 2002), and Forbath (2001).

6. THE NEW DEAL INDUSTRIAL RELATIONS SYSTEM

1. For overviews of each piece of legislation, see the chapters in Goldberg et al. (1976) or Goldman (1996). The legislative development of the NLRA is described in Bernstein (1950), Gross (1974), and Vittoz (1987). For the Social Security Act, see Berkowitz (1995) and Coll (1995), and for the FLSA, see Nordlund (1997) and Paulsen (1996). These three acts are not exhaustive. Other legislation includes significant amendments to the Railway Labor Act (1934), the Walsh-Healy Public Contracts Act (1936), and the National Apprenticeship Act (1937). The term New Deal industrial relations system is from Kochan, Katz, and McKersie (1986). For a general overview of the New Deal period, see Kennedy (1999). In the 1960s, U.S. public policy for private sector employment shifted from a labor law to an employment focus (such as the Civil Rights Act and the Occupational Safety and Health Act), which promotes equity but not voice.

2. The best modern descriptions of the labor problem are by Bruce Kaufman (e.g., 1993, 1997b, forthcoming). Texts from that era include Commons (1905, 1921), Cummins (1932), Daugherty (1933), and Estey (1928).

3. Even Adam Smith, with his famous example of the eighteen steps used to make a single pin, recognized that this extreme division of labor had both efficiency advantages and, because it renders human beings "stupid and ignorant," negative social consequences (Smith 1776, bk. 5, chap. 1, article 2d, p. 734).

212 | *Notes to Pages 104–110*

4. Industrial relations and progressive reformers were admittedly pragmatic rather than idealistic in their outlook (Kaufman forthcoming; Pope 2002), but nevertheless the goals that they wanted to pragmatically accomplish—equity and voice—reflect certain ethical principles.

5. These are the same foundations as for human rights and it is no coincidence that President Roosevelt's wife, Eleanor Roosevelt, was a major figure in the development of the United Nations' Universal Declaration of Human Rights (see chapter 2). It's also no coincidence that John R. Commons was active in the Christian Socialists, with their emphasis on improving society rather than on individual salvation, in the 1890s (Dombrowski 1936; Harter 1962).

6. According to Kaufman (forthcoming), the early views of John R. Commons were consistent with Senator Wagner's views, but after 1918 Commons saw monetary, credit, and banking stability as the keys to macroeconomic stabilization.

7. As employers were viewed as the problem, the unfair labor practices in the NLRA in 1935 only pertained to management actions, not union actions.

8. Although the New Deal industrial relations system is the product of a certain environment, this was admittedly a multifaceted and complex relationship (Ernst 1995; Gerber 1997; O'Brien 1998). The discussion here is only intended to capture the importance of balancing efficiency, equity, and voice.

9. This argument reinforces the usefulness of the framework developed here—orderly resolution of disputes is an efficiency concern, and Tomlins (1985a, 1985b) is implicitly arguing that efficiency concerns won out over voice. The contrast between the AFL and NLRA models also highlights differing conceptions of employee voice—a republican, self-government model in the AFL case, a shared system of industrial democracy in the NLRA case.

10. *Livingston Shirt Corporation,* 107 NLRB 400 (1953).

11. *Excelsior Underwear, Inc.,* 156 NLRB 1236 (1966). *NLRB v. Babcock and Wilcox Company,* 351 U.S. 105 (1956). *Lechmere, Inc. v. NLRB,* 502 U.S. 527 (1992). Union access is provided in rare situations where union organizers have no alternative access to employees such as isolated resort hotels, logging camps, mining camps, or petroleum facilities.

12. *NLRB v. Wooster Division of Borg-Warner Corp.,* 356 U.S. 342 (1958). *H. K. Porter Company v. NLRB,* 397 U.S. 99 (1970). This balancing is not without critics (Weiler 1984).

13. *NLRB v. Katz,* 369 U.S. 736 (1962). U.S. legal doctrine also explicitly seeks a balance between union information requests and a company's need to protect confidential information (*Detroit Edison v. NLRB,* 440 U.S. 301, 1979). Other examples include questions over wearing union insignia at work (e.g., *Northeast Industrial Service Company,* 320 NLRB No. 117, 1996), employer surveillance of premises (e.g., *National Steel and Shipbuilding Company,* 324 NLRB No. 85, 1997), and employee use of a company's e-mail system (e.g., *Timekeeping Systems, Inc. and Lawrence Leinweber,* 323 NLRB 244, 1997).

14. *NLRB v. Fleetwood Trailer Co.,* 389 U.S. 375 (1967). *NLRB v. Mackay Radio and Telegraph Co.,* 304 U.S. 333 (1938). As with the other examples used here, U.S. strike replacement doctrine is controversial; labor law attempts to achieve a balance does not mean that the outcome is universally accepted as balanced in a normative sense (Estreicher 1994b; LeRoy 1995).

15. 420 U.S. 251 (1975).

16. Union contracts with just cause discharge clauses essentially protect employee free speech that does not affect job performance, but otherwise individual voice is subject to the employment-at-will doctrine.

17. This argument is important because if the reason for banning nonunion employee representation is that these plans are too weak to increase wages and therefore fail to provide macroeconomic stabilization, then a continued ban might be difficult to justify if unions are a poor vehicle for macroeconomic stabilization (Kaufman 1996, 2000b). However, that nonunion employee representation plans are unable to increase wages on an aggregate level calls into question their ability to protect labor standards and provide equity on a micro level.

18. More accurately, section 8(a)(2) of the NLRA makes it illegal for employers to "to dominate or interfere with the formation or administration of any labor organization or contribute financial or other support to it." I suspect that the standards held by Commons of due process and employee power in nonunion employee representation plans could be phrased as "not dominated by management." If so, there may be less of a difference between Commons and Leiserson than portrayed in Kaufman (2000b). In other words, I doubt whether contemporary versions of representation plans in which management, not the employees, typically controls how the plans are

structured, when they meet, what topics are covered, and even whether they continue to exist would meet with Commons's approval.

19. It's legitimate to question whether the NLRA framework ever had a chance to prove itself. There was virile resistance to, and outright flouting of, the law until it was found constitutional by the U.S. Supreme Court in 1937. And then the 1940s were dominated by the concerns and institutions of World War II.

20. See Millis and Brown (1950) for a discussion of the Taft-Hartley Act's legislative history and provisions. For a critical analysis of the experience under the Taft-Hartley Act, see Gross (1995).

21. Although there is considerable debate over whether unions positively or negatively affect productivity, there is little debate that unions reduce profits and returns to shareholders (Becker and Olson 1989; Freeman and Medoff 1984).

22. For example, Leiserson (1922, 75) wrote, "Whether carved on stone by an ancient monarch or written in a Magna Charta [sic] by a King John, or embodied in collective agreement between a union and employer; the intent is the same, to subject the ruler to definite laws to which subjects or citizens may hold him when he attempts to exercise arbitrary power."

23. Much has been written about these two topics. To cite just a few examples, see Craver (1993), Estlund (1994), Estreicher (1994b), Friedman et al. (1994), Gould (1993), LeRoy (1995), and Weiler (1983, 1990).

24. *NLRB v. Mackay Radio and Telegraph Co.*, 304 U.S. 333 (1938).

25. *NLRB v. Fleetwood Trailer Co.*, 389 U.S. 375 (1967).

26. Scholarship that questions various assumptions of the New Deal industrial relations system from a variety of perspectives also includes Edwards (1993), Epstein (1983), Heckscher (1988), Hogler (1989), Kaufman (1993), Klare (1978), Kochan (1998), Kochan, Katz, and McKersie (1986), Stone (1981), Tomlins (1985a, 1985b), and Troy (1999).

27. Alternatively, adversarial U.S. labor relations might result from inherent conflicts of interest in the employment relationship between labor and management.

28. If corporations really want flexibility rather than true employee participation, then this is more of a critique of the union strategy of job-control unionism (in response to management's own bureaucratic work methods) than of the NLRA per se (see chapter 8).

29. 309 NLRB 990 (1992). Discussion of this ruling and several other closely related cases is extensive; for example, see Estreicher (1994a) or LeRoy (1996, 1999).

30. The TEAM Act would have amended section 8(a)(2) to open the door to more nonunion employee representation plans, but it was vetoed by President Clinton in 1996. A revised version of the TEAM Act was introduced in Congress in 1997, but it was not voted on; LeRoy (1999) discusses the differences between the two bills. Neither bill contained any changes to the union representation election process.

7. THE GEOMETRY OF COMPARATIVE INDUSTRIAL RELATIONS

1. Other aspects of employment systems from around the world, such as public policies on nondiscrimination or social safety nets, as well as human resource management practices are equally important. But to highlight the importance of adding voice to efficiency and equity, this chapter focuses on industrial relations systems.

2. Bargaining can range from centralized to decentralized under exclusive representation and voluntarism and is ranked here based on the most frequently observed patterns in practice. Moreover, this ordering is simply for exposition; it is not important for the major points of the chapter.

3. Hyman (2001) discusses the origins and different meanings of the sometimes ambiguous term "social partnership."

4. This evaluation is for sectoral bargaining in isolation. In Germany, for example, sectoral bargaining is combined with workplace-level codetermination, which increases the fulfillment of employee voice for the German industrial relations system considered as a whole.

5. Working conditions were established through bargaining, often informally and with high levels of wildcat strikes in the workplace.

6. Because the arbitration process revolves around disputes, even if just paper disputes, arbitration awards apply only to the parties to the proceedings. If an employers' association is a party to the arbitration, the award applies to all of its members.

7. Legislative changes in the 1990s decentralized industrial relations in both Australia and New Zealand. In Australia, the powers and scope of the arbitration commissions have been curtailed and the emphasis has shifted to enterprise bargaining. Australian workplace agreements, which are nonunion agreements negotiated by employers directly with employees, have also been legalized. At the federal level, the arbitration commission (now the Australian Industrial Relations Commission) is now primarily limited to issuing a national minimum wage award and making sure that the enterprise agreements and the nonunion workplace agreements meet a small number of minimum standards (Katz and Darbishire 2000). In New Zealand, the arbitration system has been abandoned (see the section on voluntarism later in this chapter).

8. In fact, Japanese labor law was modeled after the New Deal industrial relations system by the Allied occupation after World War II. As such, enterprise unions are not mandated by law, and isolated examples of industrial and other types of unions exist (Kuwahara 1998). An estimated 85 percent of union members belong to an enterprise union (Araki 1994).

9. Structurally, supervisors are members of the enterprise union and union leaders often move into management after being a union leader. Depending on one's perspective, this either undermines the independence of the union or provides greater shared interests (and greater appreciation for labor issues among upper management—the former union leaders).

10. Although Summers (1990) argues that U.S. unions have some nonbargaining rights as a minority union under the NLRA, he also notes that in practice this type of representation rarely occurs in the United States.

11. German corporations have a dual board structure. The supervisory board sets strategic policies and appoints upper-level managers and generally only meets four times per year. The management board controls the day-to-day management of the firm and reports to the supervisory board.

12. This is not true parity because shareholders elect the chairperson who has the power to decide deadlocked issues. In the coal and steel industry, employees have true parity on the supervisory board and can also appoint a labor director to the management board.

13. That French law struggles with trying to balance efficiency, equity, and voice is captured by this description of reforms in the early 1980s: "The Auroux laws were intended to foster a mutual learning process within the enterprise, with employers becoming more aware of their social employment responsibilities and unions more attentive to the firm's economic constraints" (Goetschy 1998, 379).

14. This description of the British industrial relations systems relies on Edwards et al. (1998), Goodman et al. (1998), and Towers (1997).

15. Britain is also a good example of the perils of importing industrial relations policies—the 1971 Industrial Relations Act enacted National Labor Relations Act-type provisions regarding unfair labor practices, secondary labor activity, enforceability of contracts, and some notion of sufficient bargaining unit support and was promptly ignored and/or boycotted by labor and management. It was repealed in 1974, though the provision regarding unfair dismissal remains in force today.

16. The voluntarist systems in Britain and New Zealand are not pure libertarian systems because there is some regulation of industrial relations. In both countries, collective representation is slightly protected—for example, by immunities from common law liabilities in Britain—as well as regulated—for example, by forbidding closed shops.

17. Jacoby (2001) complements these workplace-focused proposals with a reform agenda for corporate governance that is motivated in part by European board-level employee representation. The reforms, however, stop short of advocating equivalent representation for U.S. workers except for employee-owners. In contrast, Adams (1995) proposes several corporate board seats for employee-elected representatives.

18. The platform of reforms described by Adams (1995) includes annual wage bargaining modeled after *shunto* on the premise that coordinated bargaining that takes place in a very public forum is more responsive to overall economic conditions.

8. ALTERNATIVES TO JOB CONTROL UNIONISM

1. Hoxie's (1917, 45–46) description of business unionism remains apt three-quarters of a century later:

It aims chiefly at more, here and now, for the organized workers of the craft or industry, in terms mainly of higher wages, shorter hours, and better working conditions, regardless for the most part of the welfare of the workers outside the particular organic group, and regardless in general of political and social considerations, except in so far as these bear directly upon its own economic ends. It is conservative in the sense that it professes belief in natural rights, and accepts as inevitable, if not as just, the existing capitalistic organization and the wage system, as well as existing property rights and the binding force of contract. It regards unionism mainly as a bargaining institution and seeks its ends chiefly through collective bargaining, supported by such methods as experience from time to time indicates to be effective in sustaining and increasing its bargaining power.

2. For various perspectives, see Bluestone and Bluestone (1992), Clark (2000), Heckscher (1988), Lichtenstein (2002), Nissen (1997), Tillman and Cummings (1999), Turner, Katz, and Hurd (2001), and Wheeler (2002).

3. Admittedly, this may also require broader labor law and corporate governance reforms to sufficiently empower employees.

4. Piore and Sabel (1984) call this the mass-production model of shop-floor control. Perlman (1928, 262–272) uses the term "job control" to apply to union control over jobs through closed shops, apprenticeship programs, and union members with hiring and firing authority as foremen. This craft union conception of job control is different from the New Deal industrial relations system usage (industrial union control over jobs through seniority rights, restrictions on nonbargaining unit work, and grievance procedures). An early example of the transition from Perlman's job control to New Deal job control is the experiences of the Sidney Hillman-led Amalgamated Clothing Workers in the clothing industry in the 1920s (Fraser 1983; Lichtenstein 1993).

5. Union formalization of preexisting informal managerial practices is not limited to issues of job control. In southern paper mills in the immediate postwar period, unions formalized preexisting informal racial job segregation patterns (Minchin 2001).

6. Flexible employment, or atypical employment, includes part-time employment and temporary or contract work and other methods for varying the number of employees and hours worked. Wage, or pay, flexibility includes pay for performance, profit-sharing, and other methods for relating pay to changes in productivity and competitive pressures. Functional flexibility is the ability to shift workers as needed, through the use of cross-training and very few job classifications, for example. Procedural flexibility is the ability to introduce changes, such as new technology.

7. This is not to say that unions are to blame. In the logic of a mass manufacturing system with narrow job classifications, both labor and management were served by the stability and predictability of job control unionism; to a large degree, job control unionism is the product of union reaction to management decisions (Bluestone and Bluestone 1992; Kochan, Katz, and McKersie 1986).

8. Note further that Katz and Darbishire (2000) identify four key, growing employment relationship patterns across a number of countries—a low wage pattern, a human resource management pattern, a Japanese-oriented pattern, and a joint team-based pattern. The traditional job control (or New Deal) pattern is not among them.

9. Job control unionism is sometimes associated with a process focus because of the importance of seniority-based processes for layoffs, promotions, and the like. However, as these processes are designed to limit discretion, outcomes are largely predetermined by seniority and job ladders. Moreover, and most graphically, wage rates for each job are often specified in union contracts. Job control unionism has an outcome-based focus, albeit with a strong sense of procedural justice.

10. In particular, see Rubinstein (2000, 2001), Rubinstein and Kochan (2001), and Bluestone and Bluestone (1992). The discussion here is largely based on these sources.

11. The plant is now owned by a Shell joint venture, Montell Polyolefins. The Energy and Chemical Workers Union is now part of the Communications, Energy, and Paperworkers Union of Canada. For a less favorable perspective on the Sarnia plant, see Wells (1993).

12. A seventh craft team comprised of skilled tradespeople is responsible for nonroutine maintenance.

13. Interestingly, the solidaristic work policy can complement rather than undermine the sol-

idaristic wage policy (Mahon 1991). In the traditional solidaristic wage policy, equal pay for equal work was advocated across firms independent of ability to pay, but the general concept of equal pay for equal work contradicts the second part of the solidaristic wage policy: reduction of wage differentials between occupations. A solidaristic work policy in which workers are compensated for increased skills and responsibilities is seen as a way to reinvigorate the equal pay for equal work component of the solidaristic wage policy.

14. Paralleling the experience of the local UAW union at Saturn, Mahon (1999) discusses how a solidaristic work policy required changing the traditional representation structures in the Swedish labor movement.

15. More generally, in noting that nurses are caught between the need for a professional organization to evaluate and license skills and the need for a union to protect employee rights, Armstrong (1993, 318) advocates the spirit of employee empowerment unionism: "Or better yet, we could figure out new ways of providing autonomy while defending the collective rights of both workers and clients, students and patients." See also Heckscher's (1988) model of associational unionism.

16. The collective bargaining agreements contain a set of sometimes complicated minimum rates, the framework for individual negotiations, and industrywide standards on residual payments (Paul and Kleingartner 1996). In principle, this type of self-representation is akin to European sectoral bargaining in which collective bargaining establishes industrywide minimum standards and workplace representation implements the provisions and sometimes negotiates supplements above the industrywide minimums.

17. Until their demise in the 1970s, waitress unions negotiated minimum pay rates and some waitresses received higher rates (Cobble 1991).

18. More specifically, a grassroots effort started in the medical area in the early 1970s and these organizers then affiliated with District 65. District 65 joined the UAW in 1979 but remained largely autonomous and continued to fund the ongoing Harvard organizing drive. In 1984, the UAW transferred the local organizers to its own payroll and took over management of the drive. Unsuccessful representation elections for the medical area employees were held in 1977 and 1981; in 1984, the National Labor Relations Board redefined the appropriate bargaining unit to be all Harvard University clerical and technical employees.

19. The HUCTW affiliated with the American Federation of State, County, and Municipal Workers (AFSCME) in 1987 but remains largely autonomous.

20. Otherwise, individuals are not treated as an end in themselves in violation of Kantian principles and Aristotelian conceptions of human flourishing (see chapter 4).

21. Apprenticeship programs frequently sponsored by craft unions are another example of developing capabilities.

22. The terms social unionism and social movement unionism are often used interchangeably. My usage is more precise—social unionism is used as a general term for unionism that involves a broader social agenda than business unionism; social movement unionism is used to denote a specific form of social unionism that emphasizes grassroots participation.

23. The CGT is moving away from the Communist Party, but the extensive sharing of leaders between the two organizations has slowed the process.

24. To underscore the veracity of the internal dispute, the local was placed in trusteeship by the national leadership. Note, however, that centralization of union governance is a complex issue. Although the Justice for Janitors campaigns relied heavily on grassroots participation, centralized support was also critical. The campaigns were created and funded by the national SEIU leadership and were often resisted by conservative local leaders (Milkman and Wong 2001; Waldinger et al. 1998).

25. This is not to say that workers have no voice in a job control unionism system. They are able to participate in contract ratification deliberations and votes, elect leaders, and sometimes help process their own grievances. But compared to some alternative models of unionism, job control unionism is not centered on active rank-and-file participation and voice.

26. Handling issues "on the floor" in this quote referred to wildcat strikes; Brody (1980) and Klare (1985) also use this quote to support the need for increased worker activism. These are more militant actions or visions than the employee empowerment unionism model articulated in this chapter, but all focus on increasing the participation of workers in matters affecting their work lives.

9. BALANCING THE GLOBAL WORKPLACE

1. As a further parallel between today and the late nineteenth century, there was also back-lash against globalization prior to World War I (Williamson 1998). Moreover, although immigration was arguably less restrictive in the earlier period, immigration contributes to today's backlash because of a sense of imbalance between the international mobility of capital and the limited mobility of labor (Rodrik 1997).

2. For example, see the research on wages and import competition (Abowd and Lemieux 1993); trade protection (Gaston and Trefler 1994); foreign ownership (Aitken, Harrison, and Lipsey 1996); international rent sharing (Budd and Slaughter forthcoming; Budd, Konings, and Slaughter 2001); trade and deunionization (Baldwin 2003); and job loss (Kletzer 2001). Slaughter (1999) contrasts the labor economics and international trade economics approaches to analyzing globalization and wages. This research generally finds that trade is responsible for only a small part (around 10 percent) of recent wage trends and increases in inequality. Less attention on the relative skill premium and additional attention on increased labor demand elasticity and outsourcing, however, may reveal greater contributions of globalization toward explaining labor market outcomes (Feenstra 1998; Rodrik 1997).

3. As described by Slaughter (1999), labor economists and trade economists differ on their approaches to analyzing the relationship between trade and wages, but both assume competitive labor markets. There is also a large literature on international trade with imperfect product markets (Grossman 1992), but an industrial relations approach would analyze globalization with imperfect labor markets that favor employers.

4. The preamble to the International Labour Organization's constitution, dating back to 1919, promotes fair trade: "The failure of any nation to adopt humane conditions of labor is an obstacle in the way of other nations which desire to improve the conditions in their own countries."

5. For a detailed case study of one company's seventy–year search for lower labor costs (and a nonunion workforce) and its use of relocation threats to extract concessions, see Cowie (1999).

6. The GATT was initially intended as an interim agreement pending the creation of the International Trade Organization, but the United States failed to ratify the charter to establish this organization (Gilpin 2000; Rothgeb 2001). Subsequent major rounds of the GATT include the Kennedy round (1964–67), Tokyo round (1973–79), and Uruguay round (1986–93).

7. It is also telling that the World Bank and the International Monetary Fund have observer status in the WTO, while the International Labour Organization does not (Blackett 1999).

8. Both labor and environmental standards involve what the GATT refers to as "process and production methods"—how a product is produced rather than the qualities of the final product (Charnovitz 2002).

9. A 2001 ruling upholding a French ban on importing asbestos from Canada was made on narrow grounds and does not, by itself, constitute a shift toward allowing exceptions to free trade for health and safety reasons (Gaines 2001).

10. In a limited sense, this ruling is a minor victory for proponents of environmental and labor standards because previous rulings struck down environmental standards as not even included in the content of Article 20. The Shrimp-Turtle case admits that the protection of turtles falls within sections (b) and (g) of Article 20 and therefore shifts attention away from these sections to the provisions of the preamble (the "chapeau"). Nevertheless, the Shrimp-Turtle ruling ultimately takes a very narrow view of the chapeau (Gaines 2001). Put differently, the Shrimp-Turtle ruling reveals that not all "process and production methods" restrictions are automatically illegal (Charnovitz 2002), though to date the exceptions are quite narrow.

11. Higher standards need to be justified on the basis of scientific evidence (Kennedy 2000). In a 1998 WTO ruling, the United States successfully challenged a European Union ban on importing hormone-treated beef as lacking sufficient scientific support for the need to regulate hormone-treated meat. This is argued to be backward: rather than needing to prove a product safe, the WTO requires proof that it is dangerous (Wallach and Sforza 2000).

12. The OECD and ILO statements are available in full on each organization's web site (www.oecd.org and www.ilo.org).

13. An example of a national government corporate code of conduct is the Model Business Principles developed by the Clinton administration in 1995. This code was developed to temper

opposition to the U.S. renewal of China's most favored nation status, but there is little evidence that this code was anything but nonexistent in practice (Baker 2001).

14. The Workplace Code of Conduct is available at www.fairlabor.org.

15. Another product-labeling initiative is the RUGMARK program to certify that rugs made in Asia were not made with child labor (Liubicic 1998).

16. www.reebok.com/Reebok/US/HumanRights/business (accessed July 24, 2002).

17. For example, inspected factories were not selected at random, the companies scheduled the inspections (so they were not a surprise) and also paid for the inspection. These procedures were changed in April 2002 to improve the transparency and independence of the monitoring process.

18. Compa and Darricarrère (1996) provide concrete suggestions for improving enforcement to make corporate codes of conduct credible.

19. For additional discussion of the ILO, see Bartolomei de la Cruz, von Potobsky, and Swepston (1996), Cooney (1999), Lorenz (2001), and Valticos (1982).

20. Some would also add a living wage requirement to the set of core labor standards (e.g., Spectar 2000). Alben (2001) shows that wage standards, rather than the current core standards, were discussed in earlier GATT rounds.

21. When evaluating the developing countries' opposition to labor standards, it is important to remember that the developed countries have often disproportionately pushed for removing trade barriers that benefit themselves, such as lowering barriers for financial services, while retaining barriers for industries in which developing countries are competitive, such as textiles and agriculture (Ganesan 2000; Stiglitz 2002).

22. The ILO's tripartite structure provides labor and employers with a direct voice, and employer representatives from developed countries have also opposed ILO consideration of trade-labor linkages (Leary 1996). In the ILO Declaration on Fundamental Principles and Rights at Work, the ILO membership

> stresses that labor standards should not be used for protectionist trade purposes, and that nothing in this Declaration and its follow-up shall be invoked or otherwise used for such purposes; in addition, the comparative advantage of any country should in no way be called into question by this Declaration and its follow-up.

23. The U.S.-Jordan Free Trade agreement (2001) is the first trade agreement that explicitly includes labor and environmental standards in the text of the agreement. The United States and Jordan pledged to refrain from relaxing domestic standards to encourage trade and to uphold the principles of the ILO and internationally recognized labor rights. The parties agreed to strive to uphold these standards through domestic legislation. It is noteworthy that the "internationally recognized labor rights" enumerated in the agreement exclude the ILO core standard of nondiscrimination.

24. Rules of origin specify the minimum amount of North American content that products must contain to qualify for inclusion in the North American free trade zone.

25. More completely, there are also complex provisions for additional hearings and even arbitration with penalties if consultation fails to resolve certain complaints, but these provisions are full of limitations, restrictions, and provisos. For example, issues related to union activity cannot progress past the ministerial consultation stage, and only health and safety, minimum wage, and child labor issues can go to arbitration. There are also requirements that must be satisfied pertaining to trade-related issues, patterns of practice, and other issues. It is easy to question whether these provisions will ever be utilized (e.g., Mazey 2001), and most analyses of the NAALC procedures focus on NAO submissions and the subsequent possibility of ministerial consultations. Of the twenty-two submissions filed in the first six years of the NAALC, less than half reached the ministerial consultation stage and no submissions advanced past this stage (Bognanno and Lu 2003).

26. Illustrative cases include those involving General Electric, Honeywell, Hyundai, Maxi-Switch, Sony, and Sprint. See Bognanno and Lu (2003), Summers (1999), and Tsogas (2001).

27. Because the EU is more than a free trade zone, EU-level political institutions can enact binding laws that member countries must comply with. Directives are binding pieces of legislation that specify required results, but not processes. Individual countries use their own policies and laws to achieve the results required by directives. For a brief introduction to EU institutions, see Addison and Siebert (1991) and Bellace (1997); Dinan (1999) provides additional details.

Also, the European Works Council directive was initially enacted under the auspices of the non-binding 1989 Community Charter of Fundamental Social Rights of Workers (or "Social Charter") and its incorporation in the 1992 Maastricht Treaty. Great Britain opted out of the Social Charter and opposed its inclusion in the treaty, so initially the European Works Council directive did not apply to British establishments or workers. As a result of the Transnational Information and Consultation of Employees Regulations, Britain became a party to the European Works Council directive in 2000. See Addison and Siebert (1991, 1994) for a discussion of the Social Charter; for European labor law more generally, see Blainpain (1999).

28. More precisely, companies had a two-year window to negotiate an agreement with their employees that would specify the procedure for transnational consultation and information. These councils are referred to as voluntary or Article 13 EWCs and include transnational councils that predate the directive. The standards cited in the text apply to those companies that failed to negotiate a voluntary agreement within the two-year window. Voluntary agreements were not bound by these standards (Streeck 1997), but the resulting procedures could be challenged later on (Bellace 1997). Part of the reason for allowing voluntary agreements was to respect preexisting transnational works councils. These councils are analyzed in Streeck and Vitols (1995).

29. One exception is the European Works Councils directive under which unions can use EWCs to develop networks and alliances with other unions (Hancké 2000).

30. The Canadian region of the UAW (except one local) broke away from the U.S. parent union in 1985 because the Canadians believed they were being forced by the international UAW leadership to accept contract settlements that were responsive to U.S. conditions and constraints but not to conditions in Canada (Budd 1998). The Canadian members of the International Woodworkers of America similarly formed an autonomous Canadian union in 1987 (Widenor 1995).

31. Free trade is also consistent with the libertarian ethical belief system.

CONCLUSION

1. This broad level of analysis complements other levels of analysis, such as Hodson's (2001) examination of how workers pursue dignity at work on an individual level and Kelly's (1998) research on how workers mobilize collectively.

2. This is not to say that comparative research does not reveal intriguing ideas for components of a broader system. For example, a country that emphasizes free political speech as greatly as the United States should take stock of the protection of workers' right of expression by French law.

3. Stiglitz (2000) more explicitly discusses labor issues.

4. More generally, see Estes (1996).

5. "Special Report: The Enron Scandal," *Business Week,* January 28, 2002.

6. See, for example, Flexner (1989), Greider (1997), Hartmann (2002), Kelly (2001), Korten (1995, 1999), Phillips (2002), Soros (2000), and Yergin and Stanislaw (1998).

EPILOGUE: THE LATE MIDDLE AGES OF INDUSTRIAL RELATIONS

1. These two periods were when management demanded concessions in early 1994 and when permanent strike replacements were used in 1996 (Krueger and Mas 2002). For an example from aircraft manufacturing, see Kleiner, Leonard, and Pilarski (2002).

2. Strauss and Feuille (1981) and Kaufman (1993) both use the term "golden age of industrial relations" and while they differ on the starting point, they agree that it ended in the late 1950s. Godard (1994) makes the point that industrial relations is at a crossroads (see also Kaufman 1993; Godard and Delaney 2000).

3. There are also methodological differences among various groups, but by treating different methodologies as complementary, these differences can be more easily reconciled than can normative differences. For a recent discussion of methodological approaches to researching work, see Whitfield and Strauss (1998). Godard (1994) is critical of the dominant logical empiricism methodology, but nevertheless explicitly advocates a broadening of methodological approaches rather than a rejection of existing ones.

4. To be more explicit, if industrial relations is simply the study of unions, then its viability is in serious doubt. To industrial relations academics, the field is certainly much broader that this, but the perceptions of outsiders must not be overlooked. And this perception is often quite narrow. Further complicating this issue is that some industrial relations programs are located in business schools (and others have been shuttered by business school deans) and that higher education is increasingly reliant on private sources of financial support. Business, of course, can afford to contribute more than unions, and therefore potentially exert more influence, implicitly or explicitly.

5. In world history, the Late Middle Ages spanned roughly the 1300s and 1400s in Europe and was marked by conflict, social turbulence, and uncertainty. This period included the Hundred Years War between England and France, the Black Death, and a schism in the Catholic Church with competing popes. This was followed by the Renaissance, which included the invention of the printing press by Gutenberg and the creation of famous works of art by Leonardo de Vinci, Michelangelo, and others. The Late Middle Ages was also followed by the reformations: the split of the Protestants from the Catholic Church in the Protestant Reformation led by Martin Luther, Henry VIII's split from the Catholic Church (so he could annul his marriage to Catherine of Aragon) in the English Reformation, and the renewed Papal inquisitions during the Counter Reformation. Without intending to be melodramatic, the question for industrial relations is whether it can unite with human resource management and create a renaissance, or whether the schism will deepen into a permanent split as in the reformations. Some might even argue that human resource management has split from industrial relations to annul its marriage with organized labor, but this might be pushing the metaphor too far.

6. As "industrial relations" is popularly associated with unions and "human resource management" can be associated with union-busting, both of these terms are too value-laden to be used as the label for an inclusive field of study of the employment relationship. The term "employment relations" has also been proposed (Kaufman 1993) and is also commonly used in Great Britain, but I prefer "human resources and industrial relations" for several reasons. One, it provides greater continuity with existing terms. Two, "employment relations" may already be exclusionary. In Great Britain, it is not clear that human resource management is included within this term (Edwards 1995). In the United States, "employment relations" can be closely associated with unionized employment because some states have employment relations boards or commissions that handle representation elections, unfair labor practices, and mediation for public sector bargaining units. Three, "human resource and industrial relations" is already starting to be used. For example, the graduate degree programs at the University of Minnesota, the University of Illinois, and others were renamed "human resources and industrial relations" in the late 1990s.

7. The need for theory is unquestioned, but the quest for a *single* theory as the defining characteristic of the field is problematic, especially as this quest becomes intellectually exclusionary rather than inclusive. Kaufman (1993) argues the drive for a single theory weakened rather than strengthened the discipline by degrading important intellectual schools as evidenced by Dunlop's (1958) emphasis on the external environment over the internal, on unionized situations over nonunion, and on institutional labor economics over behavioral sciences.

8. Representative is Somers (1969b, 39): "The survival of industrial relations as a separate discipline and its growth as a respectable field of study require a broad conceptual or theoretical framework." Similar views are echoed outside of traditional industrial relations. Ferris et al. (1995, 3) lament that "the science of HRM has been marked by an absence of an integrative theory or general conceptual system."

9. As discussed in chapter 3, Kochan, Katz, and McKersie (1986) added a three-tier strategic choice component to Dunlop's (1958) systems model, but did not claim this as a general model of industrial relations. Other contributions toward industrial relations theory include Adams and Meltz (1993), Barbash (1984), Barbash and Barbash (1989), Dabscheck (1994), Hills (1995), and Somers (1969a). In a different vein, see Kelly (1998).

10. The defining feature of economics is the study of the pricing and allocation of scarce resources, not a single neoclassical theory (major alternatives include classical, institutional, Keynesian, and Marxist economic thought). Psychology studies human behavior from cognitive, biological, psychoanalytic, humanistic, behavioral, and sociocultural approaches. Ritzer (1980, 7) identifies three broad paradigms in sociology: a social facts paradigm, a social definition par-

adigm, and a social behavior paradigm. Although each of these paradigms has at least two major theories and its own dominant methodology, the status of sociology as a discipline or single field of study is not questioned.

11. Kaufman (1993) discusses organizational and social issues such as declines in academic programs, journals, and Industrial Relations Research Association membership.

12. The overlap between HRIR and economics, psychology, sociology, history, and the like as well as liberal application of "their" theories and methodologies does not disqualify HRIR as a field of study.

13. Krueger (2002) cites a variety of economic treatments of equity, but is also a rare example that goes beyond pure neoclassical concerns. The classic treatment of instrumental voice is Hirschman (1970).

14. My apologies to history and law, which also contribute immensely to the understanding of the employment relationship.

15. In fact, it can be argued that the development of industrial relations is closely linked to efforts to create equity and voice when efficiency was the sole goal of employers while the development of human resource management arose from the resulting need to highlight efficiency in these equitable employment practices.

16. There are many significant debates in economics: the effectiveness of monetary policy or tax cuts, the explanatory power of standard models of international trade, the existence of natural monopolies, structural versus reduced form econometrics, and the degree to which individuals are rational utility maximizers. Psychologists continue to debate the extent to which the Big Five personality dimensions are adequately comprehensive and meaningful as a portrait of a person's personality. The existence of these debates does not prevent identification with a single discipline; in fact, the debates are greatly enriched by the interaction of scholars with differing perspectives.

17. Bemmels and Zaidi (1989) describe the intellectual foundations of Minnesota's program.

18. In fact, one of the leading textbooks is simply called *The Labor Relations Process* (Holley, Jennings, and Wolters 2001). I trace the lineage of today's labor relations and collective bargaining textbooks back to Dunlop (1949). Earlier texts focused more broadly on the labor problem (Estey 1928; Daugherty 1933) and gave almost equal weight to unions, government regulation, and human resource management. The first two textbooks that appear to have "labor relations" in the title, Watkins and Dodd (1938) and Yoder (1938), ironically are the forerunners of today's human resource management textbooks. Dunlop (1949) briefly compares collective bargaining with alternative market and government mechanisms for setting wages, but a process-based focus is clearly apparent and a majority of the text is devoted to case exercises. Two other early texts that went into multiple editions were also process focused (Chamberlain 1951; Davey 1951). Davey (1951) devotes six chapters to the content of collective bargaining agreements. Current textbooks generally continue this process-based focus. An exception is Kochan and Katz (1988), which explicitly departs from a process focus and uses the strategic choice framework of Kochan, Katz, and McKersie (1986) as the textbook's main theme. Their theme emphasizes the level of decision making whereas the thematic approach developed herein emphasizes the objectives of the employment relationship.

19. In the teaching context, the decline in U.S. union density over the last fifty years also begs the question of how many students will be working in a unionized context and therefore need to be trained in the details of the labor relations processes. I am not advocating that we abandon teaching the current labor relations processes; I am questioning whether we lose the forest for the trees by focusing almost exclusively, and in great detail, on the existing processes.

20. Updated pedagogies based on contemporary learning theory can also be used successfully in labor relations courses; see Budd (2002) for examples based on new technologies.

21. An emphasis on work rules in industrial relations is a hallmark of the postwar industrial pluralism school (Stone 1981). Often overlooked, however, are Dunlop's (1958) rules for making rules or Clegg's (1979) procedural rules. This is the question of workplace governance.

22. This is not to say that no linkages exist in the fields mentioned in this paragraph. For instance, examples of collaboration between industrial relations and theology include Ogle and Wheeler (2001) and the industrial relations programs in some Jesuit colleges such as LeMoyne, Loyola University Chicago, and Rockhurst. With respect to human rights, Adams (2001), Gross

(1999), and Wheeler (2000) are examples that begin to incorporate human rights scholarship into industrial relations, but industrial relations scholarship ought to be able to provide contributions in the other direction as well.

23. Unfortunately, institutional economics is used as a label for more than one school of thought. The institutional school referenced here is the one that traces back to John R. Commons, Thorstein Veblen, and Wesley C. Mitchell and for which the *Journal of Economic Issues* is the primary journal. This is not to be confused with the "new institutional economics" associated with Coase (1937) and Williamson (1975) in which market imperfections such as transactions costs and asymmetric information give rise to the importance of institutions (webs of rules). The school maintains the neoclassical economics emphasis on individual utility maximization and efficiency, and therefore has a general skepticism about the benefits of government regulation (Dow 1997). Closely related is the neoinstitutional paradigm associated with North (1990). All of these institutional schools share a common conception of "institutions" as the rules of human interaction or a web of rules; "institutions" in this context, therefore, should not be narrowly equated with "organizations." For more on institutional versus new institutional economics, see Hodgson (1998).

References

Abbott, Andrew. 2001. *Chaos of Disciplines.* Chicago: University of Chicago Press.

Abowd, John M., and Thomas Lemieux. 1993. "The Effects of Product Market Competition on Collective Bargaining Agreements: The Case of Foreign Competition in Canada." *Quarterly Journal of Economics* 108 (November): 983–1014.

Abrams, Roger I. 2000. *The Money Pitch: Baseball Free Agency and Salary Arbitration.* Philadelphia: Temple University Press.

Adams, Edward S., and John H. Matheson. 2000. "A Statutory Model for Corporate Constituency Concerns." *Emory Law Journal* 49 (fall): 1085–1135.

Adams, J. Stacy. 1965. "Inequity in Social Exchange." In *Advances in Experimental Social Psychology,* vol. 2, edited by Leonard Berkowitz, 267–99. New York: Academic Press.

Adams, Roy J. 1991. "Universal Joint Regulation: A Moral Imperative." In *Proceedings of the Forty-Third Annual Meeting,* edited by John F. Burton, 319–27. Madison, Wis.: Industrial Relations Research Association.

——. 1993. "'All Aspects of People at Work': Unity and Division in the Study of Labor and Labor Management." In *Industrial Relations Theory: Its Nature, Scope, and Pedagogy,* edited by Roy J. Adams and Noah M. Meltz, 119–60. Metuchen, N.J.: IMLR Press/Rutgers University.

——. 1995. *Industrial Relations under Liberal Democracy: North America in Comparative Perspective.* Columbia: University of South Carolina Press.

——. 2001. "Choice or Voice? Rethinking American Labor Policy in Light of the International Human Rights Consensus." *Employee Rights and Employment Policy Journal* 5: 521–48.

——. 2002. "The Wagner Act Model: A Toxic System beyond Repair." *British Journal of Industrial Relations* 40 (March): 122–27.

Adams, Roy J., and Noah M. Meltz, eds. 1993. *Industrial Relations Theory: Its Nature, Scope, and Pedagogy.* Metuchen, N.J.: IMLR Press/Rutgers University.

Adams, Roy J., and Parbudyal Singh. 1997. "Early Experience with NAFTA's Labour Side Accord." *Comparative Labor Law Journal* 18 (winter): 161–81.

Addison, John T., and Barry T. Hirsch. 1997. "The Economic Effects of Employment Regulation: What Are the Limits?" In *Government Regulation of the Employment Relationship,* edited by Bruce E. Kaufman, chap. 4. Madison, Wis.: Industrial Relations Research Association.

Addison, John T., and W. Stanley Siebert. 1991. "The Social Charter of the European Community: Evolution and Controversies." *Industrial and Labor Relations Review* 44 (July): 597–625.

——. 1994. "Recent Developments in Social Policy in the New European Union." *Industrial and Labor Relations Review* 48 (October): 5–27.

Aitken, Brian, Ann Harrison, and Robert E. Lipsey. 1996. "Wages and Foreign Ownership: A Comparative Study of Mexico, Venezuela, and the United States." *Journal of International Economics* 40 (May): 345–71.

Alben, Elissa. 2001. "GATT and the Fair Wage: A Historical Perspective on the Labor-Trade Link." *Columbia Law Review* 101 (October): 1410–47.

Alchian, Armen A. 1965. "Some Economics of Property Rights." *Il Politico* 30: 816–29.

Alexander, Gregory S. 1997. *Commodity and Proprietary: Competing Visions of Property in American Legal Thought, 1776–1970.* Chicago: University of Chicago Press.

Alexander, Robin, and Peter Gilmore. 1999. "A Strategic Organizing Alliance across Borders." In *The Transformation of U.S. Unions: Voices, Visions, and Strategies from the Grassroots,* edited by Ray M. Tillman and Michael S. Cummings, chap. 14. Boulder, Colo.: Lynne Rienner.

Alford, Helen J., and Michael J. Naughton. 2001. *Managing as If Faith Mattered: Christian Social Principles in the Modern Organization.* Notre Dame: University of Notre Dame Press.

Altmann, Morris, 2001. *Worker Satisfaction and Economic Performance.* Armonk, N.Y.: M. E. Sharpe.

Appelbaum, Eileen, and Rosemary Batt. 1994. *The New American Workplace: Transforming Work Systems in the United States.* Ithaca: ILR Press.

Araki, Takashi. 1994. "The Japanese Model of Employee Representational Participation." *Comparative Labor Law Journal* 15 (winter): 143–54.

Aristotle. 1980. *The Nicomachean Ethics.* Rev. ed. Edited by William David Ross. Oxford: Oxford University Press.

Armstrong, Pat. 1993. "Professions, Unions, or What? Learning from Nurses." In *Women Challenging Unions: Feminism, Democracy, and Militancy,* edited by Linda Briskin and Patricia McDermott, chap. 15. Toronto: University of Toronto Press.

Arthur, Jeffrey B. 1992. "The Link between Business Strategy and Industrial Relations Systems in American Steel Minimills." *Industrial and Labor Relations Review* 45 (April): 488–506.

Ashenfelter, Orley, and George E. Johnson. 1969. "Bargaining Theory, Trade Unions, and Industrial Strike Activity." *American Economic Review* 59 (March): 35–49.

Atleson, James B. 1993. "Wartime Labor Regulation, the Industrial Pluralists, and the Law of Collective Bargaining." In *Industrial Democracy in America: The Ambiguous Promise,* edited by Nelson Lichtenstein and Howell John Harris, chap. 7. Washington, D.C.: Woodrow Wilson Center Press.

——. 1998. *Labor and the Wartime State: Labor Relations and Law during World War II.* Urbana: University of Illinois Press.

——. 2002. "The Voyage of the *Neptune Jade:* Transnational Labour Solidarity and the Obstacles of Domestic Law." In *Labour Law in an Era of Globalization: Transformative Practices and Possibilities,* edited by Joanne Conaghan, Richard Michael Fischl, and Karl Klare, chap. 19. Oxford: Oxford University Press.

Austin, James T., and Howard J. Klein. 1996. "Work Motivation and Goal Striving." In *Individual Differences and Behavior in Organizations,* edited by Kevin R. Murphy, chap. 6. San Francisco: Jossey-Bass.

Autor, David H., Lawrence F. Katz, and Alan B. Krueger. 1998. "Computing Inequality: Have Computers Changed the Labor Market?" *Quarterly Journal of Economics* 113 (November): 1169–1213.

Babson, Steve. 1995. *Lean Work: Empowerment and Exploitation in the Global Auto Industry.* Detroit: Wayne State University Press.

——. 1999. *The Unfinished Struggle: Turning Points in American Labor, 1877–Present.* Lanham, Md.: Rowman and Littlefield.

Bainbridge, Stephen M. 1998. "Corporate Decision Making and the Moral Rights of Employees: Participatory Management and Natural Law." *Villanova Law Review* 43: 741–828.

Baird, Charles W. 2000. "Unions and Antitrust." *Journal of Labor Research* 21 (fall): 584–600.

Baker, Mark B. 2001. "Tightening the Toothless Vise: Codes of Conduct and the American Multinational Enterprise." *Wisconsin International Law Journal* 20 (winter): 89–142.

Bal, Salman. 2001. "International Free Trade Agreements and Human Rights: Reinterpreting Article XX of the GATT." *Minnesota Journal of Global Trade* 10 (winter): 62–108.

Baldwin, Robert E. 2003. *The Decline of U.S. Labor Unions and the Role of Trade.* Washington, D.C.: Institute for International Economics.

Baldwin, R. W. 1966. *Social Justice.* Oxford: Pergamon Press.

Ballam, Deborah A. 1995. "The Development of the Employment at Will Rule Revisited: A Challenge to Its Origins as Based in the Development of Advanced Capitalism." *Hofstra Labor Law Journal* 13 (fall): 75–107.

Bandura, Albert. 1986. *Social Foundations of Thought and Action: A Social Cognitive Theory.* Englewood Cliffs, N.J.: Prentice-Hall.

Banks, Andrew, and John Russo. 1999. "The Development of International Campaign-Based Network Structures: A Case Study of the IBT and ITF World Council of UPS Unions." *Comparative Labor Law and Policy Journal* 20 (summer): 543–68.

Banks, Andy, and Jack Metzgar. 1989. "Participating in Management: Union Organizing on a New Terrain." *Labor Research Review* 14 (fall): 1–55.

Barbash, Jack. 1984. *The Elements of Industrial Relations.* Madison: University of Wisconsin Press.

——. 1989. "Equity as Function: Its Rise and Attrition." In *Theories and Concepts in Comparative Industrial Relations,* edited by Jack Barbash and Kate Barbash, chap. 8. Columbia: University of South Carolina Press.

——. 1993. "The Founders of Industrial Relations as a Field of Study: An American Perspective." In *Industrial Relations Theory: Its Nature, Scope, and Pedagogy,* edited by Roy J. Adams and Noah M. Meltz, 67–80. Metuchen, N.J.: IMLR Press.

Barbash, Jack, and Kate Barbash, eds. 1989. *Theories and Concepts in Industrial Relations.* Columbia: University of South Carolina Press.

Barling, Julian, Clive Fullagar, and E. Kevin Kelloway. 1992. *Organizational Behavior and the Psychology of Unions.* New York: Oxford University Press.

Barnett, Tim, and Cheryl Vaicys. 2000. "The Moderating Effect of Individuals' Perceptions of Ethical Work Climate on Ethical Judgments and Behavior Intentions." *Journal of Business Ethics* 27 (October II): 351–62.

Baron, Robert A. 1996. "Interpersonal Relations in Organizations." In *Individual Differences and Behavior in Organizations,* edited by Kevin R. Murphy, chap. 9. San Francisco: Jossey-Bass.

Barreto, José, and Reinhard Naumann. 1998. "Portugal: Industrial Relations under Democracy." In *Changing Industrial Relations in Europe,* edited by Anthony Ferner and Richard Hyman, chap. 14. Oxford: Blackwell.

Barrick, Murray R., and Michael K. Mount. 1991. "The Big Five Personality Dimensions and Job Performance: A Meta-Analysis." *Personnel Psychology* 44 (spring): 1–26.

Bartl, Timothy J. 2002. *Work and Pay in the New Century: Upgrading Our Wage and Hour Laws to Meet the Needs of Today's Employees.* Washington, D.C.: Labor Policy Association.

Bartolomei de la Cruz, Héctor, Geraldo von Potobsky, and Lee Swepston. 1996. *The International Labor Organization: The International Standards Systems and Basic Human Rights.* Boulder, Colo.: Westview Press.

Beauchamp, Tom L., and Norman E. Bowie, eds. 1997. *Ethical Theory and Business.* 5th ed. Upper Saddle River, N.J.: Prentice-Hall.

Becher, Tony. 1989. *Academic Tribes and Territories: Intellectual Enquiry and the Cultures of Disciplines.* Milton Keynes, England: Open University Press.

Becker, Brian E., and Mark A. Huselid. 1998. "High Performance Work Systems and Firm Performance: A Synthesis of Research and Managerial Implications." In *Research in Personnel and Human Resources Management,* vol. 15, edited by Gerald R. Ferris, 53–101. Stamford, Conn.: JAI Press.

Becker, Brian E., and Craig A. Olson. 1989. "Unionization and Shareholder Interests." *Industrial and Labor Relations Review* 42 (January): 246–62.

Becker, Craig. 1993. "Democracy in the Workplace: Union Representation Elections and Federal Labor Law." *Minnesota Law Review* 77 (February): 495–603.

Befort, Stephen F. 2002. "Labor and Employment Law at the Millennium: A Historical Review and Critical Assessment." *Boston College Law Review* 43 (March): 351–460.

Bellace, Janice R. 1983. "A Right of Fair Dismissal: Enforcing a Statutory Guarantee." *University of Michigan Journal of Law Reform* 16 (winter): 202–47.

———. 1997. "The European Works Council Directive: Transnational Information and Consultation in the European Union." *Comparative Labor Law Journal* 18 (spring): 325–61.

Belman, Dale, and Michael H. Belzer. 1997. "The Regulation of Labor Markets: Balancing the Benefits and Costs of Competition." In *Government Regulation of the Employment Relationship,* edited by Bruce E. Kaufman, chap. 5. Madison, Wis.: Industrial Relations Research Association.

Belzer, Michael H. 2000. *Sweatshops on Wheels: Winners and Losers in Trucking Deregulation.* New York: Oxford University Press.

Bemmels, Brian. 1997. "Exit, Voice, and Loyalty in Employment Relationships." In *The Human Resource Management Handbook, Part 2,* edited by David Lewin, Daniel J. B. Mitchell, and Mahmood Zaidi, 245–59. Greenwich, Conn.: JAI Press.

Bemmels, Brian G., and Mahmood Zaidi. 1989. "Industrial Relations: The Minnesota Model." In *Theories and Concepts in Industrial Relations,* edited by Jack Barbash and Kate Barbash, chap. 13. Columbia: University of South Carolina Press.

Bendiner, Burton. 1987. *International Labour Affairs: The World Trade Unions and the Multinational Companies.* Oxford: Clarendon Press.

Ben-Ner, Avner, and Derek C. Jones. 1995. "Employee Participation, Ownership, and Productivity: A Theoretical Framework." *Industrial Relations* 34 (October): 532–54.

Ben-Ner, Avner, and Louis Putterman. 1998. "Values and Institutions in Economic Analysis." In *Economics, Values, and Organization,* edited by Avner Ben-Ner and Louis Putterman, 3–69. Cambridge: Cambridge University Press.

Bennett, James T., and Jason E. Taylor. 2001. "Labor Unions: Victims of Their Political Success?" *Journal of Labor Research* 22 (spring): 261–73.

Berkowitz, Edward D. 1995. *Mr. Social Security: The Life of Wilbur J. Cohen.* Lawrence: University Press of Kansas.

Berman, Eli, John Bound, and Stephen Machin. 1998. "Implications of Skill-Biased Technological Change: International Evidence." *Quarterly Journal of Economics* 113 (November): 1245–79.

Bernstein, Irving. 1950. *The New Deal Collective Bargaining Policy.* Berkeley: University of California Press.

Bethell, Tom. 1998. *The Noblest Triumph: Property and Prosperity through the Ages.* New York: St. Martin's.

Blackett, Adelle. 1999. "Whither Social Clause? Human Rights, Trade Theory, and Treaty Interpretation." *Columbia Human Rights Law Review* 31 (fall): 1–80.

Blades, Lawrence E. 1967. "Employment at Will vs. Individual Freedom: On Limiting the Abusive Exercise of Employer Power." *Columbia Law Review* 67 (December): 1404–35.

Blair, Margaret M. 1995. *Ownership and Control: Rethinking Corporate Governance for the Twenty-First Century.* Washington, D.C.: Brookings.

Blair, Margaret M., and Mark J. Roe, eds. 1999. *Employees and Corporate Governance.* Washington, D.C.: Brookings.

Blank, Rebecca M., ed. 1994. *Social Protection versus Economic Flexibility: Is There a Trade-Off?* Chicago: University of Chicago Press.

Blanpain, Roger. 1999. *European Labour Law.* 6th ed. The Hague: Kluwer.

Bliss, Christopher, and Nicholas Stern. 1978. "Productivity, Wages, and Nutrition: Part I: The Theory." *Journal of Development Economics* 5 (December): 331–62.

Bloomfield, Meyer. 1923. "The Place of Personnel Work in Modern Management." In *Problems in Personnel Management,* edited by Daniel Bloomfield, chap. 1. New York: H. W. Wilson.

Bluestone, Barry, and Irving Bluestone. 1992. *Negotiating the Future: A Labor Perspective on American Business.* New York: Basic Books.

Boatright, John R. 2000. *Ethics and the Conduct of Business.* 3rd ed. Upper Saddle River, N.J.: Prentice-Hall.

Bognanno, Mario F., and Robert A. Kearney. 1994. "Industrial Relations and Technological Change in the Workplace: Lessons from a 911 Emergency Communications Field Study." In *Advances in Industrial and Labor Relations,* vol. 6, edited by David Lewin and Donna Sockell, 111–32. Greenwich, Conn.: JAI Press.

Bognanno, Mario F., and Jiangfeng Lu. 2003. "NAFTA's Labor Side Agreement: Withering as an Effective Labor Law Enforcement and MNC Compliance Strategy?" In *Multinational Companies and Global Human Resource Strategies,* edited by William N. Cooke, chap. 18. Westport, Conn.: Quorum Books.

Bolton, Gary E., and Axel Ockenfels. 2000. "ERC: A Theory of Equity, Reciprocity, and Competition." *American Economic Review* 90 (March): 166–93.

Bonacich, Edna. 2000. "Intense Challenges, Tentative Possibilities: Organizing Immigrant Garment Workers in Los Angeles." In *Organizing Immigrants: The Challenge for Unions in Contemporary California,* edited by Ruth Milkman, chap. 5. Ithaca: ILR Press.

Bonacich, Edna, and Richard P. Appelbaum. 2000. *Behind the Label: Inequality in the Los Angeles Apparel Industry.* Berkeley: University of California Press.

Booth, Alison L. 1997. "An Analysis of Firing Costs and Their Implications for Unemployment Policy." In *Unemployment Policy: Government Options for the Labour Market,* edited by Dennis J. Snower and Guillermo de la Dehesa, chap. 12. Cambridge: Cambridge University Press.

Bordo, Michael D., Barry Eichengreen, and Douglas A. Irwin. 1999. "Is Globalization Today Really Different from Globalization a Hundred Years Ago?" In *Brookings Trade Forum, 1999,* edited by Susan Collins and Robert Z. Lawrence, 1–50. Washington, D.C.: Brookings Institution.

Borjas, George J. 1999. *Heaven's Door: Immigration Policy and the American Economy.* Princeton: Princeton University Press.

Bowie, Norman E. 1999. *Business Ethics: A Kantian Perspective.* Malden, Mass.: Blackwell.

Bowie, Norman E., and Ronald F. Duska. 1990. *Business Ethics.* 2d ed. Englewood Cliffs, N.J.: Prentice Hall.

Bowles, Samuel, Herbert Gintis, and Melissa Osborne. 2001. "The Determinants of Earnings: A Behavioral Approach." *Journal of Economic Literature* 39 (December): 1137–76.

Boyer, George R., and Robert S. Smith. 2001. "The Development of the Neoclassical Tradition in Labor Economics." *Industrial and Labor Relations Review* 54 (January): 199–223.

Bradley, Curtis A., and Jack L. Goldsmith. 1997. "Customary International Law as Federal Common Law: A Critique of the Modern Position." *Harvard Law Review* 110 (February): 815–76.

Braverman, Harry. 1974. *Labor and Monopoly Capital: The Degradation of Work in the Twentieth Century.* New York: Monthly Review Press.

Brest, Paul. 1988. "Further Beyond the Republican Revival: Toward Radical Republicanism." *Yale Law Journal* 97 (July): 1623–31.

Brody, David. 1980. *Workers in Industrial America: Essays on the Twentieth Century Struggle.* New York: Oxford University Press.

———. 1993. "Workplace Contractualism in Comparative Perspective." In *Industrial Democracy in America: The Ambiguous Promise*, edited by Nelson Lichtenstein and Howell John Harris, chap. 8. Washington, D.C.: Woodrow Wilson Center Press.

———. 2001. "Labour Rights as Human Rights: A Reality Check." *British Journal of Industrial Relations* 39 (December): 601–5.

Bronfenbrenner, Kate, Sheldon Friedman, Richard W. Hurd, Rudolph A. Oswald, and Ronald L. Seeber, eds. 1998. *Organizing to Win: New Research on Union Strategies.* Ithaca: ILR Press.

Bronfenbrenner, Kate, and Tom Juravich. 1998. "It Takes More than House Calls: Organizing to Win with a Comprehensive Union-Building Strategy." In *Organizing to Win: New Research on Union Strategies*, edited by Kate Bronfenbrenner et al., chap. 1. Ithaca: ILR Press.

Brown, Clair, and Ben Campbell. 2001. "Technical Change, Wages, and Employment in Semiconductor Manufacturing." *Industrial and Labor Relations Review* 54 (March): 450–65.

Brown, Douglass V., and Charles A. Myers. 1962. "Historical Evolution." In *Public Policy and Collective Bargaining*, edited by Joseph Shister, Benjamin Aaron, and Clyde W. Summers, chap. 1. New York: Harper and Row.

Brown, Drusilla K. 2001. "Labor Standards: Where Do They Belong on the International Trade Agenda?" *Journal of Economic Perspectives* 15 (summer): 89–112.

Buchmueller, Thomas C., and Robert G. Valletta. 1996. "The Effects of Employer-Provided Health Insurance on Worker Mobility." *Industrial and Labor Relations Review* 49 (April): 439–55.

Budd, John W. 1995. "The Internal Union Political Imperative for UAW Pattern Bargaining." *Journal of Labor Research* 16 (winter): 43–55.

———. 1998. "The Effect of International Unions on Wage Determination in Canada." *British Journal of Industrial Relations* 36 (March): 1–26.

———. 2002. "Teaching Labor Relations: Opportunities and Challenges of Using Technology." *Journal of Labor Research* 23 (summer): 355–74.

Budd, John W., Jozef Konings, and Matthew J. Slaughter. 2002. "International Rent Sharing in Multinational Firms." Working Paper 8809. Cambridge, Mass.: National Bureau of Economic Research.

Budd, John W., and Brian P. McCall. 1997. "The Effect of Unions on the Receipt of Unemployment Insurance Benefits." *Industrial and Labor Relations Review* 50 (April): 478–92.

———. 2001. "The Grocery Stores Wage Distribution: A Semi-Parametric Analysis of the Role of Retailing and Labor Market Institutions." *Industrial and Labor Relations Review* 54 (March): 484–501.

Budd, John W., and Matthew J. Slaughter. Forthcoming. "Are Profits Shared across Borders? Evidence on International Rent Sharing." *Journal of Labor Economics.*

Burns, James MacGregor, and Stewart Burns. 1991. *A People's Charter: The Pursuit of Rights in America.* New York: Alfred A. Knopf.

Burton, John F., Jr., and James R. Chelius. 1997. "Workplace Safety and Health Regulations: Rationale and Results." In *Government Regulation of the Employment Relationship*, edited by Bruce E. Kaufman, chap. 7. Madison, Wis.: Industrial Relations Research Association.

Camerer, Colin F., and Richard H. Thaler. 1995. "Ultimatums, Dictators, and Manners." *Journal of Economic Perspectives* 9 (spring): 209–19.

Cameron, Lisa A. 1999. "Raising the Stakes in the Ultimatum Game: Experimental Evidence from Indonesia." *Economic Inquiry* 37 (January): 47–59.

Campbell, John P., and Robert D. Pritchard. 1976. "Motivation Theory in Industrial and Organizational Psychology." In *Handbook of Industrial and Organizational Psychology*, edited by Marvin D. Dunnette, chap. 3. Chicago: Rand McNally.

Cappelli, Peter. 1985. "Competitive Pressures and Labor Relations in the Airline Industry." *Industrial Relations* 24 (fall): 316–38.

——, ed. 1995. *Airline Labor Relations in the Global Era: The New Frontier.* Ithaca: ILR Press.

——. 1999. *The New Deal at Work: Managing the Market-Driven Workforce.* Boston: Harvard Business School Press.

Cappelli, Peter, and David Neumark. 2001. "Do 'High-Performance' Work Practices Improve Establishment-Level Outcomes?" *Industrial and Labor Relations Review* 54 (July): 737–75.

Cappelli, Peter, and Harbir Singh. 1992. "Integrating Strategic Human Resources and Strategic Management." In *Research Frontiers in Industrial Relations and Human Resources,* edited by David Lewin, Olivia S. Mitchell, and Peter D. Sherer, chap. 5. Madison, Wis.: Industrial Relations Research Association.

Card, David. 2001. "The Effect of Unions on Wage Inequality in the U.S. Labor Market." *Industrial and Labor Relations Review* 54 (January): 296–315.

Card, David, and Alan B. Krueger. 1995. *Myth and Measurement: The New Economics of the Minimum Wage.* Princeton: Princeton University Press.

Catholic Church. 1943. *Two Basic Social Encyclicals.* New York: Benzinger Brothers.

Chaison, Gary N., and Barbara J. Bigelow. 2002. *Unions and Legitimacy.* Ithaca: ILR Press.

Chaison, Gary N., and Joseph B. Rose. 1991. "The Macrodeterminants of Union Growth and Decline." In *The State of the Unions,* edited by George Strauss, Daniel G. Gallagher and Jack Fiorito, chap. 1. Madison, Wis.: Industrial Relations Research Association.

Chamberlain, Neil W. 1951. *Collective Bargaining.* New York: McGraw-Hill.

Charnovitz, Steve. 2002. "The Law of Environmental 'PPMs' in the WTO: Debunking the Myth of Illegality." *Yale Journal of International Law* 27 (winter): 59–110.

Charny, David. 1999. "Workers and Corporate Governance: The Role of Political Culture." In *Employees and Corporate Governance,* edited by Margaret M. Blair and Mark J. Roe, chap. 3. Washington, D.C.: Brookings.

Chelius, James, and James Dworkin, eds. 1990. *Reflections on the Transformation of Industrial Relations.* Metuchen, N.J.: IMLR Press.

Cialdini, Robert B., and Melanie R. Trost. 1998. "Social Influences: Social Norms, Conformity, and Compliance." In *The Handbook of Social Psychology,* vol. 2, edited by Daniel T. Gilbert, Susan T. Fiske, and Gardner Lindzey, chap. 21. Boston: McGraw-Hill.

Clark, Paul F. 2000. *Building More Effective Unions.* Ithaca: ILR Press.

Clegg, H. A. 1975. "Pluralism in Industrial Relations." *British Journal of Industrial Relations* 13 (November): 309–16.

——. 1979. *The Changing System of Industrial Relations in Great Britain.* Oxford: Basil Blackwell.

Coase, Ronald H. 1937. "The Nature of the Firm." *Economica* 4 (November): 386–405.

——. 1960. "The Problem of Social Cost." *Journal of Law and Economics* 3 (October): 1–44.

Cobble, Dorothy Sue. 1991. *Dishing It Out: Waitresses and Their Unions in the Twentieth Century.* Urbana: University of Illinois Press.

Cohen, Joshua, and Joel Rogers. 1983. *On Democracy.* New York: Penguin.

Cohen, Larry, and Steve Early. 2000. "Globalization and De-unionization in Telecommunications: Three Case Studies in Resistance." In *Transnational Cooperation among Labor Unions,* edited by Michael E. Gordon and Lowell Turner, chap. 10. Ithaca: ILR Press.

Cohen, Lizabeth. 1990. *Making a New Deal: Industrial Workers in Chicago, 1919–1939.* Cambridge: Cambridge University Press.

Cohen, Michael D., James G. March, and Johan P. Olsen. 1972. "A Garbage Can Model of Organization Choice." *Administrative Science Quarterly* 17 (March): 1–25.

Cohn, Marjorie. 2001. "The World Trade Organization: Elevating Property Interests above Human Rights." *Georgia Journal of International and Comparative Law* 29 (summer): 427–40.

Cole, Sarah Rudolph. 2001. "Uniform Arbitration: 'One Size Fits All' Does Not Fit." *Ohio State Journal on Dispute Resolution* 16: 759–90.

Coleman, James S. 1986. "Norms as Social Capital." In *Economic Imperialism: The Economic Approach Applied Outside the Field of Economics,* edited by Gerard Radnitzky and Peter Bernholz, 133–55. New York: Paragon House.

Coll, Blanche D. 1995. *Safety Net: Welfare and Social Security, 1929–1979.* New Brunswick, N.J.: Rutgers University Press.

Colvin, Alexander J. S. 2001. "The Relationship between Employment Arbitration and Workplace Dispute Resolution Procedures." *Ohio State Journal on Dispute Resolution* 16: 643—68.

Commission on the Future of Worker-Management Relations. 1994. *Report and Recommendations.* Washington, D.C.: U.S. Departments of Labor and Commerce.

Commons, John R., ed. 1905. *Trade Unionism and Labor Problems.* Boston: Ginn and Company.

——. 1919. *Industrial Goodwill.* New York: McGraw-Hill.

——, ed. 1921. *Trade Unionism and Labor Problems.* 2d series. Boston: Ginn and Company.

——. 1924. *Legal Foundations of Capitalism.* New York: Macmillan.

——. 1934. *Institutional Economics: Its Place in Political Economy.* New York: Macmillan.

——. 1950. *The Economics of Collective Action.* New York: Macmillan.

Compa, Lance. 2002. "Author's Reply to Getman-Wheeler-Brody Papers." *British Journal of Industrial Relations* 40 (March): 114–21.

Compa, Lance A., and Tashia Hinchliffe Darricarrère. 1996. "Private Labor Rights Enforcement through Corporate Codes of Conduct." In *Human Rights, Labor Rights, and International Trade,* edited by Lance A. Compa and Stephen F. Diamond, chap. 9. Philadelphia: University of Pennsylvania Press.

Conner, Daryl R. 1998. *Leading at the Edge of Chaos: How to Create the Nimble Organization.* New York: John Wiley and Sons.

Conquest, Robert. 1991. *Stalin: Breaker of Nations.* New York: Viking.

Cooke, William N., and David G. Meyer. 1990. "Structural and Market Predictors of Corporate Labor Relations Strategies." *Industrial and Labor Relations Review* 43 (January): 280–93.

Cooney, Sean. 1999. "Testing Times for the ILO: Institutional Reform for the New International Political Economy." *Comparative Labor Law and Policy Journal* 20 (spring): 365–99.

Cornfield, Daniel B., Karen E. Campbell, and Holly J. McCammon, eds. 2001. *Working in Restructured Workplaces: Challenges and New Directions for the Sociology of Work.* Thousand Oaks, Calif.: Sage.

Cowie, Jefferson. 1999. *Capital Moves: RCA's Seventy-Year Quest for Cheap Labor.* Ithaca: Cornell University Press.

Craver, Charles B. 1993. *Can Unions Survive? The Rejuvenation of the American Labor Movement.* New York: New York University Press.

Cravey, Altha J. 1998. *Women and Work in Mexico's Maquiladoras.* Lanham, Md.: Rowman and Littlefield.

Creighton, Breen. 1999. "Transformation of Labor and Future of Labor Law in Europe: An Australian Perspective." *Comparative Labor Law and Policy Journal* 20 (summer): 635–80.

Cropanzano, Russell, Deborah E. Rupp, Carolyn J. Mohler, and Marshall Schminke. 2001. "Three Roads to Organizational Justice." In *Research in Personnel and Human Resources Management,* vol. 20, edited by Gerald R. Ferris, 1–113. Amsterdam: JAI Press.

Cross, Frank B. 2001. "The Error of Positive Rights." *UCLA Law Review* 48 (April): 857–924.

Cummins, E. E. 1932. *The Labor Problem in the United States.* New York: D. Van Nostrand.

Dabscheck, Braham. 1989. *Australian Industrial Relations in the 1980s.* Melbourne: Oxford University Press.

———. 1994. "A General Theory of (Australian) Industrial Relations." *Journal of Industrial Relations* 36 (March): 3–17.

———. 1995. *The Struggle for Australian Industrial Relations.* Melbourne: Oxford University Press.

Dahl, Robert A. 1998. *On Democracy.* New Haven: Yale University Press.

Dailey, Virginia. 2000. "Sustainable Development: Reevaluating the Trade vs. Turtles Conflict at the WTO." *Journal of Transnational Law and Policy* 9 (summer): 331–83.

Daley, Anthony. 1999. "The Hollowing Out of French Unions: Politics and Industrial Relations After 1981." In *The Brave New World of European Labor: European Trade Unions at the Millennium,* edited by Andrew Martin and George Ross, chap. 5. New York: Berghahn Books.

Daniels, Norman, ed. 1975. *Reading Rawls: Critical Studies on Rawls' A Theory of Justice.* New York: Basic Books.

Dannin, Ellen J. 1997. *Working Free: The Origins and Impact of New Zealand's Employment Contracts Act.* Auckland: Auckland University Press.

Dark, Taylor E. 2001. *The Unions and the Democrats: An Enduring Alliance.* Ithaca: ILR Press.

Daugherty, Carroll R. 1933. *Labor Problems in American Industry.* Boston: Houghton Mifflin.

Davey, Harold W. 1951. *Contemporary Collective Bargaining.* New York: Prentice-Hall.

Davis, Edward M., and Russell D. Lansbury. 1998. "Employment Relations in Australia." In *International and Comparative Employment Relations: A Study of Industrialised Market Economies,* edited by Greg J. Bamber and Russell D. Lansbury, chap. 5. London: Sage.

Dawkins, Richard. 1976. *The Selfish Gene.* New York: Oxford University Press.

Delaney, John, and Susan Schwochau. 1993. "Employee Representation through the Political Process." In *Employee Representation: Alternatives and Future Directions,* edited by Bruce E. Kaufman and Morris M. Kleiner, chap. 8. Madison, Wis.: Industrial Relations Research Association.

Demsetz, Harold. 1967. "Toward a Theory of Property Rights." *American Economic Review* 57 (May): 347–59.

Derber, Milton. 1970. *The American Idea of Industrial Democracy, 1865–1965.* Urbana: University of Illinois Press.

Devinatz, Victor G. 1999. "The Real Difference between the Old Unionism and the New Unionism: A New Strategy for U.S. Public Sector Unions." *Journal of Collective Negotiations in the Public Sector* 28: 29–39.

Dickens, William T. 1983. "The Effect of Company Campaigns on Certification Elections: Law and Reality Once Again." *Industrial and Labor Relations Review* 36 (July): 560–75.

Dinan, Desmond. 1999. *Ever Closer Union: An Introduction to European Integration.* 2d ed. Boulder, Colo.: Lynne Rienner.

DiNardo, John, Nicole Fortin, and Thomas Lemieux. 1996. "Labor Market Institutions and the Distribution of Wages, 1973–1992: A Semi-Parametric Approach." *Econometrica* 64 (September): 1001–44.

Dombrowski, James. 1936. *The Early Days of Christian Socialism in America.* New York: Columbia University Press.

Donaldson, Thomas, and Lee E. Preston. 1995. "The Stakeholder Theory of the Corporation: Concepts, Evidence, and Implications." *Academy of Management Review* 20 (January): 65–91.

Donn, Clifford B., and G. Phelan. 1991. "Australian Maritime Unions and Flag of Convenience Vessels." *Journal of Industrial Relations* 33 (September): 329–39.

Donnelly, Jack. 1989. *Universal Human Rights in Theory and Practice*. Ithaca: Cornell University Press.

Dow, Gregory K. 1997. "The New Institutional Economics and Employment Regulation." In *Government Regulation of the Employment Relationship,* edited by Bruce E. Kaufman, chap. 2. Madison, Wis.: Industrial Relations Research Association.

Downey, Ezekiel H. 1924. *Workmen's Compensation*. New York: Macmillan.

Dunfee, Thomas W. 1999. "Challenges to Corporate Governance: Corporate Governance in a Market with Morality." *Law and Contemporary Problems* 62 (summer): 129–57.

Dunlop, John T. 1949. *Collective Bargaining: Principles and Cases*. Chicago: Irwin.

——. 1958. *Industrial Relations Systems*. New York: Holt.

——. 1961. "Consensus and National Labor Policy." In *Proceedings of the Thirteenth Annual Meeting of the Industrial Relations Research Association,* edited by Gerald G. Somers, 2–15. Madison, Wis.: Industrial Relations Research Association.

——. 1993. *Industrial Relations Systems*. Rev. ed. Boston: Harvard Business School Press.

Dunlop, John T., Frederick H. Harbison, Clark Kerr, and Charles A. Myers. 1975. *Industrialism and Industrial Man Reconsidered*. Princeton: The Inter-university Study of Human Resources in National Development.

Dworkin, Terry Morehead. 1997. "'It's My Life—Leave Me Alone': Off The-Job Employee Associational Privacy Rights." *American Business Law Journal* 35 (fall): 47–104.

Eagly, Alice H., and Shelly Chaiken. 1993. *The Psychology of Attitudes*. Fort Worth, Texas: Harcourt Brace Jovanovich.

Eaton, Adrienne E., and Paula B. Voos. 1994. "Productivity-Enhancing Innovations in Work Organization, Compensation, and Employee Participation in the Union versus the Nonunion Sectors." In *Advances in Industrial and Labor Relations,* vol. 6, edited by David Lewin and Donna Sockell, 63–109. Greenwich, Conn.: JAI Press.

Eaton, Susan C. 1996. "'The Customer Is Always Interesting': Unionized Harvard Clericals Renegotiate Work Relationships." In *Working in the Service Society,* edited by Cameron Lynne Macdonald and Carmen Sirianni, chap. 12. Philadelphia: Temple University Press.

Economic Report of the President. annual. Washington, D.C.: U.S. Government Printing Office.

Edelman, Peter B. 1987. "The Next Century of Our Constitution: Rethinking Our Duty to the Poor." *Hastings Law Journal* 39 (November): 1–61.

Edwards, P. K. 1995. "From Industrial Relations to the Employment Relationship: The Development of Research in Britain." *Relations Industrielles* 50 (winter): 39–63.

Edwards, Paul, Mark Hall, Richard Hyman, Paul Marginson, Keith Sisson, Jeremy Waddington, and David Winchester. 1998. "Great Britain: From Partial Collectivism to Neo-liberalism to Where?" In *Changing Industrial Relations in Europe,* edited by Anthony Ferner and Richard Hyman, chap. 1. Oxford: Blackwell.

Edwards, Richard. 1993. *Rights at Work: Employment Relations in the Post-Union Era*. Washington, D.C.: Brookings.

——. 1997. "Alternative Regulatory Approaches to Protecting Employees' Workplace Rights." In *Government Regulation of the Employment Relationship,* edited by Bruce E. Kaufman, chap. 11. Madison, Wis.: Industrial Relations Research Association.

Ehrenberg, Daniel S. 1996. "From Intention to Action: An ILO-GATT/WTO Enforcement Regime for International Labor Rights." In *Human Rights, Labor Rights, and International Trade,* edited by Lance A. Compa and Stephen F. Diamond, chap. 8. Philadelphia: University of Pennsylvania Press.

Elliott, Kimberly A. 2000. "Getting Beyond No . . . ! Promoting Worker Rights and Trade." In *The WTO After Seattle,* edited by Jeffrey J. Schott, chap. 12. Washington, D.C.: Institute for International Economics.

Ely, James W. 1998. *The Guardian of Every Other Right: A Constitutional History of Property Rights*. New York: Oxford University Press.

Epstein, Richard A. 1983. "A Common Law for Labor Relations: A Critique of the New Deal Labor Legislation." *Yale Law Journal* 92 (July): 1357–1408.

———. 1984. "In Defense of the Contract at Will." *University of Chicago Law Review* 51 (fall): 947–82.

———. 1995. *Simple Rules for a Complex World.* Cambridge: Harvard University Press.

Erickson, Christopher L., and Sarosh Kuruvilla. 1994. "Labor Costs and the Social Dumping Debate in the New European Union." *Industrial and Labor Relations Review* 48 (October): 27–47.

Ernst, Daniel R. 1995. *Lawyers against Labor: From Individual Rights to Corporate Liberalism.* Urbana: University of Illinois Press.

Escobar, Modesto. 1995. "Spain: Works Councils or Unions?" In *Works Councils: Consultation, Representation, and Cooperation in Industrial Relations,* edited by Joel Rogers and Wolfgang Streeck, chap. 6. Chicago: University of Chicago Press.

Estes, Ralph. 1996. *Tyranny of the Bottom Line: Why Corporations Make Good People Do Bad Things.* San Francisco: Berrett-Koehler.

Estey, J. A. 1928. *The Labor Problem.* New York: McGraw-Hill.

Estlund, Cynthia L. 1994. "Labor, Property, and Sovereignty after *Lechmere.*" *Stanford Law Review* 46 (January): 305–59.

———. 2000. "Working Together: The Workplace, Civil Society, and the Law." *Georgetown Law Journal* 89 (November): 1–96.

———. 2002. "How Wrong Are Employees About Their Rights, and Why Does It Matter?" *New York University Law Review* 77 (April): 6–35.

Estreicher, Samuel. 1993. "Labor Law Reform in a World of Competitive Product Markets." *Chicago-Kent Law Review* 69: 3–46.

———. 1994a. "Employee Involvement and the 'Company Union' Prohibition: The Case for Partial Repeal of Section 8(a)(2) of the NLRA." *New York University Law Review* 69 (April): 125–61.

———. 1994b. "Collective Bargaining or 'Collective Begging'?: Reflections On Anti-strikebreaker Legislation." *Michigan Law Review* 93 (December): 577–608.

———. 1996. "Freedom of Contract and Labor Law Reform: Opening Up the Possibilities for Value-Added Unionism." *New York University Law Review* 71 (June): 827–49.

Esty, Daniel C. 2001. "Bridging the Trade-Environment Divide." *Journal of Economic Perspectives* 15 (summer): 113–30.

European Industrial Relations Observatory. 1998. "Portugal: Collective Bargaining and Strikes in 1997." *EIRO On-line.* Dublin: European Foundation for the Improvement of Living and Working Conditions. Accessed June 25, 2002 at http://www.eiro.eurofound.ie/1998/02/feature/PT9802164F.html.

———. 2002a. "Corporate Governance Systems and the Nature of Industrial Restructuring." *EIRO On-line.* Dublin: European Foundation for the Improvement of Living and Working Conditions. Accessed December 13, 2002 at http://www.eiro.eurofound.ie/2002/09/study/TN0209101S.html.

———. 2002b. "Collective Bargaining Coverage and Extension Procedures." *EIRO On-line.* Dublin: European Foundation for the Improvement of Living and Working Conditions. Accessed December 31, 2002 at http://www.eiro.eurofound.ie/2002/12/study/TN0212102S.html.

Ewing, K. D. 2002. "Human Rights and Industrial Relations: Possibilities and Pitfalls." *British Journal of Industrial Relations* 40 (March): 138–49.

Farber, Henry S. 2001. "Union Success in Representation Elections: Why Does Unit Size Matter?" *Industrial and Labor Relations Review* 54 (January): 329–48.

Farber, Henry S., and Alan B. Krueger. 1993. "Union Membership in the United States: The Decline Continues." In *Employee Representation: Alternatives and Future Directions,* edited by Bruce E. Kaufman and Morris M. Kleiner, chap. 3. Madison, Wis.: Industrial Relations Research Association.

Feenstra, Robert C. 1998. "Integration of Trade and Disintegration of Production in the Global Economy." *Journal of Economic Perspectives* 12 (fall): 31–50.

Feinman, Jay M. 1976. "The Development of the Employment at Will Rule." *American Journal of Legal History* 20: 118–35.

Ferner, Anthony, and Richard Hyman, eds. 1998. *Changing Industrial Relations in Europe.* Oxford: Blackwell.

Ferris, Gerald R., Darold T. Barnum, Sherman D. Rosen, L. Holleran, and J. Dulebohn. 1995. "Toward Business-University Partnerships in Human Resource Management: Integration of Science and Practice." In *Handbook of Human Resource Management,* edited by Gerald R. Ferris, Sherman D. Rosen, and Darold T. Barnum, 1–16. Cambridge, Mass.: Blackwell.

Ferriss, Susan, and Ricardo Sandoval. 1997. *The Fight in the Fields: Cesar Chavez and the Farmworkers Movement.* New York: Harcourt Brace.

Feuille, Peter, and Robert L. Hildebrand. 1995. "Grievance Procedures and Dispute Resolution." In *Handbook of Human Resource Management,* edited by Gerald R. Ferris, Sherman D. Rosen, and Darold T. Barnum, chap. 18. Cambridge, Mass.: Blackwell.

Fink, Leon. 1987. "Labor, Liberty, and the Law: Trades Unionism and the Problems of the American Constitutional Order." *Journal of American History* 74 (December): 904–25.

Fletcher, Bill, and Richard W. Hurd. 1998. "Beyond the Organizing Model: The Transformation Process in Local Unions." In *Organizing to Win: New Research on Union Strategies,* edited by Kate Bronfenbrenner et al., chap. 2. Ithaca: ILR Press.

Flexner, Kurt F. 1989. *The Enlightened Society: The Economy with a Human Face.* Lexington, Mass: Lexington Books.

Folger, Robert, and Russell Cropanzano. 1998. *Organizational Justice and Human Resource Management.* Thousand Oaks, Calif.: Sage.

Folger, Robert, and Mary A. Konovsky. 1989. "Effects of Procedural and Distributive Justice on Reactions to Pay Raise Decisions." *Academy of Management Journal* 32 (March): 115–30.

Forbath, William E. 1985. "The Ambiguities of Free Labor: Labor and the Law in the Gilded Age." *Wisconsin Law Review* 1985 (July/August): 767–817.

——. 1991. *Law and the Shaping of the American Labor Movement.* Cambridge: Harvard University Press.

——. 1999. "Caste, Class, and Equal Citizenship." *Michigan Law Review* 98 (October): 1–91.

——. 2001. "The New Deal Constitution in Exile." *Duke Law Journal* 51 (October): 165–222.

Forgas, Joseph P., and Jennifer M. George. 2001. "Affective Influences on Judgments and Behavior in Organizations: An Information Processing Perspective." *Organizational Behavior and Human Decision Processes* 86 (September): 3–34.

Fossum, John A., and Brian P. McCall. 1997. "Pay and Reward for Performance." In *The Human Resource Management Handbook, Part 3,* edited by David Lewin, Daniel J. B. Mitchell, and Mahmood Zaidi, 111–43. Greenwich, Conn.: JAI Press.

Fox, Alan. 1974. *Beyond Contract: Work, Power and Trust Relations.* London: Farber and Farber.

Frank, Thomas. 2000. *One Market under God: Extreme Capitalism, Market Populism, and the End of Economic Democracy.* New York: Doubleday.

Frankel, Jeffrey A. 2001. "Assessing the Efficiency Gains from Further Liberalization." In *Efficiency, Equity, and Legitimacy: The Multilateral Trading System at the Millennium,* edited by Roger B. Porter, Pierre Sauvé, Arvind Subramanian, and Americo Beviglia Zampetti, chap. 6. Washington, D.C.: Brookings Institution.

Fraser, Steve. 1983. "Dress Rehearsal for the New Deal: Shop-Floor Insurgents, Political Elites, and Industrial Democracy in the Amalgamated Clothing Workers." In *Working-Class America: Essays on Labor, Community, and American Society,* edited by Michael H. Frisch and Daniel J. Walkowitz, 212–55. Urbana: University of Illinois Press.

Freeden, Michael. 1991. *Rights*. Minneapolis: University of Minnesota Press.

Freeman, Richard B., and Edward P. Lazear. 1995. "An Economic Analysis of Works Councils." In *Works Councils: Consultation, Representation, and Cooperation in Industrial Relations*, edited by Joel Rogers and Wolfgang Streeck, chap. 2. Chicago: University of Chicago Press.

Freeman, Richard B., and James L. Medoff. 1984. *What Do Unions Do?* New York: Basic Books.

Freeman, Richard B., and Joel Rogers. 1993. "Who Speaks for Us? Employee Representation in a Nonunion Labor Market." In *Employee Representation: Alternatives and Future Directions*, edited by Bruce E. Kaufman and Morris M. Kleiner, chap. 1. Madison, Wis.: Industrial Relations Research Association.

——. 1999. *What Workers Want*. Ithaca: ILR Press.

Friedman, Milton. 1962. *Capitalism and Freedom*. Chicago: University of Chicago Press.

Friedman, Milton, and Rose Friedman. 1980. *Free to Choose: A Personal Statement*. New York: Harcourt Brace Jovanovich.

Friedman, Sheldon, Richard W. Hurd, Rudolph A. Oswald, and Ronald L. Seeber, eds. 1994. *Restoring the Promise of American Labor Law*. Ithaca: ILR Press.

Gabin, Nancy F. 1990. *Feminism in the Labor Movement: Women and the United Auto Workers, 1935–1975*. Ithaca: Cornell University Press.

Gaines, Sanford. 2001. "The WTO's Reading of the GATT Article XX Chapeau: A Disguised Restriction on Environmental Measures." *Journal of International Economic Law* 22 (winter): 739–862.

Gall, Gregor, ed. 2003. *Union Organizing: Campaigning for Trade Union Recognition*. London: Routledge.

Gallagher, Daniel G., and George Strauss. 1991. "Union Membership Attitudes and Participation." In *The State of the Unions*, edited by George Strauss, Daniel G. Gallagher, and Jack Fiorito, 139–74. Madison, Wis.: Industrial Relations Research Association.

Ganesan, A.V. 2000. "Seattle and Beyond: Developing-Country Perspectives." In *The WTO After Seattle*, edited by Jeffrey J. Schott, chap. 7. Washington, D.C.: Institute for International Economics.

Garcia, Frank J. 1999. "The Universal Declaration of Human Rights at Fifty and the Challenge of Global Markets: Trading Away the Human Rights Principle." *Brooklyn Journal of International Law* 25: 51–97.

Gaston, Noel, and Daniel Trefler. 1994. "Protection, Trade, and Wages: Evidence from U.S. Manufacturing." *Industrial and Labor Relations Review* 47 (July): 574–93.

Gerber, Larry G. 1997. "Shifting Perspectives on American Exceptionalism: Recent Literature on American Labor Relations and Labor Politics." *Journal of American Studies* 31 (August): 253–74.

Gersuny, Carl, and Gladis Kaufman. 1985. "Seniority and the Moral Economy of U.S. Automobile Workers, 1934–1946." *Journal of Social History* 18 (spring): 463–75.

Gewirth, Alan. 1996. *The Community of Rights*. Chicago: University of Chicago Press.

Ghilarducci, Teresa. 1986. "When Management Strikes: PATCO and the British Miners." *Industrial Relations Journal* 17 (summer): 115–28.

——. 1990. "Pensions and the Uses of Ignorance by Unions and Firms." *Journal of Labor Research* 11 (spring): 203–16.

Gifford, Daniel J. 1997. "Labor Policy in Late Twentieth Century Capitalism: New Paradoxes for the Democratic State." *Hofstra Law Review* 26 (fall): 85–160.

Giles, Anthony, and Gregor Murray. 1997. "Industrial Relations Theory and Critical Political Economy." In *Theorizing in Industrial Relations: Approaches and Applications*, edited by Jack Barbash and Noah M. Meltz, 77–120. Sydney: Australian Centre for Industrial Relations Research and Teaching.

Gilligan, Carol. 1982. *In a Different Voice: Psychological Theory and Women's Development*. Cambridge: Harvard University Press.

Gilliland, Stephen W., and David Chan. 2001. "Justice in Organizations: Theory, Methods, and Applications." In *Handbook of Industrial, Work, and Organizational Psychology,* vol. 2, edited by Neil Anderson, Deniz S. Ones, Handan Kepir Sinangil, and Chockalingam Viswesvaran, chap. 8. London: Sage.

Gilpin, Robert. 2000. *The Challenge of Global Capitalism: The World Economy in the Twenty-first Century.* Princeton: Princeton University Press.

Gist, Marilyn E., and Terence R. Mitchell. 1992. "Self-Efficacy: A Theoretical Analysis of Its Determinants and Malleability." *Academy of Management Review* 17 (April): 183–211.

Gitelman, Howard M. 1988. *Legacy of the Ludlow Massacre: A Chapter in American Industrial Relations.* Philadelphia: University of Pennsylvania Press.

Glendon, Mary Ann. 1991. *Rights Talk: The Impoverishment of Political Discourse.* New York: Free Press.

——. 1998. "Knowing the Universal Declaration of Human Rights." *Notre Dame Law Review* 73 (May): 1153–82.

Glomb, Theresa M., Piers D. G. Steel, and Richard D. Arvey. 2002. "Office Sneers, Snipes, and Stab Wounds: Antecedents, Consequences, and Implications of Workplace Violence and Aggression." In *Emotions in the Workplace: Understanding the Structure and Role of Emotions in Organizational Behavior,* edited by Robert G. Lord, Richard J. Klimoski, and Ruth Kanfer, chap. 7. San Francisco: Jossey-Bass.

Godard, John. 1993. "Theory and Method in Industrial Relations: Modernist and Postmodernist Alternatives." In *Industrial Relations Theory: Its Nature, Scope, and Pedagogy,* edited by Roy J. Adams and Noah M. Meltz, 283–306. Metuchen, N.J.: IMLR Press/Rutgers University.

——. 1994. "Beyond Empiricism: Towards a Reconstruction of IR Theory and Research." In *Advances in Industrial and Labor Relations,* vol. 6, edited by David Lewin and Donna Sockell, 1–35. Greenwich, Conn.: JAI Press.

——. 1997. "Whither Strategic Choice: Do Managerial IR Ideologies Matter?" *Industrial Relations* 36 (April): 206–28.

——. 2000. *Industrial Relations, the Economy, and Society.* 2d ed. North York, Ontario: Captus Press.

——. 2002. "Institutional Environments, Employer Practices, and States in Liberal Market Economies." *Industrial Relations* 41 (April): 249–86.

Godard, John, and John Delaney. 2000. "Reflections on the 'High Performance' Paradigm's Implications for Industrial Relations as a Field." *Industrial and Labor Relations Review* 53 (April): 482–502.

——. 2002. "On the Paradigm Guiding Industrial Relations Theory and Research: Reply to Thomas A. Kochan." *Industrial and Labor Relations Review* 55 (April): 542–44.

Goetschy, Janine. 1998. "France: The Limits of Reform." In *Changing Industrial Relations in Europe,* edited by Anthony Ferner and Richard Hyman, chap. 13. Oxford: Blackwell.

Goldberg, Joseph P., Eileen Ahern, William Haber, and Rudolph A. Oswald, eds. 1976. *Federal Policies and Worker Status Since the Thirties.* Madison, Wis.: Industrial Relations Research Association.

Golden, Clinton S., and Harold J. Ruttenberg. 1942. *The Dynamics of Industrial Democracy.* New York: Harper and Brothers.

Goldman, Alvin L. 1996. *Labor and Employment Law in the United States.* Boston: Kluwer Law International.

Goodin, Robert E. 1985. *Protecting the Vulnerable: A Reanalysis of Our Social Responsibilities.* Chicago: University of Chicago Press.

Goodman, John, Mick Marchington, John Berridge, Ed Snape, and Greg J. Bamber. 1998. "Employment Relations in Britain." In *International and Comparative Employment Relations: A Study of Industrialised Market Economies,* edited by Greg J. Bamber and Russell D. Lansbury, chap. 2. London: Sage.

Gordon, Michael E. 2000a. "Export Processing Zones." In *Transnational Cooperation among Labor Unions,* edited by Michael E. Gordon and Lowell Turner, chap. 4. Ithaca: ILR Press.

——. 2000b. "The International Confederation of Free Trade Unions: Bread, Freedom, and Peace." In *Transnational Cooperation among Labor Unions,* edited by Michael E. Gordon and Lowell Turner, chap. 5. Ithaca: ILR Press.

Gordon, Michael E., and Lowell Turner. 2000. "Going Global." In *Transnational Cooperation among Labor Unions,* edited by Michael E. Gordon and Lowell Turner, chap. 1. Ithaca: ILR Press.

Gould, William B. 1977. *Black Workers in White Unions: Job Discrimination in the United States.* Ithaca: Cornell University Press.

——. 1993. *Agenda for Reform: The Future of Employment Relationships and the Law.* Cambridge: MIT Press.

Greenberg, Jerald. 1987. "A Taxonomy of Organizational Justice Theories." *Academy of Management Review* 12 (January): 9–22.

Greenfield, Patricia A., and Robert J. Pleasure. 1993. "Representatives of Their Own Choosing: Finding Workers' Voice in the Legitimacy and Power of Their Unions." In *Employee Representation: Alternatives and Future Directions,* edited by Bruce E. Kaufman and Morris M. Kleiner, chap. 5. Madison, Wis.: Industrial Relations Research Association.

Greenstone, J. David. 1969. *Labor in American Politics.* New York: Knopf.

Gregg, Paul, and Alan Manning. 1997. "Labour Market Regulation and Unemployment." In *Unemployment Policy: Government Options for the Labour Market,* edited by Dennis J. Snower and Guillermo de la Dehesa, chap. 13. Cambridge: Cambridge University Press.

Greider, William. 1997. *One World, Ready or Not: The Manic Logic of Global Capitalism.* New York: Simon and Schuster.

Grenier, Guillermo J. 1988. *Inhuman Relations: Quality Circles and Anti-Unionism in American Industry.* Philadelphia: Temple University Press.

Gross, James A. 1974. *The Making of the National Labor Relations Board: A Study in Economics, Politics, and the Law.* Albany: State University of New York Press.

——. 1995. *Broken Promise: The Subversion of U.S. Labor Relations Policy, 1947–1994.* Philadelphia: Temple University Press.

——. 1998. "The Broken Promises of the National Labor Relations Act and the Occupational Safety and Health Act: Conflicting Values and Conceptions of Rights and Justice." *Chicago-Kent Law Review* 73: 351–87.

——. 1999. "A Human Rights Perspective on U.S. Labor Relations Law: A Violation of the Freedom of Association." *Employee Rights and Employment Policy Journal* 3: 65–103.

——. 2001. "A Human Rights Perspective on U.S. Education: Only Some Children Matter." *Catholic University Law Review* 50 (summer): 919–56.

Grossman, Gene M., ed. 1992. *Imperfect Competition and International Trade.* Cambridge: MIT Press.

Grossman, Gene M., and Alan B. Krueger. 1995. "Economic Growth and the Environment." *Quarterly Journal of Economics* 110 (May): 353–77.

Gunnigle, Patrick. 1997. "More Rhetoric Than Reality: Enterprise Level Industrial Relations Partnerships in Ireland." *Economic and Social Review* 28 (October): 179–200.

Gunnigle, Patrick, Gerard McMahon, and Gerard Fitzgerald. 1999. *Industrial Relations in Ireland: Theory and Practice.* 2d ed. Dublin: Gill and Macmillan.

Gutmann, Amy, ed. 1998. *Freedom of Association.* Princeton: Princeton University Press.

Hackman, J. Richard. 1992. "Group Influences on Individuals in Organizations." In *Handbook of Industrial and Organizational Psychology,* vol. 3, 2d ed., edited by Marvin D. Dunnette and Leaetta M. Hough, chap. 4. Palo Alto: Consulting Psychologists Press.

Halpern, Jennifer J. 1998. "Bonded Rationality: The Rationality of Everyday Decision Making in a Social Context." In *Debating Rationality: Nonrational Aspects of Organi-*

zational Decision Making, edited by Jennifer J. Halpern and Robert N. Stern, chap. 9. Ithaca: Cornell University Press.

Halpern, Jennifer J., and Robert N. Stern, eds. 1998. *Debating Rationality: Nonrational Aspects of Organizational Decision Making.* Ithaca: Cornell University Press.

Hamermesh, Daniel S. 1993. *Labor Demand.* Princeton: Princeton University Press.

Hammer, Tove Helland. 2000. "Nonunion Representational Forms: An Organizational Behavior Perspective." In *Nonunion Employee Representation: History, Contemporary Practice, and Policy,* edited by Bruce E. Kaufman and Daphne Gottlieb Taras, chap. 8. Armonk, N.Y.: M. E. Sharpe.

Hancké, Bob. 2000. "European Works Councils and Industrial Restructuring in the European Motor Industry." *European Journal of Industrial Relations* 6 (March): 39–59.

Harlan, Sharon L., and Pamela M. Robert. 1998. "The Social Construction of Disability in Organizations: Why Employers Resist Reasonable Accommodation." *Work and Occupations* 25 (November): 397–435.

Harper, Michael C. 2001. "A Framework for the Rejuvenation of the American Labor Movement." *Indiana Law Journal* 76 (winter): 103–33.

Harris, Howell John. 1982. *The Right to Manage: Industrial Relations Policies of American Business in the 1940s.* Madison: University of Wisconsin Press.

——. 1993. "Industrial Democracy and Liberal Capitalism, 1890–1925." In *Industrial Democracy in America: The Ambiguous Promise,* edited by Nelson Lichtenstein and Howell John Harris, chap. 3. Washington, D.C.: Woodrow Wilson Center Press.

Harris, Seth D. 2000. "Conceptions of Fairness and the Fair Labor Standards Act." *Hofstra Labor and Employment Law Journal* 18 (fall): 19–166.

Hart, Peter M., and Cary L. Cooper. 2001. "Occupational Stress: Toward a More Integrated Framework." In *Handbook of Industrial, Work and Organizational Psychology,* vol. 2, edited by Neil Anderson, Deniz S. Ones, Handan Kepir Sinangil, and Chockalingam Viswesvaran, chap. 5. London: Sage.

Harter, Lafayette G. 1962. *John R. Commons: His Assault on Laissez-Faire.* Corvallis: Oregon State University Press.

Hartley, Fred A. 1948. *Our New National Labor Policy: The Taft-Hartley Act and the Next Steps.* New York: Funk and Wagnalls.

Hartmann, Thom. 2002. *Unequal Protection: The Rise of Corporate Dominance and the Theft of Human Rights.* Emmaus, Penn.: Rodale.

Haskel, Jonathan E., and Matthew J. Slaughter. 2002. "Does the Sector Bias of Skill-Biased Technological Change Explain Changing Skill Premia?" *European Economic Review* 46 (December): 1757–83.

Hauerwas, Stanley. 1983. "Work as Co-Creation: A Critique of a Remarkably Bad Idea." In *Co-Creation and Capitalism: John Paul II's Laborem Exercens,* edited by John W. Houck and Oliver F. Williamson, chap. 2. Washington, D.C.: University Press of America.

Hausman, Daniel M., and Michael S. McPherson. 1996. *Economic Analysis and Moral Philosophy.* Cambridge: Cambridge University Press.

Hebdon, Robert P., and Robert N. Stern. 1998. "Tradeoffs among Expressions of Industrial Conflict: Public Sector Strike Bans and Grievance Arbitrations." *Industrial and Labor Relations Review* 51 (January): 204–21.

Heckscher, Charles C. 1988. *The New Unionism: Employee Involvement in the Changing Corporation.* New York: Basic Books.

Heldman, Dan C., James T. Bennett, and Manuel H. Johnson. 1981. *Deregulating Labor Relations.* Dallas: Fisher Institute.

Henle, R. J. 1980. "A Catholic View of Human Rights: A Thomistic Reflection." In *The Philosophy of Human Rights: International Perspectives,* edited by Alan S. Rosenbaum, chap. 3. Westport, Conn.: Greenwood Press.

Hepple, Bob. 1999. "A Race to the Top? International Investment Guidelines and Corporate Codes of Conduct." *Comparative Labor Law and Policy Journal* 20 (spring): 347–63.

Herman, Barbara. 1993. *The Practice of Moral Judgment.* Cambridge: Harvard University Press.

Herman, E. Edward. 1998. *Collective Bargaining and Labor Relations.* 4th ed. Upper Saddle River, N.J.: Prentice-Hall.

Herzberg, Frederick, Bernard Mausner, and Barbara B. Snyderman. 1959. *The Motivation to Work.* 2d ed. New York: Wiley.

Hill, John Lawrence. 1997. "Law and the Concept of the Core Self: Toward a Reconciliation of Naturalism and Humanism." *Marquette Law Review* 80 (winter): 289–390.

Hills, Stephen M. 1995. *Employment Relations and the Social Sciences.* Columbia: University of South Carolina Press.

Hirschman, Albert O. 1970. *Exit, Voice, and Loyalty: Responses to Declines in Firms, Organizations, and States.* Cambridge: Harvard University Press.

Hodgson, Geoffrey M. 1998. "The Approach of Institutional Economics." *Journal of Economic Literature* 36 (March): 166–92.

Hodson, Randy. 2001. *Dignity at Work.* Cambridge: Cambridge University Press.

Hoerr, John P. 1997. *We Can't Eat Prestige: The Women Who Organized Harvard.* Philadelphia: Temple University Press.

Hogan, Robert T. 1992. "Personality and Personality Measurement." In *Handbook of Industrial and Organizational Psychology,* vol. 2, 2d ed., edited by Marvin D. Dunnette and Leaetta M. Hough, chap. 13. Palo Alto: Consulting Psychologists Press.

Hogan, Robert, and Rex J. Blake. 1996. "Vocational Interests: Matching Self-Concept with the Work Environment" In *Individual Differences and Behavior in Organizations,* edited by Kevin R. Murphy, chap. 3. San Francisco: Jossey-Bass.

Hogler, Raymond L. 1989. "Labor History and Critical Labor Law: An Interdisciplinary Approach to Workers' Control." *Labor History* 30 (spring): 165–92.

Holley, William H., Kenneth M. Jennings, and Roger S. Wolters. 2001. *The Labor Relations Process.* 7th ed. Mason, Ohio: South-Western.

Honey, Michael K. 1999. *Black Workers Remember: An Oral History of Segregation, Unionism, and the Freedom Struggle.* Berkeley: University of California Press.

Horne, Thomas A. 1990. *Property Rights and Poverty: Political Arguments in Britain, 1605–1834.* Chapel Hill: University of North Carolina Press.

Hough, Leaetta M., and Deniz S. Ones. 2001. "The Structure, Measurement, Validity, and Use of Personality Variables in Industrial, Work, and Organizational Psychology." In *Handbook of Industrial, Work and Organizational Psychology,* vol. 1, edited by Neil Anderson, Deniz S. Ones, Handan Kepir Sinangil, and Chockalingam Viswesvaran, chap. 12. London: Sage.

Howse, Robert. 1999. "The World Trade Organization and the Protection of Workers' Rights." *Journal of Small and Emerging Business Law* 3 (summer): 131–72.

Hoxie, Robert F. 1917. *Trade Unionism in the United States.* New York: D. Appleton.

Human Rights Watch. 2000. *Unfair Advantage: Workers' Freedom of Association in the United States under International Human Rights Standards.* Washington, D.C.

Humphrey, John P. 1988. "The Magna Carta of Mankind." In *Human Rights,* edited by Peter Davies, chap. 3. London: Routledge.

Hunter, Larry W., Annette Bernhardt, Katherine L. Hughes, and Eva Skuratowicz. 2001. "It's Not Just the ATMs: Technology, Firm Strategies, Jobs, and Earnings in Retail Banking." *Industrial and Labor Relations Review* 54 (March): 402–24.

Hurd, Richard W. 1998. "Contesting the Dinosaur Image: The Labor Movement's Search for a Future." *Labor Studies Journal* 22 (winter): 5–30.

Husslein, Joseph. 1924. *Bible and Labor.* New York: Macmillan.

Huthmacher, J. Joseph. 1968. *Senator Robert F. Wagner and the Rise of Urban Liberalism.* New York: Atheneum.

Hyman, Richard. 1975. *Industrial Relations: A Marxist Introduction*. London: Macmillan.

———. 2001. *Understanding European Trade Unionism: Between Market, Class, and Society*. London: Sage.

ICFTU. 2001. *A Trade Union Guide to Globalization*. Brussels: International Confederation of Free Trade Unions.

Interchurch World Movement of North America. 1920. *Report on the Steel Strike of 1919*. New York: Harcourt, Brace and Howe.

International Labour Organization. 1999. *Decent Work*. Geneva.

Irwin, Douglas A. 2002. *Free Trade under Fire*. Princeton: Princeton University Press.

Isen, Alice M. 2000. "Positive Affect and Decision Making." In *Handbook of Emotions*, 2d ed., edited by Michael Lewis and Jeannette M. Haviland-Jones, chap. 27. New York: Guilford Press.

Jacobi, Otto, Berndt Keller, and Walther Müller-Jentsch. 1998. "Germany: Facing New Challenges." In *Changing Industrial Relations in Europe*, edited by Anthony Ferner and Richard Hyman, chap. 7. Oxford: Blackwell.

Jacoby, Sanford M. 1985. *Employing Bureaucracy: Managers, Unions, and the Transformation of Work in American Industry, 1900–1945*. New York: Columbia University Press.

———. 1991. "American Exceptionalism Revisited: The Importance of Management." In *Masters to Managers: Historical and Comparative Perspectives on American Employers*, edited by Sanford M. Jacoby, chap. 8. New York: Columbia University Press.

———. 1997. *Modern Manors: Welfare Capitalism Since the New Deal*. Princeton: Princeton University Press.

———. 2001. "Employee Representation and Corporate Governance: A Missing Link." *University of Pennsylvania Journal of Labor and Employment Law* 3 (spring): 449–89.

Jacoby, Sanford M., and Anil Verma. 1992. "Enterprise Unions in the United States." *Industrial Relations* 31 (winter): 137–58.

Jennings, Kenneth M. 1997. *Swings and Misses: Moribund Labor Relations in Professional Baseball*. Westport, Conn.: Praeger.

John Paul II, Pope. 1981. *On Human Work: Encyclical Laborem Exercens*. Washington, D.C.: United States Catholic Conference.

———. 2000. "Centensimus Annus." In *A Free Society Reader: Principles for the New Millennium*, edited by Michael Novak, William Brailsford, and Cornelius Heesters, 333–86. Lanham, Md.: Lexington Books.

Jones, Derek C. 1980. "Producer Co-operatives in Industrialised Western Economies." *British Journal of Industrial Relations* 28 (July): 141–54.

Jones, Thomas M. 1991. "Ethical Decision-Making by Individuals in Organizations: An Issue-Contingent Model." *Academy of Management Review* 16 (April): 366–95.

Judge, Timothy A., and Joyce E. Bono. 2001. "Relationship of Core Self-Evaluation Traits: Self-Esteem, Generalized Self-Efficacy, Locus of Control, and Emotional Stability." *Journal of Applied Psychology* 86 (February): 80–92.

Judge, Timothy A., Kathy A. Hanisch, and Richard D. Drankowsi. 1995. "Human Resources Management and Employee Attitudes." In *Handbook of Human Resource Management*, edited by Gerald R. Ferris, Sherman D. Rosen, and Darold T. Barnum, chap. 29. Cambridge, Mass.: Blackwell.

Judge, Timothy A., Daniel Heller, and Michael K Mount. 2002. "Five-Factor Model of Personality and Job Satisfaction: A Meta-Analysis." *Journal of Applied Psychology* 87 (June): 530–41.

Kahneman, Daniel, Jack L. Knetsch, and Richard Thaler. 1986. "Fairness as a Constraint on Profit Seeking: Entitlements in the Market." *American Economic Review* 76 (September): 728–41.

Kanfer, Ruth. 1992. "Motivation Theory and Industrial and Organizational Psychology." In *Handbook of Industrial and Organizational Psychology*, vol. 1, 2d ed., edited by Marvin D. Dunnette and Leaetta M. Hough, chap. 3. Palo Alto: Consulting Psychologists Press.

Kant, Immanuel. 1998 [1781]. *Critique of Pure Reason.* Edited by Paul Guyer and Allen W. Woods. Cambridge: Cambridge University Press.

———. 1998 [1785]. *Groundwork of the Metaphysics of Morals.* Edited by Mary Gregor. Cambridge: Cambridge University Press.

Kaplan, Abraham. 1980. "Human Relations and Human Rights in Judaism." In *The Philosophy of Human Rights: International Perspectives,* edited by Alan S. Rosenbaum, chap. 2. Westport, Conn.: Greenwood Press.

Katz, Harry C. 1985. *Shifting Gears: Changing Labor Relations in the U.S. Automobile Industry.* Cambridge: MIT Press.

Katz, Harry C., and Owen Darbishire. 2000. *Converging Divergences: Worldwide Changes in Employment Systems.* Ithaca: ILR Press.

Katz, Harry C., Thomas A. Kochan, and Robert B. McKersie. 1990. "A Reaction to the Debate." In *Reflections on the Transformation of Industrial Relations,* edited by James Chelius and James Dworkin, chap. 8. Metuchen, N.J.: IMLR Press.

Kaufman, Bruce E. 1988. "The Postwar View of Labor Markets and Wage Determination." In *How Labor Markets Work: Reflections on Theory and Practice by John Dunlop, Clark Kerr, Richard Lester, and Lloyd Reynolds,* edited by Bruce E. Kaufman, chap. 5. Lexington, Mass.: Lexington Books.

———. 1989. "Models of Man in Industrial Relations Research." *Industrial and Labor Relations Review* 43 (October): 72–88.

———. 1993. *The Origins and Evolution of the Field of Industrial Relations in the United States.* Ithaca: ILR Press.

———. 1996. "Why the Wagner Act? Reestablishing Contact with Its Original Purpose." In *Advances in Industrial and Labor Relations,* vol. 7, edited by David Lewin, Bruce E. Kaufman, and Donna Sockell, 15–68. Greenwich, Conn.: JAI Press.

———, ed. 1997a. *Government Regulation of the Employment Relationship.* Madison, Wis.: Industrial Relations Research Association.

———. 1997b. "Labor Markets and Employment Regulation: The View of the 'Old' Institutionalists." In *Government Regulation of the Employment Relationship,* edited by Bruce E. Kaufman, chap. 1. Madison, Wis.: Industrial Relations Research Association.

———. 1999. "Expanding the Behavioral Foundations of Labor Economics." *Industrial and Labor Relations Review* 52 (April): 361–92.

———. 2000a. "Accomplishments and Shortcomings of Nonunion Employee Representation in the Pre-Wagner Act Years: A Reassessment." In *Nonunion Employee Representation: History, Contemporary Practice, and Policy,* edited by Bruce E. Kaufman and Daphne Gottlieb Taras, chap. 2. Armonk, N.Y.: M. E. Sharpe.

———. 2000b. "The Case for the Company Union." *Labor History* 41 (August): 321–50.

———. 2001a. "Human Resources and Industrial Relations: Commonalities and Differences." *Human Resource Management Review* 11 (winter): 339–74.

———. 2001b. "The Practice and Theory of Strategic HRM and Participative Management: Antecedents in Early Industrial Relations." *Human Resource Management Review* 11 (winter): 505–33.

———. 2003. "The Organization of Economic Activity: Insights from the Institutional Theory of John R. Commons." *Journal of Economic Behavior and Organization.*

———. Forthcoming. "John R. Commons and the Wisconsin School on Industrial Relations Strategy and Policy." *Industrial and Labor Relations Review.*

Kaufman, Bruce E., and Morris M. Kleiner, eds. 1993. *Employee Representation: Alternatives and Future Directions.* Madison, Wis.: Industrial Relations Research Association.

Kaufman, Bruce E., and David I. Levine. 2000. "An Economic Analysis of Employee Representation." In *Nonunion Employee Representation: History, Contemporary Practice, and Policy,* edited by Bruce E. Kaufman and Daphne Gottlieb Taras, chap. 7. Armonk, N.Y.: M. E. Sharpe.

Kaufman, Bruce E., and Daphne Gottlieb Taras, eds. 2000. *Nonunion Employee Representation: History, Contemporary Practice, and Policy.* Armonk, N.Y.: M. E. Sharpe.

Kawanishi, Hirosuke. 1992. *Enterprise Unionism in Japan*. London: Keegan Paul International.

Kelly, John E. 1998. *Rethinking Industrial Relations: Mobilization, Collectivism, and Long Waves*. London: Routledge.

Kelly, Marjorie. 2001. *The Divine Right of Capital: Dethroning the Corporate Aristocracy*. San Francisco: Berrett-Koehler.

Kennedy, David M. 1999. *Freedom from Fear: The American People in Depression and War, 1929–1945*. New York: Oxford University Press.

Kennedy, Kevin C. 2000. "Resolving International Sanitary and Phytosanitary Disputes in the WTO: Lessons and Future Directions." *Food and Drug Law Journal* 55: 81–104.

Keyserling, Leon H. 1945. "Why the Wagner Act?" In *The Wagner Act: After Ten Years*, edited by Louis G. Silverberg, 5–33. Washington, D.C.: Bureau of National Affairs.

Khalil-ur-Rehman. 1995. *The Concept of Labour in Islam*. Karachi: Arif Publications.

Kim, Pauline T. 1997. "Bargaining with Imperfect Information: A Study of Worker Perceptions of Legal Protection in an At-Will World." *Cornell Law Review* 83 (November): 105–60.

Klare, Karl E. 1978. "Judicial Deradicalization of the Wagner Act and the Origins of Modern Legal Consciousness, 1937–1941." *Minnesota Law Review* 62: 265–339.

———. 1985. "Traditional Labor Law Scholarship and the Crisis of Collective Bargaining Law: A Reply to Professor Finkin." *Maryland Law Review* 44: 731–840.

———. 1988. "Workplace Democracy and Market Reconstruction: An Agenda for Legal Reform." *Catholic University Law Review* 38 (fall): 1–68.

Klein, Philip A. 1993. "The Institutional Challenge: Beyond Dissent." In *Institutional Economics: Theory, Method, Policy*, edited by Marc R. Tool, chap. 2. Boston: Kluwer.

Kleiner, Morris M., Jonathan S. Leonard, and Adam M. Pilarski. 2002. "How Industrial Relations Affects Plant Performance: The Case of Commercial Aircraft Manufacturing," *Industrial and Labor Relations Review* 55 (January): 195–218.

Kleiner, Morris M., Robert A. McLean, George F. Dreher. 1988. *Labor Markets and Human Resource Management*. Glenview, Ill.: Scott, Foresman.

Kletzer, Lori G. 2001. *Job Loss from Imports: Measuring the Costs*. Washington, D.C.: Institute for International Economics.

Koch-Baumgarten, Sigrid. 1998. "Trade Union Regime Formation under the Conditions of Globalization in the Transport Sector: Attempts at Transnational Trade Union Regulation of Flag-of-Convenience Shipping." *International Review of Social History* 43 (December): 369–402.

Kochan, Thomas A. 1980. *Collective Bargaining and Industrial Relations: From Theory to Policy and Practice*. Homewood, Ill.: Irwin.

———. 1982. "Collective Bargaining and Industrial Relations: Reply." *Industrial Relations* 21 (winter): 115–22.

———. 1998. "What Is Distinctive about Industrial Relations Research?" In *Researching the World of Work: Strategies and Methods in Studying Industrial Relations*, edited by George Strauss and Keith Whitfield, chap. 2. Ithaca: ILR Press.

———. 2000. "On the Paradigm Guiding Industrial Relations Theory and Research: Comment on John Godard and John T. Delaney, 'Reflections on the 'High Performance' Paradigm's Implications for Industrial Relations as a Field,'" *Industrial and Labor Relations Review* 53 (July): 704–11.

Kochan, Thomas A., and Harry C. Katz. 1988. *Collective Bargaining and Industrial Relations: From Theory to Policy and Practice*. 2d ed. Homewood, Ill.: Irwin.

Kochan, Thomas A., Harry C. Katz, and Robert B. McKersie. 1986. *The Transformation of American Industrial Relations*. New York: Basic Books.

Kochan, Thomas A., Robert B. McKersie, and Peter Cappelli. 1984. "Strategic Choice and Industrial Relations Theory." *Industrial Relations* 23 (winter): 16–39.

Kohlberg, Lawrence. 1984. *The Psychology of Moral Development: The Nature and Validity of Moral Stages*. San Francisco: Harper and Row.

Korsgaard, Christine M. 1996. *Creating the Kingdom of Ends*. New York: Cambridge University Press.

Korten, David C. 1995. *When Corporations Rule the World*. San Francisco: Brett-Koehler Publishers.

———. 1999. *The Post-Corporate World: Life After Capitalism*. San Francisco: Brett-Koehler Publishers.

Koven, Adolph M., and Susan L. Smith. 1992. *Just Cause: The Seven Tests*. Washington, D.C.: Bureau of National Affairs.

Krueger, Alan B. 2002. "Inequality, Too Much of a Good Thing." Industrial Relations Section Working Paper No. 466. Princeton: Princeton University.

Krueger, Alan B., and Alexandre Mas. 2002. "Strikes, Scabs, and Tread Separations: Labor Strife and the Production of Defective Bridgestone/Firestone Tires." Industrial Relations Section Working Paper No. 461. Princeton: Princeton University.

Kurtz, Sharon. 2002. *Workplace Justice: Organizing Multi-Identity Movements*. Minneapolis: University of Minnesota Press.

Kuwahara, Yasuo. 1998. "Employment Relations in Japan." In *International and Comparative Employment Relations: A Study of Industrialised Market Economies*, edited by Greg J. Bamber and Russell D. Lansbury, chap. 10. London: Sage.

Kuznets, Simon. 1955. "Economic Growth and Income Inequality." *American Economic Review* 45 (March): 1–28.

La Luz, José, and Paula Finn. 1998. "Getting Serious about Inclusion: A Comprehensive Approach." In *A New Labor Movement for the New Century*, edited by Gregory Mantsios, 197–211. New York: Garland.

Lauck, W. Jett, and Edgar Sydenstricker. 1917. *Conditions of Labor in American Industries: A Summarization of the Results of Recent Investigations*. New York: Funk and Wagnalls.

Lauren, Paul Gordon. 1998. *The Evolution of International Human Rights: Visions Seen*. Philadelphia: University of Pennsylvania Press.

Lawler, John J. 1990. *Unionization and Deunionization: Strategy, Tactics, and Outcomes*. Columbia: University of South Carolina Press.

Leader, Sheldon. 1992. *Freedom of Association: A Study in Labor Law and Political Theory*. New Haven: Yale University Press.

Leary, Virginia A. 1996. "Workers' Rights and International Trade: The Social Clause (GATT, ILO, NAFTA, U.S. Laws)." In *Fair Trade and Harmonization: Prerequisites for Free Trade?*, vol. 2: *Legal Analysis*, edited by Jagdish Bhagwati and Robert E. Hudec, chap. 4. Cambridge: MIT Press.

Lecher, Wolfgang, Hans-Wolfgang Platzer, Stefan Rüb, and Klaus-Peter Weiner. 2001. *European Works Councils: Developments, Types, and Networking*. Aldershot, England: Gower.

Legge, Karen. 1995. *Human Resource Management: Rhetorics and Realities*. Basingstoke, England: Macmillan.

———. 1998. "Is HRM Ethical? Can HRM Be Ethical?" In *Ethics in Organizations*, edited by Mike Parker, chap. 7. London: Sage.

Leiserson, William M. 1922. "Constitutional Government in American Industries." *American Economic Review* 12 (May): 58–79.

Leitch, John. 1919. *Man to Man: The Story of Industrial Democracy*. New York: Forbes.

LeRoy, Michael H. 1995. "Employer Treatment of Permanently Replaced Strikers, 1935–1991: Public Policy Implications." *Yale Law and Policy Review* 13: 1–43.

———. 1996. "Can TEAM Work? Implications of an Electromation and DuPont Compliance Analysis for the TEAM Act." *Notre Dame Law Review* 71: 215–62.

———. 1999. "Employee Participation in the New Millennium: Redefining a Labor Organization under Section 8(a)(2) of the NLRA." *Southern California Law Review* 72 (September): 1651–1723.

Lester, Richard. 1941. *Economics of Labor*. New York: Macmillan.

Levine, David I. 1995. *Reinventing the Workplace: How Business and Employees Can Both Win*. Washington, D.C.: Brookings.

——. 1997. "They Should Solve Their Own Problems: Reinventing Workplace Regulation." In *Government Regulation of the Employment Relationship,* edited by Bruce E. Kaufman, chap. 13. Madison, Wis.: Industrial Relations Research Association.

Levine, Peter. 2001. "The Legitimacy of Labor Unions." *Hofstra Labor and Employment Law Journal* 18 (spring): 527–71.

Lewin, David. 1987. "Industrial Relations as a Strategic Variable." In *Human Resources and Firm Performance,* edited by Morris M. Kleiner, Richard N. Block, Myron Roomkin, and Sidney W. Salsburg, chap. 1. Madison, Wis.: Industrial Relations Research Association.

Lewin, David, Peter Feuille, Thomas A. Kochan, and John Thomas Delaney, eds. 1988. *Public Sector Labor Relations: Analysis and Readings.* 3rd ed. Lexington, Mass.: D. C. Heath.

Lichtenstein, Nelson. 1982. *Labor's War at Home: The CIO in World War II.* Cambridge: Cambridge University Press.

——. 1989. "'The Man in the Middle': A Social History of Automobile Industry Foremen." In *On the Line: Essays in the History of Auto Work,* edited by Nelson Lichtenstein and Stephen Meyer, chap. 7. Urbana: University of Illinois Press.

——. 1993. "Great Expectations: The Promise of Industrial Jurisprudence and Its Demise, 1930–1960." In *Industrial Democracy in America: The Ambiguous Promise,* edited by Nelson Lichtenstein and Howell John Harris, chap. 6. Washington, D.C.: Woodrow Wilson Center Press.

——. 2002. *State of the Union: A Century of American Labor.* Princeton: Princeton University Press.

Lichtenstein, Nelson, and Howell John Harris, eds. 1993. *Industrial Democracy in America: The Ambiguous Promise.* Washington, D.C.: Woodrow Wilson Center Press.

Lilja, Kari. 1998. "Finland: Continuity and Modest Moves Towards Company-Level Corporatism." In *Changing Industrial Relations in Europe,* edited by Anthony Ferner and Richard Hyman, chap. 6. Oxford: Blackwell.

Lillich, Richard B. 1984. "Civil Rights." In *Human Rights in International Law: Legal and Policy Issues,* edited by Theodor Meron, chap. 4. Oxford: Oxford University Press.

Linder, Marc, and Ingrid Nygaard. 1998. *Void Where Prohibited: Rest Breaks and the Right to Urinate on Company Time.* Ithaca: ILR Press.

Littler, Craig R. 1993. "Industrial Relations Theory: A Political Economy Perspective." In *Industrial Relations Theory: Its Nature, Scope, and Pedagogy,* edited by Roy J. Adams and Noah M. Meltz, 307–331. Metuchen, N.J.: IMLR Press/Rutgers University.

Liubicic, Robert J. 1998. "Corporate Codes of Conduct and Product Labeling Schemes: The Limits and Possibilities of Promoting International Labor Rights through Private Initiatives." *Law and Policy in International Business* 30 (fall): 111–58.

Locke, John. 1960 [1690]. *Two Treatises of Government.* Edited by Peter Laslett. Cambridge: Cambridge University Press.

Loe, Terry W., Linda Ferrell, and Phylis Mansfield. 2000. "A Review of Empirical Studies Assessing Ethical Decision Making in Business." *Journal of Business Ethics* 25 (June I): 185–204.

Lord, Robert G., Richard J. Klimoski, and Ruth Kanfer, eds. 2002. *Emotions in the Workplace: Understanding the Structure and Role of Emotions in Organizational Behavior.* San Francisco: Jossey-Bass.

Lorenz, Edward C. 2001. *Defining Global Justice: The History of U.S. International Labor Standards Policy.* Notre Dame, Ind.: University of Notre Dame Press.

Lowenstein, George. 1996. "Out of Control: Visceral Influences on Behavior." *Organizational Behavior and Human Decision Processes* 65 (March): 272–92.

Lucena, Hector. 1992. "Venezuela." In *Industrial Relations around the World: Labor Relations for Multinational Companies,* edited by Miriam Rothman, Dennis R. Briscoe, and Raoul C. D. Nacamulli, 401–414. Berlin: Walter de Gruyter.

Mahon, Rianne. 1991. "From Solidaristic Wages to Solidaristic Work: A Post-Fordist Historic Compromise for Sweden?" *Economic and Industrial Democracy* 12 (August): 295–325.

———. 1999. "'Yesterday's Modern Times Are No Longer Modern': Swedish Unions Confront the Double Shift." In *The Brave New World of European Labor: European Trade Unions at the Millennium,* edited by Andrew Martin and George Ross, chap. 4. New York: Berghahn Books.

Mahoney, Thomas A., and Mary R. Watson. 1993. "Evolving Modes of Work Force Governance: An Evaluation." In *Employee Representation: Alternatives and Future Directions,* edited by Bruce E. Kaufman and Morris M. Kleiner, chap. 4. Madison, Wis.: Industrial Relations Research Association.

Mangum, Garth L., and R. Scott McNabb. 1997. *The Rise, Fall, and Replacement of Industrywide Bargaining in the Basic Steel Industry.* Armonk, N.Y.: M. E. Sharpe.

Mangum, Garth L., and Peter Philips, eds. 1988. *Three Worlds of Labor Economics.* Armonk, N.Y. M. E. Sharpe.

March, James G., and Herbert A. Simon. 1958. *Organizations.* New York: Wiley.

Marshall, Alfred. 1920. *Principles of Economics.* 8th ed. New York: Macmillan.

Maslow, Abraham H. 1943. "A Theory of Human Motivation." *Psychological Review* 50 (July): 370–96.

———. 1968. *Toward a Psychology of Being.* Princeton: Van Nostrand.

Masterman, Margaret. 1970. "The Nature of a Paradigm." In *Criticism and the Growth of Knowledge,* edited by Imre Lakatos and Alan Musgrave, 59–89. Cambridge: Cambridge University Press.

Mazey, Edward. 2001. "Grieving through the NAALC and the Social Charter: A Comparative Analysis of Their Procedural Effectiveness." *Journal of International Law* 10 (summer): 239–79.

McClelland, Peter D. 1990. *The American Search for Justice.* Cambridge, Mass.: Basil Blackwell.

McKenna, Eugene F. 1987. *Psychology in Business: Theory and Applications.* London: Lawrence Erlbaum.

McMahon, Martin J., and Alice G. Abreu. 1998. "Winner-Take-All Markets: Easing the Case for Progressive Taxation." *Florida Tax Review* 4: 1–81.

Meltz, Noah M. 1989. "Industrial Relations: Balancing Efficiency and Equity." In *Theories and Concepts in Comparative Industrial Relations,* edited by Jack Barbash and Kate Barbash, chap. 7. Columbia: University of South Carolina Press.

Meron, Theodor. 1986. "On a Hierarchy of Human Rights." *American Journal of International Law* 80 (January): 1–23.

Merrill, Thomas W., and Henry E. Smith. 2001. "What Happened to Property in Law and Economics?" *Yale Law Journal* 111 (November): 357–98.

Meyer, John P., and Natalie J. Allen. 1997. *Commitment in the Workplace: Theory, Research, and Application.* Thousand Oaks, Calif.: Sage.

Meyer, Stephen. 1981. *The Five Dollar Day: Labor, Management, and Social Control in the Ford Motor Company, 1908–1921.* Albany: State University of New York Press.

Michelman, Frank I. 1969. "The Supreme Court 1968 Term—Foreword: On Protecting the Poor through the Fourteenth Amendment." *Harvard Law Review* 83 (November): 7–59.

Milgrom, Paul, and John Roberts. 1992. *Economics, Organization, and Management.* Englewood Cliffs, N.J.: Prentice-Hall.

Milkman, Ruth, ed. 2000. *Organizing Immigrants: The Challenge for Unions in Contemporary California.* Ithaca: ILR Press.

Milkman, Ruth, and Kent Wong. 2001. "Organizing Immigrant Workers: Case Studies from Southern California." In *Rekindling the Movement: Labor's Quest for Relevance in the Twenty-First Century,* edited by Lowell Turner, Harry C. Katz, and Richard W. Hurd, chap. 5. Ithaca: ILR Press.

Miller, Howard E., and Joseph G. Rosse. 2002. "Emotional Reserve and Adaptation to Job

Disatisfaction." In *The Psychology of Work: Theoretically Based Empirical Research,* edited by Jeanne M. Brett and Fritz Drasgow, chap. 10. Mahwah, N.J.: Lawrence Erlbaum.

Millis, Harry A., and Emily Clark Brown. 1950. *From the Wagner Act to Taft-Hartley: A Study of National Labor Policy and Labor Relations.* Chicago: University of Chicago Press.

Minchin, Timothy J. 2001. *The Color of Work: The Struggle for Civil Rights in the Southern Paper Industry, 1945–1980.* Chapel Hill: University of North Carolina Press.

Mishel, Lawrence, Jared Bernstein, and John Schmitt. 2001. *The State of Working America, 2000–2001.* Ithaca: ILR Press.

Montgomery, David. 1979. *Workers' Control in America: Studies in the History of Work, Technology, and Labor Struggles.* Cambridge: Cambridge University Press.

Moody, Kim. 1988. *An Injury to All: The Decline of American Unionism.* London: Verso.

Morris, Charles J. 1989. "NLRB Protection in the Nonunion Workplace: A Glimpse at a General Theory of Section 7 Conduct." *University of Pennsylvania Law Review* 137 (May): 1673–1754.

Müller-Jentsch, Walther. 1995. "Germany: From Collective Voice to Co-Management." In *Works Councils: Consultation, Representation, and Cooperation in Industrial Relations,* edited by Joel Rogers and Wolfgang Streeck, chap. 3. Chicago: University of Chicago Press.

Murphy, Kevin R. 1996. "Individual Differences and Behavior in Organizations: Much More Than *g.*" In *Individual Differences and Behavior in Organizations,* edited by Kevin R. Murphy, chap. 1. San Francisco: Jossey-Bass.

Nasr, Seyyed Hossein. 1980. "The Concept of Reality and Freedom in Islam and Islamic Civilization." In *The Philosophy of Human Rights: International Perspectives,* edited by Alan S. Rosenbaum, chap. 4. Westport, Conn.: Greenwood Press.

Naughton, Michael J. 1995. "Participation in the Organization: An Ethical Analysis from the Papal Social Tradition." *Journal of Business Ethics* 14 (November): 923–35.

Neale, Margaret A., and Max H. Bazerman. 1985. "The Effects of Framing and Negotiator Overconfidence on Bargainer Behavior." *Academy of Management Journal* 28 (March): 34–49.

———. 1991. *Cognition and Rationality in Negotiation.* New York: Free Press.

Nedelsky, Jennifer. 1990. *Private Property and the Limits of American Constitutionalism.* Chicago: University of Chicago Press.

Neisser, Ulric, et al. 1996. "Intelligence: Knowns and Unknowns." *American Psychologist* 51 (February): 77–101.

Nissani, Moti. 1995. "Fruits, Salads, and Smoothies: A Working Definition of Interdisciplinarity." *Educational Thought* 29 (August): 121–28.

Nissen, Bruce, ed. 1997. *Unions and Workplace Reorganization.* Detroit: Wayne State University Press.

Noddings, Nel. 1984. *Caring: A Feminine Approach to Ethics and Moral Education.* Berkeley: University of California Press.

Noe, Raymond A., John R. Hollenbeck, Barry Gerhart, and Patrick M. Wright. 2000. *Human Resource Management: Gaining a Competitive Advantage.* 3rd ed. Boston: McGraw-Hill/Irwin.

Nordlund, Willis J. 1997. *The Quest for a Living Wage: The History of the Federal Minimum Wage Program.* Westport, Conn.: Greenwood Press.

Norman, Richard. 1998. *The Moral Philosophers: An Introduction to Ethics.* 2d ed. Oxford: Oxford University Press.

North, Douglass C. 1990. *Institutions, Institutional Change, and Economic Performance.* Cambridge: Cambridge University Press.

Nozick, Robert. 1974. *Anarchy, State, and Utopia.* New York: Basic Books.

Nussbaum, Martha. 1993. "Non-Relative Virtues: An Aristotelian Approach." In *The*

Quality of Life, edited by Martha Nussbaum and Amartya Sen, 242–69. Oxford: Oxford University Press.

——. 2000. *Women and Human Development: The Capabilities Approach.* Cambridge: Cambridge University Press.

O'Brien, Ruth. 1998. *Workers' Paradox: The Republican Origins of New Deal Labor Policy, 1886–1935.* Chapel Hill: University of North Carolina Press.

Obstfeld, Maurice. 1998. "The Global Capital Market: Benefactor or Menace?" *Journal of Economic Perspectives* 12 (fall): 9–30.

Ogle, George E. 1994. "Employee Rights and Industrial Justice: Religious Dimensions." *Bulletin of Comparative Labour Relations* 28: 19–27.

Ogle, George E., and Hoyt N. Wheeler. 2001. "Collective Bargaining as a Fundamental Human Right." In *Proceedings of the Fifty-Third Annual Meeting,* edited by John F. Burton, 246–253. Champaign, Ill.: Industrial Relations Research Association.

Okun, Arthur M. 1975. *Equality and Efficiency: The Big Tradeoff.* Washington, D.C.: Brookings Institution.

Ó'Móráin, Séamus. 2000. "The European Employment Strategy: A Consideration of Social Partnership and Related Matters in the Irish Context." *International Journal of Comparative Labour Law and Industrial Relations* 16 (spring): 85–101.

O'Neill, Bonnie S., and Mark A. Mone. 1998. "Investigating Equity Sensitivity as a Moderator of Relations between Self-Efficacy and Workplace Attitudes." *Journal of Applied Psychology* 83 (October): 805–16.

O'Neill, Onora. 1989. *Constructions of Reason.* New York: Cambridge University Press.

Osterman, Paul, Thomas Kochan, Richard Locke, and Michael J. Piore. 2001. *Working in America: A Blueprint for the New Labor Market.* Cambridge: MIT Press.

Ostmann, LaDawn L. 2001. "Comment: Union Rights, No Dues: *In Re Epilepsy Foundation* and the NLRB's Extension of *Weingarten* Rights to Nonunion Employees." *Saint Louis University Law Journal* 45 (fall): 1309–47.

O'Sullivan, Mary. 2000. *Contests for Corporate Control: Corporate Governance and Economic Performance in the United States and Germany.* Oxford: Oxford University Press.

Ozaki, Muneto, ed. 1999. *Negotiating Flexibility: The Role of the Social Partners and the State.* Geneva: International Labour Office.

Painter, Sidney. 1947. "Magna Carta." *American Historical Review* 53 (October): 42–49.

Pateman, Carole. 1970. *Participation and Democratic Theory.* London: Cambridge University Press.

Paul, Alan, and Archie Kleingartner. 1996. "The Transformation of Industrial Relations in the Motion Picture and Television Industries: Talent Sector." In *Under the Stars: Essays on Labor Relations in Arts and Entertainment,* edited by Lois S. Gray and Ronald L. Seeber, chap. 5. Ithaca: ILR Press.

Paulsen, George E. 1996. *A Living Wage for the Forgotten Man: The Quest for Fair Labor Standards, 1933–1941.* Selinsgrove, Pa.: Susquehanna University Press.

Pencavel, John. 1999. "The Appropriate Design of Collective Bargaining Systems: Learning from the Experience of Britain, Australia, and New Zealand." *Comparative Labor Law and Policy Journal* 20 (spring): 447–81.

Perlman, Selig. 1928. *A Theory of the Labor Movement.* New York: Macmillan.

Perry, Michael J. 1998. *The Idea of Human Rights: Four Inquiries.* New York: Oxford University Press.

Perry, Michael S. 1993. *Labor Rights in the Jewish Tradition.* New York: Jewish Labor Committee.

Peters, Ronald, and Theresa Merrill. 1998. "Clergy and Religious Persons' Roles in Organizing at O'Hare Airport and St. Joseph Medical Center." In *Organizing to Win: New Research on Union Strategies,* edited by Kate Bronfenbrenner et al., chap. 10. Ithaca: ILR Press.

Pfeffer, Jeffrey. 1998. "Understanding Organizations: Concepts and Controversies." In *The*

Handbook of Social Psychology, vol. 2, edited by Daniel T. Gilbert, Susan T. Fiske, and Gardner Lindzey, chap. 33. Boston: McGraw-Hill.

Phillips, Kevin. 2002. *Wealth and Democracy: A Political History of the American Rich.* New York: Broadway Books.

Phillips, Michael J. 1998. "The Progressiveness of the *Lochner* Court." *Denver University Law Review* 75: 453–505.

Pincoffs, Edmund L. 1977. "Due Process, Fraternity, and a Kantian Injunction." In *Due Process: Nomos XVIII,* edited by J. Roland Pennock and John W. Chapman, chap. 5. New York: New York University Press.

——. 1986. *Quandaries and Virtues: Against Reductivism in Ethics.* Lawrence: University of Kansas Press.

Pinder, Craig C., and Karen P. Harlos. 2001. "Employee Silence: Quiescence and Acquiescence as Responses to Perceived Injustice." In *Research in Personnel and Human Resources Management,* vol. 20, edited by Gerald R. Ferris, 331–369. Amsterdam: JAI Press.

Piore, Michael J., and Charles F. Sabel. 1984. *The Second Industrial Divide: Possibilities for Prosperity.* New York: Basic Books.

Pollis, Adamantia, and Peter Schwab. 1979. "Human Rights: A Western Construct with Limited Applicability." In *Human Rights: Cultural and Ideological Perspectives,* edited by Adamantia Pollis and Peter Schwab, chap. 1. New York: Praeger.

Pope, James Gray. 1997. "Labor's Constitution of Freedom." *Yale Law Journal* 106 (January): 941–1032.

——. 2002. "The Thirteenth Amendment versus the Commerce Clause: Labor and the Shaping of American Constitutional Law, 1921–1957." *Columbia Law Review* 102 (January): 1–122.

Porter, Michael E. 1980. *Competitive Strategy.* New York: Free Press.

Porter, Roger B. 2001. "Efficiency, Equity, and Legitimacy: The Global Trading System in the Twenty-First Century." In *Efficiency, Equity, and Legitimacy: The Multilateral Trading System at the Millennium,* edited by Roger B. Porter, Pierre Sauvé, Arvind Subramanian, and Americo Beviglia Zampetti, chap. 1. Washington, D.C.: Brookings Institution.

Posner, Richard A. 1986. *Economic Analysis of Law.* 3rd ed. Boston: Little, Brown.

Potter, Edward E., and Judith A. Youngman. 1995. *Keeping America Competitive: Employment Policy for the Twenty-First Century.* Lakewood, Colo.: Glenbridge Publishing.

Provis, Chris. 2000. "Ethics, Deception, and Labor Negotiation." *Journal of Business Ethics* 28 (November): 145–58.

Puette, William J. 1992. *Through Jaundiced Eyes: How the Media View Organized Labor.* Ithaca: ILR Press.

Putnam, Robert D. 2000. *Bowling Alone: The Collapse and Revival of American Community.* New York: Simon and Schuster.

Rachels, James. 1993. "Subjectivism." In *A Companion to Ethics,* edited by Peter Singer, chap. 38. Oxford: Blackwell.

Rachleff, Peter. 1993. *Hard-Pressed in the Heartland: The Hormel Strike and the Future of the Labor Movement.* Boston: South End Press.

Ramstad, Yngve. 1993. "Institutional Economics and the Dual Labor Market Theory." In *Institutional Economics: Theory, Method, Policy,* edited by Marc R. Tool, chap. 5. Boston: Kluwer.

Rankin, Tom. 1990. *New Forms of Work Organization: The Challenge for North American Unions.* Toronto: University of Toronto Press.

Rawls, John. 1971. *A Theory of Justice.* Cambridge: Harvard University Press.

——. 1993. *Political Liberalism.* New York: Columbia University Press.

——. 2001. *Justice as Fairness: A Restatement.* Cambridge: Harvard University Press.

Rest, James R. 1986. *Moral Development: Advances in Research and Theory.* New York: Praeger.

———. 1994. "Background: Theory and Research." In *Moral Development in the Professions: Psychology and Applied Ethics,* edited by James R. Rest and Darcia Narváez, chap. 1. Hillsdale, N.J.: Lawrence Erlbaum.

Reynolds, Lloyd G. 1988. "Labor Economics Then and Now." In *How Labor Markets Work,* edited by Bruce E. Kaufman, chap. 4. Lexington, Mass.: Lexington Books.

Reynolds, Morgan. 1996. "A New Paradigm: Deregulating Labor Relations." *Journal of Labor Research* 17 (winter): 121–28.

Ritzer, George. 1980. *Sociology: A Multiple Paradigm Science.* Boston: Allyn and Bacon.

Rockefeller, John D., Jr. 1923. *The Personal Relation in Industry.* New York: Boni and Liveright.

Rodrik, Dani. 1997. *Has Globalization Gone Too Far?* Washington, D.C.: Institute for International Economics.

Rogers, Joel, and Wolfgang Streeck, eds. 1995. *Works Councils: Consultation, Representation, and Cooperation in Industrial Relations.* Chicago: University of Chicago Press.

Rosenbaum, Alan S., ed. 1980a. *The Philosophy of Human Rights: International Perspectives.* Westport, Conn.: Greenwood Press.

———. 1980b. Introduction to *The Philosophy of Human Rights: International Perspectives,* edited by Alan S. Rosenbaum, 3–41. Westport, Conn.: Greenwood Press.

Rosenberg, Alexander. 1995. *Philosophy of Social Science.* Boulder, Colo.: Westview Press.

Rosenblum, Nancy L. 1998. *Membership and Morals: The Personal Uses of Pluralism in America.* Princeton: Princeton University Press.

Ross, Arthur M. 1948. *Trade Union Wage Policy.* Berkeley: University of California Press.

Ross, W. D. 1923. *Aristotle.* London: Methuen and Company.

Rothgeb, John M. 2001. *U.S. Trade Policy: Balancing Economic Dreams and Political Realities.* Washington, D.C.: CQ Press.

Royle, Tony. 1999. "Where's the Beef? McDonald's and its European Works Council." *European Journal of Industrial Relations* 5 (November): 327–47.

Rubinstein, Saul A. 2000. "The Impact of Co-Management on Quality Performance: The Case of the Saturn Corporation." *Industrial and Labor Relations Review* 53 (January): 197–218.

———. 2001. "A Different Kind of Union: Balancing Co-Management and Representation." *Industrial Relations* 40 (April): 163–203.

Rubinstein, Saul A., and Thomas A. Kochan. 2001. *Learning from Saturn: Possibilities for Corporate Governance and Employee Relations.* Ithaca: ILR Press.

Russell, Thaddeus. 2001. *Out of the Jungle: Jimmy Hoffa and the Remaking of the American Working Class.* New York: Knopf.

Ryan, Alan. 1987. *Property.* Minneapolis: University of Minnesota Press.

Ryan, John A. 1912. *A Living Wage: Its Ethical and Economic Aspects.* New York: Macmillan.

Sandberg, Åke. 1994. "Justice at Work: Solidaristic Work Policy as a Renewal of the Swedish Labor Market Model?" *Social Justice* 21 (winter): 102–14.

Sandel, Michael J. 1982. *Liberalism and the Limits of Justice.* Cambridge: Cambridge University Press.

———. 1996. *Democracy's Discontent: America in Search of a Public Philosophy.* Cambridge: Harvard University Press.

Sashkin, Marshall. 1984. "Participative Management Is an Ethical Imperative." *Organizational Dynamics* 12 (spring): 5–22.

Scheve, Kenneth F., and Matthew J. Slaughter. 2001. *Globalization and the Perception of American Workers.* Washington, D.C.: Institute for International Economics.

Schlatter, Richard. 1951. *Private Property: The History of an Idea.* New Brunswick, N.J.: Rutgers University Press.

Schmidt, Frank L., and John E. Hunter. 1998. "The Validity and Utility of Selection Methods in Personnel Psychology: Practical and Theoretical Implications of Eighty-five Years of Research Findings." *Psychological Bulletin* 124 (September): 262–74.

Schott, Jeffrey J., ed. 2000. *The WTO After Seattle*. Washington, D.C.: Institute for International Economics.

Schumann, Paul. 2001. "A Moral Principles Framework for Human Resource Management Ethics." *Human Resource Management Review* 11 (spring/summer): 93–111.

Schumpeter, Joseph A. 1947. *Capitalism, Socialism, and Democracy*. New York: Harper and Brothers.

Schwab, Stewart J. 1997. "The Law and Economics Approach to Workplace Regulation." In *Government Regulation of the Employment Relationship*, edited by Bruce E. Kaufman, chap. 3. Madison, Wis.: Industrial Relations Research Association.

Scoville, James G. 1993. "The Past and Present of Ethics in Industrial Relations." In *Proceedings of the Forty-Fifth Annual Meeting*, edited by John F. Burton, 198–206. Madison, Wis.: Industrial Relations Research Association.

——. 1995. "New Tasks for a Theory of the Labor Movement: New Beginnings in Eastern Europe." *Labour* 9 (Autumn): 463–80.

Sen, Amartya. 1980. "Equality of What?" In *The Tanner Lectures on Human Values*, vol. 1, edited by Sterling M. McMurrin, 195–220. Salt Lake City: University of Utah Press.

——. 1993. "Capability and Well-Being." In *The Quality of Life*, edited by Martha Nussbaum and Amartya Sen, 30–53. Oxford: Oxford University Press.

Sen, Amartya, and Bernard Williams, eds. 1982. *Utilitarianism and Beyond*. Cambridge: Cambridge University Press.

Servais, Jean-Michel. 2000. "Labor Law and Cross-Border Cooperation among Unions." In *Transnational Cooperation among Labor Unions*, edited by Michael E. Gordon and Lowell Turner, chap. 3. Ithaca: ILR Press.

Shestack, Jerome J. 1984. "The Jurisprudence of Human Rights." In *Human Rights in International Law: Legal and Policy Issues*, edited by Theodor Meron, chap. 3. Oxford: Oxford University Press.

Simmons, A. John. 1992. *The Lockean Theory of Rights*. Princeton: Princeton University Press.

Simon, Herbert A. 1982. *Models of Bounded Rationality*. Cambridge: MIT Press.

Slaughter, Matthew J. 1999. "Globalization and Wages: A Tale of Two Perspectives." *World Economy* 22 (July): 609–30.

Slichter, Sumner H. 1941. *Union Policies and Industrial Management*. Washington, D.C.: Brookings.

Slichter, Sumner H., James J. Healy, and E. Robert Livernash. 1960. *The Impact of Collective Bargaining on Management*. Washington, D.C.: Brookings.

Slomp, Hans. 1996. *Between Bargaining and Politics: An Introduction to European Labor Relations*. Westport, Conn.: Praeger.

Sloss, David. 1999. "The Domestication of International Human Rights: Non-Self-Executing Declarations and Human Rights Treaties." *Yale Journal of International Law* 24 (winter): 129–221.

Smith, Adam. 1937 [1776]. *An Inquiry Into the Nature and Causes of the Wealth of Nations*. Edited by Edwin Cannan. New York: Modern Library.

Solomon, Lewis D. 1996. "Perspectives on Human Nature and Their Implications for Business Organizations." *Fordham Urban Law Journal* 23 (winter): 221–56.

Solomon, Robert C. 1992. *Ethics and Excellence: Cooperation and Integrity in Business*. New York: Oxford University Press.

Somers, Gerald G., ed. 1969a. *Essays in Industrial Relations Theory*. Ames: Iowa State University Press.

——. 1969b. "Bargaining Power and Industrial Relations Theory." In *Essays in Industrial Relations Theory*, edited by Gerald G. Somers, chap. 3. Ames: Iowa State University Press.

Soros, George. 2000. *Open Society: Reforming Global Capitalism*. New York: Public Affairs.

Spectar, J. M. 2000. "Pay Me Fairly, Kathie Lee! The WTO, the Right to a Living Wage, and a Proposed Protocol." *New York Law Journal of International and Comparative Law* 20: 61–92.

Squire, Madelyn C. 1990. "The Prima Facie Tort Doctrine and a Social Justice Theory: Are They a Response to the Employment-at-Will Doctrine?" *University of Pittsburgh Law Review* 51 (spring): 641–72.

Stanger, Howard R. 2002. "Newspapers: Collective Bargaining amidst Technological Change." In *Collective Bargaining in the Private Sector,* edited by Paul F. Clark, John T. Delaney, and Ann C. Frost, chap. 5. Champaign, Ill.: Industrial Relations Research Association.

St. Antoine, Theodore J. 1988. "A Seed Germinates: Unjust Discharge Reform Heads toward Full Flower." *Nebraska Law Review* 67: 56–81.

Stephens, Beth. 2001. "Taking Pride in International Human Rights Litigation." *Chicago Journal of International Law* 2 (fall): 485–93.

Sterba, James P. 1988. *How to Make People Just: A Practical Reconciliation of Alternative Conceptions of Justice.* Totowa, N.J.: Rowman and Littlefield.

Stewart, Andrew. 1989. "Employment Protection in Australia." *Comparative Labor Law Journal* 11 (fall): 1–47.

Stiglitz, Joseph. 2000. "Democratic Development as the Fruits of Labor." *Perspectives on Work* 4: 31–37.

———. 2002. *Globalization and Its Discontents.* New York: W. W. Norton.

Stone, Deborah A. 2001. *Policy Paradox: The Art of Political Decision Making.* New York: W. W. Norton.

Stone, Katherine V. W. 1981. "The Post-War Paradigm in American Labor Law." *Yale Law Journal* 90 (June): 1509–80.

———. 1996. "Mandatory Arbitration of Individual Employment Rights: The Yellow Dog Contract of the 1990s." *Denver University Law Review* 73: 1017–50.

———. 1999. "Rustic Justice: Community and Coercion under the Federal Arbitration Act." *North Carolina Law Review* 77 (March): 931–1036.

———. 2001. "The New Psychological Contract: Implications of the Changing Workplace for Labor and Employment Law." *UCLA Law Review* 48 (February): 519–661.

Strauss, George. 1962. "The Shifting Balance of Power in the Plant." *Industrial Relations* 1 (May): 65–96.

Strauss, George, and Peter Feuille. 1981. "Industrial Relations Research in the United States." In *Industrial Relations in International Perspective: Essays on Research and Policy,* edited by Peter B. Doeringer, chap. 3. New York: Holmes and Meier.

Streeck, Wolfgang. 1997. "Neither European Nor Works Councils: A Reply to Paul Knutsen." *Economic and Industrial Democracy* 18 (May): 325–37.

Streeck, Wolfgang, and Sigurt Vitols. 1995. "The European Community: Between Mandatory Consultation and Voluntary Information." In *Works Councils: Consultation, Representation, and Cooperation in Industrial Relations,* edited by Joel Rogers and Wolfgang Streeck, chap. 9. Chicago: University of Chicago Press.

Sturmthal, Adolf. 1966. "Economic Development and the Labour Movement." In *Industrial Relations and Economic Development,* edited by Arthur M. Ross, 165–81. London: Macmillan.

Sturmthal, Adolf, and James G. Scoville, eds. 1973. *The International Labor Movement in Transition: Essays on Africa, Asia, Europe, and South America.* Urbana: University of Illinois Press.

Sullivan, Roger J. 1989. *Immanuel Kant's Moral Theory.* Cambridge: Cambridge University Press.

Summers, Clyde W. 1976. "Individual Protection against Unjust Dismissal: Time for a Statute." *Virginia Law Review* 62 (April): 481–532.

———. 1990. "Unions without Majority: A Black Hole?" *Chicago-Kent Law Review* 66: 531–48.

——. 1993. "Employee Voice and Employer Choice: A Structured Exception to Section 8(a)(2)." *Chicago-Kent Law Review* 69: 129–48.

——. 1999. "NAFTA's Labor Side Agreement and International Labor Standards." *Journal of Small and Emerging Business Law* 3 (summer): 173–87.

——. 2000. "Employment at Will in the United States: The Divine Right of Employers." *University of Pennsylvania Journal of Labor and Employment Law* 3 (fall): 65–86.

——. 2001. "The Battle in Seattle: Free Trade, Labor Rights, and Societal Values." *University of Pennsylvania Journal of International Economic Law* 22 (spring): 61–90.

Swygert, Michael I., and Katherine Earle Yanes. 1998. "A Unified Theory of Justice: The Integration of Fairness into Efficiency." *Washington Law Review* 73 (April): 249–328.

Szabo, Imre. 1982. "Historical Foundations of Human Rights and Subsequent Developments." In *The International Dimension of Human Rights,* vol. 1, edited by Karel Vasek, chap. 2. Westport, Conn.: Greenwood Press.

Tannenbaum, Frank. 1951. *A Philosophy of Labor.* New York: Alfred A. Knopf.

Taras, Daphne Gottlieb. 1997. "Collective Bargaining Regulation in Canada and the United States: Divergent Cultures, Divergent Outcomes." In *Government Regulation of the Employment Relationship,* edited by Bruce E. Kaufman, chap. 8. Madison, Wis.: Industrial Relations Research Association.

——. 2000. "Contemporary Experience with the Rockefeller Plan: Imperial Oil's Joint Industrial Council." In *Nonunion Employee Representation: History, Contemporary Practice, and Policy,* edited by Bruce E. Kaufman and Daphne Gottlieb Taras, chap. 11. Armonk, N.Y.: M. E. Sharpe.

Tchobanian, Robert. 1995. "France: From Conflict to Social Dialogue?" In *Works Councils: Consultation, Representation, and Cooperation in Industrial Relations,* edited by Joel Rogers and Wolfgang Streeck, chap. 5. Chicago: University of Chicago Press.

Thibaut, John, and Laurens Walker. 1975. *Procedural Justice: A Psychological Analysis.* Hillsdale, N.J.: Lawrence Erlbaum.

Tillich, Paul. 1959. *Theology of Culture.* New York: Oxford University Press.

Tillman, Ray M. 1999. "Reform Movement in the Teamsters and United Auto Workers." In *The Transformation of U.S. Unions: Voices, Visions, and Strategies from the Grassroots,* edited by Ray M. Tillman and Michael S. Cummings, chap. 8. Boulder, Colo.: Lynne Rienner.

Tillman, Ray M., and Michael S. Cummings, eds. 1999. *The Transformation of U.S. Unions: Voices, Visions, and Strategies from the Grassroots.* Boulder, Colo.: Lynne Rienner.

Tomlins, Christopher L. 1985a. *The State and the Unions: Labor Relations, Law, and the Organized Labor Movement, 1880–1960.* Cambridge: Cambridge University Press.

——. 1985b. "The New Deal, Collective Bargaining, and the Triumph of Industrial Pluralism." *Industrial and Labor Relations Review* 39 (October): 19–34.

Tool, Marc R., ed. 1993. *Institutional Economics: Theory, Method, Policy.* Boston: Kluwer.

Toulmin, Stephen. 1972. *Human Understanding.* Princeton: Princeton University Press.

Towers, Brian. 1997. *The Representation Gap: Change and Reform in the British and American Workplace.* Oxford: Oxford University Press.

Traxler, Franz. 1998. "Austria: Still the Country of Corporatism." In *Changing Industrial Relations in Europe,* edited by Anthony Ferner and Richard Hyman, chap. 8. Oxford: Blackwell.

Troy, Leo. 1999. *Beyond Unions and Collective Bargaining.* Armonk, N.Y.: M. E. Sharpe.

Tsogas, George. 2001. *Labor Regulation in a Global Economy.* Armonk, N.Y.: M. E. Sharpe.

Turner, Lowell. 1991. *Democracy at Work: Changing World Markets and the Future of Labor Unions.* Ithaca: Cornell University Press.

Turner, Lowell, Harry C. Katz, and Richard W. Hurd, eds. 2001. *Rekindling the Movement: Labor's Quest for Relevance in the Twenty-First Century.* Ithaca: ILR Press.

Turner, Ronald. 2000. "Employment Discrimination, Labor and Employment Arbitration, and the Case against Union Waiver of the Individual Worker's Statutory Right to a Judicial Forum." *Emory Law Journal* 49 (winter): 135–204.

United Nations. 2000. *Trade and Development Report, 2000*. New York.

United Nations Development Programme. 1999. *Human Development Report 1999*. New York: Oxford University Press.

United States Industrial Commission. 1901. *Report of the Industrial Commission on the Relations and Conditions of Capital and Labor Employed in Manufactures and General Business*, vol. 7. Washington, D.C.: Government Printing Office.

Valticos, Nicolas. 1982. "The International Labour Organization (ILO)." In *The International Dimension of Human Rights*, vol. 1, edited by Karel Vasek, chap. 12. Westport, Conn.: Greenwood Press.

van Boven, Theodoor C. 1982. "Distinguishing Criteria of Human Rights." In *The International Dimension of Human Rights, Volume 1*, edited by Karel Vasek, chap. 3. Westport, Conn.: Greenwood Press.

Vandevelde, Kenneth J. 1980. "The New Property of the Nineteenth Century: The Development of the Modern Concept of Property." *Buffalo Law Review* 29 (spring): 325–67.

Velasquez, Manuel G. 1998. *Business Ethics: Concepts and Cases*. 4th ed. Upper Saddle River, N.J.: Prentice-Hall.

Verma, Anil, and Joel Cutcher-Gershenfeld. 1993. "Joint Governance in the Workplace: Beyond Union-Management Cooperation and Worker Participation." In *Employee Representation: Alternatives and Future Directions*, edited by Bruce E. Kaufman and Morris M. Kleiner, chap. 6. Madison, Wis.: Industrial Relations Research Association.

Victor, Bart, and John B. Cullen. 1988. "The Organizational Bases of Ethical Work Climates." *Administrative Science Quarterly* 33 (March): 101–25.

Vittoz, Stanley. 1987. *New Deal Labor Policy and the American Industrial Economy*. Chapel Hill: University of North Carolina Press.

Wailes, Nick, and Russell D. Lansbury. 1999. "Collective Bargaining and Flexibility: Australia." LEG/REL Working Paper. Geneva, Switzerland: International Labour Organization.

Waldinger, Roger, Chris Erickson, Ruth Milkman, Daniel J. B. Mitchell, Abel Valenzuela, Kent Wong, and Maurice Zeitlin. 1998. "Helots No More: A Case Study of the Justice for Janitors Campaign in Los Angeles." In *Organizing to Win: New Research on Union Strategies*, edited by Kate Bronfenbrenner et al., chap. 6. Ithaca: ILR Press.

Wallach, Lori, and Michelle Sforza. 2000. *The WTO: Five Years of Reasons to Resist Corporate Globalization*. New York: Seven Stories Press.

Walton, Richard E., and Robert B. McKersie. 1965. *A Behavioral Theory of Labor Negotiations*. New York: McGraw-Hill.

Watkins, Gordon S., and Paul A. Dodd. 1938. *The Management of Labor Relations*. New York: McGraw-Hill.

Watson, Tony J. 1995. *Sociology, Work, and Industry*. 3rd ed. London: Routledge.

Webb, Sidney, and Beatrice Webb. 1897. *Industrial Democracy*. London: Longmans, Green, and Co.

Weil, David. 1996. "Regulating the Workplace: The Vexing Problem of Implementation." In *Advances in Industrial and Labor Relations*, vol. 7, edited by David Lewin, Bruce E. Kaufman, and Donna Sockell, 247–86. Greenwich, Conn.: JAI Press.

———. 1997. "Implementing Employment Regulation: Insights on the Determinants of Regulatory Performance." In *Government Regulation of the Employment Relationship*, edited by Bruce E. Kaufman, chap. 12. Madison, Wis.: Industrial Relations Research Association.

Weiler, Paul. 1983. "Promises to Keep: Securing Workers' Rights to Self-Organization under the NLRA." *Harvard Law Review* 96 (June): 1769–1827.

———. 1984. "Striking a New Balance: Freedom of Contract and the Prospects for Union Representation." *Harvard Law Review* 98 (December): 351–420.

——. 1990. *Governing the Workplace: The Future of Labor and Employment Law.* Cambridge: Harvard University Press.

Weintraub, Sidney. 1997. "The North American Free Trade Agreement." In *Economic Integration Worldwide,* edited by Ali M. El-Agraa, chap. 8. New York: St. Martin's.

Weisfeld, Israel. 1974. *Labor Legislation in the Bible and Talmud.* New York: Yeshiva University Press.

Weiss, Howard M. 2002. "Conceptual and Empirical Foundations for the Study of Affect at Work." In *Emotions in the Workplace: Understanding the Structure and Role of Emotions in Organizational Behavior,* edited by Robert G. Lord, Richard J. Klimoski, and Ruth Kanfer, chap. 2. San Francisco: Jossey-Bass.

Weissbrodt, David. 1988. "Human Rights: An Historical Perspective." In *Human Rights,* edited by Peter Davies, chap. 1. London: Routledge.

——. 2000. "Principles Relating to the Human Rights Conduct of Companies." New York: United Nations Commission on Human Rights, E/CN.4/Sub.2/2000/WG.2/WP.1.

Wellington, Harry, and Ralph K. Winter, Jr. 1971. *The Unions and the Cities.* Washington, D.C.: Brookings Institution.

Wells, Donald. 1993. "Are Strong Unions Compatible with the New Model of Human Resource Management?" *Relations Industrielles* 48 (winter): 56–85.

West, Robin. 2001. "Rights, Capabilities, and the Good Society." *Fordham Law Review* 69 (April): 1901–32.

Wever, Kirsten S. 1995. *Negotiating Competitiveness: Employment Relations and Organizational Innovation in Germany and the United States.* Boston: Harvard Business School Press.

Wheeler, Hoyt N. 1985. *Industrial Conflict: An Integrative Theory.* Columbia: University of South Carolina Press.

——. 1994. "Employee Rights as Human Rights." *Bulletin of Comparative Labour Relations* 28: 9–18.

——. 2000. "Viewpoint: Collective Bargaining Is a Fundamental Human Right." *Industrial Relations* 39 (July): 535–39.

——. 2002. *The Future of the American Labor Movement.* Cambridge: Cambridge University Press.

Wheeler, Hoyt N., and John A. McClendon. 1991. "The Individual Decision to Unionize." In *The State of the Unions,* edited by George Strauss, Daniel G. Gallagher and Jack Fiorito, chap. 2. Madison, Wis.: Industrial Relations Research Association.

White, Stuart. 1998. "Trade Unionism in a Liberal State." In *Freedom of Association,* edited by Amy Gutmann, chap. 12. Princeton: Princeton University Press.

Whitfield, Keith and George Strauss, eds. 1998. *Researching the World of Work: Strategies and Methods in Studying Industrial Relations.* Ithaca: ILR Press.

Whitley, Richard. 2000. *The Intellectual and Social Organization of the Sciences.* Oxford: Oxford University Press.

Whittall, Michael. 2000. "The BMW European Works Council: A Cause for European Industrial Relations Optimism?" *European Journal of Industrial Relations* 6 (March): 61–83.

Whyte, William F. 1999. "The Mondragon Cooperatives in 1976 and 1998." *Industrial and Labor Relations Review* 52 (April): 478–81.

Widenor, Marcus R. 1995. "Diverging Patterns: Labor in the Pacific Northwest Wood Products Industry." *Industrial Relations* 34 (July): 441–63.

Williams, Jane. 1999. "Restructuring Labor's Identity: The Justice for Janitors Campaign in Washington, D.C." In *The Transformation of U.S. Unions: Voices, Visions, and Strategies from the Grassroots,* edited by Ray M. Tillman and Michael S. Cummings, chap. 11. Boulder, Colo.: Lynne Rienner.

Williamson, Jeffrey G. 1998. "Globalization, Labor Markets, and Policy Backlash in the Past." *Journal of Economic Perspectives* 12 (fall): 51–72.

Williamson, Oliver E. 1975. *Markets and Hierarchies, Analysis and Antitrust Implications: A Study in the Economics of Internal Organization.* New York: Free Press.

Wills, Jane. 2000. "Great Expectations: Three Years in the Life of a European Works Council." *European Journal of Industrial Relations* 6 (March): 85–107.

Wimbush, James C., Jon M. Shepard, and Steven E. Markham. 1997. "An Empirical Examination of the Multi- Dimensionality of Ethical Climate in Organizations." *Journal of Business Ethics* 16: 67–77.

Windmuller, John P. 2000. "The International Trade Secretariats." In *Transnational Cooperation among Labor Unions,* edited by Michael E. Gordon and Lowell Turner, chap. 6. Ithaca: ILR Press.

Witt, Matt, and Rand Wilson. 1999. "The Teamsters' UPS Strike of 1997: Building a New Labor Movement." *Labor Studies Journal* 24 (spring): 58–72.

Witte, John F. 1980. *Democracy, Authority, and Alienation in Work: Workers' Participation in an American Corporation.* Chicago: University of Chicago Press.

Witte, John, Jr. 1996. "Law, Religion, and Human Rights." *Columbia Human Rights Law Review* 28 (fall): 1–31.

Wong, David. 1993. "Relativism." In *A Companion to Ethics,* edited by Peter Singer, chap. 39. Oxford: Blackwell.

Wright, Patrick M., Lee D. Dyer, John W. Boudreau, and George T. Milkovich, eds. 1999. *Research in Personnel and Human Resources Management, Supplement 4: Strategic Human Resources Management in the Twenty-First Century.* Stamford, Conn.: JAI Press.

Wuerffel, Kristin Nadasdy. 1998. "Discriminating among Rights?: A Nation's Legislating a Hierarchy of Human Rights in the Context of International Human Rights Customary Law." *Valparaiso University Law Review* 33 (fall): 369–412.

Yergin, Daniel, and Joseph Stanislaw. 1998. *The Commanding Heights: The Battle between Government and the Marketplace That is Remaking the Modern World.* New York: Simon and Schuster.

Yoder, Dale. 1938. *Personnel and Labor Relations.* New York: Prentice-Hall.

Yonay, Yuval P. 1998. *The Struggle over the Soul of Economics: Institutionalist and Neoclassical Economists in America between the Wars.* Princeton: Princeton University Press.

Zietlow, Rebecca E. 1998. "A Substantive Approach to Equal Justice under Law." *New Mexico Law Review* 28 (summer): 411–50.

Zinn, Kenneth S. 2000. "Solidarity across Borders: The UMWA's Corporate Campaign against Peabody and Hanson PLC." In *Transnational Cooperation among Labor Unions,* edited by Michael E. Gordon and Lowell Turner, chap. 11. Ithaca: ILR Press.

Index